W9-AUH-313

Behind East Asian Growth

The reasons behind the dynamic emergence and continued rise of Asian prosperity are often subject to heated debate. There have been plenty of theories put forward to explain Asia's success, but these explanations have often come from a narrow perspective.

In this new study the contributors have a wide range of disciplinary backgrounds that help provide the reader with a unique survey of the fundamental reasons behind East Asian growth. These are shown to be historical legacies combined with contemporary politics, but also highlighted are four key factors:

- Effective governance: motivating factors such as external threats to the nation and nearby successful models.
- Achieving and learning societies: solid commitment to education, particularly universal primary and secondary schooling.
- Growth with equity: the lowest disparity of incomes in the world for any developing region.
- External influences: threats from communism, Japan's early industrialisation and protection by the US.

Behind East Asian Growth is a distinctive and comprehensive survey of the factors influencing the region's unique economic success. It will be welcomed by academics, the business community and policy-makers alike.

Henry S. Rowen is Director of the Asia/Pacific Research Center, Senior Fellow at the Hoover Institution and Emeritus Professor at the Graduate School of Business, Stanford University. He was previously President of the RAND Corporation and Assistant Secretary of Defense.

Behind East Asian Growth

The political and social foundations
of prosperity

Edited by
Henry S. Rowen

London and New York

First published 1998
by Routledge
11 New Fetter Lane, London EC4P 4EE

Simultaneously published in the USA and Canada
by Routledge
29 West 35th Street, New York, NY 10001

© 1998 Salzburg Seminar

Typeset in Times by Florencetype Ltd, Stoodleigh, Devon
Printed and bound in Great Britain by
Creative Print and Design (Wales), Ebbw Vale

British Library Cataloguing in Publication Data
A catalogue record for this book is available from the British Library

Library of Congress Cataloging in Publication Data
Rowen, Henry S.
  Behind East Asian growth: the political and social foundations of
prosperity/Henry S. Rowen.
    p. cm.
  Includes bibliographical references (p.   ) and index.
  1. East Asia – Economic policy – Case studies. 2. East Asia –
Economic conditions – Case studies. I. Title.
HC460.5.R69 1998
338.95 – dc21   97–26883
                                                                           CIP

ISBN 0–415–16519–9 (hbk)
ISBN 0–415–16520–2 (pbk)

Contents

Figures

Tables

Contributors

Dipak Dasgupta is a Senior Economist at the World Bank.

Stephan M. Haggard is Professor at the Graduate School of International Relations and Pacific Studies, University of California at San Diego.

Sung-Yeal Koo is Professor, Department of Economics, Yonsei University, Seoul.

Yutaka Kosai is President, Japan Center for Economic Research, Tokyo.

Otto C.C. Lin is Vice President for R&D, the Hong Kong University of Science and Technology.

Minxin Pei is Assistant Professor of Politics at Princeton University, New Jersey.

Jon S.T. Quah is Head of the Department of Political Science and Coordinator of the European Studies Program at the National University of Singapore.

James H. Raphael is Director of Research at the Asia/Pacific Research Center, Stanford University, California.

Thomas P. Rohlen is a Senior Fellow at the Asia/Pacific Research Center and Professor at the School of Education, Stanford University, California.

Hilton L. Root is a Senior Research Fellow at the Hoover Institution, Stanford University, California.

Henry S. Rowen is a Senior Fellow at the Hoover Institution, Emeritus Professor of Public Policy and Management at the Graduate School of Business, Stanford University, California and Director, Asia/Pacific Research Center, Stanford University.

Donald R. Snodgrass is a Fellow at the Harvard Institute for International Development, Massachusetts.

Harold W. Stevenson is Professor of Psychology and a Fellow at the Center for Human Growth and Development, University of Michigan.

Fumihide Takeuchi is an Economist in the Asian Research Bureau, Japan Center for Economic Research, Tokyo.

Ali Wardhana is a Senior Advisor to the Indonesian Government.

Meredith Jung-En Woo-Cumings is Professor of political science, Northwestern University, Illinois.

Editor's foreword

The genesis of this book is a multi-year project titled The Rise of Industrial East Asia and Its Implications for the Developing World, conducted since 1994 by the Salzburg Seminar and financed by the Sasakawa Peace Foundation. After a gathering of experts in Singapore and Stanford University in 1994, plans proceeded for holding a series of seminars as part of the Salzburg Seminar's core program. The first two seminars were held in April of 1996 and 1997; a third is scheduled for April, 1998. A book on this topic was planned from the outset of the program.

Its focus on the social and political foundations of East Asia's remarkable rise stems from the great attention paid in recent years to the economic policies of these governments, ones clearly superior to those adopted elsewhere in the developing world. This raised the question as to why this had happened and also as to other factors that have contributed to such successes. In visits to the region I found much interest in this topic so we decided to make this the central theme of the book.

The content of this work encompasses several disciplines: economics, politics, psychology, anthropology, engineering, a mixture determined by the multifaceted nature of the topic. This is why the contributors include former officials and an international civil servant as well as academics. This multidisciplinary, cross-cutting approach enables readers to view topics in particular countries from several different perspectives.

Gail Neale of the Salzburg Seminar provided the inspiration for this project and, as the result of the careful attention and commitment of Shirasu Takashi, the Sasakawa Peace Foundation provided financial support. I want also to thank the participants in the planning meetings for advice on the topics; contributors to the book for supplying interesting ideas and observations; and my colleagues in Stanford's Asia/Pacific Research Center, the Institute for International Studies and the Hoover Institution for advice and comments. Dr Peter Lewis, a National Fellow at the Hoover Institution in 1995–6 was especially helpful on possible lessons from East Asia for countries in Africa.

Chapter 4, "Business, Politics and Policy in East and Southeast Asia" by Stephan Haggard, is an adaptation of his contribution to Andrew

MacIntyre's *Business and Government in Industrializing Asia* (Ithaca, Cornell University Press, 1994). The publishing house, Allen and Unwin, has graciously permitted us to use this material.

Finally, and definitely not least, my assistants, George Wilson, Amy Searight and Asha Jadeja provided invaluable help in research and production.

1 The political and social foundations of the rise of East Asia: an overview

Henry S. Rowen

This book addresses this question: why have so many East Asian countries had such remarkably strong and sustained economic growth? The conventional – and clearly correct – answer is that they adopted unusually good policies. But why did they do so? Their record of development is so exceptional, not only in comparison to other developing regions but in world history, that it has recently attracted the attention of scholars from many fields. Because no single discipline has provided a persuasive explanation, this book draws on several in an effort to produce a more convincing explanation than has heretofore been advanced.

The current interest in what can be called the new Asian exceptionalism is juxtaposed against a long-standing puzzle about China: why – when it advanced to the threshold of a systematic experimental investigation of nature and created the world's earliest mechanized industry from the tenth to the fourteenth century – was it unable to sustain that progress?[1] Although Japan was the first non-European-culture country to break out of the near universal pattern of slow development in the mid-nineteenth century, almost another 100 years passed before other East Asian nations followed suit. Despite this lag they were still ahead of the rest of the developing world.

These countries' economic policies have been consistently better than those in other developing regions. Their strategies have varied, with some governments strongly shaping their industrial structures (notably South Korea) and others being hands-off (notably Hong Kong); nonetheless, the area of consensus among experts on the merits of these strategies is much greater than that of dissonance.

This only pushes the inquiry one stage further: why were good policies so widely adopted and adhered to so consistently? Were favorable social (including political) factors responsible for their adoption, and might such factors independently have helped to produce exceptional results?

Such success was not predicted. The newly independent South Korea suffered great damage from war. Given the record of the Kuomintang on the mainland, there was no strong basis for optimism in 1949 about Taiwan's economic prospects. Hong Kong was the destination for many poor and unskilled refugees from China and there was uncertainty about Beijing's behavior towards it after 1949. Singapore's prospect under the rule of a socialist-oriented party in a troubled region was problematical. The Indonesian economy under Sukarno was thoroughly mismanaged. China's progress in industrializing was disrupted by the Great Leap Forward and the Cultural Revolution, and its overall performance through the end of the 1970s was unimpressive. Japan aside, the Philippines in 1950 seemed to have the brightest prospect, an assessment that turned out to be spectacularly wrong.

THEIR PERFORMANCE

The region's six fastest-growing economies (Japan, South Korea, Taiwan, Hong Kong, Singapore, and China) experienced about 5 percent a year per capita growth (in international purchasing power parity, PPP) from 1965–95 while three Southeast Asian countries (Thailand, Malaysia and Indonesia) averaged about 3.5 percent a year. The average for the rest of the developing world was only 1.5 percent per year. Seven East Asian countries – North Korea, Mongolia, Vietnam, Cambodia, Laos, the Philippines, and Myanmar – performed poorly. (Oil-rich Brunei is appropriately omitted from most such comparisons.) Vietnam has been on a promising track since 1986, but that is too short a record to warrant inclusion among the sustained, high-growth economies.

Growth in the trade of the nine high-performing countries has been remarkable. Between 1965 and 1990, the region's developing countries more than doubled their share both of total world exports (from 8 to 18 percent) and of world manufactured exports (from 9 to 21 percent). By 1990, these nine countries had 56 percent of all developing country exports and 73 percent of all manufactured ones; these proportions had increased five-fold over the preceding 25 years.

To underscore the magnitude of their accomplishments, during those years *all* of the large-population, high-performing countries, were in East Asia; the other four top performers (Botswana, Malta, Cyprus and Mauritius) are tiny.

A growth rate of 5 percent per capita for over three decades is without precedent, although the "miracle" growth years of the 1950s and 1960s in Germany, Italy and France came close; there has been no other nearly comparable performance in history. Japan's annual per capita growth from the Meiji Restoration to 1940 was respectable at 1.5 percent but that was no better than that of the US and Sweden over the period.[2] In the rest of the world, Egypt was the only large country whose performance was close to that of the Southeast Asians over the period from 1965, but it stagnated after 1980.

These fast-growing countries fall into four groups. Already industrialized Japan is in a class by itself. A second group has two of its former colonies, Taiwan and South Korea, who modeled their development strategies largely on Japan (especially South Korea) and the two city-states, Hong Kong and Singapore, each exploiting its locational advantages as entrepôts. These countries have some cultural similarities, inherited some common institutions from the period of Japanese colonialism; are ethnically homogenous (less so in Singapore); and are poor in natural resources; long ago they were labeled the Newly Industrialized Economies (NIEs). The third group, Thailand, Malaysia and Indonesia, have more natural resources than those in the Northeast and more ethnic diversity. Fourth is China – almost a world unto itself, one in which development is proceeding rapidly, but unevenly, within the country.

Their present levels of development vary greatly. Japan, with a GDP of $21,000 per capita in 1995 (at 1995 international prices), is highly developed, as are Hong Kong and Singapore, at $21,000 and $20,000 respectively. At the other end of the scale is China, at (approximately) $2,300 in 1995. It is the rapid and sustained *growth rates* that distinguish several of these nations from the rest of the developing world more than their current per capita income *levels*. Mexico and Argentina in the 1990s were at levels comparable to Malaysia, above Thailand, and well ahead of Indonesia and China, but the Latins have been growing much more slowly.

Economic statistics do not capture all that matters. For example, they omit such positives as improvements in health and longevity. They also leave out of account such negatives as pollution and other kinds of environmental damage that have grown together with economic output. Fixing them requires large investments that will be a drag on future growth. However, there is no good reason to believe that allowing for these omitted factors greatly changes the conclusion that, for the most part, these are remarkably successful countries.

EXPLANATIONS

It has been argued that the NIEs were lucky in their timing. The international environment was highly favorable for developing countries after World War II: for 25 years the Bretton Woods system provided a stable international financial system; the industrial countries were booming; the US provided a large, relatively open market; development assistance was available; and American military protection was supplied. Not everyone was accorded equal opportunity or help but the environment favored development-oriented and competent governments, those that avoided the off-ramp of socialism and that were not crippled by domestic or foreign conflicts. The NIEs exploited these opportunities. Although the world economy grew more slowly after the early 1970s they continued to do well, world trade continued to grow strongly and multinational companies continued to transfer technology to countries offering good opportunities.

Anyone in a poor country who complains that the good old days ended in the early 1970s should be reminded that the Southeast Asians began to grow strongly about then, as did China after 1979 and Vietnam after 1986.

This seems to leave three major explanations: (1) better policies were adopted; (2) their social capabilities are greater; and (3) external influences played important roles.

Policies

Much progress is being made, theoretically and empirically, on the sources of growth and there is a wide consensus on economic policies that are good, albeit with some disputes at the margin. There is, however, no adequate theory that enables one to predict which countries will adopt good policies.

Social capabilities

Successful countries also have social attributes that appear favorable. This category encompasses institutions that less directly – but often profoundly – affect the key requisites of growth: physical investment, the formation of human capital, and the acquisition of technology. A crucial institution is the character and the stability of the politics and laws under which economic activity is carried out; this cluster is addressed below under the heading of effective governance. Another is the set that deter- mines the distribution of incomes, especially through the distribution of opportunities. Still another is the value people put on achievement and learning.

External influences

Influences from outside individual countries – including from outside the entire region – were also important. Historically, Europe's extension of power from the sixteenth century on had huge effects wherever it im- pinged. So did Japan's activities from the late nineteenth century on. More recently, the competition between the communist and non-communist powers was played out in the region with varying degrees of intensity and conflict. And the United States was important as a market, as an occupying and reforming power, and as a protector.

Methodological difficulties

There are problems with some aspects of the literature on East Asia's rise. Some scholar identifies a possible explanatory factor such as a pattern of initially authoritarian regimes or government micro-management of the economy and asserts its importance.[3] Such claims need to be validated by comparisons among the largest feasible set of countries, and, as Minxin Pei points out in Chapter 2, this is not always done. When it is, such claims sometimes fail to stand up. For instance, the governments of all of the recently successful countries in the region (Japan being an earlier one) were authoritarian 35 years ago at the onset of growth. But there have been many such regimes in the world and the data show no growth advantage to them. Also, the tendency of governments to favor some industries over others through preferential access to credit, subsidies and trade protection is nearly universal; such interventions are usually judged to have contributed much to the poverty of nations. Either the parameters at issue actually differed (e.g. Asian "authoritarianism" or "industrial policies" were not the same as Latin American or South Asian ones) or other influences were at work – or both. A finer grained description and analysis is needed. In any case, single factor explanations do not take us very far; it is the interaction of several, perhaps many – which ones is an open question – that accounts for the outcomes we observe.

A similar problem arises with cultural explanations. The successes of the Chinese-cultural-sphere countries (China, Japan, Korea, Vietnam, Taiwan, Hong Kong, and Singapore) are sometimes attributed to a factor called "Confucianism." There are several difficulties here. Most obviously, 35 years ago all of these countries except Japan were poor and some still are. Has Confucianism basically changed in that short interval? If Confucianism did contribute to success, it clearly did so in conjunction with other factors. More importantly, how can one identify a potential positive factor without examining countries that do not have it? (This is the same methodological point made above.) There does seem to be much in the position that culture can affect behavior in ways important for development, but Confucianism consists of a bundle of attributes that need to be (and generally are not) defined precisely.

In the absence of an accepted theory encompassing all of these varied factors, the best that can be done – and the approach taken by this book – is to present them, argue their plausibility, make comparisons with other countries and regions, and await the reaction of the reader. With further research some of these factors – and perhaps others neglected here – will doubtless be seen as much more important than others.

THEIR ECONOMIC POLICIES

Consider several basic policy categories:

Macroeconomic stability

East Asia has the best record of any developing region on inflation and exchange rate stability.

Openness

Exporting forces domestic firms to learn about foreign markets and importing brings in technology, creates competition and lessens the scope for rent-seeking behavior. The East Asians are distinguished among developing regions by their engagement with the world economy, in particular their pushing of exports. The resource-poor NIEs had little choice but to export manufactured goods to pay for raw materials; the Southeast Asians had more resources and therefore more options, but by 1990 manufacturing's contribution was 27 percent of GDP for Malaysia, 25 percent for Thailand, and 19 percent for Indonesia. Although all were heavily engaged in trade, their policies varied. Korea strenuously promoted exports and Taiwan subsidized them; both limited imports to certain channels. Hong Kong was *laissez-faire*, and the others were in between. Openness to foreign direct investment – a major source of badly-needed technology – also varies. Hong Kong has virtually no restrictions and Korea has many; but Korea has worked hard to acquire foreign technology, including licensing it on a large scale.

The allocation of resources

The share of national resources consumed by these governments, and therefore their taxes, has been low; the tax administration has varied in efficiency and honesty but has been good in the NIEs; and investment in infrastructure has been high. There has been some financial repression (interest rates held below a competitive level), implying rationing of credit, but highly negative real interest rates have been avoided. Although many state enterprises were created in the 1950s and 1960s and few have been privatized, their shares of national output have sharply declined. Unlike in most developing countries, economically damaging regulations were not pervasive and did not create high obstacles for new enterprises; nor was agriculture drained of resources to support urban areas.[4]

Property and other economic rights

According to one analysis, "No country with a persistently high economic freedom rating during the two decades [1975–95] failed to achieve a high level of income. In contrast, no country with a persistently low rating was able to achieve even middle income status."[5] These freedoms include (with variations among evaluators) protection of the value of money, the ability to move it abroad, free exchange of property, low levels of taxation, a fair judiciary, few trade restrictions, labor market freedom, ability to start a business, freedom from economic coercion by political opponents, and absence of large-scale corruption.

Several East Asian countries rate amongst the highest in the world on these freedoms.[6] From 1975–95, only two non-OECD (Organization for

Economic Cooperation and Development) countries, Hong Kong and Singapore, had consistently high ratings. In 1993–95, five other East Asian countries were in the top 20 (out of 102 that were rated).

Such policies, together with other influences, affected direct inputs to growth:

Physical capital

The fast-growing East Asian countries had low savings rates several decades ago, inevitably given their poverty, but their savings grew to become the world's highest at 30–40 percent of GDP. For some this might reflect a Confucian propensity to save and the earlier widespread destruction and redistribution of wealth might have led to increased savings as people restored their ratio of wealth to income.[7] All the governments encouraged savings and Singapore introduced a forced savings system (the Provident Fund). In any case, when countries grow fast for whatever reasons, good investment opportunities provide a high payoff from deferring consumption; moreover, consumption tends to lag behind income growth.

Human capital

According to Williamson, "a good share of the differences in growth performance along the Asia-Pacific Rim, or between it and Latin America, can also be explained by human capital and demographic forces."[8] (This topic, a fundamental contributor to the region's successes, is discussed further below.)

Technology

Firms in developing countries have two main disadvantages regarding technology: (1) they are behind, have poorly developed industrial and academic infrastructures and are far from the centers of science and innovation; (2) they are outside of mainstream international markets, domestic markets are small and they have unsophisticated users. They need strategies to overcome these technological and market barriers.[9] Engaging in trade is one mechanism. Another is to allow foreign firms to invest directly, perhaps jointly with domestic ones. A third is to emphasize licensing and indigenous development. All these methods entail building domestic competencies.

Japan, long before, had created trading companies that specialized in knowing foreign markets. After World War II, the Northeast Asians, especially Japan and Korea, opted for a licensing and indigenous development path. The others chose to acquire technology mainly via foreign direct investment. In Chapter 9, Otto Lin describes Taiwan's remarkably successful strategy for building technical competencies.

What was the Miracle?

The World Bank's *East Asian Miracle* report credited success mainly to getting the above fundamentals right.[10] It also identified important roles for various institutions, including intermediaries between government and the private sector, as well as relatively equal income distributions.

In accordance with the near universal pattern, most of these governments found ways to intervene extensively in favor of particular industries and firms, through state-owned banks, varying degrees of import protection, subsidies, restrictions on foreign investment, controls over trade unions, and spending on applied research. (Even Hong Kong subsidizes housing.) *Miracle* graded these activities positively in Northeast Asia and negatively in Southeast Asia (as elsewhere in the world), attributing the difference to the competence and honesty of bureaucrats and their insulation from rent-seeking politics.

These findings produced much controversy. Some critics held that the study did not adequately make the case on the dominant role of the fundamentals; others criticize its treatment of government micro-intervention in Northeast Asia.[11] Ian Little faults *Miracle* for using shaky data as the basis for finding significant gains in total factor productivity; *a fortiori*, those analysts that give even more credit to government industrial policies he finds to be in still greater error. He finds that rapid growth was mainly based on labor-intensive manufacturing that employed well-educated, hard-working, docile labor forces. In short, these achievements are fully explicable in conventional terms: high rates of material and human investment plus avoiding macroeconomic disasters, and not governments favoring shipbuilding, steel, autos, etc.

A related line of investigation asserts that high levels of physical and human capital accumulation account for almost all of their growth (excepting Japan).[12] But there remains the question as to how these countries managed such large capital accumulations. As Lau says "the miracle lies ... in the ability to mobilize the savings and use them efficiently."[13]

Aoki *et al.* adopt a view distinct from both the "market-friendly" view, which holds that markets were decisive in the successes, and the "developmental state" view, which gives credit to the state. They define an alternative position labeled "market-enhancing" in which government supports or complements private actions.[14] Examples include fostering financial institutions; the hard-budget, fiscal federalist practices in China; and government coordination of actions by private entities. Their perspective is compatible with much of the material presented in this book. However, to the degree that it is valid, the question remains: how did these countries avoid the extremes – or the damaging consequences – of incompetence, rent-seeking, and corruption that marked government behavior elsewhere?

THEIR SOCIAL CAPABILITIES

A description of Tokugawa Japan (1603–1868) helps us to understand the meaning of social capability and the importance of good institutions. According to Ohkawa and Rosovsky, it was backward economically but advanced socially.[15] Although crop yields were low and many peasants lived near the border of subsistence, especially early in that era, crafts were well-developed and services were sophisticated. Nearly half of all males had some formal schooling. It was a vigorous, advanced, and effective traditional society, "in many ways more advanced than many countries in Africa or Latin America today." Edo, Kyoto, and Osaka were among the largest cities in the world. There were good roads, inns, and restaurants. Housing was usually well-designed and made, dress was beautiful and functional, and the cuisine was nutritional and attractive. Japan lacked one essential for wealth: the technology being created in Europe and North America. Its effective institutions enabled it rapidly to reduce this technological gap once it made the decision to do so.

Simon Kuznets, in his pioneering work on modern economic growth, identified three social requisites for development: "Secularism," defined as a concentration of life on earth with a high priority towards economic progress; "Equalitarianism," the denial of inborn differences among human beings except insofar as they manifest themselves in human activities; and "Nationalism," based on the claim of a community of feeling grounded in the past which overrides particularist attitudes and ideologies.[16]

These attributes are found in greater abundance in East Asia than in other developing regions. The Confucian countries clearly warrant the label 'Secular' and the Islamic ones of this region have not displayed the damaging radicalism of those in the Middle East. On Equalitarianism, this region is famous for having narrow income differences. And internal divisions along lines of clan, language groups or religion – a common source of political instability and poor policies – are muted; i.e. Nationalism tends to override particular interests.

Social capabilities are expressed in institutions. According to the economic historian and Nobel laureate, Douglass North:

> Institutions are the humanly devised constraints that structure human interaction. They are made of formal constraints (e.g., rules, laws, constitutions), informal constraints (e.g., norms of behavior, conventions, self-imposed codes of conduct), and their enforcement characteristics. Together they define the incentive structure of societies and specifically economies.[17]

> Economic history is overwhelmingly a story of economies that failed to produce a set of rules of the game (with enforcement) that induce sustained economic growth.[18]

According to North, institutions reduce uncertainty by providing a structure to everyday life; once established, many activities can then be carried out more predictably and at a low-marginal cost. (Whether or not they remain socially efficient over time is another matter.) They affect the costs of doing business; costs are increased if there are uncertain or poorly structured property rights, if contracts are weakly protected, if information is scarce and access to it highly skewed, and if corruption is endemic. These conditions lead to transactions being kept smaller than optimal out of people's aversion to risk, to capital being kept in liquid form, and to long-term agreements being avoided.

We identified above one set of institutions in which the region is remarkably strong: those involving economic rights. Other valuable ones are discussed below: "Effective governance"; "Achieving and learning societies"; "Growth with equity"; and "External influences". The performance and institutions of the Philippines provide a contrast and are discussed in the section, "Why the Philippines has lagged".

Effective governance

The high-growth countries have development-focused regimes. Such an observation might be a tautology: governments that have good results can, *ex post*, be called "developmental." As we have seen, also unhelpful is the observation that 35 years ago most of these countries were authoritarian. It is more useful to distinguish among the *motivations* of leaders to produce better economic results, their *scope* for doing so, and their *understanding* of how best to proceed.

Motivations

Aims

One might assume that all leaders wanted their countries to develop rapidly. At some level of abstraction no doubt that was true but they also had other things in mind including surviving in power and building a national identity. Many were struggling to create new states and surviving in power often entailed distributing rents on a scale that hurt productive investment. Decisions that did not have early payoffs but did have short-term costs were unappealing.

Most post-independence leaders were charismatic founders of their countries or leaders of political and social revolutions, usually populist and some communist in ideology, ignorant of economics, and hostile to the West. They are legendary figures: Castro, Ho Chi Minh, Kenyatta, Kim Il-Sung, Mao, Nasser, Nehru, Nkrumah, Qaddafi, and Sukarno. As Mason *et al.* put it about South Korea's first president:

President Rhee was more interested in other things than in economic development. As in so many of the new states, the leader who fought for independence proved not to be a man capable of effective administration. Like others with similar careers – Sukarno, Nkrumah, Sheik Mujib – Rhee was more adept at bringing a new nation into being than directing its development.[19]

Although Latin America's independence had come a century earlier, it continued to throw up populist leaders such as Peron in Argentina, Allende in Chile, and Garcia in Peru. Lee Kuan Yew stands out as a rare, economically rational, exception among the founders.

Legitimacy

Political legitimacy is not an acute problem in democracies, the system many newly independent countries inherited from their metropoles; but many were weak and were soon succeeded by authoritarian regimes that had such problems. Having played a central role in achieving independence provided enough legitimacy for most first-generation leaders, but in time the aura wore off and even some of them ran into difficulties as their economies languished. Some, such as Nasser in Egypt, offered socialist ideology; this was adequate for a time but did not put bread or rice on the table. Among Latin American intellectuals and politicians a common line was to blame the "core" industrial, imperialist countries and their multinational corporations but eventually this lost credibility. As Mario Vargas Llosa said of his Peruvian countrymen, "one of our worst defects – our best fictions – is to believe that our miseries have been imposed upon us from abroad."[20] Some Arabs have had a similar tendency but, as Bent Hansen put it, "Egypt's main enemy has been Egypt."[21]

In East Asia, regimes that came to power through the use of force also had legitimacy problems: in South Korea, Indonesia, Taiwan (where the Nationalist Party of China, the KMT's problem was mitigated by comparison with that in Beijing) and, periodically, in Thailand. Their leaders perceived that a cure was raising the people out of poverty – and found strategies for doing so. It helped that they spread the benefits of growth widely. And, not least, their regimes became politically more inclusive over time, as Minxin Pei describes in Chapter 2.

External Threats

A distinctive contribution of Meredith Jung-En Woo-Cumings in Chapter 14 is the weight she attaches to external security threats. Several countries faced them, including domestic insurgencies supported from outside. Taiwan and South Korea had such powerful enemies that survival required becoming economically strong. They were at war. Beijing could survive doing a mediocre economic job (up to a point) but Taipei could not. Singapore, a predominantly Chinese outcast in a sea of Malays, also had to prosper. Malaysia, while still Malaya, had suppressed an internal insurgency as well as hostility from Indonesia and for some years worried about a revival of these troubles. Thailand had externally-supported communists in the countryside and faced direct threats from Vietnam and Cambodia, and Indonesia worried about the revival of the communists – supported by China.

These threats created an incentive for leaders to recruit all possible sources of support. In Thailand, they caused the regime for the first time in its history to pay attention to the condition of the peasants. There and elsewhere they provided an incentive to invest in rural infrastructure and education. Although countries elsewhere were also seriously threatened, including Turkey, Israel, Egypt, and Pakistan, the threat of hanging, as Samuel Johnson put it, was not always sufficient to motivate rational policies. This is yet another illustration of the proposition that single factor explanations are inadequate. In any case, as Campos and Root put it, "[n]owhere else in the developing world has there been a confrontation between communist and Western forces on such a large scale involving so many countries."[22]

One result was to stimulate military spending. Landau finds that military spending below 9 percent of GDP – a larger share than the NIEs spent – is associated with a positive effect on growth, and spending above that a negative one.[23] Positive mechanisms might be the above-mentioned motivations to succeed, the modernizing influence of the military, and the sharing of benefits of growth for reasons of political solidarity. A negative effect of military spending, one that dominates with a high enough level of such spending, is the diverting of resources from investment.

Forestalling competing power centers

Economically destructive behavior can be motivated by the aim of destroying obstacles to power or potential competing ones. Thus, with the aim of weakening opposition to his rule Stalin destroyed the kulaks, thereby greatly damaging Soviet agriculture, and, in Egypt, Nasser systematically undermined the efficacy of its many state-owned enterprises because of fear that they might challenge his power. In India, Nehru's view was that the state had to keep basic industries out of the private sector:

> because not only they might prove to be very profitable but because it gives them economic power. I think it is highly objectionable that economic power should be in the hands of a small group of persons, however able or good they might be. Such a thing must be prevented.[24]

The contrast with Park Chung Hee's view is striking; Park controlled these industries but he understood that having efficient ones entailed their being in private hands. The KMT in Taiwan arranged matters such that very large private firms did not develop, but its many small firms became highly productive.[25]

In general, potential dangers from competing power centers were forestalled by various combinations of repression and sharing of benefits.

Positive models in the neighborhood

East Asia had a superb role model nearby in Japan. That was true of no other developing region with the possible exceptions of Turkey, the Maghreb countries, and Mexico, *vis-à-vis* Western Europe and the US; but cultural distances were large in these cases.

Here, one, and then successively more, countries geographically close and of similar culture were succeeding. This must have served both as an embarrassment to the leaders of those still doing poorly and as models to emulate. Words written on Beijing's Democracy Wall in 1979 expressed the point concisely: "East Germany is not doing as well as West Germany, North Korea as well as South Korea, or China's mainland as well as Taiwan."

A history of greatness

Japan's success was proof that you did not need to be white in order to be successful. Moreover, not long after its modernizing began, it defeated one of the great powers of the era, Russia, an event that sent shock waves through Asia. Kishore Mahbubani (personal communication) suggests that Japan's success broke a psychological barrier for the East Asians. It increasingly led to the question: "If they can do it why can't we?"

Is there something to the idea that a common knowledge of earlier greatness that has been lost but might be recovered, is a motivator? This clearly was so in post-World War II Japan, a nation determined to come back but as a great economic power not a great military one. It also plausibly applies to the Chinese who had for centuries the world's most advanced empire and who had then suffered many humiliations from the early-nineteenth century on. Of course, other developing nations have great accomplishments in their pasts, including Egypt and Turkey. Evidently more than a memory of greatness is needed.

Scope for action

Leaders need political support to survive and even more to carry out policies that, at least initially, inevitably hurt some interests. Being a founding father, having been elected, or having support of the military helps, but these are sometimes inadequate. Dysfunctional institutions pose obstacles, including class structures that support privileges, block advances on the basis of merit, and cause public funds to be wasted. Some countries have rooted systems of privilege, for instance the Philippines and Latin American and Arab ones. When they are dysfunctional enough, people fall back on informal, largely family and clan-based activities that limit the scope of business activities. Some countries have such sharp differences among groups – usually ethnically based – that governance is ineffective. Through varying mixes of historical legacies, political skills, and a capacity to learn and adapt, most East Asian countries were not severely afflicted by these ills or managed to overcome them.

The destruction of old orders

Large systemic changes which undermine existing distributional coalitions, such as wars, revolutions, or entry into radically new trading arrangements, weaken or destroy growth-inhibiting institutions and have a liberating effect.[26]

This happened widely in East Asia. There was destruction through Japanese occupation, wars, decolonization and revolutions in Japan, Korea, Taiwan, China (twice, in 1949 and during the Cultural Revolution), Singapore, Malaysia, and Indonesia. Indonesia had a terrible bloodletting in 1965–66. Singapore was removed from Malaysia. Land reforms in Japan, Korea, and Taiwan reduced the potential blocking power of landholders. And in Japan the Americans weakened the power of the *zaibatsu*.

These events removed potential obstacles to regimes motivated to produce results. With a few exceptions, there were no dominant economic classes to protect and seek rents. These events – some of them grave crises – opened the way for changes in leaders and new policies.

Bureaucratic competencies – and honesties

Most newly independent countries had few competent civil servants to manage their ambitious programs, with the occasional exception of finance ministries and central banks. These deplorable situations were worsened by poor systems of recruiting talent and low pay with the wide result of incompetent and corrupt administrations.

In contrast, Japan has a long tradition of excellence in its administration. The British left a legacy of competent and honest administration in Singapore, Hong Kong and Malaysia, and Thailand has a hundred-years plus history of being a bureaucratically-run state, although the quality of its civil service has suffered from low pay. In the Chinese-cultural-sphere countries, a bureaucratic career – becoming a mandarin – was long the main path for success and attracted the most able young men. Jon Quah, in Chapter 5, describes the steps taken in Singapore to create an exemplary civil service (one with the world's highest pay). In Korea, Park Chung Hee promptly appointed able technocrats and began to revitalize the civil service. The KMT in Taiwan had talented people from the mainland. Under Deng Xiaoping, the former balance in favor of "Reds" was tipped in favor of "Experts" and the ancient tradition of the examination system was revived. And in Indonesia, Suharto brought in the "Berkeley Mafia" economic technocrats to manage macroeconomic policy.

However, it would certainly be an error to assume that bureaucrats and politicians have been highly competent and honest everywhere, especially in the industry-focused departments. For example, an authoritative account of Thailand's bureaucracy describes it as being "marked often by patronage and rent-seeking".[27]

Corruption, a universal – but unequally distributed – phenomenon, is damaging in itself and highly correlated with bureaucratic inefficiency; one can make money out of red tape.[28] Unlike taxes, bribes must be kept secret and this leads to greater distortions of resources. A lack of well-defined and continuing authority by corrupt officials in their powers sometimes means that many of them need to be bribed. In the Philippines under Marcos, corruption flowed to the top, but after his demise the reported number of independent bribe takers increased and social efficiency probably declined further.[29]

Recent public revelations in Korea raise questions not only about the honesty of politicians (a widely problematic class) but also of some bureaucrats. There have been disturbing charges in Taiwan. And, according to President Jiang Zemin, China is rife with corruption at all levels of government. In 1996, Transparency International reported Thailand to be the 37th, Indonesia the 45th, and China the 50th most corrupt countries out of 54 surveyed, yet these have been some of the most rapidly growing nations.[30] What is one to make of such evidence? Insofar as it is valid, evidently if countries have enough other positive social factors and have adopted good policies, as all these countries have, they can overcome this negative factor. Even so, the most successful countries rank in the upper tier including Singapore (rated number 7 in honesty) and Hong Kong (number 18 – ahead of France) probably would not have become so rich without high standards of probity.

Shared growth

The propensity of these regimes to spread the benefits of growth widely not only boosted their legitimacy; it reduced obstacles to adopting policies that entailed short-term costs for long-term benefits. (Recall that one of Kuznets' attributes for success is Equalitarianism.) We expand on this theme below.

Weakness or destruction of the political Left

In many developing countries, the radical Left, often supported by Moscow or Beijing, created political instabilities and supported growth-retarding policies. It was different here. The basic conservatism of the Japanese kept the Left parties marginal. The Korean War wiped out the radical Left in the South and the KMT assured a non-Left for Taiwan. Lee Kuan Yew saw to its emasculation in Singapore. As Quah reports in Chapter 5, the advice reportedly given to Lee in 1961 by the Dutch economist Albert Winsemius was: "Number one, is get rid of the Communists; how you get rid of them does not interest me as an economist, but get them out of the government, get them out of the unions, get them off the streets. How you do it, is your job." The massive killings in Indonesia destroyed it there. As Pei observes in Chapter 2, there were also self-destructions of the Left, including China's Cultural Revolution and the abortive move by Indonesia's Communist Party in 1965. In both Indonesia and China the winners adopted equity-enhancing policies that both helped development and undermined the political Left.

Again, external threats

These not only supplied an urgent motivation for development, they supplied a political basis for removing obstacles to that end.

Governments' relations with business

In most developing countries, government–business relations have had a rent-seeking, sometimes even predatory, character. That characteristic has not been absent in this region, most notably in the Philippines and elsewhere in Southeast Asia; however, on the whole they seem to have been positive. In Chapter 3, Hilton Root reports that bureaucracies became partners with business in promoting growth. The reasons included governments' tight fiscal controls that limited available funds, merit-based bureaucracies and their firm political foundations. Root highlights the important role of functional intermediaries between government and business, industrial associations and consultative bodies. These were vehicles for sharing information and reducing uncertainty and political risks.

Stephan Haggard in Chapter 4 focuses on the political character of relations between government and business. In Taiwan and Korea, strong state institutions gave government elites scope for reforms. In Taiwan, the arms-length relation between the KMT and largely native Taiwanese businesses caused the government initially to build state enterprises, while in Korea the government's greater dependence on the private sector led to more support to private business and to a concentrated industrial structure. In both, the power of business expanded over time and the autonomy of technocrats declined. In Southeast Asia, the bureaucracies were less competent and governments were less insulated from political pressures. Particularly striking there are the close personal links between Chinese capitalists and governments; these entail extensive networks of rent seeking, but also much productive investment.

Why did favorable institutions emerge in some settings and not in others? Haggard argues that they are affected by broad political relations, especially the reliance of government elites on business for political support. He proposes the idea of an optimum distance between them: where it is too great, anti-growth policies are likely but if the government-business nexus is too close the result is capture and rent-seeking. The larger political structures limited business influence in Korea, Taiwan and Thailand; provided scope for ethnic rent-seeking in Malaysia; fostered personalistic ties in Indonesia; and provided opportunities for nearly unchecked plunder in the Philippines.

Nationalism versus ethnic diversity and conflict

Differences along lines of class or ethnicity (i.e., racial, tribal, linguistic, or religious) are often an obstacle to effective governance. Most East Asian countries have few of them. The Northeast Asians and China are ethnically highly homogeneous (with China's several different spoken languages not a source of deep divisions). Indonesia has many distinct language groups and has had troubles in Sumatra, Timor and Irian Jaya, but, perhaps because so many live on separate islands, such tensions have not been disabling. There is also some (largely latent) hostility there to the role of the ethnic Chinese. In Malaysia, the division between the Malays and Chinese erupted in violence in 1969 but has been managed adequately since. Singapore has a large minority of ethnic Malays and Indians; as Quah reports, it has adopted policies of decent housing for all, universal education and other policies supportive of its minorities. For the region, overall, nationalisms have overcome particularisms.

The transformation of political institutions

Pei describes how most of these countries went through transformations in which political order was restored by autocratic regimes, over time a monopoly of power by the military or a party was allowed to erode, the treatment of dissidents gradually became less harsh, and some political opposition was permitted. All of this involved the slow building of institutions, formal and informal. Alternative groups were allowed to participate in politics, usually first at the local level, but initially they were not allowed to win many positions. He poses two puzzles: why did strong development occur under weak rule of law? And what forces restrained predation of these autocratic regimes? (A partial answer is supplied above: the existence of grave external threats.)

Eventually, South Korea, Taiwan, Thailand, and the Philippines joined Japan among the "Free" nations (Singapore among the "Partly Free" ones) as rated by Freedom House.[31] Despite assertions, emanating mostly from Singapore and Malaysia, that Asian democracy is different from the Western kind, Freedom House ratings show the same positive correlation between incomes and democracy (of the Western kind) as the rest of the world (which is not to argue that there are no differences between them). This evolution of political institutions – parties, bureaucracies, semi-open electoral procedures, some rule of law – promoted political stability and property rights. These political transitions paralleled market-opening events with the arrival of a second generation of leaders committed to development and with adequate scope to act.

Understanding good and avoiding or abandoning bad policies

The third main attribute of governance effective for development is knowing the right things to do. "Right" in this context depends on leaders' goals. For example, although the Stalinist central planning system was inefficient overall, it was effective in building heavy industry and military power. For development, understanding means understanding the importance of the economic policies described above.

For several decades after World War II, "good" policies were widely understood to mean something quite different: pervasive state involvement. This usually resulted in insecurity of property rights, government ownership of industry, heavy regulation, and autarky. The communist countries were the worst but statist countries such as India and Mexico were abundant. Mexico's experience is illustrative. Its GDP per capita before its 1910 revolution was about equal to that of Japan.[32] It had a high level of foreign investment and free trade; in 1900 its export/GDP ratio was about 20 percent. After the revolution it restricted foreign trade and investment and by the 1970s had an inefficient, corrupt system with a small wealthy class and a huge poor one. Even after nearly a decade of opening its economy from the mid-1980s, its export/GDP ratio in 1991 was only 7 percent. By then its per capita GDP was about one-third that of Japan.

The two most damaging ideas for development have been economic autarky and collectivism – which in extreme form requires autarky. The power of the collectivist ethos is shown by the fact that in the mid-1980s over 80 percent of the world population lived in socialist countries (about one-third of the total) or in highly state-controlled ones (about one-half), almost all of which had performed poorly. Leaders came to favor domestically-produced goods over imports; restrictions, sometimes near-bans on foreign investment; and extensive nationalizations and domestic controls.

The destructiveness of socialism is displayed in the countries divided after World War II. North Korea's level of development was no less than that of the South before separation. Since 1945, its rate of decline relative to the South has been 4–5 percent a year to a level about one-fifth as much per capita. Despite forced industrialization, Chinese per capita GDP grew at about 3 percent annually from 1949–79, modestly better than average for a developing country but markedly inferior to its high-speed neighbors.

How did the East Asian either avoid these errors or, having committed them, manage to escape? (Not all did, as North Korea illustrates.) History played a large role. Perhaps Japanese society is too intelligent and conservative ever to have accepted socialism, but occupation by US forces ruled out that possibility. The US also saw to the survival of South Korea as a capitalist society and, less directly, to that of Taiwan which under the KMT – although Leninist in original style – became strongly anti-communist. The defeat of communist insurgents in most of Southeast Asia left that region capitalist. As for China's escape, the self-destruction of its radical left in the Cultural Revolution helped greatly, as did the examples of nearby successes.

Japan has been important in this process both as proof of what Asians can accomplish and as a source of specific lessons, although as James Raphael and Thomas Rohlen observe in Chapter 12, there are several different possible interpretations of "The Japanese Model."

These factors have produced the world's most effective governments for development. Chapter 6 by Ali Wardhana provides an authoritative, inside account of one of the most important cases, that of Indonesia.

Achieving and learning societies

We have observed above the influence of some major historical developments from the nineteenth century on. It is often claimed that more ancient traditions have been of singular importance, especially in the Sinitic countries.

Systematic and large differences in values both within the region and with those outside are revealed in surveys and behavior. The Japanese by comparison with Americans, and to a lesser extent the Europeans, are much less individualistic, more attuned to duties than rights, more hierarchical and deferential to authority, have more elaborate institutions of social control, place more value on loyalty and stability, and are much less religious.[33]

One might expect such cultural differences to be expressed in economic institutions. For instance, it has been said that the typical Japanese firm today is less like a Western one than in 1900 (when the Japanese were vigorously adopting foreign institutions). It is no accident that a Japanese firm invented the just-in-time system of manufacturing, one that depends on close cooperation and trust among workers. Aoki describes a model of the Japanese firm with wide sharing of information at low levels and broad job specifications, all imbedded in a main bank (*keiretsu*) system in which the bank takes charge when things go badly.[34] It suffices to say that this model is not recognizably American in character nor even German. He holds that neither the US nor the Japanese model may be superior in all dimensions and for every industry – but it is distinctive.

Another prominent institution is the Chinese family firm and its networks. It is a productive one. However, few have professional managers or have institutionalized themselves (although this is beginning to happen in Singapore). Redding and Fukuyama emphasize the Chinese limitation of trust to the family as a major reason. [35] Perhaps its main source was the insecurity of property in traditional China along with no history of feudal responsibilities; this meant that even more than elsewhere the family was all-important. In contrast, the Japanese firm long ago made a transition from being wholly within the family, first through the custom of adopting sons, then by bringing in professional managers, and eventually to public ownership. Such firms can grow large and live indefinitely. Korea's *chaebols* are still family-run but it seems likely that their evolution will follow the Japanese pattern. In short, even among the Sinitic countries there is not a single model. However, there is a pattern of more reliance on personal relations than arms-length dealing (one also found more in continental Europe than in the Anglo-Saxon countries).

Another important, distinctive, and rapidly growing institution in China is the town and village enterprise. These are predominantly local government owned or collective firms, mostly in manufacturing. They express Chinese entrepreneurship and are also a byproduct of the rapid increase in agricultural productivity after (partial) privatization from 1979, one that made many more workers and new market opportunities available.

How important have these institutions been in the region's successes? Although a precise answer is beyond reach, they are creative and productive responses to the environments in which people have found themselves.

Confucianism

It is often asserted that Confucianism has been an important factor in the successes of those East Asian countries within the Chinese cultural sphere (Japan, Korea, Taiwan, Hong Kong, Singapore, Vietnam, and of course China). Consider this story:

> When Confucius went to the state of Wei, Zan Yu acted as driver of his carriage. Confucius observed, "How numerous are the people!" Zan Yu asked, "Since they are thus numerous, what more shall be done for them?" "Enrich them," was the reply. "And when they have been enriched, what more shall be done?" Confucius replied, "Teach them."[36]

These precepts, although not always obeyed over the past two thousand years, are evidently alive today.

Of course, Confucius was not the only influence on these peoples; depending on the country, one should also consider Taoism, Mahayana Buddhism, Shintoism, Christianity, and Islam. In short, "Confucianism" is shorthand for a bundle of values and predispositions for behavior. The first question to ask is: "What is it?" The answer is not obvious because its values are numerous: benevolence, moral-rightness, conscientiousness, filial piety, respect for authority, brotherly respect, propriety, sincerity, self-cultivation, human knowledge, uprightness, and more. At bottom, it is a creed that extols merit and concern for the welfare of others. It is often observed that Confucianism consists of a set of moral norms that centers primarily on relations among humans and not those between man and God or spirits. It is primarily a personal ethic, centered on relations within the family. Its secular focus (again, corresponding to one of Kuznets' precepts for development) has averted clashes of the kind that marked medieval Christianity and affects Islam to this day. East Asian governments have not had to deal with serious religious strife.

Confucianism in Japan acquired a different character from that of its place of origin; one more overtly nationalistic (another of Kuznets' key attributes), paternalistic and group-oriented and without the role for "benevolence" in the Chinese original.[37] Indeed, Japan is often held to have several attributes quite different from those of China. As we have seen, the primary unit of affiliation or loyalty in China is the family while in Japan it extends beyond the family to the "village" – under modern conditions represented by the company and the political faction.[38]

Max Weber attributed China's poverty to the inhibiting influence of traditional Confucianism with its rigid social and family hierarchies at the core. He wrote that it is "opposite to the development of rational economic corporate enterprise."[39] In addition, "the poise and harmony of the [Confucian] soul are shaken by the risks of acquisitiveness." To Weber, the family piety and strong cohesion of the system prevented impersonal economic rationalization.

> It is very striking that out of this unceasing and intensive economic ado and the much bewailed crass "materialism" of the Chinese, there failed to originate on the economic plane those great and methodical business conceptions which are rational in nature and are presupposed by modern capitalism ... [China is] a typical land of profiteering ... Confucianism has not favored the rise of modern capitalism.

Overall, the Confucians lacked what Weber termed the "mighty enthusiasms" of the Puritans. Moreover, Confucianism did not provide protection for property. Local officials could exploit merchants and peasants for increased taxes and bribes without their having any recourse to the law.

(Indeed, there is little protection of intellectual property in Chinese tradition.)[40]

Insofar as there is a plausible answer to Confucianism's long delayed – but in hindsight arguably positive – role in development, it lies in the path taken by history. China had been the world's most technologically advanced country for hundreds of years through about the fifteenth century, at which time it stagnated – at about the time Europe began to advance. Political events had led to an inward focus that became stultifying. In any case, traditional Confucian society did not esteem the merchant but rather the mandarin. It also seems that the tradition of respect for scholars eroded in the Ming Dynasty (1368–1744); they were reduced in professional ranking to the "smelly number nine position."[41] It was not until these countries acquired political centers oriented towards development that it occurred, first in Japan; then in others through colonialism, communist rule in China, and the other processes described here.[42]

Under the heading "Industrial neo-Confucianism," Vogel identifies four clusters of institutions and attitudes common to the four NIEs: Meritocratic Elites, Entrance Exam Systems, Importance of the Group, and Self-Cultivation (the drive for self-improvement reflected in hard work and other achievement-focused activities).[43] Of Vogel's four clusters, those other than the Importance of the Group can be subsumed under the heading of a high value attached to achievement through education and the other forms of learning discussed below.

As Root mentions, there are also negatives in Confucian tradition. Family loyalty can justify nepotism, for example. Respect for authority implies a passivity that allows scope to political leaders that can cause mistakes to be larger and more persistent; China under Mao's rule is a case in point. Relying on personal networks, which has important benefits, also constrains the growth of firms especially in technologically advanced industries. And reliance on relationships rather than rules fosters corruption, a phenomenon not limited to Confucian countries but apparent in them.

Is "shared growth" an expression of Confucian values? It is consistent with them but events that destroyed established interests, the motivation of leaders to exclude alternative power centers, and the need for social cohesion in the face of serious external threats were other influences.[44]

Learning

Growth accounting estimates attribute varying proportions (20 to 60 percent) of the increased output between 1960 and 1985 in eight of the region's high-performing countries to increased human capital.[45] Countries that had primary and secondary school enrollment rates above the worldwide norm for their incomes at an earlier date grew faster later than those with lower initial levels and the high-growth East Asian countries had done just that.[46] They also spent smaller shares of their education budgets on higher education and larger shares on primary and secondary schooling than others.

Williamson asks: "What attributes of earlier economic and social history explain the above average commitment of some countries to human resource development, like schooling, in some countries and the below average commitment in others?"[47] Is it simply a cultural value or are there other explanations, such as the aim of achieving a more equal income distribution?

Understanding requires a long time-perspective. Japan, Thailand, Korea (then a colony of Japan), and the Philippines increased their primary enrollment rates more rapidly after 1900 than almost all the developing nations in the twentieth century.[48] Williamson reports that the East Asian countries have always invested more (South Korea, Japan, and Taiwan far more) and Latin America less in secondary education than other countries for which data are available. For example, South Korea had a far higher secondary schooling enrollment rate than Brazil in the early 1970s when Brazil's income was higher and its teachers less well paid than Korea's (implying a lower cost of schooling). The difference seems to stem from much greater income inequality in Brazil and an unexplained factor which can be called a 'cultural bias' *against* education in Brazil even greater than that *favoring* education in Korea.[49]

These actions reflected deeply held values in the Confucian countries. Basic education was available through temple schools in the Tokugawa era and Japan had one of the world's highest levels of literacy in 1868. Education thereafter received high national priority and, by 1950, the average farm worker had seven years of schooling while the average manufacturing one had ten years. The high quality of manpower contributed greatly to Japan's postwar success. When the Chinese moved to the Straits Settlements they promptly created schools. In colonized Korea, more than 50 percent of primary age children were attending school by the mid-1940s and South Korea had a literacy rate equal to that of Japan by the early 1950s.[50] In contrast, China, despite the traditional high standing of education, had among the lowest schooling levels at the beginning of the postwar era in part because schooling had only been for children of the elite to ready them for the civil service examinations.[51]

Elsewhere in the region, at the beginning of World War II literacy in the Philippines (influenced by the American push for education) was, at 60 percent, probably the highest in Asia after Japan. Malaysia was not far behind (at 58 percent in 1960), due largely to Chinese private education. Thailand's literacy was at about the same level as Malaysia's due to the efforts of Buddhist priests and, beginning in the 1880s, government public schools there, "in the 1930s the Japanese system of moral and vocational education was brought in to inculcate the duties and responsibilities of citizenship – patriotism and national solidarity."[52] By 1940, Thailand had rapidly rising primary enrollments although it lagged later in secondary education. In contrast, the Dutch in Indonesia, like the British in Malaysia, did little for public education.

After World War II, unlike many nations elsewhere, these countries all emphasized primary and secondary education over tertiary education until development was well advanced. There is also much private spending on schooling; in Chapter 8, Donald Snodgrass shows how important this spending has been in Korea. And, unlike many others, they invested in schooling in rural areas, a policy that helped equalize incomes.

Women's education is especially beneficial in several ways: in the labor market; in helping to reduce birth rates; and in the educational development of children. In 1960, females in the nine East Asia countries had one-half as many years of education as males (far behind Latin America's 80 percent, but far ahead of South Asia's 30 percent). The female to male ratio had grown by 1985 to 70 percent, a larger change than in any other region.[53]

Table 1.1 shows that the educational attainments of the Confucian nations in 1960 were in the middle range of all regions/civilizations, a high level given their low incomes then. They then increased these attainments by more than any other group of countries defined broadly by culture, by nearly 3 years, between 1960 and 1985 (although the Eastern Orthodox set of countries came close).

Such results, together with the observation that non-wealthy Japanese, Korean, and Chinese families often pay for extra schooling of their children and in many other ways encourage their children's studies, suggest systemic differences among cultures. This shows up at home. Mothers' estimates of the time spent on homework by first-graders in Sendai, Japan were three times as high and for Taipei children seven times as high, as for Minneapolis children. At the fifth grade, the discrepancies were equally dramatic.[54]

Table 1.1 Average years of schooling (population age 25+) in seven regions/ "civilizations" (1960 and 1985)

Region/"civilizations"	1960	1985
Western European and offshoots	6.5	8.7
Latin American	3.0	4.9
Eastern Orthodox	5.0	7.6
Sub-Saharan Africa	1.3	2.8
Confucian	4.3	7.1
Buddhist	2.6	4.2
Islamic	1.1	3.1
Developing regions' average:	2.9	5.0
Average increase: 2.1 years		

Source: Robert J. Barro and Jong-Wha Lee, "International Comparisons of Educational Attainment," *Journal of Monetary Economics* 32 (1993): 363–94

Learning goes on at all levels of these societies. Japan from at least the mid-nineteenth century became an avid learning society and the Koreans display a similar capacity. Much knowledge is acquired both from outside the region and within it: Japanese learning from Americans and Europeans, Koreans learning from Japanese and Americans, Chinese on the mainland learning from many sources, Southeast Asians learning from the Northeast Asians, etc. In South Korea and Taiwan the proportion of the government elite with advanced degrees from American universities is striking. Indonesia has the famous Berkeley Mafia. And Lee Kuan Yew, then called Harry Lee, received a double first at Cambridge.

There is further evidence of East Asia's human capital advantages from tests of achievement and of cognitive skills. As Harold Stevenson reports in Chapter 7, students from this region excel in international comparisons. Mathematics tests of 13-year-old children from OECD countries plus South Korea ranked the Korean students ahead of the others. Another comparison ranked Japanese children at the top in mathematics, Hong Kong's in the top half of the distribution, and Thai and Nigerian ones near the bottom. Yet another comparison of mathematics achievements put in rank order Chinese, Japanese, Asian-Americans and Caucasian-Americans.[55] In the US, Asian-Americans are far over-represented in National Merit Scholarships, Presidential Scholarships, Arts Recognition and Talent Search scholarships, and Westinghouse Science Talent Search scholarships. They comprise five times their proportion in the overall population in the student bodies of leading universities and are over-represented in college faculties and as architects, scientists, engineers, school teachers, and physicians. These accomplishments are also displayed by the ethnic Chinese in Southeast Asia.

The argument has been advanced that the Confucian peoples are more intelligent, at least as measured in non-verbal tests, notably those that measure visio-spatial abilities.[56] However, Stevenson reports finding no significant difference in the intellectual abilities of children in Japan, Taiwan and the US. Also, a comparison of Chinese-Americans and Japanese-Americans with Caucasians shows no significant difference in mean IQs but does show large differences in academic achievements and career choices. One estimate of the degree of over-achievement relative to their IQs from these two factors is about 21 points for the Chinese and 10 points for the Japanese; i.e. their achievements are equivalent to their having IQs that much higher than their actual ones.[57]

Whence comes this impetus to achieve? Flynn conjectures that the Pearl River Delta, the origin of most of his sample of Chinese in America, was perhaps the most work-intensive environment in the world for thousands of years. And traditional China made education the "foundation on which rested the entire political, social, economic and cultural life of the Chinese people ... [T]he traditional Chinese examination system was the only way a village youth could rise to the Mandarin class."[58]

In Chapter 11, Sung-Yeal Koo documents the rapid demographic transition experienced by these countries and the role of education in this transition. Between the early 1960s and the 1990s, population growth rates declined from about 2.7 percent annually (aside from Japan) to 0–1 percent for Northeast Asia plus Singapore and in Southeast Asia from 2–3 percent earlier to 1–2.5 percent. "Virtuous circles" were at work.[59] Early high educational levels, including education of females, caused desired family size to decrease; increased incomes enabled more money to be spent on schools; reduced numbers of children enabled more money to be spent per child and allowed more mother's time per child; this increased the quality of education. And more equal distribution of incomes enabled more children, especially in rural areas, to be enrolled. More women entered the market labor force. And given their rapidly growing savings, the demographic transition meant that more physical capital became available per worker.

A story told by Ross Garnaut reflects the Chinese taste for education. While Australian ambassador there, he was jogging early one morning in an industrial city in North China when he came across children sitting outside their houses. They were studying outside to catch the first light of day because their houses had no electricity.

The ethnic Chinese in Southeast Asia

The role of the ethnic Chinese is similar to that of many outsiders elsewhere with the one difference that they are much more numerous than others; there are about 30 million of them in Southeast Asia (outside of Taiwan and Hong Kong). In Malaysia, the Chinese comprise 35 percent of the population; in Thailand, where they are more assimilated, the standard estimate is 10 percent and it is 3–4 percent in Indonesia. They dominate commerce and industry; the business acumen, ability to mobilize capital, and networks are highly productive.

Their importance for national performance is difficult to judge given limited information about their activities, understandably so, given latent hostility to them along with the implausibility of any guess at how well the region would have done in their absence. Some facts that help put their contributions into perspective are that good policies on macroeconomics, agriculture and education deserve much of the credit, and those came from leaders paying attention to their economic technocrats.

This is not to deny the doubtless large contribution of the Chinese. When the international product cycle caused first Japanese, then Korean and Taiwanese, businessmen to look for cheap and malleable labor elsewhere as their labor became costly, they found it mainly in Southeast Asia. Chinese entrepreneurs helped the transfers go there rather than to Brazil, Mexico, or Egypt.

Other sources of information

A different kind of transfer – and increasingly exchange – involves knowledge about economic and management policies and institutions. Within the region there have been such organizations as the Asian Development Bank, Japanese aid agencies, the Korean Development Institute and the Thai Development Research Institute. Those outside of the region include the World Bank, the IMF, the Ford Foundation, the Asia Foundation, US AID, the Harvard Institute for International Development, and many others. These organizations provided much counsel and training. (For example, the advanced education of the Berkeley Mafia technocrats of Indonesia was supported by the Ford Foundation.)

In sum, countries that are providing education universally are laying the basis for more equal incomes and this will pay off in faster productivity growth and probably greater political stability. The growth-negative way, common elsewhere, is to spend much of the nation's educational budget on schooling for a small elite, to tax agriculture, or to adopt populist policies that (usually unsuccessfully) attempt to tax the rich to give to the poor (which is not an argument against a safety net for the very poor).

Growth with equality

All of the countries that combined high growth and high income equality from 1965–89 are in East Asia. (Only Malaysia had relatively high inequality.)[60] Moreover, as Dipak Dasgupta reports in Chapter 10, between 1970 and 1993 the share of the population below a postulated poverty line in Indonesia fell from 60 percent in 1970 to 14 percent in 1993. Taiwan in the 1970s became known for "growth with equity," and the concept of "shared growth" is familiar throughout the region. We have discussed the role of the wide availability of schooling and the relatively favorable treatment accorded agriculture. Hong Kong and Singapore saw to the provision of decent housing. Singapore has been sensitive to ethnic politics from the beginning and helps less productive peoples.

Inequality in outcomes might be the product of several influences: (1) an historically derived distribution of wealth perpetuated in a system of privilege; (2) differences in the distribution of talents or class or ethnic discrimination; and (3) the product (perhaps unintended) of economic policies.[61]

Wealth, initially mainly in the form of land, was highly concentrated in Latin America and the Philippines; this contributed to inequalitarian norms. The pattern of subsidizing higher education in Latin America and Africa while neglecting primary schooling reflects the fact that the children of elites benefit from the former and many of those short-changed are far away and powerless; this bias perpetuates differences in income. In contrast, land holdings in the rice-growing parts of Asia are typically small; only Malaysia and parts of Indonesia had much plantation agriculture. Moreover, there were the wartime devastations and large-scale land redistributions described above. Such redistributions are a "taking," a violation of economic freedoms; why, then, are they often credited with contributing to later successes? The answer is that some of the land had been owned by the dispossessed Japanese; also, compensation in the form of equity in state enterprises in Taiwan rose in value and this diminished the scope for grievances. Wealth reallocation worked tolerably well in Malaysia because much of it involved British holdings and because rapid growth was sustained. Campos and Root also observe that a redistribution of assets (that is unlikely to recur, for example of land) is less distorting than an ongoing redistribution of income.[62]

Differences in the distribution of talents are familiar. We have discussed the varying tastes for and talents in education. Those talents and others have led to the Chinese becoming the most successful ethnic group in the region. Lucian Pye has written: "In colonial Malaya ... Chinese workers on the rubber plantations collected sap from the trees at more than twice the rate of Malay workers." They are the commercial capitalists of the region and their successes, not surprisingly, arouse envy on the part of other groups. As he puts it:

> The Chinese are an urban people, interested in money and market activities, and they are committed to self-improvement and they have strong family ties. The Malays are rural, are contemptuous of merchants, prefer service careers in the army and police, are more easygoing in social relations, and are tolerant of divorce.[63]

Such differences are by no means growth-preventing but they can inspire resentment and violence that is bad for business, although the social consequences in Southeast Asia do not seem to have been great.

On the third explanation, economic policies, populist governments in Argentina, Peru and Chile adopted redistributive policies that created distortions and tensions while East Asian governments did relatively little of it. Instead, they took advantage of the fact that their abundant production factor was cheap, hard-working, usually docile, labor. Pushing exports increased the demand for labor and helped to narrow income differences. New skills were being learned and worker productivity increased.[64] Such a policy is equalitarian but not redistributive. Those countries that more-or-less isolated themselves from the world economy, consciously or not, perpetuated inequalities.

Evidence has been accumulating that income inequality is bad for growth.[65] In 1960, not only were the countries that were to grow fast well ahead of others in human capital, their inequalities of land and income were much lower than for a set of comparison countries. One of the costs of extreme inequality is political instability, a deterrent to investment. Also, it:

> leads to social pressures that governments have attempted to relieve through populist policies. After one or two years of economic expansion inflation soars, real wages fall, unemployment starts to increase, and output declines. The policies prove unsustainable, and the government has to switch to another set of policies. Many countries in the [Latin American] region have suffered this populist cycle, some of them more than once. In East Asia, the situation has been the opposite. A very equitable income distribution has facilitated macro-economic stability.[66]

Extreme inequality is associated with the absence of a substantial middle class, arguably one needed for sustained progress through its role in generating demand for manufactured products; and greater equality usually generates less political pressure for wasteful redistribution.[67]

More equalitarian societies may find it easier to accumulate human capital despite the well-known proposition due to Kuznets that only the rich are capable of saving and the initial stage of growth increases their share of national income. In contrast, Birdsall and Sabot *et al.* have proposed a mechanism by which policies that increase the earning capacity of the poor, increases their productivity, savings and the demand for domestic goods.[68] Moreover, the ownership of land by many smallholders in Korea helped them finance the education of their children and lessened hostility to nearly universally authoritarian regimes.

A key distinction concerns how greater equality of incomes is achieved: through the more even distribution of *opportunity* (e.g., to schools or the judicial system) or through government redistribution of *outcomes* (e.g., money incomes). Achieving greater equality via the former route is likely to increase the national income and foster social harmony whereas the latter risks lowering the national income and encouraging social disharmony.

External influences

External influences here refer to those from outside individual countries, including from outside the region. Several have been mentioned: ancient ones from China, those from Spain and America on the Philippines, those of capitalism and democracy from Europe and America, and socialism from Europe.

There have been others, some common to the developing world such as the boom of the 1950s–60s and the oil shocks of the 1970s and some narrower. Military threats are also external influences and, as we have seen, they played a large role both in motivating governments to develop and in increasing their political scope for doing so. And although any developing nation could, in principle, learn from Japan's success and from those of Korea and Taiwan, neighboring countries have benefited most.

Japan's early modernization and its later influence on others

Here two kinds of influence are of interest: external influences on Japan's modernization, and then its contribution to the modernization of others. Important early external influences on Japan came from China, mostly via Korea with significant modifications en route, including a written language and the Confucianist ethic. Later, there was the thin link to modern technology via the Dutch in Nagasaki, then the reaction to the perceived threat from Europe and America followed by the adaptation of many of their institutions.

After World War II the US helped during the occupation with economic aid, sound fiscal and monetary policies, land reform, and – inadvertently – through procurements in the Korean War. For all that, Japan's achievements were largely home-grown. Although it continued to acquire much technology from abroad, it demonstrated organizational creativity, including inventing the main bank–*keiretsu* system and just-in-time manufacturing.

Before World War II, Japan had a strong impact on East Asia through its colonial activities. Although those on the receiving end suffered greatly, Korea and Taiwan also benefited from infrastructure, schools and some (relatively low level) industrial and government experiences. Korea, especially, acquired institutions useful for development and from 1920–40 Korea was one of the world's most rapidly growing nations; for instance, between 1912 and 1945 the number of factory workers rose from 12,000 to 300,000.[69] Park Chung Hee was thoroughly exposed to Japanese ways of doing things and Korea's development strategy became modeled largely on Japan's.[70] Park also became familiar with the American management style while working with the US military.

Japan's influence has been less direct but nonetheless important to Southeast Asia. Being an occupying power gave the Japanese familiarity with these countries, and their increasing direct investments have had a large impact. A familiar image is that of "flying geese," with Japan in the lead; perhaps a more apposite one is of "waves" of development that have moved from northeast to southwest. Chapter 12 by James Raphael and Thomas Rohler addresses the complexities involved in trying to construct such a model of Japan's development – they offer several that could be relevant.

Neighborhood effects

The good performers got on the growth track in sequence, starting in the North and moving South. This process involved nearby countries (separated at most by one time zone), with many cultural similarities and past interactions (albeit often unwilling ones).

Although this sequence helps an understanding of East Asia's performance, it is somewhat oversimplified. For example, although Chinese large-scale industrialization began after 1949, the coastal parts of China, notably Shanghai, were making industrial progress in the 1920s and 1930s up to the Japanese invasion in 1937. As Mark Elvin puts it (personal communication), in that period, Shanghai – with the presence of Europeans, Americans, and Japanese – provided a non-stop, year-round exhibition of textile and other industrial machinery. This history implies the existence of social capabilities, at least along the Chinese coast, that would have been expressed earlier in sustained development but for unfortunate political events.

There is an exceptionally high level of trade within the region. Any given pair of countries there in 1990 tended to trade over four times more with each other than otherwise similar countries.[71] This activity could reflect the fact that manufactured goods are traded mainly through networks and mostly not, like commodities, through impersonal markets.[72] Networks, prominent in this region, are most easily formed where trust exists; i.e. within families and ethnic groups such as the ethnic Chinese throughout the region. It also has many organizations that specialize in bringing buyers and sellers together including the large Japanese and Korean trading organizations and the many traders in Hong Kong.

Why the Philippines has lagged

The poor economic performance of the Philippines provides a sharp contrast. Its long rule by Spain left it with institutions that were negative for development while the Americans, aside from promoting education and democracy, decided early to delegate administration to the Philippine elite.

Unlike almost all of the region's economically successful countries, Philippine political culture has been class-stratified and patron–client based with a small number of families dominating politics and the economy. In this regard there are similarities to Indonesia but that country has allowed its technocrats more scope, especially in the management of macroeconomic policy. Until recently, Philippine economic policies have been poor, notably under the long rule of Marcos who pursued the politics of cronyism to a destructive extreme. Timberman describes an opaque system: "[o]ne leading Filipino businessman later likened government ministries under Marcos to the spokes of a wheel, with Marcos at the hub. All the spokes were attached to the hub but none of them knew what the others were doing."[73]

The main developmental asset of the Philippines has been its high educational level, one that doubtless kept its economic performance from being even worse.

THE STRUCTURE OF THE BOOK

The following chapters are grouped according to the four broad themes discussed above:

- Effective governance
- Achieving and learning societies
- Growth with equality
- External influences

The final chapter addresses this question: What useful lessons might developing countries in other regions derive from the East Asian experience?

NOTES

1 Elvin, 1973
2 Maddison, 1994
3 On the alleged developmental advantage of authoritarian regimes, see Fukuyama, 1992. For the alleged virtues of government micro-management, see Johnson, 1982; Wade, 1990; and Amsden, 1989.
4 Teranishi (1995) reports a net drain on agriculture in the Latin America and Africa but not in East Asia.
5 Gwartney *et al.*, 1996: xvii (emphasis in original).
6 Gwartney *et al.*, 1996. See Freedom House, 1996, for broadly similar findings but with lower ratings for Singapore and South Korea.
7 Williamson, 1993: 146.
8 Williamson, 1993: 131.
9 Hobday, 1995.
10 World Bank, 1993.
11 Rodrik, 1994; Little, 1996.
12 Young, 1992; Kim and Lau, 1994a: 235–71; and Krugman, 1994: 62–78.
13 Lau, 1994b.
14 Aoki *et al.*, 1995
15 Ohkawa and Rosovsky, 1973.
16 Kuznets, 1966: 13.
17 North, 1994: 359–69.
18 North, 1991: 98.
19 Mason *et al.*, 1980: 253.
20 Vargas Llosa, 1995: 54.
21 Hansen, 1991: 254.
22 Campos and Root, 1996: 31.
23 Landau, 1993.
24 Waterbury, 1993: 18.
25 Campos and Root, 1996: 110.
26 Olson, 1982.
27 Christiansen *et al.*, 1992.
28 Shleifer and Vishny, 1993; and Mauro, 1995.
29 Shleifer and Vishny, 1993.
30 *Financial Times* (June 3, 1996).
31 Freedom House, 1996.
32 Maddison, 1994.

33 Lipset, 1996.
34 Aoki, 1995.
35 Redding, 1990; and Fukuyama, 1995.
36 Analects, XIII, ch. 9, quoted from Hou, 1995: 243.
37 Morishima, 1982.
38 Nakone, 1970.
39 Weber, 1962.
40 Alford, 1995.
41 Lin and Ho, 1995.
42 Metzger, 1995.
43 Vogel, 1991.
44 Aoki *et al.,* 1995: 31.
45 World Bank, 1993; Lau, 1994a.
46 Baumol *et al.,* 1989: 205 and Barro, 1991.
47 Williamson, 1993: 131.
48 Easterlin, 1981.
49 Williamson, 1993: 157.
50 Naohiro Ogawa and Noriko O. Tsuya, "Demographic Change and Human Resources Development in the Asia-Pacific Region: Trends of the 1960s to 1980s and Future Prospects," in Ogawa, *et al.,* ibid., p. 60.
51 Oshima, 1993.
52 Oshima, 1993.
53 World Bank, 1993: 47.
54 Stevenson and Stigler, 1992: 55.
55 Chen and Stevenson, 1996.
56 Lynn, 1991.
57 Flynn, 1991.
58 Ibid., p. 128.
59 Birdsall *et al.,* 1995.
60 World Bank, 1993: 30. The ratio of total incomes of the richest 20 percent of the population to the bottom 20 percent is 4–11 times in a set of East Asian countries and 11–26 times in a set of Latin American ones.
61 Williamson, 1993: 144.
62 Campos and Root, 1996: 45.
63 Pye, 1985: 250.
64 Birdsall and Sabot, 1995.
65 Alesina and Rodrik, 1994: 465–91; and Alesina and Rodrik, 1991.
66 Larrain and Vergara, 1993: 259–60; also Rodrik, 1994.
67 Murphy *et al.,* 1989.
68 Birdsall *et al.* (1995) estimate that the net effect of broadly-based educational expansion is to narrow income inequalities, and that lower inequalities – controlling for the direct effects of education – have a significant effect on growth.
69 Mason *et al.,* 1980: 76–7.
70 Kohli, 1994.
71 This observation is based on use of a gravity model of international trade wherein trade between two countries is proportional to the product of their GDPs and inversely proportional to the distance between them. (Frankel *et al.,* 1993).
72 Rauch, 1996.
73 Timberman, 1991: 92–3.

REFERENCES

Alesina, Alberto and Dani Rodrik (1991) "Distributive Politics and Economic Growth" National Bureau of Economic Research Working Paper No. 3668 (March).

—— (1994) "Distributive Politics and Economic Growth" *Quarterly Journal of Economics*, 109 (May): 465–91.

Alford, William P. (1995) *To Steal a Book is an Elegant Offense*, Stanford: Stanford University Press.

Amsden, Alice H. (1989) *Asia's Next Giant: South Korea and Late Industrialization*, New York: Oxford University Press.

Aoki, Masahiko (1995) "Evolutionary Organizational Diversity and Its Implications for Reform in Transitional Economies," mimeo, Stanford University.

Aoki, Masahiko, Kevin Murdock, and Masahiro Okuno-Fujiwara (1995) "Beyond the East Asian Miracle: Introducing the Market Enhancing View," Stanford University Center for Economic Policy Research Publication No. 442 (Oct).

Barro, Robert J. (1991) "Economic Growth in a Cross Section of Countries," *Quarterly Journal of Economics*, 106 (May), pp. 407–44.

Baumol, William J., Blackman, Sue Anne Batey, and Wolff, Edward N. (1989) *Productivity and American Leadership: The Long View*, Cambridge, MA: MIT Press.

Birdsall, Nancy, David Ross, and Richard Sabot (1995) "Inequality and Growth Reconsidered," unpublished paper prepared for the annual meeting of the American Economic Association, May 1995.

Campos, Jose Edgardo and Hilton Root (1996) *The Key to the Asian Miracle: Making Shared Growth Credible*, Washington: Brookings Institution.

Chen, Chuansheng and Harold W. Stevenson (1996) "Motivation and Mathematics Achievement: A Comparative Study of Asian American, Caucasian American, and East Asian High School Students," *Child Development* 66 (4).

Christiansen, Scott R., David Dollar, Ammar Siamwalla, and Pakorn Vichyanond (1992) "Institutional and Political Bases of Growth-Inducing Policies in Thailand," draft paper prepared for the World Bank project on the East Asian Development Experience, October, 1992.

Easterlin, Richard A. (1981) "Why Isn't the Whole World Developed?" *Journal of Economic History*, vol. XLI, March, no. 1.

Elvin, Mark (1973) *The Pattern of the Chinese Past*, Stanford: Stanford University Press.

Flynn, James R. (1991) *Asian Americans: Achievement Beyond IQ*, Hillsdale, NJ: Lawrence Erlbaum Associates.

Frankel, Jeffrey, Ernesto Stein, and Shang-jin Wei (1993) "Continental Trading Blocs: Are They Natural or Super-Natural?", National Bureau of Economic Research Working Paper No. 4588.

Freedom House (1996), *World Survey of Economic Freedom, 1995–1996*, Richard E. Messick (ed.), New Brunswick, NJ: Transaction Publishers.

Fukuyama, Francis (1992) *The End of History and the Last Man*, New York: Free Press.

—— (1995) *Trust: The Social Virtues and the Creation of Prosperity*, New York: Free Press.

Gwartney, James, Robert Lawson, and Walter Block (1996) *Economic Freedom of the World: 1975–1995*, Vancouver: Fraser Institute.

Hansen, Bent (1991) *The Political Economy of Poverty, Equity and Growth*, Oxford: Oxford University Press.

Hobday, Michael (1995) *Innovation in East Asia*, Brookfield, VT: Edward Elgar.

Hou, Chia-Chu (1995) "The Influence of Confucianism on Economic Policies and

Entrepreneurship in Taiwan," in Tzong-shian Yu and Joseph S. Lee (eds) *Confucianism and Economic Development*, Taipei: Chung-Hua Institution for Economic research.

Johnson, Chalmers (1982) *MITI and the Japanese Miracle*, Stanford: Stanford University Press.

Kim, Jong-Il and Lawrence J. Lau (1994) "The Sources of Economic Growth of the East Asian Newly Developing Countries," *Journal of the Japanese and International Economies*, 8 (Sept.), pp. 235–71.

Kohli, Atul (1994) "Where Do High Growth Political Economies Come From? The Japanese Lineage of Korea's 'Developmental State'," *World Development*, vol. 22, no. 9: 1269–93.

Krugman, Paul (1994) *Modern Economic Growth*, New Haven: Yale University Press.

Landau, Daniel (1993) "The Economic Impact of Military Expenditures," World Bank Policy Research Working Paper No. 1138.

Larrain, Felipe and Rodrigo Vergara (1993) "Investment and Macro-Economic Adjustment: The Case of East Asia," in Luis Serven and Andres Solimano, eds, *Striving for Growth after Adjustment: the Role of Capital Formation*, Washington, DC: World Bank, pp. 259–60.

Lau, Lawrence J. (1994a) "The Sources of Long-Term Economic Growth: Observations from the Experience of Developed and Developing Countries," Department of Economics, Stanford University.

—— (1994b) "How the East Grew Rich," paper prepared for the Salzburg Seminar, Salzburg, Austria, December 1994.

Lin, Tzong-Biau and Ho, Lok-Sang (1995) "Is There a Link Among Confucianism, Institutions and Economic Performance?", in Tzong-shian Yu and Joseph S. Lee (eds) *Confucianism and Economic Development*, Taipei: Chung-Hua Institution for Economic Research.

Lipset, Seymour Martin (1996) *American Exceptionalism*, New York: Norton.

Little, Ian (1996) "Picking Winners: The East Asian Experience," London: Social Market Foundation.

Lynn, Richard (1991) "Race Differences in Intelligence: A Global Perspective," *Mankind Quarterly*, 31: 254–96.

Maddison, Angus (1994) "Explaining the Economic Performance of Nations, 1820–1989," in William J. Baumol, Richard R. Nelson, and Edward N. Wolff, eds, *Convergence of Productivity: Cross-National Studies and Historical Evidence*, London: Oxford University Press.

Mason, Edward S., Mahn Je Kim, Dwight H. Perkins, Kwang Suk Kim, David C. Cole, Leroy Jones, Il Sakong, Donald R. Snodgrass, and Noel F. McGinn (1980) *The Economic and Social Modernization of the Republic of Korea*, Cambridge, MA: Council on East Asian Studies, Harvard University, 1980.

Mauro, Paulo (1995) "Corruption and Growth," *Quarterly Journal of Economics*, 110 (August): 681–712.

Metzger, Thomas A. (1995) "Confucian Culture and Economic Modernization: An Historical Approach," in Tzong-shian Yu and Joseph S. Lee (eds) *Confucianism and Economic Development*, Taipei: Chung-Hua Institution for Economic Research.

Morishima, Michio (1982) *Why Has Japan Succeeded? Western Technology and the Japanese Ethos*, Cambridge: Cambridge University Press.

Murphy, Kevin M., Andrei Shleifer, and Robert W. Vishny (1989) "Income Distribution, Market Size, and Industrialization," *Quarterly Journal of Economics*, 104 (Aug.): 537–65.

Nakone, Chie (1970) *Japanese Society*, Berkeley: University of California Press.

——(1991) "Institutions," *Journal of Economic Perspectives*, 5 (Winter): 98.

North, Douglass C. (1994) "Economic Performance Through Time," *American Economic Review*, 84 (June): 359–69 (Nobel lecture).

Ogawa, Naohiro and Tsuya, Noriko O. (1993) "Demographic Change and Human Resources Development in the Asia-Pacific Region: Trends of the 1960s to 1980s and Future Prospects," in Naohiro Ogawa, Gavin W. Jones, and Jeffrey G. Williamson (eds) *Human Resources in Development along the Asia-Pacific Rim*, Singapore: Oxford University Press.

Ogawa, Naohiro, Gavin W. Jones, and Jeffrey G. Williamson (eds) (1993) *Human Resources in Development Along the Asia-Pacific Rim*, Singapore: Oxford University Press.

Olson, Mancur (1982) *The Rise and Decline of Nations: Economic Growth, Stagflation, and Social Rigidities*, New Haven: Yale University Press.

Oshima, Harry T. (1993) *Strategic Processes in Monsoon Asia's Economic Development*, Baltimore: Johns Hopkins University Press.

Pye, Lucian W. (1985) *Asian Power and Politics: The Cultural Dimensions of Authority*, Cambridge, MA: Harvard University Press.

Rauch, James E. (1996) "Trade and Search: Social Capital, Sogos Shosa, and Spillovers," National Bureau of Economic Research Working Paper No. 5618, June.

Redding, Gordon S. (1990) *The Spirit of Chinese Capitalism*, Berlin: De Gruyter.

Rodrik, Dani (1994) "King Kong Meets Godzilla: The World Bank and The East Asian Miracle," in "Miracle or Design," Overseas Development Council Policy Essay No. 11.

Shleifer, Andrei and Robert W. Vishny (1995) "Corruption," *Quarterly Journal of Economics*, 43 (Aug. 1993).

Stevenson, Harold W. and James W. Stigler (1992) *The Learning Gap*, New York: Simon and Schuster.

Teranishi, Juro (1995) "Sectoral Resource Transfer, Conflict, and Macro-stability in Economic Development: A Comparative Analysis," in Masahiko Aoki, Kevin Murdock, and Masahiro Okuno-Fujiwara (eds) *Beyond the East Asian Miracle: Introducing the Market Enhancing View*, Stanford University Center for Economic Policy Research Publication No. 442.

Timberman, David G. (1991) *A Changeless Land: Continuity and Change in Philippine Politics*, Armonk, NY: M.E. Sharpe.

Vargas Llosa, Mario, in James Como (1995) "Hero Storyteller," *National Review*, 47 (April 17).

Vogel, Ezra (1991) *The Four Little Dragons: The Spread of Industrialization in East Asia*, Cambridge, MA: Harvard University Press.

Wade, Robert (1990) *Governing the Market: Economic Theory and the Role of the Government in East Asian Industrialization*, Princeton: Princeton University Press.

Waterbury, John (1993) *Exposed to Innumerable Delusions*, Cambridge: Cambridge University Press.

Weber, Max (1962) *The Religion of China: Confucianism and Taoism*, New York: Free Press.

Williamson, Jeffrey G. (1993) "Human Capital Deepening, Inequality, and Demographic Events along the Asia-Pacific Rim," in Naohiro Ogawa, Gavin W. Jones, and Jeffrey G. Williamson (eds) *Human Resources in Development along the Asia-Pacific Rim*, Singapore: Oxford University Press.

World Bank (1993) *The East Asian Miracle: Economic Growth and Public Policy*, New York: Oxford University Press.

Young, Alwyn (1992) "A Tale of Two Cities: Factor Accumulation and Technical Change in Hong Kong and Singapore," *National Bureau of Economic Research Macro-Economic Annual*.

Yu, Tzong-shian and Joseph S. Lee, eds (1995) *Confucianism and Economic Development*, Taipei: Chung-Hua Institution for Economic Research.

Part I

Effective governance

Most governments of developing countries after World War II attempted to do too many things and did them badly. The communist countries were the worst in this respect but the many others with much state ownership of the economy, regulation and autarkic policies also did poorly. In contrast, the successful ones, and these were overwhelmingly located in East Asia, had effective governments that understood that they had to support their private sectors. These were strong, effective governments that focused their considerable powers on the essentials for development. Their dynamism was not limited to economics; success brought about large changes, including in politics.

2 Constructing the political foundations of an economic miracle

Minxin Pei

The rapid growth of East Asian economies since the end of World War II has fundamentally altered the distribution of global wealth and political power. In the scholarly community, the economic ascendence of East Asia has received intense attention and aroused heated debates in recent years.[1] Social scientists have attempted to explain the causes of the dramatic economic transformation of East Asia, and their efforts have spawned a vast (and still growing) literature on the political economy of East Asia.[2] The most influential argument, eloquently articulated in the works of Chalmers Johnson, Alice Amsden, and Robert Wade, questions some of the basic tenets of neo-classical economic theories and focuses, instead, on the effectiveness of state intervention in the economy through industrial policy, credit control, and investment targeting. Such state intervention is found to be especially prominent and efficacious in Japan and the first-generation newly-industrialized countries (NICs) in East Asia (Korea, Taiwan, and Singapore). It has also been further argued that these countries were able to adopt export-oriented industrialization strategy with active participation by the state primarily due to the "insulation" of the state (especially the economic bureaucracy) from societal rent-seeking groups.

This *state-centered* explanation for the rapid economic growth in East Asia, while strongly buttressed by the solid evidence of extensive state intervention, has one serious flaw: a perceived methodological weakness manifested in its proponents' inability to apply rigorous methods of theory-testing on the basis of systematically gathered data. In most studies on government-business cooperation in East Asia, evidence tends to be presented in an anecdotal fashion. Even in the best works on the subject, rigorous statistical tests are rarely, if at all, performed to validate theoretical hypotheses.[3] This weakness leaves the theorists of the developmental state vulnerable to criticism by neoclassical economists who employ apparently more rigorous methodological tools to support their claim that market forces, rather than government intervention, were the real miracle-maker in East Asia. The most influential work produced to counter the claims made by the theorists of the developmental state is the 1993 World Bank's report entitled *The East Asian Miracle: Economic Growth and Public Policy*. Amassing a wealth of comparative data on economic development in East Asia and other developing countries, the re-revisionist school represented by the Bank's report cites sound macro-economic and other public policies (conservative fiscal policy, high savings rates, and investment in human capital) adopted by East Asian countries as the basic sources of developmental success; it concedes, with much reservation, on only one point namely, that in northeast Asian states, government manipulation of credit supplies may have played some role in spurring certain investment activities.

A third perspective on the East Asian Miracle is centered on the cultural values and organization of production in East Asia. This approach credits communitarian values, the Confucian work ethic, emphasis on education and equity, long-term relational contracting, and informal corporate and ethnic networks in many East Asian countries (especially in societies with strong Confucian cultural heritage), with fostering a cultural environment conducive to rapid economic growth. The most successful efforts at employing the cultural-sociological perspective have produced several notable works, all derived from Japanese examples.[4]

The scholarship based on these three differing and, in certain senses complementary, explanations is now rich and extensive. It, however, has failed to probe the deeper political foundations of the so-called East Asian Miracle – the evolution and operation of the governing institutions in these countries. The developmental state perspective tends to assert the autonomy of the state and seldom investigates its historical or political origins.[5] This approach has given excessive emphasis to how the state governed the *market* but paid scant attention to how the state governed *itself* in East Asia. It has all but overlooked the process of political insti-tutionalization and completely missed the story of institutional develop-ment in East Asian states since the end of World War Two that has been a critical part of the region's developmental success. For the neoclassical and cultural-sociological perspectives, the issue of the political foundations of rapid economic growth is largely irrelevant and consequently ignored.

A renewed focus on the evolution and operation of the ruling institu-tions in East Asian states may illuminate several important issues that the literature on East Asian political economy has not yet sufficiently addressed:

1 the process in which the ruling political institutions (political parties, the legal system, representative organs, and electoral systems) were developed and consolidated in East Asian countries and the cross-country similarities and differences in this process;
2 the mechanisms through which these institutions resolved conflicts among competing political forces and helped maintain political order;

3 the role played by key individual leaders in initiating crucial institutional reforms and enforcing the new norms conducive to rapid economic development.

These questions require detailed investigation not only because such inquiries will further our understanding of the political factors behind the East Asian Miracle, but because they will generate new insights into two important theoretical issues in political development and economic growth: laying the institutional foundations for political stability and curbing the predatory behavior of the (autocratic) state.[6]

In retrospect, the lack of scholarly attention to the political foundations of the East Asian Miracle is all the more remarkable because in the 1950s and through much of the 1960s, politics in many newly constituted political systems in East Asia resembled that of the contemporary post-colonial developing world; it was ruled by high levels of political instability, intra-elite intrigues, leftist insurgencies, urban radicalism, political violence, ethnic conflicts, and governmental corruption.[7] In the last 40 years, however, political order has gradually been restored in these countries, creating the essential political preconditions to sustained rapid economic growth. To be sure, the restoration of political order and consolidation of new ruling institutions occurred earlier in some countries (such as Taiwan, South Korea, and Singapore) than in others (Indonesia, Malaysia and Thailand).[8] Moreover, the precise patterns of restoration also differed among the countries in the region (as shall be discussed later). The net effect of the restoration of political order was similar across the entire region: it ushered in long periods of rapid economic growth.

This chapter does not attempt to provide a theory of political development based on the East Asian experience. Its goal is to offer some insights into the commonalities and differences in the political evolution of East Asian countries since World War II. These observations will provoke more questions focusing on the development of political institutions in East Asia and on the extent to which the *political* lessons from the East Asian Miracle may be applicable to other developing regions.

EVOLUTION OF POLITICAL INSTITUTIONS IN EAST ASIA

An unmistakable feature of political development in East Asia since World War II (see Table 2.1) is the gradual process of "authoritarian institutionalization" in nearly all the high-performance East Asian countries. At the center of this process was the slow emergence of modern political institutions exercising formal and informal constraining power through dominant parties, bureaucracies, semi-open electoral procedures, and a legal system that steadily acquired a measure of autonomy. This long evolutionary process created institutional mechanisms that defined the

Table 2.1 The evolution of major political systems in East and Southeast Asia since World War II

	Authoritarian–democratic continuum			
	Hard authoritarianism and orthodox Communism	Soft authoritarianism	Democratizing regimes/ fragile democracies	Established democracy
High		Singapore (1965–) Taiwan (1974–86) South Korea (1981–87) Malaysia (1970–) Thailand (1976–92) South Korea (1962–71) Indonesia (1971–)	Taiwan (1986–) South Korea (1987–) Thailand (1992–)	Japan (1947–)
Political institutionalization				
Low	China (1949–79) Vietnam (1954–86) North Korea (1947–) Myanmar (Burma) (1962–)	Taiwan (1949–74) South Korea (1972–80)	China (1979–) Vietnam (1986–) The Philippines (1972–86) Indonesia (1959–70) Thailand (1947–73)	Singapore* (1955–63) South Korea (1953–61) Malaysia (1963–69) Myanmar (Burma) (1948–61) The Philippines (1946–71 & 1986–) Indonesia (1950–58) Thailand (1974–76)

Note: Singapore became part of Malaysia during 1963–65

rules of politics with greater clarity and helped stabilize expectations among competing political forces, producing two beneficial outcomes – a higher level of political stability and security of property rights (due to the increasing constraints placed on the rulers by the power of market forces and new political norms).

As depicted by Table 2.1, in a few countries, the process of institutionalization assumed a linear characteristic (Taiwan being the most exemplary case); political development generally proceeded from under-institutionalized autocracy to institutionalized autocracy and to new democracy. Although the process of political institutionalization has been slow in China and Vietnam, both countries seem to be evolving along a similar path. In a majority of the East Asian countries that emerged from decolonization in the 1950s, the general pattern was, initially, a movement away from unconsolidated democracy to relatively institutionalized autocracy (with an interlude of under-institutionalized authoritarianism) and, in the case of South Korea and Thailand, to new democracy. Both patterns of political development, in retrospect, seem to reconfirm the theoretical propositions made in Samuel Huntington's seminal works on political development and democratization.[9] More than any other region in the developing world, the East Asian case offers a wealth of empirical data to test Huntington's controversial thesis that the most critical cause of the breakdown of political order in new states undergoing rapid socio-economic changes was the underdevelopment of governing institutions and the most effective treatment of this political pathology was the construction of these institutions.

From a comparative perspective, the transition from weak democracies to authoritarian rule in East Asia in the 1960s and 1970s differed fundamentally from a similar contemporary trend in South America. In the case of South America, as analyzed by Guillermo O'Donnell and others, the emergence of bureaucratic-authoritarianism was caused chiefly by the exhaustion of the import–substitution industrialization and economic crisis produced by unsustainable populist economic policies.[10] Although most "soft authoritarian" regimes in East Asia shared many of the institutional characteristics of bureaucratic-authoritarianism, the factors contributing to their ascendance were diverse.[11] The pre-eminent cause was the underdevelopment of critical political institutions (parties, bureaucracies, and the judiciary) and the political crisis caused by the failure of existing political institutions to mediate conflicts among diverse political forces in these countries. Purely economic factors (such as the developmental crisis set off by the end of the "easy" import–substitution phase) played a relatively minor role.[12]

The rise of autocracies with a relatively high level of institutionalization in East Asia coincided with the most rapid phase of economic growth in the region. Although the positive relationship between rapid economic growth and authoritarian rule in East Asia has often been asserted, this claim has been challenged both on theoretical and empirical grounds.[13] This controversy aside, the more mature form of authoritarianism in East Asia was characterized by a set of distinctive behavioral patterns that revealed a rising degree of the constraints of the rule law and of the binding political constraints on the rulers, some of them self-imposed by the ruling elite and others imposed by countervailing political and economic forces, and emerging institutional norms. Under mature authoritarianism, the ruling elite became more diverse, and the oligarchy grew more competitive internally, especially with generational changes within the ruling elite (a development leading, in most cases, to the ascendance of moderate technocrats) and the rising level of institutional autonomy accorded to development agencies and local governments which increasingly grew assertive over their prerogatives. This process of "creeping institutionalism" that defined authority relations within the various domains of the state and set the rules governing elite politics also spilled over into state–society relations. Most notable in this respect was the unexpected durability of semi-open electoral procedures (most of them initially introduced by authoritarian rulers to reduce the direct costs of harsh political repression) and their effects on the political process itself and the calculations of the ruling elite.

This development resulted in a gradual expansion of the public space, usually marked by the state's reduction of its intervention in routine social activities and a significant increase of civil liberties. The semi-open electoral process also afforded the nascent democratic opposition a ready and relatively low-risk institutional forum to challenge their authoritarian rulers and establish their political base. The combination of creeping institutionalism under authoritarian rule and the dramatic expansion of the social base of democracy (especially the middle-class) due to the rapid economic development constituted a powerful force behind the surge of democratization in several East Asian states in the late 1980s and early 1990s (Taiwan, South Korea, and Thailand).

Another notable feature of political development in East Asia since World War II was that the transition from hard to soft authoritarianism (and from weak democracy to soft authoritarianism) coincided (and in some instances, overlapped) with the beginning of the implementation of market-friendly economic policies, structural-institutional reforms, and the immediate economic take-off in these states (most markedly in Taiwan, South Korea, Indonesia, Vietnam, and China). Of course, the exact timing of this subtle shift differed among these countries. It may be argued that Taiwan, South Korea and Singapore (the first-generation NICs) were the first to undertake this shift (in the early 1960s), followed by Indonesia, Malaysia, and Thailand in the early 1970s (which are generally considered the second-generation NICs), with China and Vietnam attempting to take the same route in the 1980s.[14]

In nearly all the East Asian countries where the transition from poorly institutionalized autocracy to relatively institutionalized autocracy occurred, the shift was, again characterized by several striking similarities.

The transition was precipitated by a horrendous domestic crisis that called into question the political legitimacy and viability of the governing elite. In the case of Taiwan, Kuomintang's thorough defeat in the civil war on the mainland (1946–49) and a bloody local uprising against government corruption and incompetence (1947) forced the regime to undertake a set of wide-ranging reforms, including the re-organization of the ruling party, a purge of corrupt and incompetent officials, and land reform. In South Korea, the watershed event precipitating this shift was the failed attempt by an unpopular ruler (Syngman Rhee) to steal an election in 1960, which sparked a nationwide revolt spearheaded by students and eventually led to the takeover by the military.

In Indonesia, an abortive coup in 1965 and the subsequent massacre of the communists and their supporters nearly plunged the country into complete chaos. For Singapore, its unsuccessful union with Malaysia in 1965 was the political crisis that created the favorable opportunities for the People's Action Party (PAP) under the leadership of Lee Kuan Yew to consolidate its rule. In Malaysia, the political crisis was triggered by the breakdown of ethnic peace and the collapse of the grand political coalition among the Malays, Chinese and Indians in 1969, leading to severe restrictions on political competition and restructuring of political institutions in the new federation. In Thailand, which was perhaps the most stable polity in Southeast Asia, government performance declined dramatically in the early 1970s and led to rising political violence and riots in the streets, ultimately resulting in the 1976 takeover of power by the Thai military.

In China, two decades of extremist economic policies (embodied in the Great Leap Forward) and political movement (which culminated in the Cultural Revolution) did much to discredit the Old Regime and were responsible for the initiation of reforms in 1979. In Vietnam, the Old Regime's crisis originated in its military misadventure in Cambodia and radical economic policies adopted after the reunification of the country in 1975; the regime's initiation of economic reforms in 1986 was motivated by its desire to remedy its past mistakes. Even in Myanmar (Burma), the military regime's economic reforms and attempts at political reconciliation with the opposition in the early 1990s can be traced to the student-led bloody uprising against the failed military socialist dictatorship in 1988 and the subsequent international isolation of the junta.

These political and economic crises played a critical role in (1) bringing new leadership to power and (2) discrediting old policies so dramatically that radical institutional reforms, once inconceivable under the old regime, became acceptable and were adopted. These institutional reforms led to new and more efficient property rights arrangements that became the foundation of sustained economic growth.[15] The most dramatic examples in this respect were land reforms initiated by right-wing regimes in Taiwan and South Korea (in the 1950s), and agrarian decollectivization launched by communist-authoritarian regimes in China (in 1979) and Vietnam (in 1986).[16]

RESTORING POLITICAL ORDER

As noted, the severe political and economic crises that precipitated the process of political institutionalization in East Asia served to discredit the old regimes and bring in new political leaders committed to a new course of action. Indeed, in nearly all cases, the process of restoration of political order was led and managed by a new leadership. In some instances, this change of leadership was peaceful (Vietnam, China, and Malaysia); in others, it was violent and accomplished through military coups (South Korea, Indonesia, and Thailand). With the exception of Thailand, Singapore, and Malaysia, the old leadership consisted primarily of first-generation nationalist or communist revolutionaries whose governments were initially legitimized on the basis of successful nationalist or communist revolutions, but whose legitimacy was progressively eroded by radical politics and economic stagnation caused by market-unfriendly policies.[17]

The process of institutionalizing politics, however, was more complicated, turbulent, and costly in countries where the radical Left had gained political dominance or ready access to political power (e.g., China, Vietnam, Indonesia under Sukarno, and Myanmar (Burma)).[18] In these countries, the self-destruction of the radical Left took place at enormous costs, ranging from China's Great Leap Forward and the Cultural Revolution, to Vietnam's miserable economic failure and international isolation in the mid-1980s, to the bloody elimination of Indonesia's Communist Party (PKI) in 1965, and to Burma's progressive political and economic decay resulting from its three decades of self-imposed isolation and socialist economic policies (1962–92). In these countries, the transition from hard to soft-authoritarianism tended to encounter greater difficulties and face much higher levels of uncertainty. The process of political institutionalization was also more tenuous. Despite the reversal of radical politics and socialist economic policies, key political institutions, especially legal institutions, political parties, and technocracy, remained fragile and lacked autonomy.

In other East Asian countries, the radical Left failed to gain access to political power. In Malaysia, the defeat of the communist insurgency under British colonial rule eliminated the Left as a viable political force in the post-independence era. In Singapore, the PAP's internal split and the government's subsequent *blitzkrieg* strike against the Barisan Sosialis in 1963 also effectively marginalized the Left. In Thailand, the Left never had a chance of becoming a significant political force due to the absence of a nationalist revolution (which global experience suggests was perhaps the most conducive to the rise of the Left). In South Korea, the Korean

War destroyed the Left and weakened its base of political support in the South. In Taiwan, the indigenous Left was a negligible force, and the Kuomintang's repression of and vigilance against the communists as a security threat made the rise of the Left a total impossibility. Such fortuitous circumstances spared these countries prolonged ideological and class conflicts and provided favorable conditions for building effective political institutions to guide rapid economic development. An important political lesson from these five countries (Malaysia, Singapore, Thailand, South Korea, and Taiwan) is that the Right that controlled the government, after destroying the Left as a political force, wisely adopted certain equity-enhancing policies championed by the Left, because such policies (e.g., land reform, shared growth, and investment in human capital) undermined social support for the Left and contributed to economic development.

The process of political institutionalization is not restricted narrowly to the consolidation of key political organizations and procedures. These are the formal manifestations of institutionalization; they are an important part of the institutionalization process, but not the only part. As Douglass North noted, institutions also include customs and norms that do not assume procedural or legal forms, although they equally restrain and influence human behavior.[19] In East Asia, the actual course of political institutionalization has borne out North's insights. Formal political organizations and procedures were strengthened; informal norms also gained greater binding power. With no exception, all new regimes immediately initiated a substantial reorganization of the ruling apparatus and a process of establishing political norms.

The most notable and far-reaching measure in increasing the effectiveness of government was the co-optation and empowerment of technocrats chosen through rigorous examinations and scrutiny of their professional qualifications.[20] To be sure, in some countries, thanks to the legacy of previous colonial regimes, the level of technocratization of government bureaucracies was already quite high and so was the quality of civil service (e.g., South Korea, Singapore and, to a lesser extent, Malaysia).[21] This positive political legacy of colonialism did not fall victim to post-independence politics; the principle of meritocracy was preserved. The new regimes took extraordinary steps to insure the high quality of technocrats charged with making important economic decisions.[22] In Taiwan, the Kuomintang's efforts to strengthen the state bureaucracy were further aided by the withdrawal of large numbers of the government's senior technocrats from the mainland. Most of the key economic policy-makers in Taiwan were from this group.[23] In South Korea, President Park Chunghee instituted the Higher Civil Service Examination in 1962 and relentlessly pushed the process of technocratization of government once he gained political power.[24] This trend was most pronounced in countries where the level of technocratization of government was relatively low under the old regime. In Indonesia, as soon as General Suharto consolidated his power he recruited talented technocrats into the government.[25] Under Deng Xiaoping's reformist regime, the government largely abandoned the Maoist policy of discriminating against technocrats and placed the recruitment of qualified professionals as a top political priority. This measure quickly raised the overall level of professional qualifications of government personnel.[26] A similar process seemed to be underway in Vietnam after *doi moi* (renewal) was launched in 1986.

The improvement of the technocratic capacities of the state took place simultaneously with a process of political "normalization." A central feature of this process was the decline of charismatic leaders and devaluation of personality cult. Charismatic leaders such as Mao Zedong and Sukarno have, in recent history, made significant contributions to the nationalist revolutions in developing countries. But such charismatic leaders have turned out to be, without a single exception, disastrous failures in governing the post-revolution developmental process, mostly because these charismatic leaders were unwilling to subject themselves to any institutional norms and constraints. In East Asia, an important mark of political normalization and maturity achieved by the new development-oriented regimes was their success in preventing the emergence of the personal cult of individual leaders; the ruling elites of these regimes seemed to be well aware of the inherent conflict between charismatic leadership and institutional stability. It is worth noting that while autocratic strongmen (such as Chiang Ching-kuo, Park Chong-hee, Lee Kuan Yew, Deng Xiaoping, and Suharto) ruled many East Asian states during economic take-off, they all showed a deep aversion to personality cults.

Another central characteristic of political normalization was the gradual hardening of institutional constraints on the behavior of the ruling elite and state apparatus. New leaders initiated measures to subject intra-elite conflicts to codified or informal procedures to provide greater security for each other, while changing the winner-take-all approach to intra-elite power struggles to a new *modus operandi* characterized by mutual compromise and accommodation. Arbitrary use of violence against political rivals was thus severely curtailed; penalties for losers in intra-elite power struggles were also reduced. For example, the new regimes ended extremely violent practices prevalent under the old regime, such as execution of or long jail terms for defeated political foes and persecution of their family members. Instead, milder forms of penalty, such as retirement with generous benefits, were favored. These initiatives ended the vicious cycle of violence and conspiracy that plagued elite politics in the developing world; they drastically lowered the costs of political defeat. The added sense of personal security derived from these new norms further contributed to political moderation and self-restraint among competing members of the ruling elite.

Significantly, the regime's moderate tactics in resolving intra-elite conflict also trickled down and was reflected in the adoption of less harsh methods of repression against opposition forces. In East Asian countries ruled by soft authoritarian regimes, "white terror" and "red terror" subsided, although the overall human rights record was poor by contemporary Western standards (however, the general level of repression may not be significantly higher than that in most competitive oligarchies in early nineteenth Europe). This trend was evident in the government's more selective and strategic use of the state's repressive capacity, and the subsequent dramatic decline of political repression against the population and the opposition. The scope of repression was reduced (as shown in the steep fall in numbers of political prisoners and arrests), as was its level (as revealed in shorter jail terms and some improvement in the treatment of dissidents). The single most important mark in this respect was the *de facto* abolition of the death penalty against political offenders. Increasingly, the East Asian soft authoritarian regimes favored the tactic of "exporting dissent" to remove leadership of the opposition.[27] In retrospect, the regimes' own initiative to reduce the level of political repression seemed to induce rising political moderation on the part of oppositions. It is worth noting that, after the adoption of such tactics, opposition-organized violence against the regime almost disappeared in the region.[28]

RE-SHAPING RULING ARRANGEMENTS

Two types of ruling arrangements were predominant in East Asia during the rapid phase of economic development: military dictatorships (South Korea between 1961–87, Indonesia after 1965, Thailand before 1992, and Myanmar in the early 1990s) and one dominant-party or one-party regimes (Kuomintang (KMT) in Taiwan since 1949, the PAP in Singapore since 1957, the UMNO coalition in Malaysia since 1971, the post-1979 CCP (Chinese Communist Party), and the post-1986 Workers' Party in Vietnam). In countries where a political party played the leading role in the nationalist revolution and gained control over the military prior to the founding of the nation (such as in China, Taiwan, Vietnam, and Singapore), dominant or one-party rule has tended to prevail.[29] In contrast, if the military played the leading role in the country's nationalist revolution (as in Indonesia and Burma) or founding experience (as during the Korean War in South Korea), military dictatorships tended to predominate.[30] Although no systematic investigation has been made to determine whether a dominant-party or one-party regime is more effective in promoting economic development than a military dictatorship (or vice versa), numerous studies have concluded that dominant-party regimes may enjoy an institutional advantage in managing conflicts among groups during periods of economic transition.[31] The military dictatorships in Indonesia and South Korea were also apparently aware of the institutional inadequacy of the military as an effective governing institution; both founded political parties (Golkar in Indonesia and the Democratic Republican Party in South Korea) to compete in elections.

In analyzing the behavior of the more mature dominant parties in East Asia one notes three instructive features.[32] First, despite the undisputed political supremacy of the dominant parties, there seemed to be some self-imposed restrictions on the scope of power of the ruling party and differentiation of political functions (as separate from technocratic functions). Increasingly, the ruling party's division of labor was to insure its monopoly of political power, leaving more administrative discretion to the technocratic agencies of the state.[33]

Second, these dominant party regimes rearranged their ruling institutions to *economize* on political resources, creating controlled participatory arrangements to accommodate popular demands for political participation. In contrast to one-party regimes where open political competition was completely suppressed (at great enforcement costs to the regime itself), the mature authoritarian regimes in East Asia avoided the diminishing political returns of total control of the political process. Instead of aiming at complete elimination of political opposition or winning unnecessarily large (and costly) electoral margins (over 90 percent), these dominant party regimes (or military-sponsored dominant parties) were willing to settle for comfortable winning margins (typically around 65 percent of the votes).[34] The ruling elite seemed to have recognized certain political advantages of popular participation, especially in terms of ascertaining the degree of popularity of the government and providing a safety valve to divert public frustration (as it is a well-known fact that democratic governments are practically immune to social revolutions).

Third, as an insurance policy, these regimes devised schemes to allow some forms of democratic participation but severely limit its political impact. Such political institutional arrangements and schemes varied widely. In Taiwan, the Kuomintang allowed semi-open local elections but banned organized opposition. In Malaysia and Singapore, relatively open elections were held under rules that favored the ruling party. In nearly all cases, the ruling parties were insured victory thanks to the government's control of vital media and organizational resources, and severe restrictions on political campaigns (such as limits on the length of campaigns to create hurdles for the opposition in its mobilization, coordination, and coalition-building efforts, and on the type of campaign activities). In some countries, elections were held only for symbolic political offices (such as in Indonesia, China, and Vietnam). In Thailand, the military frequently exercised a veto over election results.

In functional terms, these elections were a signalling device providing the ruling elite valuable information about the public's political sentiment and allowing them to make policy adjustment. Another hidden benefit of such controlled democracy was to keep the dominant party occupied with activities that were less costly to economic development; a politically idle dominant party was more likely to intrude into the economic affairs of the state. In retrospect, these semi-open elections created a valuable political legacy upon which more genuine democratic institutions of political participation could later be built. The remarkably successful transition to democratic rule in Taiwan and South Korea owed much to these past elections.

FORGING GROWTH ALLIANCES

The state's activist involvement in achieving rapid capital accumulation through high levels of investment and even direct ownership of strategic industrial enterprises, in assisting domestic private firms in gaining competitive advantages in the world markets, and in aggressively courting foreign capital, has been widely documented.[35] However, the political and historical origins of various types of the state-capital growth alliances have not been adequately investigated. In fact, a quick review of the recent histories of these fast-growing economies shows that such alliances did *not* exist prior to the advent of soft authoritarian rule. On the contrary, due to political factors, the relationship between the state and capital (both foreign and domestic) was weak in some countries, and tense or even hostile in others. In nearly all East Asian countries, the state–capital growth alliances did not fully emerge until the critical transition from hard to soft authoritarianism.

In the first-generation NICs (except Hong Kong), unhindered by ideological hostility against capital, the new regimes (South Korea's military dictatorship under Park, Taiwan's quasi-Leninist regime under the Chiangs, and Singapore's PAP under Lee) assumed a far more supportive stance in improving the ties with the private sector. There were, to be sure, substantial differences in terms of their preferential policies directed towards different types of firms. In Taiwan, the growth alliance appeared to be the product of a shrewd political strategy by the ruling KMT to seek reconciliation with the ethnic Taiwanese population through an implicit contract. The KMT, transplanted from mainland China, maintained absolute control of the state's apparatus while allowing local business elites a free hand in the private sector in exchange.[36] Thanks to its high domestic savings rate, the Taiwanese government did not have to reply on foreign capital as a major source of accumulation. The international capital was used mainly as a source of technology transfer. On the other hand, a critical component in the growth alliance in Taiwan was the large number of small and medium-sized private firms. The government operated an extensive program to support these enterprises through preferential loans, technical support, and trade and information services to enhance their export competitiveness.[37]

In contrast, the South Korean growth alliance was centered on the state–*chaebol* nexus, with the government providing preferential credit access to large domestic conglomerates and enhancing their international competitiveness with trade protection. This industrial policy favoring large domestic firms reduced the role played by foreign capital, especially direct investment by multinational corporations (which would have competed directly with weaker indigenous firms in the country's highly protected market).[38] Instead, the South Korean government opted for international debt-financing to sustain its strategic alliance with the *chaebols*.[39]

The political support for similar growth alliances was, however, much weaker in other East Asian countries until more recently. The leftist Old Regimes in Maoist China, pre-1986 Vietnam, Ne Win's Burma, and, to a less extent, Sukarno's Indonesia, all exhibited strong hostility to capitalists for ideological reasons. The critical turn towards soft authoritarianism (a process that was unfolding in Indonesia, China, Vietnam and, to a less extent, Myanmar (Burma)) was accompanied by a fundamental shift in the state's policy toward domestic and international capital. This change was especially striking in these governments' treatment of foreign capital: their old hostility was replaced with an unabashed aggressiveness in courting foreign investment.

Equally significant was these regimes' new policy in encouraging the growth of domestic capital. In Indonesia and Malaysia, the soft authoritarian regimes resisted populist appeals for redistributive measures that would have severely harmed the interests of minority ethnic-Chinese capitalists. Instead, a new bargain was struck to permit the formation of mutually beneficial cooperation with ethnic-Chinese capitalists. In Malaysia, the New Economic Policy, despite its professed pro-Malay stance, was a moderate measure of redistribution acceptable to ethnic Chinese capitalists.[40] In Indonesia, the close ties between the military and ethnic-Chinese businessmen provided political insurance for these capitalists and lucrative private returns for the members of the ruling elite (although such arrangements produced massive official corruption and private rent-seeking activities).[41] In both cases, the durability of the growth alliance has been enhanced by the huge influx of foreign, mainly Japanese capital, which has been aggressively courted by the government to balance against the economic dominance of the ethnic Chinese minority. An increasingly important part of this alliance is the expanding state sector in these countries, promoted and constructed for the same purpose of achieving a tripartite balance.

In Dengist China, although the ideological battle against state-socialism was more bitter and prolonged than elsewhere, various growth alliances flourished.[42] Fiscal decentralization since the late 1970s added a powerful incentive for local governments to create favorable conditions for economic growth and protect property rights of non-state firms, resulting in a unique local state corporatist growth alliance between private entrepreneurs and lower echelons of the state apparatus.[43] Another powerful growth alliance in China has been forged between foreign capital (mainly overseas Chinese investors with extensive ties to local elites) and provincial governments in China eager to boost local growth rates. In Vietnam, the accelerated influx of foreign direct investment in the early 1990s also seemed to be creating a similar pro-growth alliance.

TENTATIVE CONCLUSIONS AND AGENDA FOR FUTURE RESEARCH

Several general observations about East Asian political development emerge from the above discussion. First, the political nationalist revolutions that initially led to the independence and state formation in developing counties were an extremely negative factor for sustained economic development in these countries later on. Nationalist revolutions tended to produce personal dictators who were leaders of such revolutions, and generate anti-Western ideologies that were translated into leftist economic mentalities and anti-market development policies which inevitably produced disastrous consequences. The East Asian political experience shows that only the political defeat (or in many cases, deaths) of the nationalist leaders and their succession by political pragmatists can meet the most crucial requirement of sustained economic development: top-level political commitment to market-friendly economic development strategies. In this sense, political nationalism must be replaced with some form of cosmopolitan economic nationalism as the foundation of the political legitimacy of these soft authoritarian regimes in the developing world.[44]

Second, it is imperative to establish a delicate balance of power and division of labor between three sets of key political actors: the supreme leader, the ruling political apparatus (whether it is the military or the dominant party), and the technocratic elite. Ideally, the supreme leader should be committed to the general direction of development, act as the ultimate deal-maker, but refrain from imposing his personal views on specific policies. The dominant party or the praetorian guards, must be limited to strictly political functions (such as political recruitment and contesting in elections), although some form of economic compensations may have to be made to them in exchange for their withdrawal from economic decision-making (however, the determination of the price for their cooperation is no easy task, and the enforceability of any resulting agreement will remain questionable in the absence of the rule of law). The technocratic dominance in economic decision-making must be established, maintained, and defended at all costs. Such autonomy should, ideally, be codified in rules enforceable by independent or semi-independent judicial bodies, although at the beginning, the most powerful force of enforcement is personal in nature: the unwavering support of the supreme leader (as in nearly all East Asian cases).

Third, a tacit agreement must also be reached with the political opposition. The ruling regime must signal that political moderation pays. The initiative thus lies with the regime – it must first lower the level of repression and convey a message to the opposition that the regime will be more selective and restrained in using violent means. In exchange, the opposition demonstrates its willingness to seek less extreme means in opposing the regime. Given the considerable capacity of opposition political entrepreneurs to mount challenges against the ruling elite in modernizing societies, it is advisable for the government to create materially rewarding exit avenues for opposition leaders, thus making the political arena less congested. Direct harsh measures against political dissent should be replaced with more subtle and less costly tactics.

Soft authoritarian regimes must not be tempted to achieve (the unachievable) total control of the political process. Up to a certain level, any marginal increase in the regime's control of the political process can only be gained at enormous enforcement and coercive costs. A more efficient alternative is to design political institutional arrangements which can accommodate moderate opposition but firmly exclude radicals.

The above discussion of the political origins of the economic success in East Asia has left unsolved several important theoretical and empirical puzzles. Two interrelated issues should receive top priority in future research:

(1) *The rule of law* – Without doubt, the most intriguing puzzle of the East Asian model is how property rights were protected when the rule of law was weak or non-existent, as was the case in most East Asian nations during their high-growth phase (except for Japan, Singapore, and Hong Kong). Theoretically, the rule of law is distinct and separate from democracy (although the latter implies the former). Empirically, it is also possible to establish the rule of law without democracy (Singapore and Hong Kong being the most important case). The fact that sustained rapid economic development has occurred in East Asia under relatively weak rule of law presents another powerful challenge to orthodox Western political economy theories. More scholarly efforts should be directed to the empirical investigation of the institutional safeguard of economic growth in East Asia that has remained unexplored.

(2) *Limiting autocratic predation* – An equally fascinating puzzle of the East Asian Miracle concerns the various forces that restrained the predation of autocratic regimes. Orthodox theories and overwhelming historical and contemporary evidence convincingly demonstrate that, unconstrained by the rule of law, the checks and balances of democratic institutions, and public scrutiny of a free press, an authoritarian regime plunders the nation's wealth for the private gains of its ruling elite.[45] The experience from East Asia in this respect is mixed, and provides examples of both relatively self-restrained non-predatory autocracies (Singapore, Malaysia, and pre-democratization Taiwan

and South Korea) and highly predatory autocracies (i.e., those regimes with a significant level of official corruption) that have managed to sustain high rates of economic growth (China, Indonesia, and Vietnam).[46] A top priority for future research, which will have far-reaching implications for understanding the political economy of development, is to uncover the hidden political and institutional factors that have constrained the autocratic rulers in these states from unchecked plunder of public wealth.

NOTES

1 Representative works include: World Bank, 1993; Amsden, 1989; Wade, 1990; Haggard, 1990; Johnson, 1982; Krugman, 1994.
2 For an excellent review of the literature, see Wade, 1992.
3 Such methodological weakness is evident in the works of Wade, Amsden, and Haggard.
4 See Womack, *et al.*, 1991; Dore, 1987; Kumon and Rosovsky, 1992.
5 For an excellent critique of this flaw and a revealing account of the historical origins of the developmental state, see Kohli, 1994.
6 It ought to be noted here that autocratic regimes presided over the period between 1960 and 1990 in East Asia, although South Korea and Taiwan began the transition toward democracy in the late 1980s, and Thailand made a similar move in the early 1990s.
7 For a brilliant and influential analysis of the lack of political order in developing countries, see Huntington, 1968.
8 China, Vietnam, and Burma, the "third-generation" NICs in the region lagged further behind in the rebuilding of political order. In China, effective political stability was restored only after the death of Mao Zedong in 1976; in Vietnam, it came about in the mid 1980s; in Burma, the military junta initiated a serious effort to re-build political order in the early 1990s.
9 At the risk of oversimplification, one may argue that the principal contribution of Huntington (1968) is the crucial role of political institutions in newly constituted political systems in the post-colonial era. Irrespective of the type of political regimes, under-institutionalized political systems are incapable of providing political order for economic development. Huntington has since been often criticized for advocating authoritarianism for developing countries as a transitional means of building political order. I believe such criticism overlooks the fact that Huntington's analysis and implicit policy prescriptions apply equally to decrepit autocracies and democracies. Also see Huntington 1991, for his analysis of the resurgence of democracy in the developing countries.
10 O'Donnell, 1973; Collier, 1979.
11 A popular term describing relatively institutionalized autocracies in East Asia is "soft authoritarianism," first coined by Edwin Winckler (1984). Chalmers Johnson (1987) later adopted the same term in analyzing the connection between political institutions in economic performance in East Asia.
12 For an analysis of the differences between East Asian bureaucratic-authoritarian regimes and their Latin American counterparts, see Im, 1987.
13 See, for example, Haggard, 1990: 254–70; Pei, 1994a; Przeworski and Limongi, 1993; Barro, 1994.
14 Myanmar in the early 1990s exhibited many familiar signs of a similar shift although the progress to date is not very reassuring. See Steinberg, 1993.

15 The East Asian experience seems to bear out Douglass North's theory linking efficient economic institutions with sustained long-run growth, see North, 1981 and 1990.

16 It seems that a more detailed study of the institutional reforms of property rights arrangements is overdue in studying the East Asian experience. To date, scholarly attention has focused exclusively on the role of developmental policies.

17 This was most evident in such countries as Indonesia under Sukarno, China under Mao, Vietnam under the pre-1986 leadership, and Burma under the military-socialist regime. In South Korea, President Syngman Rhee was also associated with the country's nationalist movement. The case of Taiwan was more ambiguous. Although Chiang Kai-shek was one of the leaders of the Chinese Nationalist movement, the defeat of his forces on the mainland effectively put an end to his nationalist project. His policies became more moderate and pragmatist after he retreated to Taiwan.

18 Burma's case is extremely unique in the comparative context. Unlike typical military-backed rightist regimes in other developing countries, Burma's military-backed authoritarian regime was leftist in its ideological and economic orientations.

19 North, 1990: 36–45.

20 East Asian governments' extensive reliance on technocrats in economic decision-making is well-known and noted in the World Bank's *The East Asian Miracle* (1993) and Vogel, 1991: 93–5.

21 Thailand's bureaucracy was also staffed with highly qualified technocrats despite the absence of colonial rule.

22 Even in Malaysia, the government's pro-Malay affirmative action program did not seem to have affected the senior levels of the bureaucracy, where well-qualified non-Malays continue to outnumber Malays, although Malays constituted an overwhelming majority in the Malaysian Civil Service (see Puthucheary, 1987: 94–110).

23 Among the six premiers who managed the Executive Yuan between 1950 and 1988, four were competent technocrats with broad experience in finance and economics. For details on the high level of technocratization of government in Taiwan, also see Tien, 1989: 119–29.

24 Han, 1986; Cho, 1972.

25 However, Suharto also gave the army many economic concessions in return for their political support. Such concessions soon became a hotbed of corruption and caused several costly scandals, although they fortunately did not derail the country's overall course of rapid development (see Crouch, 1978: 273–303, 318–30).

26 One must note, however, that because of Deng's less-than-successful effort to separate the party from the state, technocratic autonomy in China remained quite weak. For a study in China's technocratization of government, see Li and White, 1990.

27 This tactic was used most effectively by Taiwan, South Korea, and China (after Tiananmen).

28 One puzzling exception here is South Korea, where radical students were the main force in anti-government street riots (but it seems that most of the street violence occurred after the introduction of the more authoritarian Yushin constitution in the mid-1970s).

29 Although Singapore did not experience a nationalist revolution, the PAP led the independence movement.

30 The predominance of the military in Thai politics seemed to result both from the traditional weakness of political parties and the absence of a nationalist revolution. In Burma, the picture was more mixed. Although the military and

political parties shared the leadership during the country's struggle for independence, post-independence leadership in Burma allowed the political parties to atrophy in the 1950s, paving the way for the military to take over the government.

31 See Haggard and Kaufman, forthcoming. For other studies of dominant party regimes, see Pempel, 1990; Huntington and Moore, 1970. For the controversy over the effectiveness of military regimes, see Nordlinger, 1970. Nordlinger's contention that the military acted as a positive force of social change was challenged by Robert Jackman (1976). Using the same data, Jackman found no relationship between military regimes and social change.

32 I here exclude the one-party regimes in China and Vietnam, where genuine dominant party rule has yet to emerge.

33 One needs further investigation to determined how exactly the dominant party's intrusion into the technocratic functions of the state was successfully restricted in the East Asian case. This was a major problem for one-party regimes like China and Vietnam.

34 Indeed, such winning margins appeared to be the historical norm in semi-open elections in East Asia.

35 See Amsden, 1989; Wade, 1990; World Bank, 1993.

36 See Gold, 1988. Toward the end of his rule, Chiang Ching-kuo also launched a successful program of recruiting Taiwanese elites into the government.

37 The political logic of this unique industrial policy seemed to be driven by the electoral requirements of the KMT, which had to compete in frequent semi-open local elections and needed extensive patron-client networks to sustain its grass-roots support; a large number of small and medium-sized firms seemed to provide an ideal organizational base for political mobilization. This contrasted sharply with South Korea, where the military regime were not constrained by similar electoral requirements (as the most important election then was for the presidency, held only twice under military rule).

38 Russell Mardon (1990) provides a similar argument.

39 In Singapore, the growth alliance seems to be dominated by both state-controlled capital (in the form of state-owned enterprises) and foreign capital (multinational corporations); this appears to result from the country's unique position as an entrepôt well-positioned in high-tech manufacturing and international financing, and from the state's strong technocratic capacity.

40 In 1991, the Malaysian government replaced the NEP with the National Development Program, which was even less redistributive and pro-Malay than its predecessor. Part of the reason for watering down the NEP measures was due to their success. For example, since its implementation in 1970, Malay-controlled wealth rose from 2–3 percent to 18.2 percent in 1992; unexpectedly, ethnic Chinese-controlled wealth increased as well, from 25 to 38 percent, in the same period (these gains were achieved due to the relative decline of foreign holdings) (*Far Eastern Economic Review*, December 21, 1995: 26).

41 For an analysis of the pro-growth alliance in Indonesia, see Robison, 1988.

42 For a study of the quiet capitalist revolution in China in the 1980s, see Pei, 1994.

43 See Oi, 1992: 99–126; also see Andrew Walder's analysis of the organizational dynamics of the growth alliance (1995).

44 This form of economic nationalism, at least at its early stage in East Asia, may resemble a modified version of neo-mercantilism exemplified in the Japanese model.

45 See Olson, 1993.

46 The Philippines under Marcos was a typical example of utterly unrestrained autocratic predation.

REFERENCES

Ahmad, Zakaria Haji (ed.) (1987) *Government and Politics of Malaysia*, Singapore: Oxford University Press.

Amsden, Alice (1989) *Asia's Next Giant: South Korea and Late Industrialization*, New York: Oxford University Press.

Barro, Robert (1994) "Democracy and Growth," *NBER Working Paper No. 4909* (October).

Cho, Chang Hyun (1972) "Bureaucracy and Local Government in South Korea," in Se-jin Kim and Chang-Hyun Cho (eds) *Government and Politics of Korea*, Silver Spring, Maryland, 91–126.

Collier, David (ed.) (1979) *The New Authoritarianism in Latin America*, Princeton: Princeton University Press.

Crouch, Harold (1978) *The Army and Politics in Indonesia*, Ithaca: Cornell University Press.

Dore, Ronald (1987) *Taking Japan Seriously: A Confucian Perspective on Leading Economic Issues*, Stanford: Stanford University Press.

Gold, Thomas (1988) "Entrepreneurs, Multinationals, and the State," in Edwin Winckler and Susan Greenhalgh (eds) *Contending Approaches to the Political Economy of Taiwan*, Armonk, NY: M.E. Sharpe, 175–205.

Haggard, Stephan (1990) *Pathways from the Periphery: The Politics of Growth in the Newly Industrialized Countries*, Ithaca: Cornell University Press.

Haggard, Stephan, and Robert Kaufman (1995) *The Political Economy of Democratic Transitions*, Princeton, NJ: Princeton University Press.

Han, Song-joo (1986) "Political Institutionalization in South Korea, 1961–1984," in Robert A. Scalapino, Seizaburo Sato, and Jusuf Wanandi (eds) *Asian Political Institutionalization*, Berkeley, CA: Institute of East Asian Studies, 116–37.

Huntington, Samuel P. (1968) *Political Order in Changing Societies*, New Haven, CT: Yale University Press.

—— (1991) *The Third Wave: Democratization in the Late Twentieth Century*, Norman: Oklahoma University Press.

Huntington, Samuel, and Clement Moore (eds) (1970) *Authoritarian Politics in Modern Societies*, New York: Basic Books.

Im, Hyug Baeg (1988) "The Rise of Bureaucratic Authoritarianism in South Korea," *World Politics*, vol. 39, no. 2, 231–57.

Jackman, Robert (1976) "Politicians in Uniform: Military Governments and Social Change in the Third World," *American Political Science Review*, vol. 70, 1978–97.

Johnson, Chalmers (1982) *MITI and the Japanese Miracle*, Stanford, CA: Stanford University Press.

—— (1987) "Political institutions and economic performance: the government–business relationship in Japan, South Korea, and Taiwan," in Frederic Deyo (ed.) *The Political Economy of the New Asian Industrialism*, Ithaca, NY: Cornell University Press, 136–64.

Kohli, Atul (1994) "Where Do High Growth Political Economies Come From? The Japanese Lineage of Korea's 'Developmental State'," vol. 22, no. 9, 1269–93.

Krugman, Paul (1994) "The Myth of Asia's Miracle," *Foreign Affairs*, 73(6) (November/December): 62–78.

Kumon, Shumpei, and Henry Rosovsky, (eds) (1992) *The Political Economy of Japan, vol. 3: Cultural and Social Dynamics*, Stanford, CA: Stanford University Press.

Li, Cheng, and Lynn White III (1990) "Elite Transformation and Modern Change in Mainland China and Taiwan: Empirical Data and the Theory of Technocracy," *China Quarterly*, no. 121 (March), 1–35.

Mardon, Russell (1990) "The State and the Effective Control of Foreign Capital: The Case of South Korea," *World Politics*, vol. 43, no. 1, 111–38.

Nordlinger, Eric (1970) "Soldiers in Mufti: The Impact of Military Rule Upon Economic and Social Change in the Non-Western States," *American Political Science Review*, vol. 64, 1131–48.

North, Douglass (1981) *Structure and Change in Economic History*, Cambridge: Cambridge University Press.

—— (1990) *Institutions, Institutional Change and Economic Performance*, Cambridge: Cambridge University Press.

O'Donnell, Guillermo A. (1973) *Modernization and Bureaucratic Authoritarianism: Studies in South American Politics*, Berkeley, CA: Institute of International Studies, University of California, Berkeley.

Oi, Jean (1992) "Fiscal Reform and the Economic Foundations of Local State Corporatism in China," *World Politics*, vol. 45, no. 2, 99–126.

Olson, Mancur (1993) "Dictatorship, Democracy, and Development," *American Political Science Review*, vol. 87, no. 2, 99–126.

Olson, Mancur (1993) "Dictatorship, Democracy, and Development," *American Political Science Review*, vol. 87, no. 3, 567–76.

Pei, Minxin (1994a) "The Puzzle of East Asian Exceptionalism," *Journal of Democracy*, vol. 5, no. 4, 90–103.

—— (1994b) *From Reform to Revolution: the Demise of Communism in China and the Soviet Union*, Cambridge, MA: Harvard University Press.

Przeworski, Adam, and Fernando Limongi (1993) "Political Regimes and Economic Growth," *Journal of Economic Perspectives*, vol. 7, no. 3 (Summer), 51–69.

Robinson, Richard (1988) "Authoritarian States, Capital-owning Classes, and the Politics of Newly Industrializing Countries: the Case of Indonesia," *World Politics*, vol. 41, no. 1, 52–74.

Steinberg, David (1993) "Liberalization in Myanmar: How Real Are the Changes?" *Contemporary Southeast Asia*, vol. 15, no. 2, 161–78.

Tien, Hung-mao (1989) *The Great Transition*, Stanford, CA; Hoover Institution Press.

Vogel, Ezra (1991) *The Four Little Dragons: The Spread of Industrialization in East Asia*, Cambridge, MA: Harvard University Press.

Wade, Robert (1990) *Governing the Market: Economic Theory and the Role of Government in East Asian Industrialization*, Princeton, NJ: Princeton University Press.

—— (1992) "East Asia's Economic Success: Conflicting Perspectives, Partial Insights, Shaky Evidence," *World Politics*, vol. 44, no. 2 (January), 270–320.

Walder, Andrew (1995) "Local Governments as Industrial Firms: An Organizational Analysis of China's Transitional Economy," *American Journal of Sociology*, vol. 101, no. 2, 263–301.

Winckler, Edwin (1984) "Institutionalization and Participation on Taiwan: From Hard to Soft Authoritarianism?" *China Quarterly*, no. 99 (September), 481–99.

Womack, James, Daniel Jones, and Daniel Roos (1991) *The Machine that Changed the World*, New York: Harper Perenniel.

World Bank (1993) *The East Asian Miracle: Economic Growth and Public Policy*, New York: Oxford University Press.

3 Distinctive institutions in the rise of industrial Asia

Hilton L. Root

Conventional wisdom suggests that a key reason for the success of economic policy in East Asia is the authoritarian character of the political regimes. Comparison of the economic performance of nations within the region, however, indicates that a link between authoritarianism and successful growth should not be taken for granted.

Authoritarian regimes in Myanmar, the Philippines, and Vietnam, for example, consistently failed to make the tough economic decisions needed to sustain growth. The connection appears even weaker when the region's experience is compared to other developing areas, such as Africa or Latin America, where authoritarianism and growth rarely complement each other. Since regime type is a poor predictor of economic performance and the much vaunted dichotomy between democracy and autocracy provides little illumination on why economic policy succeeds, we must look to other explanations to understand the institutional foundations of East Asian growth.

In this chapter, explanations popular among various academic disciplines and policy-makers will be examined, followed by suggestions of alternative factors and relationships. The goal is to identify generalizations about the role of government in the economic development of East Asia's high-performing economies Hong Kong, Indonesia, Malaysia, Singapore, South Korea, Taiwan and Thailand.

THE ROLE OF CONFUCIANISM

Confucianism is sometimes proposed as the cultural explanation for the success of Asia's high-performing economies. But the values typically associated with Confucianism are not unique to the region.[1] Most are universal values, such as filial piety, held in reverence by cultures and belief systems throughout the world. Moreover, traditional Confucian values, such as family loyalty, can justify nepotism and thus stifle the development of modern government structures. For example, a national civil service requires performance-driven evaluations and adherence to bureaucratic norms.

While Confucian principles emphasize rule by persons of moral authority over rule by law, and paternalism over legalism, the success of the best performing economies in the region corresponds with a shift away from ascriptive standards. Even though Confucian thought links seniority to moral authority, leaders like the Republic of Korea's Park Chung Hee (44 when he took power) or Singapore's Lee Kuan Yew (35) were young men who seized power forcefully and then appointed other young men like themselves to positions of authority, disregarding their Confucian heritage.

Lee Kuan Yew expressed his non-Confucian disdain for seniority in July 1961, "I am in favour of efficient service. The brighter chap goes up and I don't care how many years he's been in or he hasn't been in. If he is the best man for the job, put him there."[2] Similarly, under Park's leadership the age structure of the Korean administration changed, so that by the middle of the 1960s, bureau directors were an average of two years younger than their subordinates.

Another cultural obstacle to be overcome was that the Confucian elite did not highly value business activities. In traditional Confucian society, business must approach government as a supplicant. A respectable image of business had to be created to surmount this bias.[3]

THE ROLE OF POLICY SELECTION

Economists, rather than relying on cultural factors to explain the success of East Asian economies, tend to emphasize the importance of choosing the "right" policy. However East Asians did not always choose the "right" policies – they did not always follow the recommendations of economists. For example, economic experts spoke out against the Republic of Korea's Seoul–Pusan Highway and the Pohang Comprehensive Steel Mill projects. Although considered inconsistent with national comparative advantage, these projects have been successful beyond any expectations.[4] Even Korea's highly leveraged chemical industry, condemned by economists in the 1980s, looks successful in the 1990s. And, in another instance, a World Bank report projected the rapid decline of Singapore after its separation from Malaysia.

East Asian leaders, like those of most developing nations, believed that national development and shared growth required executive interventions in the market. Among these interventions, land reform, significant investment in agriculture and rural infrastructure, encouragement of small- and medium-sized enterprises, and limits on inflation, are promises often heard, but rarely implemented in developing countries. Slogans in most countries, these reforms were realities that brought considerable economic rewards. Mobilization of the domestic market and reduction of income disparities between the urban and rural sectors were outcomes that East Asian leaders could be proud of, and that could be used to garner support for their governments.[5]

Measures to promote investment were commonplace throughout the region. Conscious industrial policy was practiced by a number of the high-performers and most made subsidized and directed finance available to promote investment and infant industries. Even efforts to reconfigure the ownership structure of private firms were undertaken. These familiar tactics to promote strategic industries – avenues for rent seeking and bribe taking in most developing countries – were often effectively implemented in East Asia. Even the presumed shift by the high-performing East Asians from import substitution policies, associated with Latin America or India, to export-oriented industrialization receives more credit than is perhaps warranted.[6]

Policies that presumedly worked in East Asia produced unsustainable levels of debt elsewhere, so that Latin American reformers typically respond to invitations for the renewal of state activism, "We tried it and were impoverished."[7] For instance, the articles of incorporation of Korea's National Development Bank are identical to those of Argentina's. They agreed on the same objectives: fund those activities in which private sector spending is insufficient, select activities with high social rates of return, and prepare borrowers for private capital markets. That they worked in one country, but not the other, was thus not the result of design. This prompts us to ask: does good governance emerge simply because of state "will" and official "power" or do these elements of development management need special encouragement and nurturing?

While they promoted exports, many East Asian governments maintained state-led import substitution into the early 1980s.[8] State-owned enterprises played a major role in Indonesia, Malaysia, the Republic of Korea, Singapore, Taiwan, and Thailand. Although in most developing countries such enterprises generally performed poorly, in the Republic of Korea, Singapore, and Taiwan, they sometimes out-performed private sector firms. Along with import substitution, closed economies, tariff barriers against imports, large state sectors, and state-controlled banks were all common throughout the region. In addition, with the exception of Hong Kong and Singapore, restrictions on financial markets and selective credit policies also existed. Why, then, was East Asia spared the adverse economic consequences that resulted from highly interventionist policies elsewhere?

Few governments profess a preference for inflation, unlimited printing of money, or the promotion of income inequality between sectors, regions, and social classes. Many governments borrowed internationally for deficit reduction, rural development, and small- and medium-sized enterprise promotion. How did the high-performers accomplish what so many others merely promised?[9]

One common thread to the region's growth experience, which helps distinguish it from the rest of the world, was the successful implementation of economic and social policies. This capability stands out as being so fundamental, it is the focus of this analysis. Two important components of this implementation capacity are bureaucratic capability and the existence of an effective state–society interface. Bureaucratic capability means that civil servants were subjected to performance evaluations while being expected to act as neutral referees in the development process. The existence of effective channels of communication with the government enhanced the private sector's ability to carry out policies successfully. In exchange for participation in the policy process, information provided by the private sector allowed governments to select policies that worked and to eliminate those that failed.

The quality of the dialogue between the private and public sectors did not reflect regime type. The region's democracies did not promote participation in the policy process more effectively than countries in which national leaders were not elected. In fact, many of the countries that enjoyed the most extensive functional participation in the policy process, Hong Kong, the Republic of Korea, and Singapore, shared varying degrees of undemocratic means of creating a government. Yet they rank high among all developing nations in the transparency, accountability and predictability of the public sector. The attainment of high levels of accountability and transparency without the formal trappings of democracy is a dilemma that confounds simple assumptions about the relationship of regime type to economic performance

MAKING THE BUREAUCRACY A PARTNER IN GROWTH

In most developing countries hosting authoritarian political systems, the state is a predator and public officials are among the principal beneficiaries. In such states, government interventions in the economy usually provide extensive opportunities for members of the civil service to misappropriate public wealth. Therefore, when the relationship between bureaucracy and development is examined, corruption typically is at the top of the list of defining features. In contrast, East Asia's rapid economic expansion presents a different face. More often, it is associated with successful state mobilization of national resources. Among the world's developing nations, East Asia's high-performing countries stand out for their implementation of policies that limit the effects of corruption on investment.

To see why corruption did not have a debilitating impact on economic confidence, consider that most East Asian regimes controlled one of the most irksome sources of uncertainty in business calculation, a capricious and opaque regulatory environment. Reducing the costs often associated with bureaucratic venality is one of the reasons that corruption did not impair investment. Administrative reforms that eliminated many of the sources of bureaucratic abuse were introduced in most of the high performers. Administrative structures are highly centralized, and licensing for large investment is dominated by a single agency that reports to the executive. Most East Asian high-performers keep their bureaucracy small and independent boards that administer exams determine bureaucratic career paths. Those occupying positions have a functional rather than patronage-based justification for their appointment, redundant functions are limited.

Indonesia's investment environment is an exception. There despite widespread bribery, military organization reduces economic uncertainty. Military order ensures clients get the service they are paying for. Top people get their shares and corruption is not whittled away at the bottom by a hundred takers. Concentration at the top, where it can be controlled by the actual decision-makers, provides assurances to the client that agreements will be carried out. Indonesia worries less about its reputation for a clean business environment than, for example, Singapore.[10] When investment is primarily in resource extraction, confidence in the country matters less. That, too, will change as Indonesia's industrial development becomes more dependent on attracting foreign capital.

Critical to understanding bureaucratic capability is the mix of incentives employed in the successful East Asian governments to induce civil servants to use their private expertise and knowledge gained in office to promote long-term public benefits rather than short-term personal benefits. What mix of incentives makes the gains of cooperation greater than the gains of a single defection? In effect, how are public officials persuaded that a smaller reward over a longer time period is more attractive than using information acquired through public office for rapid personal gain?

In Indonesia and in Thailand hard budget constraints give the economic bureaucracy some independence over macroeconomic policy-making while at the same time introducing a low-cost means of monitoring performance. In Thailand the Budget Bureau tightly controls the annual budget. It presents a highly compressed version of its proposed budget to the cabinet. Because ordinary members of the Parliament cannot amend the budget upward, budget allocations are partially shielded from political consideration. In countries where the legislature can make upward adjustment, the budget becomes the center piece of policy-making and politicking.[11] The budget process in Indonesia is also governed by a hard budget constraint. The balanced budget law, the review process, and the parliamentary rules inhibit politicians and private parties from tinkering with the budget. The law that balances the budget keeps the Indonesian technocrats one step removed from the political demands of legislators and other parties. The only way the latter can override the technocrats is to alter the budget law. Because the balanced budget is a foundation for the legitimacy of the New Order government, signaling competent economic management, it is unlikely to be altered. Hence, the law provides a buffer for the technocrats.[12]

By contrast, in most developing countries control over the budget is fragmented among different government agencies and legislative tinkering is common. Consequently, it becomes difficult to locate blame when problems arise. Delegating budgetary control to a well-defined and small set of experts, and agencies and giving them the necessary instruments to do their jobs, offers a low-cost way of monitoring performance.

In most of the high-performers a merit-based system of recruitment and promotion helps secure for the members of the economic bureaucracy the necessary independence to do their jobs. By establishing objective rules for appointment, the system gives bureaucrats confidence that they cannot easily be demoted, fired, or blocked from rising simply because their decisions conflict with those of powerful private sector interests. In many developing countries, such as the Philippines, influential groups (and even individuals) can ask politicians to pressure a civil servant to alter a decision that they do not like. Because politicians may influence the career of a civil servant, the latter must often accede or leave the bureaucracy. A merit system reduces such politically motivated interventions. When rules for promotion are clearly established in law, politicians have a convenient and valid excuse for refusing to intercede on a supporter's behalf.

The experience of East Asia's successful bureaucracies reveals the importance for leadership to base its commitment to growth on firm political foundations.[13] An important signal of that willingness is the credibility of the regime's promise to share the benefits of growth widely (Campos and Root, 1996). Most developing states offer such promises, but few actually deliver. Shared growth reduces the long-term danger that social movements will contest regime legitimacy and topple the government. The promotion of policies that offered broad benefits to the rural population was an important component of the commitment to shared growth.

In East Asia, the support of rural development featured policy choices that balanced indirect taxation on agriculture (overvalued exchange rates and tariff protection of non-agricultural goods) with rural infrastructure development. Rural infrastructure development, in particular, provided longer-lasting poverty alleviation than alternative policy options. Unsustainable migration to cities was prevented by building rural schools, and by increasing employment opportunities in the countryside. Relative to other developing regions (Latin America or sub-Saharan Africa), low levels of policy-based resource shifts from agriculture to urban-based industries meant that East Asia's urban population constituted a smaller proportion of the total population. Moreover, land reform (in Japan, the Republic of Korea, and Taiwan), and public housing, an urban surrogate for land reform (Hong Kong and Singapore did not have land to redistribute), concretely signaled leadership's commitment to shared growth.

Thus, while in the 1970s governments in the developing world acquired insupportable debts as they bought the political support of narrow urban coalitions by subsidizing consumption, East Asian leaders, depending upon political support more geographically and sociologically spread throughout the population, avoided high levels of international debt. Broad political foundations allowed East Asian governments to keep public sector deficits well below the averages of developing countries.[14]

The East Asian example suggests that the more convincing the government's commitment is to shared growth, the greater will be the value placed on long-term gains and capital investment by individuals and firms within the country. By undermining social support for parties that advocate revolution, equity-enhancing policies inspire confidence in the regime's survival. This in turn induces longer time horizons in the investment calculations of the private sector. It also alters the calculus of regime officials in favor of supporting long-term national goals.

Another signal of the regime's commitment to growth was effectively conveyed by leaderships' efforts to uphold standards of civil service integrity. Above all, this meant signaling that personal connections would not protect public servants from prosecution for wrongdoing and that the advancement of integrity would begin at the top. By making it clear that confusion of private with public interests would not be tolerated at any level of the administrative hierarchy, governments signaled that officials would not confuse the profits that should accrue to entrepreneurial activity with the maintenance of public order. It was only once this assurance was clearly demonstrated that government could be accepted as a reliable partner in the development process.

When leadership shows an interest in capturing the gains of private sector development for itself, short-term thinking will be engendered among investors. Despite the extensive intervention of most East Asian governments in the economy, the ruling oligarchy did not monopolize access to the market. Therefore, that intervention did not lead to predation by those who controlled the political levers. If government officials are in competition with business for the rents or profits that accrue from economic activity, a partnership between the two groups in the interests of growth cannot be forged. By ensuring a distinction between the gains of political and economic management, government created a foundation for effective cooperation with business.

In the absence of an elaborate legal system, most East Asian high performers depended upon credible bureaucracies to enforce contracts. Hong Kong, Japan, Malaysia, the Republic of Korea, Singapore, and Taiwan all took efforts to ensure that civil service appointments were based on job-related ability. In addition, recruitment within the civil Service was supervised by relatively autonomous bodies that shielded the appointment process from direct political intervention.[15] A performance bond – years spent preparing for competitive and advanced degrees – had to be posted by would-be civil servants.

To measure and enforce performance, mechanisms to ensure the responsibility of technocrats for policy outcomes were constructed, along with devices to simplify the policing of defections by public officials. In the best cases, oversight mechanisms were complemented by internal grievance procedures. The Republic of Korea and Taiwan created a structure that was flexible enough to allow officials to improvise in response to their local clientele.

THE ROLE OF POLITICAL LEADERSHIP

The sphere of neutral bureaucratic competency cannot be created entirely on the basis of formal rules. No amount of formalization will protect bureaucratic autonomy if top leadership will not gain political benefits as an outcome of stable economic policies. Therefore institutional design by itself does not explain bureaucratic performance.[16]

In East Asia, the need to establish broad coalitional foundations was the motivation for leadership to create mechanisms for the technocratic formulation of policy. The institutions to ensure technocratic neutrality worked when top political leadership derived key coalitional support from economic policies that provided broad-based economic growth.[17] Political motivation to enforce neutrality is critical. A political system featuring economic patrimonialism did not lead to gross inequality and inefficiency in Malaysia because political competition was based on being able to deliver equitably distributed growth. Indonesia's Suharto defended his technocratic team to assure international donors of a stable macro-economic policy framework, while fighting the spread of communism at home. Chiang Kai Shek, in Taiwan, courted the support of the native Taiwanese by providing economic opportunities based on growth. The Republic of Korea's General Park had to demonstrate the effectiveness of a non-communist path to industrialization and military security. Lee Kuan Yew had to ensure Singapore's economic viability despite international skepticism and the imminent danger of communist insurrection.

Thus in each case, external motivations derived from the need to build broad coalitional foundations for regime survival, explain the commitment of regime leaders to neutral economic policy-making. In each case, civil service neutrality was politically valued because the alternative, a dysfunctional bureaucracy, could impair business confidence. Lack of business confidence would undermine the government's ability to sustain growth, which in turn could cause the collapse of the ruling coalition. By contrast, despite a constitution that guaranteed the integrity of the civil service, neutral competency did not emerge in the Philippines, instead political leaders routinely intervened behind the scenes in *ad hoc* ways to aid particular clients. Protected from left-wing contestation, leadership in the Philippines made its bid for coalition support by catering to a narrow elite whose parochial concerns provided little motivation for top political leaders to defend the technocratic basis of economic policy-making. In short, economic policy-making cannot be protected from political opportunism merely through the erection of formal structures: external political motives will determine whether those structures work and if they will be created at all.

Leadership plays a critical role in inspiring bureaucratic performance. To induce the cooperation of the civil service, bureaucrats must first be convinced that leadership's commitment to growth is credible and that their expertise will be valued.

At critical points, Park and Suharto defended technocrats from political opposition, signalling their personal commitment to reform. They understood that once lost, a reputation for sound management may be lost irretrievably.

Secondly, leadership must demonstrate a commitment to addressing wrongdoing at all levels of the administration, including the very highest. Leadership must establish and consistently enforce performance criteria for entrance and promotion, instead of using the civil service as a spoils system to reward political supporters. Finally, leadership must not exempt itself from the standards it hopes to inculcate in others. Expectations generated by positive perceptions of the government's institutional capacity to implement programs are necessary to inspire private sector confidence and cooperation. This realization led Park, Lee Kuan Yew, and Chiang Kai Shek to address administrative reform immediately upon taking power. Lee Kuan Yew liked to reiterate Churchill's comment, "I worry more about my bureaucracy than about Hitler."

East Asia's most successful leaders undertook public sector reform before proposing administrative guidance of the economy. They understood that doubts about successful implementation would undermine citizens' acceptance of reforms. When uncertainty exists about a regime's ability to implement policy, citizens will defend the status quo against uncertain future benefits. Therefore, without an efficient public sector, growth is in doubt from the start. Such doubts will shift the investment horizons of the private sector away from long-term capital intensive commitments toward short-term projects with immediate payoffs. Investment also reflects private sector expectations that profits are secure. Such expectations depend heavily on the structure of the state's interface with society.

PARTICIPATORY DEVELOPMENT: THE STATE–SOCIETY INTERFACE

Curbing the predatory behavior of autocratic states is one of the major conundrums of political development. This problem is acute in developing nations, especially those governed by dictatorships, which often have difficulty committing to secure property rights and rule-bound market systems. In the absence of a rule-bound regulatory framework, clientalism[18] and secrecy arise. Both detract from economic growth.

When leadership does not recognize the constraint of law, certain kinds of information-sharing may expose firms to harm. Firms sharing information are exposed to political risk if the ruler uses information about the firm's assets to build political power or to punish opponents. Unable to prevent the use of information in ways that are prejudicial, leadership will generally receive too little information about the performance of policies from the groups targeted by the policies. To overcome these information failures, many of the region's governments, Hong Kong, Japan, Malaysia, the Republic of Korea, Singapore, and Taiwan, encouraged the expansion of functional intermediaries, such as manufacturers' associations, to broker information needed by the government. Such intermediaries can collect and certify information and pass it along to the leader or to the bureaucracy.

When the government's past behavior does not, by itself, inspire confidence, the flow of information exchanged will depend on the credibility of the intermediaries as brokers between government and industry. Since government depends on quality information for the formulation of effective policies, leadership will grant the industrial association some degree of autonomy. This will enhance the association's credibility. Thus leadership may encourage associations to appoint industrywide representatives to consult with government on an industry's behalf and to address the Press directly. When viewed as a legitimate spokesperson for the industry, an association is a more effective partner for the government. Even the rise of intermediaries does not suffice to overcome a more general political problem. Intermediaries are unlikely to share information if government can be expected to use that information opportunistically, at no political cost to itself. Therefore, mechanisms that impose costs on government officials are necessary.

Consultative bodies were one such mechanism that emerged to "tie the dictator's hands" in a number of East Asia's polities.[19] For example, deliberative councils in Japan and the Republic of Korea gave exporters a central voice in policy-making relating to their industry. Although such mechanisms must be tailormade to meet the special requirements of each society, certain fundamentals must be addressed. These mechanisms can provide a framework for the cooperation of economic actors by limiting the government's ability to change policy arbitrarily and, hence, redistribute economic rents and wealth. By making the economic rules governing an industry more predictable and secure, the deliberative council format renders profits less prone to political risk. If expected returns from future development are secure, firms and individuals are more likely to invest.

The council format facilitated bargains between constituent groups in exchange for information needed to formulate rational economic policies. The exchanges helped leadership evaluate policy performance and ensure policy-makers accurate information about private sector assets and strategies. These council formats also facilitated, with varying degrees of success, the sharing of information between firms about markets, marketing strategies, products, and new technologies. In Hong Kong and Singapore, where minimal attempts at intervening in industrial policy had occurred, institutions to generate a continuous exchange of information between business and government on the consequences of policy were of less importance to the governments.

However, advisory committees did play a major role in the governance of Hong Kong, where they were used to bolster the legitimacy of the government and build a consensus in support of new policies. Consultation took place between civil servants and advisory committees at all stages of policy-making, beginning at the proposal stage. The committee was asked to comment on draft legislation and, once it was enacted into law, the committee was involved in the drafting of any subsidiary legislation or regulations that were needed for its implementation.

Why did governments not overturn decisions *ex post* or use knowledge gained opportunistically? Tying the fortunes of many groups to the continued use of the cooperative decision-making structures raises the cost of altering the system *ex post*. Once councils permeate an economy, a government that unilaterally imposes its will on an industry or sector will risk undermining the value of councils for other groups, thus subverting the entire system of cooperative decision-making. Government, then, is unlikely to overturn only those decisions it opposes and abide only by those it prefers. Increasing the transaction costs of policy-making may also retard growth and, consequently, provoke challenges to the legitimacy of government. Thus, by institutionalizing deliberative councils, government reduces its discretionary power, but gains the confidence of business in the stability of agreed-upon policies.[20] Councils are a means to attain predictability by tying the hands of government, but they are not sufficient to sustain transparency over time. As already noted, bureaucratic capability must be nurtured and leadership must resist the temptation to use control over the economy to build a narrow support base.

Channels for information exchange between business and government are essential if government seeks to play an activist role in economic management. The local and field-specific knowledge of economic interest groups will surpass the expert knowledge of the bureaucracy in any economy. Whereas the survival of business depends on exact knowledge of a particular sector or market, errors made by government officials rarely result in dismissal or the collapse of the state. State officials can generally find the means to compensate for mistakes through taxation or coercion.

In contrast, errors may jeopardize the very survival of private enterprises. Normally they cannot bail themselves out by accessing the public trough. Although competition in the marketplace induces business to gather accurate information, competition motivates business to treat that information as proprietary. Improper information disclosure may enable a rival firm to capture markets, imitate product design, or intercept strategies; or it might enable government officials to punish the political defection of firms and to impose conditions of political loyalty. To avert being outmaneuvered, business has a high incentive to keep vital information secret, which makes economic planning or coordination by the state difficult. To program or coordinate national development, government must be able to overcome these anxieties about the opportunistic use of information by providing assurances of relative policy and procedural transparency.

During the rapid development stage, leaders of most high-performers called upon interest group participation in policy-making to gain a comprehensive image of the economy. Regular continuous sessions in a formal setting with influential private sector leaders were needed. Occasional, intermittent consultations were rarely adequate. For example, the export promotion councils of the Republic of Korea placed the concrete experience of interest groups at the disposal of officials.[21] The credibility of these formal meetings depended upon bureaucratic neutrality to separate public from private interests in a systematic manner. By chairing the meetings, the government bureaucracy enhanced its authority, allowing policy to reflect the rational administration of trained officials. In the Philippines during the 1970s government representatives did not play a role that inspired private sector confidence.

Several East Asian regimes developed methods to share benefits with labor and induce labor to accept sacrifices in the hope of seeing broader opportunities. The Republic of Korea and Singapore, for example, developed methods to bring the general public into the policy debate and to increase public awareness of general policy concerns, through such strategies as the creation of a five-year plan and the imperative to balance the budget and control inflation. In Taiwan, local participatory forums were used to generate a consensus for the support of government programs and to encourage broad involvement in the growth process.

The emergence of consultative forums that offer functional groups a high degree of participation in the policy-making process highlights a noteworthy generalization about information symmetry and government in Asia. A cross-country comparison of the Asian experience suggests that the standards of sound economic management are indifferent to regime type and are not the monopoly of any particular political system. Moreover, only a weak correlation exists between participation in elections and the transparency of economic policy.

Parliamentary government does not ensure accountable economic policy or procedures. In fact, regimes can use democracy as an excuse for their absence. Elections may determine the peaceful succession of one government by another, but, as the comparison of the subcontinent with East Asia suggests, multiparty elections do not necessarily ensure participation in the policy-making process by functionally relevant groups. A larger lesson might be that under-institutionalized political systems can undermine economic development in autocratic and democratic regimes alike.[22]

Participation in the policy process offers a clue as to why some countries intervene in the economy more successfully than others.[23] Interventions tended to succeed in nations that had effective frameworks for the exchange of information between the state and society. The East Asian governments that are conventionally viewed as authoritarian feature a high level of consensus building and are particularly effective at reducing information asymmetry in the economic policy dialogue. Their experience suggests that mechanisms to improve the quality of information provided by government, and ensure high-quality information from the private sector, are critical for governments to guide the economy successfully.

Leadership in Japan, Malaysia, the Republic of Korea, Singapore, and Taiwan, was able to instill the lesson that the same rules apply to everyone. When this lesson is not explicitly adhered to by those who run the government, social discipline will break down, and compliance with rules will diminish. When the population can observe that rules apply differently according to one's status, then all bets are off. Curiously, although the theme seems to reflect fundamental democratic sentiments, adherence does not reflect regime type. The region's democracies are not the best exemplars of even the most fundamental egalitarian practices.

POLICY ADAPTIVITY: MEASURING INSTITUTIONAL CHANGE

One of the least noted lessons of the "East Asian miracle" is the importance of being able to change, including the ability to recognize when change is necessary. The region's development experience makes little sense unless acknowledgement is given to how mistakes were often recognized promptly and corrective measures were taken swiftly. Changes include the reversal of heavy industry initiatives in Malaysia, the Republic of Korea, and Singapore. Korea and Thailand both privatized major banks before being told to do so. The role of the state sector diminished in Taiwan from 51 percent in 1955, to 19 percent in 1990.[24] Imbalances due to macropolicies were rarely allowed to persist in any of the high performers. The ability to change in the face of new information, and the ability to collect that information promptly and reliably, reflects the existence of effective institutions. It suggests that being able to craft and adopt new institutions is as important as the ability to formulate new policies. The introduction of new organizations, new rules, and new procedures, however, is not reflected in calculations of total factor productivity growth. As a result, institutional change is systematically underestimated. Because institutional learning and adaptation is not captured in measurements of productivity, economists may complacently argue that "The real issue is whether policies fit the economy's capacity and environment."[25]

The East Asian experience challenges an assumption – institutions are given and are not subject to change – that has profoundly shaped the development field. The transformation of key institutions responsible for the formulation and implementation of policy is central to the success of East Asia's high-performers. Corrupt bureaucracies were reformed, a dialogue between the public and private sectors was initiated, and single-party governments developed firm foundations for democratic practice. All of this suggests the need to go beyond matching policies to institutions; rather institutional innovation must become part of the development agenda.

REPLICATION

Rapid growth in East Asia was often preceded by social upheaval, war, and, sometimes, revolution. The Cold War left East Asia with some of the most politically contestable regimes among developing countries. Taiwan was in a state of war with Mainland China, and South Korea faced perpetual threat from North Korea, Singapore and Indonesia had to withstand formidable communist insurgency. Thus, among the world's developing countries East Asia's governments faced particularly acute political risk; national survival depended on making the right choices. Although tragic events completely transformed Japanese, Korean, and Taiwanese societies, no one would want to recommend that governments program social upheaval as a precursor or necessary precondition of growth. Violent social change can also be a major setback; it may take years for stable conditions to re-emerge. What, then, can be done in the absence of catastrophe or the threat of catastrophe?

Hopefully, a more open global economy will be a catalyst for progressive policy change. The globalization of world capital markets will benefit those countries that practice good governance – transparent, predictable, and accountable regulatory regimes. In fact, the countries in the region that practice good governance also have the highest percentage of per capita private sector investment. By practicing good governance countries will remove the impediments to private investment. Those that persist with poor policies and poor governance will find themselves excluded from private capital markets and unable to finance their future infrastructure requirements. A focus on good governance will move the development process to its final stage – national independence and integration into the world economy. Attention to good governance will help position countries to attract private resource flows and escape dependence on development assistance. Thus good governance should be the last mission of development banks, a way to wean countries off dependency on outside concessional aid.

NOTES

1 Those who emphasize the role of Confucianism must explain why, compared to the industrial West, economic growth has only just begun in the Confucian Hong Kong, Republic of Korea, Taiwan, the People's Republic of China and Vietnam. Moreover, why does North Korea stagnate while the Republic of Korea prospers? A Confucian explanation offers little insight into the take-off of Southeast Asia's star performers – Indonesia, Malaysia, and Thailand – and it denies the region's success of any universal relevance.

2 Quah, 1993b.

3 Curiously, the most successful country in the region, Japan, attributes less to Asian values, while the Philippines leads the region in asserting Asian values as a key factor of Asian success (*Far Eastern Economic Review*, August 10 1995: 37).

4 During the Republic of Korea's high growth period, financial activity, including access to the banking sector, interest areas, and credit allocation, was heavily regulated despite the arguments of experts that the economy would collapse due to the assumed inefficiency of the financial sector.

5 Rural political support mattered more to governments in East Asia than in most developing countries. Bangkok, Jakarta, Taipei, and Tokyo are less supportive of their respective national government than the country as a whole. Japan's Liberal Democrats, Indonesia's Golkar, and Taiwan's Kuomintang depended heavily on rural support.

6 The kind of interventions touted by East Asians resulted in corruption and other undesirable effects elsewhere (Summers and Shah, 1992). Interventionism enabled governments the means to reward followers and consolidate political support.

7 Jaramillio-Vallejo, 1994.

8 The real exchange rate index based on the gross national product deflator rose equally in Latin America and East Asia during the 1970s (Teranishi, 1994b). The Republic of Korea and Taiwan targeted industries by selectively supporting exports without cutting import barriers. Thus, they combined import barriers with export promotion balancing incentives. In addition, Korea carefully screened foreign investments.

9 Many governments said they wanted to achieve what the high performers achieved. Many non-performers even borrowed extensively from international sources using similar rhetoric, that is, the promotion of small- and medium-sized enterprises, and rural infrastructure. Ultimately, differences between nations are not in what they professed but in what they accomplished. The essential question then is: why were certain East Asian countries able to carry out policy interventions more successfully than other developing countries?

10 In a study by Transparency International of how executives perceive the integrity of business transaction, Indonesia scored lowest of 14 of the largest countries in Asia. Singapore and New Zealand scored highest with a rating of 9.7 out of 10, whereas Indonesia scored 1.9, below India at 2.6, the Philippines at 2.5, and Pakistan and the People's Republic of China at 2.1 (*Far Eastern Economic Review*, August 31, 1995: 13).

11 In Thailand the bureau submits its budget recommendations to the cabinet for approval, presenting the cabinet only with the broad expenditure outlines for each ministry. The details are obscured. The cabinet may propose changes to these broad expenditure categories. Once cabinet-level changes have been factored in, the final product is sent to Parliament by the bureau. Within Parliament, the Budget Scrutiny Committee is responsible for evaluating the budget proposal. The committee is composed of ordinary members

of Parliament (MPs) and ministerial MPs. In particular, parliamentary rules restrict the ordinary MPs to amendments that adjust the budget downward. The ordinary MPs cannot propose increases to the overall budget and can only propose minimal changes to components of the budget. The sectoral (component) changes are rarely significant.

12 Campos and Root, 1996.
13 Governments consistently have to make difficult decisions. Whether sacrifices will benefit the general population or narrow interest groups depends on the regime's political foundations. The decision by Germany's Third Reich to murder Jews was difficult, significant resources were diverted to the task, but the outcome was self-defeating. Similarly, the murders during the Marcos regime were decisions entailing great risks, such as the possibility of revenge sought by surviving family members, but these were the wrong difficult decisions because the government took risks from which few people benefited.
14 Hong Kong, Singapore, and Taiwan consistently ran budget surpluses (Thomas and Wang, 1992).
15 The Asian experience is in accord with Western fundamentals. Max Weber noted "According to experience, the relative optimism for the success and maintenance of a strict mechanization of the bureaucratic apparatus is offered by a secured money salary connected with the opportunity of a career that is not dependent upon mere accident and arbitrariness" (Weber, 1976; 208).
16 Root, 1996.
17 Campos and Root, 1996.
18 Clientalism refers to the personalized pairing of partners in recurrent exchanges. Particularistic ties are developed to cope with the costliness of contract uncertainty. Thus promises under clientalism are likely to be honoured despite the absence of a public enforcement authority. Because the exchange is highly personalized, social or political rank will heavily influence the terms of trade.
19 Root, 1989.
20 A wide range of deliberative bodies were developed, such as political councils and village associations.
21 Taiwan was a partial exception. There, officials used state-owned companies to control the commanding heights of the economy (Wade, 1990a).
22 Huntington, 1968.
23 The region's laggards cannot be distinguished from the high performers by measuring the level of government intervention in the economy. In 1955, the state sector of Taiwan accounted for 51 percent of the country's total output, a higher percentage than that of the Indian state sector. Most of the countries in the region were highly interventionist by the standards of neoclassical economics.
24 Figures by Dahlman, Carl J. and Ousa Sananikone, as cited in Petri, 1993: 16.
25 Petri, 1993. Ignoring the role of institutional and organizational innovation, Paul Krugman has evaluated East Asia's achievement in terms of capital formation (total factor productivity), which leads him to underestimate the region's achievement and to ignore one of its principle sources of growth (Krugman, 1994). Organizational capability is a form of social capital not easily acquired but easily taken for granted. The emergence of capital markets, for example, involved the acquisition of new organizational skills.

REFERENCES

Campos, J. Edgardo and Hilton Root (1996) *The Key to the East Asian Miracle: Making Shared Growth Credible*, Washington, DC: Brookings Institution.

Far Eastern Economic Review, August 10, 1995, 158: 37.

Far Eastern Economic Review, August 31, 1995, 158: 13.

Huntington, Samuel P. (1968) *Political Order in Changing Societies*, New Haven, CT: Yale University Press.

Jaramillio-Vallejo, Jaime (1994) *Proceedings of the World Bank Annual Conference on Development Economics*, Washington, DC: World Bank.

Krugman, Paul (1994) "The Myth of Asia's Miracle," *Foreign Affairs*, Nov.–Dec., 73: 62–78.

Petri, Peter A. (1993) *The Lessons of East Asia: Common Foundations of East Asian Success*, Washington, DC: World Bank.

Quah, Jon S.T. (1982) "The Public Bureaucracy and National Development in Singapore," in Tummala, K.K., ed., *Administrative Systems Abroad*, Washington, DC: University Press of America, pp. 42–75.

Quah, Jon S.T. (1991) "Promoting Accountability in Public Management: The Singapore Case," in Bahadur, Goraksha, N. Pradman, and Mila A. Reforma, eds, *Public Management in the 1990s: Challenges and Opportunities*, Manila: Eastern Regional Organization for Public Administration.

Quah, Jon S.T. (1992) Administrative Reform and National Development in Singapore," in The Changing Role of Government: Administrative Structures and Reforms, London: Commonwealth Secretariat, pp. 119–54.

Quah, Jon S.T. (1995) "Controlling Corruption in City-States: A Comparative Study of Hong Kong and Singapore," *Crime, Law and Social Change*, 22: 391–414.

Quah, Jon S.T. (1993) "The Rediscovery of the Market and Public Administration: Some Lessons from the Singapore Experience," *Australian Journal of Public Administration*, 52: 320–28.

Quah, Jon S.T., Chan Heng Chee, and Seah Chee Meow, eds (1985) *Government and Politics of Singapore*, Singapore: Oxford University Press.

Root, Hilton L. (1989) "Tying the King's Hands: Credible Commitments and Royal Fiscal Policy During the Old Regime," *Rationality and Society*, 1: 240–58.

—— (1996) *Small Countries, Big Lessons: Governance and the Rise of East Asia*, New York: Oxford University Press.

Summers, Lawrence H. and Shekhar Shah (1992) "Introduction," *Proceedings of the World Bank Annual Conference on Development Economics 1992*, Washington, DC: World Bank.

Teranishi, Juro (1994a) "Shared Growth and East Asian Miracle: A Comment on the World Bank Study," Tokyo: Hitotsubashi University, 1994, unpublished manuscript.

—— (1994b) "Sectoral Resource Transfer, Conflict and Macrostability in Economic Development: A Comparative Analysis," in Masahiko Aoki, Hyung-Ki Kim, and Masahiro Okuno-Fujiwara (eds) *The Role of Government in East Asian Economic Development: Comparative Institutional Analysis*, Oxford: Oxford University Press, pp. 279–322.

Thomas, Vinod and Yan Wang (1992) "Government Policies and Productivity Growth: Is Asia an Exemption?" in Petri, Peter A., ed., *The Lessons of East Asia: Common Foundations of East Asian Success*, Washington, DC: World Bank.

Wade, Robert (1990a) *Governing the Market: Economic Theory and the Role of Government in East Asian Industrialization*, Princeton, NJ: Princeton University Press.

—— (1990b) "Industrial Policy in East Asia: Does It Lead or Follow the Market?" in Gereffi, Gary and Donald Wyman, eds, *Manufacturing Miracles: Paths of Industrialization in Latin America and East Asia*, Princeton, NJ: Princeton University Press.

Weber, Max (1976) *From Max Weber: Essays in Sociology*. Gerth, H.H., and C. Wright Mills, trans. and eds, New York: Oxford University Press.

4 Business, politics and policy in East and Southeast Asia

Stephan M. Haggard[1]

One explanation for East Asia's rapid growth is the distinctive nature of the region's politics (Johnson, 1982, 1987; Chu, 1989; Cheng, 1990; Haggard, 1988, 1990; Wade, 1990 chs. 7 and 8; Chang, 1994; Campos and Root, 1996).[2] One version of this approach is that the East Asian newly-industrializing countries (NICs) enjoyed the advantages of competent, meritocratic bureaucracies (see for example World Bank, 1993: 174–81; but also Evans, 1992, 1995). A second line of analysis focuses on the broader institutional milieu, and particularly the "strength" of the state.

The core of these institutionalist approaches is that economic policy is a key input to long-term growth, but that the policy-making process is subject to collective action, coordination and commitment problems (Chang, 1994). Politicians are typically responsive to interest group pressures and short-term political constraints that introduce distortions, reduce the credibility of policy, and lead to sub-optimal performance.[3] Bureaucratic and political institutions can amplify or mute these dilemmas, depending on how they structure decision-making and the representation of interests.

This chapter argues that while institutions are one important element of the political matrix, equal attention must be paid to the relationship between the government and the private sector. The East Asian model is typically seen to include close business–government relations as a defining element. In contrast to other developing countries, governments in East Asia have defended property rights and provided strong incentives to private investment (Campos and Root, 1996). However successful economic reforms typically involved *conflict* between politicians and businessmen and the ability of the government to override or ignore particularistic private sector interests. Moreover, close business–government relations have not always been salutary; as elsewhere in the developing world, they have been implicated in extensive rent-seeking and corruption. I develop these arguments by reviewing the historical experience of the major developing countries of the region – Korea, Taiwan, Hong Kong, Singapore, Thailand, Indonesia, Malaysia and the Philippines – focusing on variation in the nature of business–government relations.

These differences help explain patterns of industrial organization, the balance between foreign and local investment, and the extent of corruption across the region. The review underlines that there is no single "East Asian model"; high growth emerged under a variety of political systems, albeit with very different consequences.

THE EAST ASIAN MODEL REVISITED

Recent accounts of economic growth in East Asia emphasize the fundamental role played by capital accumulation, but acknowledge that policy played an important role in both the level and efficiency of investment (Krugman, 1994). First, stable fiscal and monetary policies encouraged savings and capital accumulation and allowed the government to pursue a consistently export-oriented exchange rate policy. Second, labor markets were relatively flexible and wage levels determined largely by conditions of supply and demand; this allowed the East Asian countries to exploit their comparative advantage in low-cost labor. Finally, though trade policy did provide protection for domestic producers, it was never "overly" protectionist and simultaneously allowed access to needed inputs at world market prices. An activist industrial policy deployed a variety of additional instruments, including fiscal and financial subsidies and even direct ownership of production, but generally placed emphasis on the promotion of exports and thus exposed domestic firms to international competitive pressures.

Institutions had an effect on the politics of each of these policy areas. Coherent fiscal and monetary policies require not only technical sophistication but the political capacity to raise revenues and to limit claims on government expenditures, including those coming from the private sector. This capacity might result from institutional mechanisms that exclude or limit potential claimants from participation, as was the case with the tightly-controlled budgetary processes in Korea, Taiwan and Hong Kong, or through a process of delegation from politicians to technocrats, as in the case of Taiwan's powerful central bank. In either case, a crucial sphere of economic policy-making was depoliticized.

The position of labor has been a central point of controversy in the literature on the NICs (for a review, see Deyo, 1989). In particular, there is debate over the extent to which labor repression was a prerequisite of the export-led growth strategy. Wage determination in the NICs was driven largely by market forces, with the exception of Singapore where government intervention was somewhat more direct. During an initial period of labor abundance in the NICs, rapid absorption of labor was achieved with relatively slow real wage growth. As labor markets tightened, as they did in all of the NICs, real wages rose, signaling the private sector of the need to diversify away from labor-intensive manufacturing.

However, a pure market story ignores a variety of other actions taken by governments that allowed wage determination to function as it did. To differing degrees across the NICs we find governments limiting workers' channels of redress, curtailing or banning strikes, limiting non-wage demands, such as those surrounding working conditions, and restricting the formation of linkages between unions and other political forces, from political parties to the church. These controls clearly reflected a political environment in which the interests of management were favored over those of workers, even though the institutional mechanisms for achieving this objective varied across countries. (World Bank, 1993: 164–7).

Finally, trade and industrial policy play a big role in both neoclassical (Krueger, 1993) and heterodox (Amsden, 1989; Wade 1990) explanations of East Asian growth. In neoclassical accounts, trade liberalization was responsible for an expansion of exports, greater specialization along lines of comparative advantage, and strong pressures for technological innovation and productivity improvements, while industrial policy is considered either inconsequential or a drag on growth. In heterodox accounts, the emphasis is reversed. Doubt is cast on the extent of trade liberalization in the larger NICs, and it is in any case not seen as a major contributor to subsequent growth; to the contrary, the larger export-oriented NICs are portrayed as pursuing a policy of import-substitution cum export-promotion (Rodrik, 1995). Moreover, industrial policies of various sorts – essentially subsidies – are seen as making a positive contribution to long-run growth.

The political underpinnings of these trade and industrial policies have received little attention in economic accounts, however. On the one hand, trade liberalization exposes protectionist groups to new competitive pressures; neoclassical accounts must therefore explain why business would support such liberalizing reforms. Heterodox accounts face a different problem. As the rent-seeking literature rightly emphasizes, business can exploit an interventionist policy stance. Indeed, because of their power and organization, we would expect that organized private sector groups would constitute the *greatest* threat to a coherent, export-oriented industrial policy. This is particularly true where governments have persisted over long periods of time in pursuing policies that favor import-substituting industries or the non-tradable goods sector.

At least some of the disagreement about the East Asian model stems from efforts to generalize from individual cases. The East Asian countries combined some degree of liberalization with more directed industrial policies, but in mixes that varied from the *laissez-faire* stance of the British colonial government in Hong Kong to the highly dirigist stance of Korean governments. The key question is not only why such policies worked in economic terms, but why the government was able to support export-oriented activities – through whatever means – that provided the check of international competition. Why, in Alice Amsden's words (1989: 14–18), was the state able to "discipline" the private sector? Or, in the language of the World Bank *Miracle* study, why was it capable of running "contests" for policy favors that insured that only the efficient received them? (World Bank, 1993: 93–100).

For institutionalists, the answer is to be found in "strong" states. The state had both the capacity and instruments to discipline business, and the business-government relationship was structured to limit the opportunities for particularistic rent-seeking or for business control over the policy agenda. Peter Evans (1992, 1995), for example, emphasizes that states in East Asia were "embedded" in a network of relations with private sector actors. However, he also emphasizes that bureaucratic actors were socialized to government tasks, immune from capture, and thus "autonomous" as well. Other mechanisms of government control include the state-created industry association and the "deliberation council," through which such associations are represented to the political leadership (World Bank, 1993: 181–8). Though such channels grant business direct access to the government, they also provide the government with the organizational means for agenda-setting and control. As Wade summarizes neatly, "the state charters or creates a small number of interest groups, giving them a monopoly of representation of occupational interests in return for which it claims the right to monitor them in order to discourage the expression of narrow, conflictual demands . . . [and] maximize compliance and cooperation" (Wade, 1990: Cheng *et al.*, 1995).

The institutionalist approach can now be summarized. Growth may rest ultimately on high rates of investment, but such investment in turn hinges on effective government policy, usually taken to include some mix of stable macroeconomic policies and a growth-promoting trade and industrial policy. Such effectiveness is dependent on bureaucratic capacity, but also on institutional insulation. Though governments in the NICs were broadly pro-business, political institutions minimized capture by narrow private interests. Where they existed, industry associations did not so much represent business interests to the government as they served to communicate government intentions to the private sector.

THE EAST ASIAN MODEL: A CRITIQUE

The institutionalist approach addresses the *capacity* of the state but not its *motivations* (Moon, 1990; Doner, 1991b). Since institutionalists reject the idea that government policy can he reduced to a vector of private sector pressures, why does the government choose to do what it does? Why have the East Asian governments chosen to embrace relatively efficient and outward-oriented policies rather than exploiting their power for predatory ends?

Three answers have been advanced. The first is ideology. State officials developed, inherited or imported ideas about how to achieve economic growth and used their control over material and organizational resources to implement them. Chalmers Johnson's (1982) classic study of Japan's Ministry of International Trade and Industry emphasizes the role of alternative economic ideas, and Vogel (1991) argues that the highly-successful Japanese model played an important role in economic thinking in the NICs. Elsewhere, I have shown how American advisers played a role in both Korea and Taiwan and how a succession of British financial secretaries shaped Hong Kong's uniquely laisser-faire economic policy regime (Haggard, 1990: chapters 3–5). In general, however, this approach is unsatisfying unless it explains where ideas and ideologies come from and why politicians have an incentive to select the ones that they do.

The second option is to argue that though state elites may be relatively independent from domestic social forces, they are constrained by international pressures of various sorts. External economic agents – foreign firms and banks, international financial institutions, bilateral donors – provided assistance to all of the East Asian countries at some point, and influenced the course of policy in the process. Once the economy is more open, exposure to international markets itself constitutes a check on policy since the cost to the government of pursuing policies that reduce national competitiveness becomes both higher and more readily apparent. Pursuing an alternative theoretical Line, Kang (1995) has shown how security threats can push governments to greater efficiency.

Finally, outward-looking industrial policies might be understood in terms of the material interests of the government itself. Rent-seeking and predatory state models assume that politicians' interests conflict with economic efficiency, but there are a number of efficiency-enhancing policy reforms that benefit the government directly. For example, one reason the government pushed exports in Korea and Taiwan was not because of an interest in efficiency or growth, but because it provided government leaders access to scarce foreign exchange. Similar arguments can be advanced with reference to fiscal and financial market reform (Levi, 1988; Haggard *et al.*, 1991).

As a number of critics have pointed out (Doner, 1991b; Doner and Hawes, 1992; Haggard and Moon, 1990; MacIntyre, 1991; Chiu, 1992; Wade, 1992; Evans, 1992, 1995), these three answers to the question of government motivation all paint a relatively passive picture of the private sector. Active and successful in markets, firms are portrayed as quiescent in politics. However even if politicians are not captured by the private sector, they are dependent on them in several important respects; for resources, for information, for political support, and ultimately for the investment and growth which are a source of legitimacy in any mixed economy.[4]

These observations suggest a reconceptualization of the business–government relationship. Rather than thinking in terms of insulation and autonomy, it may be more useful to see business–government relations as an ongoing negotiation. The government seeks political support, investment, and information. The private sector seeks a predictable and stable business environment and sector – and even firm-specific incentives.[5] At least three aspects of "business–government relations" will influence the outcome of this bargaining relationship. The first is the nature of political institutions and the extent to which they provide opportunities for business access to, and control over, the policy agenda; these are the questions that drive the institutionalist agenda. Second, we need to know not only about the preferences of the private sector, but its political capacity: organizational coherence, ability to mobilize broader support from other segments of the population, and ability to withdraw political and economic support.[6]

However, these factors are themselves endogenous to the broader political relationship between the government and the private sector: the extent to which politicians rely on business support. Regional variation on this score is surprisingly wide, ranging from close alignments, to arms-length relationships, to open antagonism. In the remainder of this chapter, I place the institutional arrangements linking business and government within their broader political context, and show how variations across countries have influenced the nature of government policy, and through policy, economic outcomes.

BUSINESS–GOVERNMENT RELATIONS IN KOREA AND TAIWAN

In many ways, the KMT can be viewed as a foreign occupying force. On relocating to Taiwan following its defeat in the civil war, the party had few ties with indigenous elites; the party relied on the military and bureaucratic cadre relocated from the mainland. The government's independence was buttressed by overwhelming military and police power, a relatively large state-owned enterprise sector, and control over the financial sector. The Taiwanese business community had little formal representation in the tightly-organized ruling party (Chu, 1994). State–corporatist business organizations provided nominal channels of representation, but in fact were quiescent.

The economic reforms of the late-1950s and early 1960s shifted the policy emphasis away from the state-owned sector toward tacit support for private business through more secure property rights and various fiscal and financial incentives. New research is showing that extensive relationships developed in the 1950s between technocrats and the largest firms (Kuo, 1995). In general, however, officials were relatively unconstrained by political, personal or family loyalties to the private sector and could take a long-term view. The pressure for reform came less from domestic politics than it did from American pressures.

The arms-length nature of the political relationship with local business had implications for reform and the conduct of industrial policy. This relationship was partly a function of the island's relatively decentralized industrial structure, with a large number of small family firms. However this structure was itself the result of policy; the government self-consciously sought to check the growth and concentration of large Taiwanese capital. As a result, industrial policy does not show the same degree of sector- and firm-specific activism visible in Korea, despite the fact that the government controlled a similar array of policy instruments (Cheng, 1993). The KMT's political concerns also explain why the government showed a strong propensity to use state-owned enterprises to achieve industrial policy goals.

Korea's more interventionist policy style, by contrast, can be explained by the government's greater political vulnerability and dependence on business support. In contrast to Taiwan, the American occupation imposed democratic institutions on Korea. Though abused by Syngman Rhee, electoral politics created strong incentives to woo private sector support. The close political relationship between Rhee, the Liberal Party, and the private sector explains the extensive corruption and rent-seeking in the 1950s (Haggard *et al.*, 1991).

The student revolution of 1960 and the seizure of power by the military in 1961 substantially weakened the political position of the private sector. The military exploited popular discontent with corruption in launching its *coup d'état*, and younger colonels even called for the execution of prominent business leaders. The military exploited this reversal of political fortunes to initiate institutional changes that substantially reduced business access to government largesse, at least in the short-run. The junta closed the legislature, banned parties, and reformed the institutions of economic policy-making to increase executive control. The government established sectoral business organizations and used them to monitor and control business behavior. As in Taiwan, seizure of the financial system provided the government with a crucial instrument for enforcing its policy preferences.

Yet the military leadership was ultimately much more dependent on private sector support than was the case in Taiwan. The state-owned enterprise sector was relatively small and the military lacked a party apparatus that could provide an organized base of political support. In 1963, the Korean military came under strong American pressure to make a transition to (nominally) democratic rule. This political change increased the need for business cooperation, and Park Chung Hee quickly reached a *modus vivendi* with the large firms grouped in the relatively independent Federation of Korean Industries. The government extended various policy favors, particularly the provision of preferential credit, in return for support for the Park's ambitious development plans and large political contributions (Cheng *et al.*, 1995).

As in Taiwan, industrial organization can be partly explained by the nature of these policy choices. In the 1950s, Korean business already appeared more concentrated than in Taiwan (Fields, 1990; Hamilton and Biggart, 1988; Hamilton, 1991). But Park's political strategy encouraged the further concentration of favored private-sector partners, particularly as the political coalition supporting the regime narrowed. The most spectacular growth of the *chaebol* occurred precisely during the period of the authoritarian Yushin constitution (1973–80) (Fields, 1990; Kim, forthcoming).

In both countries, the political power of business expanded in the 1970s and 1980s. Large private groups emerged, and the organizational capabilities of the private sector increased accordingly. Both governments also forged closer relations with the private sector as part of a strategy of shifting toward more complex, capital-intensive and technology-intensive industries, a strategy that required greater business representation in the policy-making process and more differentiated forms of assistance.

Yet more purely political factors were also at work. In Taiwan, as electoral politics became a more important component of the KMT's strategy of rule in the late 1970s, the quest for sources of political funding became more intense, the barriers separating the party from the private sector blurred, and the autonomy of the technocrats *vis-à-vis* business interests declined. The KMT's reliance on business grew even more intense following the transition to democratic rule in the mid-1980s. As Chu (1994) argues, the interests of the party and of the private sector converged on a number of important points as well: both saw the need for the involvement of an active state in the process of industrial upgrading, both put economic growth before environmental considerations, both favored a slow growth in social welfare spending, and both supported continuing exclusion of organized labor from economic policy-making. These shared interests constituted the basis for a new conservative coalition that draws on extensive financial contributions from business and electoral support from the growing middle-class more interested in political and economic stability than the ethnic appeals of the Taiwanese opposition.

The 1970s were a period of new authoritarianism in Korea. Along with his new Yushin constitution, the Park government initiated a heavy and chemical industry plan, supported by a close, clientelistic relationship between the executive and the largest firms. Though apparently the initiative of a "strong" state, the *chaebol* played an important role in defining the new policy thrust, which further increased the concentration of big business and gave it effective blackmail power over government initiatives (Rhee, 1994; Moon, 1994).

In 1980–81, the military once again intervened in politics, reversing the opportunity for democratization opened by Park Chung Hee's assassination. The new military government of Chun Doo Hwan sought to stabilize the economy and reverse the highly interventionist policy course associated with the heavy industry drive. Though some of the liberalizing reforms ultimately profited big business, many were explicitly aimed to reduce the influence of, and benefits flowing to, the largest *chaebol*. These included anti-monopoly and fair trade laws, trade liberalization, reduction in preferential credit in favor of small and medium-sized firms, and the efforts to restructure a number of particular industrial sectors. Economic policy became a tool in an unsuccessful effort to construct a new growth coalition.

The transition to democracy in 1986-87 initially gave the new president Roh Tae Woo strong incentives to distance himself from big business; throughout his term in office, he periodically took initiatives to curb business power. But the open political environment also provided oppor-tunities for business groups to air their grievances and to back favored candidates. With stalemate in the legislature and continuing protests, the government moved in a conservative direction in 1990. Not until the pres-idency of Kim Young Sam were there more far-reaching efforts to reform the nature of business-government relations, yet the scandals that unfolded in 1995 and 1996 showed that business influence over politics continued.

We see both commonalities and differences in Korea and Taiwan in the 1980s and 1990s. The growth of the largest firms and of business asso-ciations provided new opportunities for business to air its grievances about government policy, lobbying for continued support in some areas, and deregulation in others. Yet the political landscape in the two countries differed. In Taiwan, the ruling KMT continued to enjoy a majority and forged a conservative coalition with business around broad continuity in policy and new opportunities for business representation in both party and state policy-making machinery. In Korea, by contrast, both Roh's conservative coalition and that of his successor Kim Young Sam were squeezed between a more vociferous Left on the one hand and a much more concentrated private sector on the other. As a result, both govern-ments' generally pro-business stance was mixed with recurrent reform efforts – only marginally successful – to reduce the overweening influence of the *chaebol.*

SINGAPORE AND HONG KONG

Comparing the city-states of Singapore and Hong Kong provides a natural experiment for demonstrating how differences in institutions and business-government relations can influence policy and economic structure.[7] As with the analysis of the larger NICs, Korea and Taiwan, such a compar-ison allows for a number of controls. Both city-states began as trading entrepôts, and both continue to perform the function of linking their hinterlands (China for Hong Kong, the Malaysian peninsula for Singapore) with the world economy. Both are constrained by their size to pursue open trade policies, both have been open to foreign direct invest-ment, and both developed substantial manufacturing sectors. There are even some institutional and cultural similarities. Both have British colonial heritages that are responsible for strong, meritocratic civil services, but both are also predominantly Chinese cities, though Singapore has substantial Indian and Malay minorities.

However the two cities could not be more different (see particularly Chiu *et al.*, 1997: 7). Hong Kong's commitment to *laissez-faire* is not limited to the foreign sector, but constitutes a more general principle of economic management. With the important exception of the property and housing markets, the government has not intervened extensively in the economy, but has rather concentrated on providing a minimum of public goods and necessary services while keeping macroeconomic policy stable and taxes low. Periodic efforts on the part of the domestic manufacturing sector to secure assistance through some kind of industrial policy have been rebuffed (Haggard, 1990: 124); outside of some limited support for industrial estates, training, and promotional activities for the city as a whole, the government comes closer to mirroring Adam Smith's "night watchman" state than any country in the world.

As a result, the industrial structure has reflected changing comparative advantage and situational factors rather than government direction. The service and trading sector has always played a prominent role in Hong Kong's development, dominated initially by large British companies headquartered in Hong Kong such as Jardine Matheson. Following the Chinese civil war, the colony enjoyed the influx of an experienced class of large manufacturers from Shanghai, concentrated in the textile and apparel industry. These sectors, offshore assembly investment by American and Japanese companies, and the growth of a myriad of small, highly-flexible Chinese firms in sectors such as toys and plastic flowers, constituted the backbone of Hong Kong's manufacturing growth.

In recent years, however, the close proximity to a rapidly-reforming China has resulted in a substantial "hollowing out" of the manufacturing sector. Chinese manufacturing firms based in Hong Kong have shifted production to Shenzen's special economic zones, or more further afield on the mainland, concentrating on design and logistics (Naughton, 1997). The result has been a marked shift toward an economic structure even more dominated by financial and commercial services (Chiu *et al.*, 1997).

In Singapore, by contrast, the government has pursued an activist industrial policy, centered primarily on attracting, servicing and supporting foreign investors (Rodan, 1989). Part of Singapore's strategy is simply to excel in the provision of public goods, infrastructure, and a hospitable business climate. However, the core industrial policy agency, the Economic Development Board, has manipulated incentives to foreign firms – its main clients – in order to attract particular types of investment as well. Since the "second industrial revolution" of the late 1970s, government control over wage policy and the inflow of immigrant labor from Malaysia has periodically been used to discourage low-end assembly operations. Direct state intervention in the economy is also extensive, particularly through the instrument of government-owned and government-linked enterprises and various statutory boards.

The result of the government's strategy has been an industrial structure largely dominated by European, American and Japanese multinationals. Although the government has always maintained various programs to support local business, they did not figure centrally in the government's strategy until the economic downturn of 1985 resulted in a dramatic upturn in local business failures. Beginning in the 1990s, however, the government has concentrated greater efforts on domestic business, including by fostering a small group of larger "promising local enterprises."

Singapore's strategy is also one in which manufacturing has thrived and undergone a substantial upgrading process that is now beginning to extend into research, design and development. In contrast to Hong Kong, where manufacturing's share of output has steadily fallen over the last decade, Singapore has made a strong commitment to maintain its manufacturing base.

These differences in strategy and structure can be traced directly to politics and the nature of business–government relations. Hong Kong remained a British colony until June 30, 1997, when Britain relinquished it to China. British colonial authorities defended property rights, provided an even-handed judiciary, and respected civil liberties. However, politics was dominated by the Governor and economics by a succession of powerful, *laissez-faire* Financial Secretaries. Representative bodies permitted both formal and informal access for segments of Hong Kong's business elite, but in general, business representation reflected commercial and financial, rather than manufacturing interests. In any case, such representation in no way challenged the authority of the Financial Secretary to conduct economic policy as he saw fit.

Politics in Singapore has been substantially more complicated, in part because of the presence of electoral constraints on government. In contrast to Hong Kong, Singapore experienced a typical nationalist movement in the 1950s, with deep divisions between centrist and leftist camps. Despite its current authoritarian and business-friendly profile, the People's Action Party (PAP) only succeeded electorally by advancing a popular nationalist program that appealed to labor and included provision of social services and employment and public investment. Adroit political strategy and outright repression allowed Lee Kuan Yew to defeat his socialist rivals, but when federation with Malaya failed in 1965, Singapore was left to its own devices; only then did the government pursue its aggressive strategy of courting foreign investors, relying in part on the party's increasingly-strict control over the labor movement.

However, the nature of the government's strategy was also based on both distance from, and lack of confidence in, the local private sector. Concentrated primarily in services and commercial activities, and of questionable political loyalty, the local Chinese business sector did not appear to have the scale or skills to provide the core for a successful development strategy. The result was much greater reliance on foreign firms and state-owned enterprises. Although the shift back toward greater emphasis on local business had primarily an economic rationale, it also overlapped with the changing of the guard in the PAP from an older to a younger generation of leadership, and particular sensitivity to retaining electoral support.

THE SOUTHEAST ASIAN CASES

Though the southeast Asian countries are moving along an export-oriented growth path, they have done so on the basis of quite different policy and political frameworks.[8] Industrial policies have played a less substantial role in the transition to export-led growth than in Korea and Taiwan, bureaucracies appear less competent, and governments less insulated from political pressures. If institutional insulation has played an important role in economic policy in Thailand, Indonesia, and Malaysia, it is probably in the area of macroeconomic policy-making. In contrast to a number of other middle-income countries, particularly in Latin America, the Southeast Asian countries have maintained relatively conservative and stable monetary and fiscal policies over the last two decades; the major exception is the Philippines under Marcos (Sachs, 1985).

The industrial policy regimes in the four larger ASEAN countries differ in ways that can be explained by the nature of the political relationship between state and business. In Thailand, government has been favorably disposed to business, but until the 1980s business organization was relatively weak and the private sector did not have institutionalized access to the government outside particular patron–client relations; in general, the government maintained tight control over the policy process. Despite substantial corruption in some areas, and the emergence of business–government cooperation on East Asian lines in other sectors (Doner, 1991a), the result has been a relatively non-interventionist industrial policy stance that has encouraged both foreign and local investment in export-oriented manufacturing.

In Malaysia and Indonesia, ethnic politics are critical and a distinction must be made between the government's relationship with the Chinese and "indigenous" (in Malaysia, *bumiputra*; in Indonesia, *pribumi*) segments of the private sector. At one level, the relationship between the government and Chinese business is conflictual because of recurrent political efforts to control its activities in order to advance "indigenous" business interests. This has been particularly true in Malaysia, where the party system generated both electoral and interest group pressure on the government to support Malay entrepreneurs. In Indonesia, the goal of advancing the *pribumi* has been a recurrent political theme, but political channels did not exist for the private sector to articulate its demands. As a result, business representation moved through informal, personalistic networks to a greater degree.

The apparent conflict between Chinese capital and the state has been mitigated by the development of close personalistic relationships between top political elites, bureaucrats, and the larger Chinese enterprises. These relationships have been based on an exchange of political support, including political funds, for protection and policy favors. Extensive networks have evolved between the state and the private sector, but these have been permeated by rent-seeking. Subsidies and protection for "indigenous" segments of the private sector in the import-substituting and non-traded goods sectors have been coupled with corrupt ties with Chinese business, particularly in Indonesia. In both countries, governments have also sought to substitute for the weakness of the "indigenous" private sector through the creation of state-owned enterprises, which in turn have become an important locus of power, patronage, and corruption.

Finally, in the Philippines, business–government relations have been exceedingly close, but under conditions of an economically-powerful and diversified oligarchy, rulers who draw little distinction between the public and private spheres, and weak institutions for structuring the business–government nexus in an efficient and growth-promoting way. The result has been an ineffective industrial policy, dominated by cronyism. Only with democratization were the excesses of this system checked.

Thailand

The comparative puzzle presented by Thailand is its long history of relatively stable macroeconomic policy coupled with a relatively non-interventionist policy style at the industry level. From the late nineteenth century until the 1930s, a combination of good agricultural performance, strong domestic participation in agricultural trade, and fear of foreign political penetration all served to limit government intervention in markets (Doner and Unger, 1993). Pressure from the domestic private sector was also minimal. The combination of business links to a highly competitive agricultural export sector, the relatively small size of manufacturing compared to commerce, and the highly institutionalized nature of the traditional Thai polity all served to bloc the emergence of a rent-seeking, import-substituting coalition.

Thailand did experience a period of greater state involvement in the economy beginning in the early 1950s when the military created a number of new state-owned enterprises and sought to curb the power of Chinese entrepreneurs.[9] Under Sarit and his successors (1957–73), however, the military reacted against the costs of the interventionist strategy and granted substantially more independence to Sino-Thai business. Not only did traditional commerce and bank-based groups thrive, but a new generation of Thai capital emerged in the manufacturing sector. The reforms of Sarit and his successors did not eliminate clientelism and corruption, but their negative consequences were bounded by centralization of budgetary policy, the independence of the central bank, and the generally high technical competence of the economic bureaucracy.

As in the East Asian NICs, the power of business continued to increase over the 1970s. The reasons lay in the growth of large business groups, increased organizational efforts by the private sector, and the gradual liberalization of politics. The government's relationship with the private sector was consolidated in 1981 through the creation of a Joint Public–Private Consultative Committee (JPPCC), which linked the prime minister and economic bureaucracy directly with representatives of the largest business associations. Laothamatas' (1992) study emphasizes that the JPPCC served as a channel for business demands on government, but also provided a base of support for the government for both political liberalization and economic reform during the 1981–84 period.

It is important to underline, however, that during Thailand's gradual transition to a more export-oriented strategy in the first half of the 1980s, business operated in a political and institutional context that granted the government substantial power over the overall economic policy agenda. With reference to the formulation and implementation of macroeconomic policy, the executive and bureaucracy were extremely powerful.[10] Prem controlled appointments to his cabinet, shielding economic decision-making from direct party and business influences to a substantial degree. The National Economic and Social Development Board (NESDB) was entirely technocratic in make-up and though party-based cabinet officials were represented on the Council of Economic Ministers, they were outnumbered by bureaucrats, advisors and non-party politicians appointed by Prem. In effect, politicians were limited to seeking pork-barrel projects for their districts within parameters controlled by the bureaucracy. This ability to control fiscal and monetary policy and to undertake needed exchange rate adjustments is a central precondition for the pursuit of an effective export-oriented growth strategy.

With reference to trade and industrial policy, Laothamatas (1992, 1994) and Christensen (1992) argue that business had more success in penetrating the government; trade liberalization measures were blocked in the 1980s and subsidies to exporters increased. Yet such policies are not necessarily a block to successful growth, and may contribute to it if they are not excessive and seek to assist the transition of competitive firms into world markets.

The parliamentary elections of 1988 marked yet another step toward genuine parliamentary rule; as we might expect, this institutional change had an influence on the pattern of economic policy-making. Chatchai, the first elected leader to head a government since 1976, quickly appointed politicians or wealthy party backers to virtually all cabinet posts and intervened in the bureaucracy in various ways. Particular business demands were now channeled to an increasing extent through the parties, in part precisely to circumvent the technocratic influence that had characterized the JPPCC system under Prem.

The limits on the ability of political parties to raise funds coupled with the traditional practice of vote-buying gave rise to closer relations between politicians and private sector supporters. Party bosses also cultivated relations with local officials who provided an important base of support and linkage with constituencies, particularly in the rural areas. To solidify, and pay for, these bases of support, politicians naturally became more aggressive in seeking government favors. In short, economic policy was characterized to a greater extent by corruption and rent-seeking.

As the 1991 coup demonstrated, however, these developments were reversible. Exploiting disaffection with parliamentary rule – including among the Bangkok business class – the military swept back into power. Though their rule proved untenable and short-lived, it is a further vindication of the approach developed here that the military government, based on an alliance with the technocracy and progressive segments of the private sector, quickly undertook some of the most wide-ranging economic reforms in recent Thai history.

It is true that the Thai bureaucracy lacked the analytic capacity or the highly differentiated policy instruments of the East Asian NICs. However, institutional arrangements and the nature of business–government relations did facilitate the government's ability to undertake quite substantial reforms; this was true both of the first half of the 1980s and again following the 1991 coup. With more democratic institutions, however, rent-seeking and corruption have become a more central element of Thai economic policy-making than in the past.

Malaysia

The situation in Malaysia and Indonesia present some revealing contrasts to Thailand, since they, too, had to respond to the "problem" of an economically powerful Chinese minority. While the Thai government had accommodated these interests by the 1960s, political elites in Malaysia and Indonesia moved in the opposite direction, constructing ruling formulae that, at least formally, exhibited a greater hostility to the Chinese. This political fact colored all aspects of economic policy.

The key set of relationships for understanding economic policy in Malaysia have been those between the Malay-dominated ruling party (UMNO – United Malays National Organization) and the allied Malayan Civil Service – which together exercised monopoly control over the government since independence – and the Chinese business community (Jesudason, 1989; Bowie, 1991; Koon, 1992). Formally, intra-ethnic relations have been mediated by a grand coalition dominated by the major Malay party (UMNO), but through which the conservative Chinese business community enjoys representation via the Malaysian Chinese Association (MCA). Yet within that overall settlement or pact, the balance of power has undergone some important shifts that have influenced industrial policy.

Before turning to that issue, however, it is worth digressing briefly on the institutions governing macroeconomic policy. As in Thailand, this policy area has remained relatively depoliticized, and thus again provides some important confirmation for institutionalist arguments. The industrial policies designed to assist the Malays contributed to large fiscal deficits in the early 1970s, but high domestic savings rates and lucrative trade taxes made it possible to finance them in a non-inflationary way. These purely economic features of the Malaysian economy, and its openness, have clearly contributed to low inflation and consistent exchange rate policies. Yet the political insulation and conservative orientation of the Malaysian monetary authorities, a legacy of the British currency board system, also contributed to the outcome. Moreover, the country's high savings rate is partly attributable to fiscal policy, including particularly the government's ability to extract forced savings through high social security contributions. As we will see, this pool of savings was used to political ends, but the capacity to tax and to control monetary policy contributed to macroeconomic stability.

With reference to industrial policy, the government has been caught between two conflicting imperatives: the political interest in fostering and responding to the interests of its Malay political base and the need to placate and promote the Chinese private sector and foreign investors in the name of economic growth. The political institutions inherited from the British play a key role in understanding the resolution of this dilemma. Malaysia's democratic political structure and the existence of a strong party apparatus have created both incentives and opportunities for rent-seeking. Moreover, and in contrast to Indonesia, they have provided the political space for the emergence of a mild form of what might be called "populist nationalism." These political factors have served the interests of a new Malay business class.

Prior to the riots of 1969, the bureaucracy had a strong, even dominant, role in formulating policy and pursued a course under which Chinese capital flourished. Government policy was focused primarily on agriculture. Industrial policy was arms-length and consisted of non-targeted incentives and provision of public goods such as infrastructure. Protection was relatively low (Lim, 1992). But a poor electoral showing by the Alliance in May 1969 and ensuing ethnic riots pushed Malay political leaders to reverse their tacit commitment not to discriminate against Chinese business. A range of government interventions ensued designed to favor both Malay business and employment.

The government faced a profound dilemma in pursuing this strategy: the growing political importance of extending support to the Malay private sector was not matched by equal economic capabilities. The government response consisted of two components, one of which increased both growth and efficiency, the other which was almost certainly a drag on them. First the government aggressively encouraged foreign direct investment in offshore processing industries, a strategy which allowed Malaysia to capture more than its share of expanding Japanese investment in the late-1980s (Jesudason, 1989: ch. 6).

The other response was to foster greater state involvement in the economy, including via state-owned enterprises and other government and even party bodies. On the surface, this dualistic strategy of courting export-oriented foreign investment while also pursuing state-led industrial development bears a superficial similarity to the Korea-Taiwan model. The difference lay precisely in politics.

The problem was not that Malaysia lacked a competent policy bureaucracy; to the contrary, Malaysia inherited a highly competent cadre of British-trained higher civil servants (Leigh, 1992: 118). The problem was that the broader political structure increasingly limited the capacity of the bureaucracy to define a coherent policy course. Instruments such as protection, the provision of finance, licensing, quotas and government contracts were used to redress the economic imbalance between Malays and Chinese, though a number of studies have noted that the Chinese held their own by forming strategic political partnerships with *bumiputra* counterparts (Ling, 1992; Koon, 1992). The government's strategy was not limited to promoting the Malay private sector. A substantial state-owned enterprise sector also emerged; it quickly grew into a sprawling political empire controlled ultimately by the ruling party but with its own independent base of support in its management, workers, and linked Malay businesses.

Much attention has been given both to Mahathir's "Look East" policy of industrial deepening and the political implications of his ascent to the Prime Ministership. Bowie (1994) suggests that both were less a departure from the New Economic Policy of the 1970s than its culmination. The new strategy was based on the same assumption of the political necessity of checking the relative power of Chinese capital while compensating for the weakness of Malay business through greater reliance on the mechanism of the state-owned enterprise. The economic results included mounting inefficiencies and losses in particular projects and erratic growth.

The political effects, however, were a further step forward in the creation of what Yoshihara Kunio (1988: 74) calls a "bureaucratic" Malay business class (see also Ling, 1992). Perhaps one of the most interesting developments – and one which reveals the importance of party politics – was the creation of a corporate vehicle by the UMNO itself and the accumulation of substantial party assets through exploitation of quotas on ownership. Bowie's (1994) analysis shows not only the erosion of lines between government, party and private sector, but also the increasing tendency toward authoritarianism required to maintain the party's political monopoly intact.

Not until the late-1980s and early 1990s – in the face of rapidly deteriorating economic performance – did the government begin to reconsider its policy course and move in the direction of liberalization. The timing was auspicious; despite the domestic shake-out among a number of politically-connected groups, Japanese foreign direct investment boomed. Bowie (1994) suggests that domestic liberalization is likely to be ersatz because of the dependence of the emergent Malay business elite (and, increasingly, their Chinese partners) on government largesse (Ling, 1992). However, it should be remembered that extensive government support for domestic entrepreneurs was also a feature of Korean and Taiwanese development in the early post-war period, and there is increasing evidence that an indigenous export-oriented manufacturing, commercial and financial class is emerging.

Indonesia

Despite numerous other differences – including the level of overall economic development and the structure of output – Indonesia shares with Malaysia certain similarities in the political dynamics of business-government relations. Political elites and corresponding political structures have shifted over time in important ways, but have consistently rested on coalitions that are suspicious of the power of Chinese-Indonesian capital. As in Malaysia, the ruling coalition's central dilemma was the relative economic weakness of the "indigenous" Indonesian private sector alternative (Robinson, 1986; MacIntyre, 1991). As a result – and again as in Malaysia – the effort to substitute for and foster local Indonesian business has been one motivating factor in patterns of government intervention.

The institutional locus of these efforts differed from those in Malaysia in several respects, with important consequences for policy. The authoritarian nature of the regime, the structure of political institutions linking government and business, and the organizational and economic weakness of the Indonesian private sector all served to increase the relative power of state actors. The dominant political party (Golkar) did not play a role in mediating business interests, rather, business representation was channeled through state-corporatist organizations and more importantly through informal, personalistic channels. The effect of this structure was an industrial policy – if it can be called that – that favored state elites directly (managers of state-owned enterprises, the military, and the president's family and, ironically, the very large Chinese firms that the government's policy was nominally designed to contain.

Business–government relations and the institutional structure for managing them evolved through several stages. Initially, the post-independence democratic system created a triangular set of linkages between party politicians, bureaucrats and segments of local capital, both indigenous and Chinese (Robison, 1986). During the late Sukarno period, the increasing concentration of power in the executive shifted the locus of rent-seeking and patronage away from the parties toward senior civil servants and the military, a pattern that was to persist and deepen following the economic and political crisis and change of regime in 1966. During this so-called Guided Economy phase, the strategy of the government also shifted in a decidedly more statist direction. Dutch assets were nationalized and the state-owned enterprise sector grew apace.

Yet the Guided Economy strategy was ultimately not sustainable. By the early 1960s, the reduced influence of the technocrats and efforts by Sukarno to placate the demands of increasingly polarized political groups resulted in massive fiscal deficits, financed largely by money creation. The Planning Council degenerated into a purely political entity, and the increasing entry of the army into the government resulted in ongoing interference in policy-making. Technocrats attempted a stabilization program in 1963, but the bureaucracy, army, communists and Sukarno's policy of military "*confrontasi*" with Malaysia all combined to derail the program. In 1965, the country slipped into hyperinflation.

Stabilization came only after a military coup resulted in Suharto's assumption of power. In 1966, Suharto's ear was captured by a group of western-trained economists who assisted in the design of a stabilization plan that included a constitutional provision that the budget be "balanced"; expenditures could not exceed revenues plus counterpart funds generated by the aid program. The stabilization signaled the willingness of the political leadership to insulate certain portions of the economic policy-making process, particularly for the purpose of enhancing the government's credibility with foreign investors and the international aid community.

This did not mean that the government had abandoned its interest either in structuring politics or intervening in the economy; to the contrary. At the political level, the New Order regime was built on an explicitly corporatist model in which the parties – including even the ruling one – were downplayed in favor of vertical, state-sponsored interest organizations, including for business. In contrast to Korea, these bodies played no discernible industrial-policy purpose. Rather, the complicated network of formal institutions were bypassed in favor of clientelistic linkages that favored the largest firms. Among these were an important group of Chinese capitalists which developed a symbiotic relationship with the top political and military leadership.

The political structure also had a further consequence: patterns of intervention in the economy tended to be even more dominated by state enterprises than in Malaysia. This was particularly true during the heyday of the oil boom years, when full government coffers provided the opportunity for the "engineers" within the economic bureaucracy to temporarily triumph over more liberal technocrats who favored government restraint and a more market-oriented approach. In the 1980s, a new form of "state" enterprise emerged in the form of nominally private firms held by members of Suharto's immediate family.

A consistent theme in studies of the Indonesian political economy is the crucial role that swings in oil prices have had for government policy (MacIntyre, 1993). Booms favor greater state intervention; foreign exchange constraints provide the motive for a more liberal policy stance. Yet MacIntyre (1991) argues that secular trends in the Indonesian political economy may come to play a more important role in supporting the trend toward liberalization as the private sector begins to organize and to press its claims on the government. While business interests vary by sector, his assessment is that their demands are not necessarily limited to rent-seeking; rather, their interests increasingly lie in "rationalizing government regulation of business, limiting gross cronyism and promoting a more consistent and predictable legal framework." Their concerns provide a good summary of the lingering weaknesses of the Indonesian industrial policy system.

The Philippines

The poor economic performance of the Philippines constitutes a major issue in the comparative analysis of the ASEAN (Association of Southeast Asian Nations) economies. In the 1950s, the country held greater economic promise than any in the region, including the NICs. By the 1980s, Philippine economic performance had been surpassed not only by Korea and Taiwan, but by Indonesia, Malaysia and Thailand, and the government was forced to wrestle with the most wrenching adjustment crisis in the region.

A number of critics on the Left have adopted a position akin to that of traditional Philippine nationalism, and argued that the country's problems stem from the adoption of outward-oriented policies at the behest of the World Bank and IMF.[11] For the most part, however, there is a surprising consensus that the problem is virtually the opposite: domestic structures rather than international pressures, and particularly a combination of deeply-entrenched class structure and weak political institutions, have *prevented* the government from adopting more open and export-oriented policies.

As Hutchcroft (1994) argues, the problem is not simply that the Philippine public administration has been poor or that the government lacks policy instruments for supporting business, though both are true; the state has even proven incapable of providing the basic legal and administrative underpinnings necessary for a market economy to function.

These characteristics of Philippine economic policy-making can be traced to the nature of business–government relations. In contrast to all of the other countries discussed here, the Philippine social elite is landed, providing it with an economic base distinct from the state. Business organization, though weak at the association level, has been facilitated by the highly concentrated nature of family groups which have diversified away from agriculture into both manufacturing and services on the basis of extensive state protection. The concentration of big business enhances its clout *vis-à-vis* both politicians and officials.

The effects of these purely sociological factors have been compounded by weak and porous institutional arrangements. The democratic institutions transplanted from the United States during the colonial period provided ample opportunity for rent-seeking. In the late-1960s, the Marcos government attempted to develop a more centralized industrial policy capacity, particularly around the Board of Investments (Doner, 1991a), but it was quickly captured by powerful oligarchic groups diversifying into import-substituting activities.

With the declaration of martial law, the relationship with the traditional oligarchy shifted. No longer beholden to traditional politicians or social elites, and no longer constrained by electoral politics, Marcos could use the instruments of office to build a new base of support among his cronies. Elsewhere, I have described the new policy system as "dualistic" (Haggard, 1989). On the one hand, Marcos drew on a handful of highly competent technocrats to assist in his quest for foreign support. But the real center of decision-making power resided with the Marcoses. The government's relations with business – always personalistic – became even more so as the first family became directly involved in a range of particular projects. Government agencies, such as the Ministry of Human Settlements, became little more than instruments for the dispensation of patronage.

With the transition to democracy, the relationship with the private sector shifted again. The cronies, many of whom had been wiped out by the financial crises of the early- to mid-1980s, saw a sharp reduction of their access to government. Other portions of the private sector, particularly the non-crony private sector opposition to Marcos, gained influence. This segment of business had a "modernizing" wing, exemplified by Jaime Ongpin, who took economic portfolios in the new government and initiated important economic reforms during the early years of the Aquino administration. With the reconvening of Congress, the interests of the dominant family-based import-substituting industries gained renewed channels of access to government, both directly through the legislature and indirectly through their support for political candidates. Though democratization arguably provided some checks on corruption, the absence of strong political alternatives to personalistic politics weakened the hand of the Aquino government in its efforts to reform relations with the private sector. Only with the ascent of a new leadership under Fidel Ramos was there evidence of a new reformism, building on the growing maturation of the Philippine private sector.

CONCLUSION

The institutionalist literature on the East Asian NICs has made an important contribution in showing how features of government and the bureaucracy influence the efficiency and credibility of economic policy. Yet a nagging question remains of why favorable institutions have emerged in some settings and not in others. In this essay, I have outlined an approach that places institutional arrangements in their broader political milieu. In particular, I have focused on the extent to which government elites rely on business for political support.

The analysis reaches a very different conclusion from those emphasizing the benefits of close business–government relations. Rather, the East and Southeast Asian cases suggest that there may be an optimum level of "distance" between the state and the private sector. We know from other regions that governments altogether lacking political ties with the private sector, or actively hostile to it, are prone to pursue policies that are inimical to growth. On the other hand, *too* close an alignment between business and government can lead to capture, rent-seeking, and corruption.

Clearly, the optimum level of political distance is not exogenous to political institutions. But the array of institutional arrangements that matter are not limited to the bureaucracy, business associations or deliberation councils; rather, they encompass such basic features of the political order as the type of regime and the party structure. These macro-political institutions limited business control over the policy agenda in Korea, Taiwan, Hong Kong, Singapore and Thailand, provided opportunities for ethnic rent-seeking in Malaysia, fostered personalistic ties between business and political elites in Indonesia, and provided virtually unchecked opportunities for plunder at various points in Philippine history.

One of the most striking features of the East and Southeast Asian political landscape in the mid-1990s is the increase in the organization and influence of the domestic private sector. This should hardly be surprising given the spectacular records of economic performance in the region, but it raises the question of how a shift in the balance of political power between the public and private sectors will affect government policy in the future.

To get at this question would take me far beyond the scope of this historical review. It is worth noting, however, that the interests of business are closely related to past patterns of government policy. In Korea, Taiwan, Hong Kong and Thailand, the policy regime encouraged the development of domestic private sectors strongly tied to world markets; similar changes are now underfoot in Malaysia, Indonesia and even the Philippines. The political voice of business in these countries may be more supportive of economic reform and further liberalization than it has been in the past.

This finding underlines the quite orthodox lesson that governments willing and able to undertake the combination of economic reform and industrial policy required to move domestic firms into international competition will, in the process, create bases of political as well as economic support. This lesson is not a trivial one, and provides additional political justification for the importance of export-oriented policies.

NOTES

1 My thanks to Tun-jen Cheng, Rick Doner, Chalmers Johnson, David Kang, Linda Lim, Andrew MacIntyre, Chung-in Moon, Henry Rowen, and Ed Winckler for extensive comments on earlier drafts. This paper drawn extensively on Haggard, 1994.

2 Of course, there are a variety of other non-economic explanations as well, including sociological factors (Vogel, 1991), corporate structures and governance (Hamilton, 1991), the changing geostrategic environment (Cumings, 1984), the role of labor (Deyo, 1989), and culture (Berger and Hsiao, 1988), to name only the major contenders.

3 This does not necessarily imply authoritarianism; democracies have to solve coordination problems as well, and have developed a variety of mechanisms for doing so. For a more extended discussion of the "authoritarian hypothesis," see Haggard 1990, chapter 9.

4 This criticism of institutionalism has been made by Haggard and Moon, 1990; Doner, 1991b; Doner and Hawes, 1992; Evans, 1992; Wade, 1992; Kim, forthcoming. I am particularly indebted to Chung-in Moon and Richard Doner for forcing me to rethink this issue.

5 This view has been advanced in recent debates about business–government relations in Japan. See particularly Samuels' conception of "reciprocal consent" (1987: 8–9).

6 Among the mechanisms through which this might occur are reduced financial backing for political campaigns, investment strikes, and capital flight. Note that the ability of private capital to flee is in part a function of the capacity of the state.

7 Comparative analyses of the city-states are few, but include Krause, 1988, Haggard, 1990: ch. 4 and Chiu, *et al.*, 1997.

8 For an early comparative review, see Mackie, 1988.

9 In fact, a number of Chinese groups advanced through forming tactical alliances with the government during this period (Suehiro, 1992: 47).

10 Party politicians in the cabinet had the right to review budgets prepared in the bureaucracy, but the proposals submitted by the Budget Bureau were rarely changed significantly, and the Senate and the House were not permitted to initiate spending bills or increase expenditures. They could set ceilings on the level of taxation, but adjustments under those ceilings remained in the hands of the economic bureaucracy. The bureaucracy's discretion, in turn, was circumscribed by a number of rules that limited the government's capacity to spend. A further check on policy was provided by the Central Bank, which despite its formal subordination to the Ministry of Finance had long enjoyed a history of independence.

11 Bello *et al.*, 1982 and Broad, 1988 are two examples. For three critiques, see Haggard, 1989; Hutchcroft, 1991; Jayasuriya, 1987.

REFERENCES

Amsden, Alice (1989) *Asia's Next Giant: South Korea and Late Industrialization*, New York and Oxford: Oxford University Press.

Bello, Walden, David Kinley and Elaine Elinson (1982) *Development Debacle*, San Francisco: Institute for Food and Development Policy.

Berger, Peter L. and Hsin-Huang Michael Hsiao (1988) *In Search of an East Asian Development Model*, New Brunswick, NJ: Transaction Books.

Bowie, Alisdair (1991) *Crossing the Industrial Divide: State, Society, and the Politics of Economic Transformation in Malaysia*, New York: Columbia University Press.

—— (1994) "The Dynamics of Business–Government Relations in Industrializing Malaysia," in Andrew MacIntyre (ed.), *Business and Government in Industrializing East and Southeast Asia*, Ithaca, NY: Cornell University Press.

Broad, Robin (1988) *Unequal Alliance: The World Bank, the International Monetary Fund, and the Philippines*, Berkeley: University of California Press.

Campos, Jose Edgardo and Hilton Root (1996) *The Key to the Asian Miracle: Making Shared Growth Work*, Washington DC: The Brookings Institution.

Campos, Jose Edgardo and Hilton Root (Forthcoming) "Institutions, Leadership, and the East Asian Miracle," unpublished ms.

Chang, Ha Joon (1994) *The Political Economy of Industrial Policy*, London: Macmillan.

Cheng, Tun-jen (1990) "Political Regimes and Development Strategies: South Korea and Taiwan", in G. Gerreffi and D. Wyman (eds), *Manufacturing Miracles: Patterns of Development in Latin America and East Asia*, Princeton, NJ: Princeton University Press.

—— (1993) "Guarding the Commanding Heights: the State as Banker in Taiwan," in Stephan Haggard, Chung Lee and Sylvia Maxfield (eds) *The Politics of Finance in Developing Countries*, Ithaca, NY: Cornell University Press.

Cheng, Tun-jen, Stephan Haggard and David Kang (1995) "Institutions, Economic Policy and Growth in Taiwan and Korea," paper prepared for the UNCTAD Project on Economic Development in East Asia, December.

Chiu, Stephen Wing-Kai (1992) "The State and the Financing of Industrialization in East Asia: Historical Origins of Comparative Divergences," unpublished PhD dissertation, Princeton University.

Chiu, Stephen Wing-Kai, K.C. Ho and Tai-lok Lui (1997) *City-States in the Global Economy: Industrial Restructuring in Hong Kong and Singapore*, Boulder, CO: Westview Press.

Christensen, Scott (1992) "Capitalism and Democracy in Thailand," paper prepared for the Association of Asian Studies, Washington DC, April 4.

Chu, Yun-han (1989) "State Structure and Economic Adjustment of the East Asian Newly Industrializing Countries," *International Organization* 43 (Autumn).

—— (1994) "The Realignment of State–Business Relations and Regime Transition in Taiwan" in Andrew MacIntyre (ed.) *Business and Government in Industrializing East and Southeast Asia*, Ithaca, NY: Cornell University Press.

Cumings, Bruce (1984) "The Origins and Development of the Northeast Asian Political Economy: Industrial Sectors, Product Cycles, and Political Consequences," *International Organization* 38, 1: 1–40.

Deyo, Fred (1987) *The Political Economy of the New Asian Industrialism*, Ithaca, NY: Cornell University Press.

—— (1989) *Beneath the Miracle: Labor Subordination in the New Asian Industrialism*, Berkeley: University of California Press.

Doner, Richard F. (1991a) *Driving a Bargain: Automobile Industrialization and Japanese Firms in Southeast Asia*, Berkeley: University of California Press.

—— (1991b) "Approaches to the Politics of Economic Growth in Southeast Asia," *Journal of Asian Studies* 50, 4 (November).

Doner, Richard F. and Gary Hawes (1992) "The Political Economy of Growth in East Asia," unpublished ms.

Doner, Richard F. and Daniel Unger (1993) "The Politics of Finance in Thai Economic Development," in Stephan Haggard, Chung Lee and Sylvia Maxfield (eds) *The Politics of Finance in Developing Countries*, Ithaca, NY: Cornell University Press.

Evans, Peter (1992) "The State as Problem and Solution: Predation, Embedded Autonomy and Structural Change," in Stephan Haggard and Robert Kaufman (eds) *The Politics of Economic Adjustment*, Princeton, NJ: Princeton University Press.

—— (1995) *Embedded Autonomy: States and Industrial Transformation*, Princeton, NJ: Princeton University Press.

Fields, Karl James (1990) "Developmental Capitalism and Industrial Organization: Business Groups and the State in Korea and Taiwan," unpublished PhD dissertation, University of California, Berkeley.

Haggard, Stephan (1988) "The Politics of Industrialization in the Republic of Korea and Taiwan," in Helen Hughes (ed.) *Achieving Industrialization in East Asia*, Cambridge: Cambridge University Press.

—— (1989) "The Political Economy of the Philippine Debt Crisis," in Joan Nelson (ed.) *Economic Crisis and Policy Choice*, Princeton, NJ: Princeton University Press.

—— (1990) *Pathways from the Periphery: The Politics of Growth in the Newly Industrializing Countries*, Ithaca, NY: Cornell University Press.

—— (1994) "Business, Politics, and Policy in East and Southeast Asia" in Andrew MacIntyre (ed.) *Business and Government in Industrializing Asia*, Ithaca, NY: Cornell University Press.

Haggard, Stephan and Tun-jen Cheng (1987) "State and Foreign Capital in the East Asian NICs," in Fred Dey (ed.) *The Political Economy of the New Asian Industrialism*, Ithaca: Cornell University Press.

Haggard, Stephan and Chung-in Moon (1990) "Institutions and Economic Policy: Theory and a Korean Case Study," *World Politics*, 42, 2: 210–37.

Haggard, Stephan, Byung-kook Kim and Chung-in Moon (1991) "The Transition to Export-led Growth in Korea, 1954–1966," *The Journal of Asian Studies* (November).

Hamilton, Gary (ed.) (1991) *Business Networks and Economic Development in East and Southeast Asia*, Hong Kong: Centre of Asian Studies, University of Hong Kong.

Hamilton, Gary and Nicole Woolsey Biggart (1988) "Market, Culture, and Authority: A Comparative Analysis of Management and Organization in the Far East," *American Journal of Sociology* 94 Supplement: S52–S94.

Hutchcroft, Paul (1991) "Oligarchs and Cronies in the Philippine State: the Politics of Patrimonial Plunder," *World Politics* 43 (April): 414–50.

—— (1994) "Booty Capitalism: Business–Government Relations in the Philippines," in Andrew MacIntyre (ed.) Business and Government in Industrializing East and Southeast Asia, Ithaca, NY: Cornell University Press.

Juyasuriya, S.K. (1987) "The Politics of Economic Policy in the Philippines during the Marcos Era," in Richard Robinson, Kevin Hewison, and Richard Higgot (eds) *Southeast Asia in the 1980s: The Politics of Economic Change*, Sydney: Allen and Unwin.

Jesudason, James V. (1989) *Ethnicity and the Economy: The State, Chinese Business, and Multinationals in Malaysia*, Singapore: Oxford University Press.

Johnson, Chalmers (1987) "Political Institutions and Economic Performance: The

Business–Government Relationship in Japan, South Korea and Taiwan," in Fred Deyo (ed.) *The Political Economy of the New Asian Industrialism*, Ithaca, NY: Cornell University Press.

Johnson, Chalmers (1990) *MITI and the Japanese Miracle: the Growth of Industrial Policy, 1925–75*, Stanford, CA: Stanford University Press.

Kang, David (1995) "Profits of Doom: Transaction Costs, Rent-Seeking, and Development in South Korea and the Philippines," unpublished PhD dissertation, University of California at Berkeley.

Kim, Eun Mee (Forthcoming) *From Dominance to Symbiosis: State and Chaebol in Korea*.

Koon, Heng Pek (1992) "The Chinese Business Elite of Malaysia," in Ruth McVey (ed.) *Southeast Asian Capitalists*, Ithaca, NY: Cornell Southeast Asia Program.

Krause, Lawrence (1988) "Hong Kong and Singapore: Twins or Kissing Cousins?" *Economic Development and Cultural Change* 36 (supplement): 45–66.

Krueger, Anne O. (1993) *The Political Economy of Policy Reform in Developing Countries*, Cambridge, MA: MIT Press.

Krugman, Paul (1994) "The Myth of Asia's Miracle," *Foreign Affairs* 73, 6 (November–December): 62–78.

Kuo, Cheng-Tian (1995) *Global Competitiveness and Industrial Growth in Taiwan and the Philippines*, Pittsburgh, PA: University of Pittsburgh Press.

Laothamatas, Anek (1992) *Business Associations and the New Political Economy of Thailand*, Boulder, CO: Westview Press.

—— (1994) "From Clientelism to Partnership: Business–Government Relations in Thailand," in Andrew MacIntyre (ed.) *Business and Government in Industrializing East and Southeast Asia*, Ithaca, NY: Cornell University Press.

Leigh, Michael (1992) "Politics, Bureaucracy, and Business in Malaysia: Realigning the Eternal Triangle," in Andrew MacIntyre and Kanishka Jayasuriya (eds) *The Dynamics of Economic Policy Reform in South-East Asia and the South-West Pacific*, Singapore: Oxford University Press.

Levi, Margaret (1988) *Of Rule and Revenue*, Berkeley: University of California Press.

Lim, David (1992) "The Dynamics and Economic Policymaking: A Study of Malaysian Trade Policy and Performance," in Andrew MacIntyre and Kanishka Jayasuriya (eds) *The Dynamics of Economic Policy Reform in South-East Asia and the South-West Pacific*, Singapore: Oxford University Press.

Ling, Sieh Lee Mei (1992) "The Transformation of Malaysian Business Groups," in Ruth McVey (ed.) *Southeast Asian Capitalists*, Ithaca, NY: Cornell Southeast Asia Program.

MacIntyre, Andrew (1991) *Business and Politics in Indonesia*, Sydney: Allen and Unwin.

—— (1993) "The Politics of Finance in Indonesia: Command, Confusion and Competition," in Stephan Haggard, Chung Lee and Sylvia Maxfield (eds) *The Politics of Finance in Developing Countries*, Ithaca, NY: Cornell University Press.

—— (ed.) (1994) *Business and Government in Industrializing East and Southeast Asia*, Ithaca, NY: Cornell University Press.

Mackie, Jamie (1988) "Economic Growth in the ASEAN Region: the Political Underpinnings," in Helen Hughes (ed.) *Achieving Industrialization in East Asia*, Melbourne: Cambridge University Press.

Moon, Chung-in (1988) "The Demise of a Developmentalist State? The Politics of Stabilization and Structural Adjustment," *Journal of Developing Societies* 4: 67–84.

—— (1990) "Beyond Statism: the Political Economy of Growth in South Korea," *International Studies Notes* 15, 1.

—— (1994) "Changing Patterns of Business–State Relations in South Korea, in Andrew MacIntyre (ed.) *Business and Government in Industrializing East and Southeast Asia*, Sydney: Allen and Unwin

Naughton, Barry (1997) *The China Circle*, Washington DC: Brookings Institution.

North, Douglass C. (1990) *Institutions, Institutional Change, and Economic Performance*, New York: Cambridge University Press.

Rhee Jong-Chan (1994) *The State and Industry in South Korea: The Limits of the Authoritarian State*, London: Routledge.

Robison, Richard (1986) *Indonesia: the Rise of Capitalism*, St Leonards, NSW: Allen and Unwin.

Rodan, Gary (1989) *The Political Economy of Singapore's Industrialization*, London: Macmillan.

Rodrik, Dani (1995) "Getting interventions right: how South Korea and Taiwan grew rich," *Economic Policy*, April, 20: 55–107.

Sachs, Jeffrey (1985) "External Debt and Macroeconomic Performance in Latin America and East Asia," *Brookings Papers on Economic Activity* 2: 397–431.

Samuels, Richard J. (1987) *The Business of the Japanese State*, Ithaca, NY: Cornell University Press.

Vogel, Ezra (1991) *The Four Little Dragons: the Spread of Industrialization in East Asia*, Cambridge, MA: Harvard University Press.

Wade, Robert (1990) *Governing the Market: Economic Theory and the Role of Government in East Asian Industrialization*, Princeton, NJ: Princeton University Press.

—— (1992) "East Asia's Economic Success: Conflicting Perspectives, Partial Insights, Shaky Evidence," *World Politics* 44, 2: 270–320.

World Bank (1993) *The East Asian Miracle: Economic Growth and Public Policy*, New York: Oxford University Press.

Yoshihara, Kunio (1988) *The Rise of Ersatz Capitalism in South-East Asia*, Manila: Ateneo de Manila University Press.

5 Singapore's model of development

Is it transferable?

Jon S.T. Quah

On June 3, 1959, when Singapore attained self-government after nearly 140 years of British colonial rule, it had a population of 1.58 million that was growing at the rate of 4 percent annually, an economy based on entrepôt trade and an unemployment rate of 5 percent. Housing was a serious problem, with half of the population living in squatter huts and only 9 percent in public housing. Its per capita GNP in 1960 was only S$1,330 or US$443.[1] In short, Singapore had the classic features of a developing country.

Nearly 37 years later, Singapore is so transformed that it has received the status of an "advanced developing country" from OECD, with a per capita GNP in 1995 of S$34,459 or US$24,614 (an increase of nearly 26 times).[2] Housing is no longer a serious problem, with 86 percent of the population living in public housing. The unemployment rate in 1995 was 2.7 percent with labor in short supply. Corruption has been minimized as a result of the comprehensive anti-corruption strategy of the People's Action Party (PAP) government.

Singapore's rapid economic growth and good record in solving such problems as public housing, traffic congestion, crime, and corruption has attracted worldwide attention. For example, 17 leaders from ten countries attended the conference on "The Relevance of Singapore's Experience for Africa" in Singapore in November 1993.[3] Why did Singapore succeed? Can lessons be learned by other countries from its experience? Is Singapore's model of development (SMD) transferable?

SMD refers to nine major policies introduced by the PAP government since 1959 to ensure a good life for all Singaporeans through political stability and economic growth. The success of the SMD is reflected in the durability and legitimacy of the PAP government; it has been re-elected eight times. This 37-year-long reign is the result of its ability to deliver the goods to the population. These are the nine policies that constitute SMD:

1 Promotion of economic development;
2 Satisfaction of the population's needs;

3 Minimization of corruption;
4 Heavy investment in education;
5 Emphasis on meritocracy;
6 Maintenance of racial harmony;
7 Learning from others;
8 Rejection of the welfare state;
9 Adoption of a comprehensive approach to curbing crime.

PROMOTION OF ECONOMIC DEVELOPMENT

When the PAP leaders assumed power in June 1959, the prospects for Singapore were unfavorable for four reasons. First, the entrepôt trade was declining because of increased trading by Singapore's neighbors, the Federation of Malaya and Indonesia. Second, unemployment was becoming a serious problem, especially given the high population growth rate. Third, there was a serious housing shortage. Finally, Singapore has no resources except for its strategic geographical location and natural harbor – and human potential.

The government focused on providing more jobs and reducing unemployment in the short run and fostering a national identity among its citizens and deepening their political allegiance in the long run. The goal of nation-building was an obvious choice, given the immigrant and multi-racial nature of the population.

The nation-building program had two purposes: to combat the twin threats of communism and communalism. The PAP leaders realized that they had to improve economic conditions to prevent the communists from exploiting the grievances of the unemployed or discontented citizens. They also knew that development was needed to enhance citizens' commitment to Singapore and thereby reduce such competing loyalties as race, language, and religion.[4]

Declining entrepôt trade, high unemployment, and no natural resources implied a strategy of industrialization. In 1960, the PAP government invited a United Nations mission led by a Dutch economist, Albert Winsemius, to devise an industrialization program. The Winsemius team recommended a crash program to reduce unemployment. It also recommended a ten-year program which included creating an investment climate for industrialization, import restrictions to protect infant industries, an export drive, and relying on private enterprise and incentives to attract foreign investment.[5]

In his discussions with Prime Minister Lee Kuan Yew, Winsemius stressed two preconditions for success:

> Number one: get rid of the Communists; how you get rid of them does not interest me as an economist, but get them out of the government, get them out of the unions, get them off the streets. How you do it, is

your job. Number two: let Raffles [the Englishman who had founded Singapore] stand where he stands today; say publicly that you accept the heavy ties with the West because you will very much need them in your economic program.[6]

Lee took Winsemius' advice seriously, neutralized the communist threat and attracted many multinational corporations from the United States, Europe, and Japan.

According to Malcolm Gillis *et al.*,[7] there are three political prerequisites for economic development. First, there must be political stability as "investors will not put their money" into a project when "a change in government could lead to the project's being confiscated or rendered unprofitable by new laws and other restrictions." Second, political independence is a precondition for promoting economic development as most colonial governments made "only limited investments in training local people, in developing electric power resources, or in promoting industry." Third, governmental support is the most important prerequisite as it is needed to formulate and implement sound economic policies. However, such policies can limit certain groups. If they "are in a position to topple the government, that government will be unwilling or unable to take the steps necessary to promote growth." This explains why some governments cannot devalue their currencies, eliminate overstaffing of public enterprises, or remove subsidies on basic consumer goods, even when such policies are needed. In short, a major reason why "many nations are still underdeveloped is that their governments have been unable or unwilling to pursue policies that would achieve development."

An important implication of Gillis *et al.*'s third precondition is the legitimacy and power of the government. The greater its legitimacy and power, the greater its willingness or ability to pursue policies that promote economic growth, for it will not be overthrown by opponents or those hurt by such policies. This is certainly true for Singapore, which has met the three prerequisites. The PAP government's success in promoting economic development is manifested in the impressive improvements in living standards during its 37 years in power.

SATISFACTION OF BASIC NEEDS

At the very least, a government is expected to provide jobs and adequate housing. The newly-elected PAP government was aware in 1959 that it had to solve the problems of unemployment and housing if it wanted to be re-elected in five years' time.

All governments face the problem of housing supply. In Singapore's case, the problem is especially serious because of its small size (646 sq. km. or 249 sq. miles) and high population density (4,536 persons per sq. km. in 1994).[8] Land is scarce and extremely expensive. Private housing is beyond the reach of most of the population and the government chose to play a pivotal role in providing affordable public housing.

The Singapore Improvement Trust was created as a statutory board in 1927 by the colonial government as a town-planning authority. The housing shortage after World War II and the SIT's failure to solve it made public housing an important political issue. The SIT built an unimpressive total of 23,264 housing units during 1928–59 and its failure can be attributed to: the fact that it was not created as a public housing authority; it had inadequate legal powers and financial assistance provided by the colonial government; many of its personnel; high building costs; public criticism; and the squatter problem.[9]

In contrast, the Housing Development Board, created in 1960, built an impressive total of 765,052 housing units during 1960–94 and increased the proportion of the population residing in its apartments from 9 percent to 86 percent.[10] The Board succeeded where the SIT failed because it learned from its predecessor's mistakes. It was created as the *de jure* public housing authority from the outset and was blessed with governmental support, enough money, competent personnel, and necessary legal powers.

The success in housing has reinforced the PAP government's legitimacy. The large proportion of the population living in public housing means that it will always be an important political issue in Singapore and any government that wishes to remain in power must take into account the wishes of these people. If housing problems worsen, those citizens affected might not vote for the ruling party. Indeed, as the population becomes more affluent, expectations regarding housing have been raised. The government has responded by upgrading the older public housing estates.

Finally, this program also has a nation-building role; it brings Singaporeans of different ethnic, linguistic, or religious groups together and thereby provides them with more opportunities for interacting with and understanding one another. In 1964, the government introduced the Home Ownership for the People Scheme to allow eligible citizens to own their homes. The rationale was obvious: it wanted as many of its citizens as possible to become property owners in the belief that their loyalty would be reinforced if they had a stake in the country.[11]

MINIMIZING CORRUPTION

The PAP leaders inherited a civil service that had been afflicted by corruption during the colonial period. The rampant inflation during and after the Japanese occupation (1942–45), coupled with the fixed and low salaries of civil servants, made most of them vulnerable to bribery. In 1950, the Commissioner of Police reported that graft was prevalent in many government departments.

The government's anti-corruption strategy was based on the following logic: since corruption is caused by *both* incentives and opportunities, "attempts to eradicate corruption must be designed to minimize or remove the conditions of both the incentives and opportunities that make individual corrupt behavior irresistible."[12]

As it could not afford in 1959 to raise salaries, the PAP began by strengthening existing legislation to reduce opportunities for corruption and to increase penalties. In 1960, the more comprehensive Prevention of Corruption Act was enacted, which also gave the government additional powers of enforcement. For example, the Corrupt Practices Investigation Bureau, established in 1952, was given additional powers of arrest, search of arrested persons, and examination of bank accounts and other assets of civil servants under investigation, and the PAP government later strengthened the POCA with amendments and new legislation to deal with unanticipated problems.

The second prong of its anti-corruption strategy was reducing incentives by improving salaries and working conditions in the 1980s, long after it had achieved good economic growth. In 1972, all civil servants were given a 13-month non-pensionable allowance comparable to the bonus in the private sector. Its aim was not to curb corruption but to prevent a drain to the private sector.

On March 22, 1985,[13] Prime Minister Lee Kuan Yew provided an eloquent justification for why the salaries of his cabinet ministers had to be raised. According to him, the choice was a simple one: "Pay political leaders the top salaries that they deserve and get honest, clear government or underpay them and risk the Third World disease of corruption." Lee concluded that the best way of tackling corruption was "moving with the market," which is "an honest, open, defensible and workable system" instead of hypocrisy, which results in duplicity and corruption.

In order to minimize salary differences with the private sector, the pay of civil servants has been repeatedly increased. In October 1994, a White Paper on "Competitive Salaries for Competent and Honest Government" was presented to Parliament to justify the pegging of the salaries of ministers and senior civil servants to the average salaries of the top four earners in six private sector professions: accounting, banking, engineering, law, local manufacturing companies and multinational corporations. It recommended formal salary benchmarks for ministers and senior bureaucrats, additional salary grades for political appointments and annual salary reviews for the civil service. The long-term formula suggested in the White Paper will not only eliminate the need to justify the salaries of ministers and senior bureaucrats "from scratch with each salary revision," but also ensure the building of "an efficient public service and a competent and honest political leadership", which have been vital for Singapore's prosperity and success.

Senior civil servants in Singapore now earn perhaps the highest salaries in the world. For example, the gross *monthly* salary for the top administrative position (Staff Grade V) is S$48,400 (or US$34,571); in contrast the top monthly salary of GS-18 (the highest salary scale for the United States Federal Service) is US$7,224 and the monthly salary of the top civil servant in the New South Wales Public Service is A$18,278.[14]

HEAVY INVESTMENT IN EDUCATION

An important feature of Confucian thinking is the "belief in the perfectibility and educability of human beings."[15] An emphasis on education is found also in Japan, South Korea, and Taiwan. Agreeing with Alfred Marshall's view of education as "a national investment" and his astute observation that "the most valuable of all capital is that invested in human beings,"[16] the governments in these countries "have rushed to invest heavily in human resources. Parents, teachers, and students treat education almost like a national religion, and government and society devote considerable resources to a frantic expansion of schools and classes."[17]

Singapore's expenditure on education has increased by 54 times from S$63 million in 1959 to S$3,400 million in 1994. Enrollment in educational institutions at the primary, secondary, and tertiary levels increased from 353,000 students in 1960 to 539,000 students in 1994.[18] In 1979, the Skills Development Fund was established to provide incentive grants to companies for training their employees. The Fund is also concerned with the retraining of redundant workers. It is financed by the collections from the skills development levy imposed on employers with workers earning S$750 or less a month.

Singapore's investment in education and training has resulted in a workforce rated the best among the ten newly industrialized economies (NIEs) by the International Institute for Management Development and the World Economic Forum in their *World Competitiveness Report* in 1991. The Singaporean workforce was rated the best in terms of the following eight criteria: compulsory education; in-company training; economic literacy; professional women in the workforce; worker motivation; labor flexibility; industrial relations; and organized labor. Since 1980, the Business Environment Risk Intelligence Report has also rated Singapore's workforce as the best in the world.

Finally, the heavy investment in education has also contributed indirectly to political stability for it has provided those from humble backgrounds with scholarships or bursaries, regardless of sex, race, or religion, and enabled them to improve themselves through education. Education thus serves as an important channel for upward social mobility.[19]

MERITOCRACY

The PAP government's emphasis on meritocracy began early. In 1959, it adopted a policy of selective retention of senior civil servants. This meant that expatriate civil servants who were competent and due for retirement were urged to stay on while their incompetent colleagues were retired prematurely. This policy, and a reduction in the variable allowance, resulted in a high turnover rate among senior civil servants, especially those on expatriate contracts.

This focus on efficiency as the sole criterion for retraining or retiring a senior civil servant was reinforced by de-emphasizing seniority in promotions. In 1961, Prime Minister Lee Kuan Yew expressed his disdain for seniority as follows: "I am in favor of efficient service. The brighter chap goes up and I don't care how many years he has been in or he hasn't been in. If he's the best man for the job, put him there."[20] This policy remains in force today and is responsible for the relative youthfulness of many permanent secretaries.

Lee's concern for meritocracy and the need to attract the "best and the brightest" to join the Singapore Civil Service (SCS) can be attributed to his experience as the legal adviser for several trade unions in Singapore in the 1950s before entering politics. He had no difficulty winning his legal cases against the incompetent and poorly paid lawyers of the colonial government. According to him, "We extracted every ounce of political and material advantage out of the disputes with the colonial government and got them maximum benefits . . . We helped them [unions] and exposed the *stupidities* and *inadequacies* of the colonial administration."[21] Hence, it was not surprising that Lee supported the role of the Public Service Commission in controlling the quality of personnel entering the SCS by "keeping the rascals out" and attracting "the best and the brightest" candidates. The Commission was formed in 1951, but only in 1956 was a board created to interview candidates for scholarships.[22]

In 1990, two additional agencies were created to deal with the personnel management of teachers and police and civil defense officers: the Education Service Commission and the Police and Civil Defense Services Commission. The PSC offers attractive undergraduate scholarships to students with excellent results in the Cambridge General Certificate of Education advanced level examination to study at the two local universities or prestigious universities abroad. After graduation, these "scholars" are bonded to serve the SCS for a mixed number of years, depending on the duration of their scholarships. The most prestigious is the President's Scholarship; 134 President's Scholars were selected from 1966 to 1994.[23] In recent years, the PSC has enhanced the competitiveness and prestige of its scholarships to meet the challenge posed by private companies that offer equally attractive scholarships to bright students.

Ezra Vogel[24] has contended that "what is unusual in Singapore is not the prominence of meritocratic administrators, but the fact that the meritocracy extends upward to include virtually all political leaders." According to him, the first generation of political leaders in Singapore "believed in meritocracy not only for bureaucrats but also for politicians;" they were regarded as "among the brightest of their generation," having distinguished themselves academically and "won competitive scholarships to study in England." Vogel coins the term "macho-meritocracy" to describe the broader notion of the meaning of meritocracy in the Singapore context thus:

For the first generation of Singapore leaders, the foundation of good government was not a government of separation of powers but a strong central meritocratic one. Since Singapore has a relatively small population, a key issue has been how to ensure that the best talent is channeled into the positions most important to Singapore society … In Singapore, meritocracy is more than a procedure for selecting talent; it creates a special awe for the top leaders and provides a basis for discrediting less meritocratic opposition almost regardless of the content of its arguments. This special awe enabled the first generation of meritocratic, impeccably honest heroes to establish what might be called a "macho-meritocracy."

The emphasis on meritocracy in the selection of electoral candidates by the PAP was manifested in 1984, when it revealed in detail its eight-stage process of selecting new candidates for the forthcoming election in a series of five newspaper articles.[25] By publicizing its selection process, the PAP leaders also demonstrated to the electorate that the 26 new candidates had been selected on the basis of competence, academic qualifications, and good track records. The attrition rate for potential candidates was high as only 21 percent of those invited to participate in the selection process were actually selected.[26]

MAINTENANCE OF RACIAL HARMONY

Singapore is a multiracial, multilingual and multi-religious society. Its population of 2.93 million people in June 1994 consisted of Chinese (77.5 percent), Malays (14.2 percent), Indians (7.1 percent), and persons of other ethnic groups (1.2 percent). There are four official languages (English, Malay, Mandarin and Tamil), plus six main Chinese dialects (Hokkien, Teochew, Cantonese, Hakka, Hainanese and Foochow) and five Indian languages (Malayalam, Punjabi, Telegu, Hindi and Bengali).

There is also great diversity in religion among the population. According to the 1990 Census, 31.1 percent of the population were Buddhist, followed by 22.4 percent Taoist, 15.4 percent Muslim, 14.3 percent no religion, 12.5 percent Christian, 3.7 percent Hindu, and 0.6 percent belonging to other religions. There is a close relationship between ethnicity and religion as Buddhism (39.3 percent) and Taoism (28.4 percent) are the major religions for the Chinese, while Islam (99.6 percent) and Hinduism (52.6 percent) are, respectively, the major religions of the Malays and Indians.

In view of this, any incumbent government needs to promote racial harmony. The second obligation of government in a plural society is to ensure that both public and private organizations are fair in their treatment of their clientele, regardless of their ethnicity, language, or religion. Hence, there exists a Presidential Council for Minority Rights, which examines bills presented in Parliament to ensure that minority rights are not endangered.

Racial/religious riots pose the most serious threat to Singapore's survival. Political instability from such riots would tear apart the social fabric and reduce foreign investment. In a plural society, riots are more likely to erupt when there is disharmony and lack of understanding and tolerance among the various groups. To date, Singapore has experienced four such riots: the Maria Hertogh racial/religious riots of December 1950; the July and September 1964 racial riots; and the racial riots resulting from the spillover effects of the May 13, 1969 racial riots in Malaysia.

The PAP leaders took measures to prevent communalism from undermining racial harmony not only by promoting economic development and providing public housing; they introduced national (or military) service, and conducted periodic national campaigns. The government also sought to "immunize" the heterogeneous population from the threat of racial and/or religious riots by restricting individuals, groups, organizations and the mass media, especially the Press, from sensationalizing and exploiting racial, linguistic, and religious issues. The rationale for these restraints on the Press can be traced to the irresponsible role played by both the English and Malay newspapers in sensationalizing the Maria Hertogh case, which resulted in three days of rioting (December 11–13, 1950) and caused 18 deaths and 173 injured persons.[27]

It is equally important to ensure religious harmony as conflicts between religious groups can be easily transformed into racial riots. The government White Paper on "Maintenance of Religious Harmony" to Parliament in December 1989 urged that the "followers of the different religions ... exercise moderation and tolerance, and do nothing to cause religious enmity or hatred" and by separating religion from politics in order "to establish working rules by which many faiths can accept fundamental differences between them, and coexist peacefully in Singapore." The Maintenance of Religious Harmony Act of 1990 gave the Minister of Home Affairs the power to issue a Prohibition Order against those who threaten racial harmony by preventing them from engaging in such activities as addressing any congregation; printing, publishing, distributing or contributing to any publication produced by that religious group, and holding office in any editorial board or committee of any publication produced by that group.

LEARNING FROM OTHERS

Instead of "reinventing the wheel," the PAP leaders and senior civil servants will examine what has been done elsewhere to identify relevant solutions for policy problems in Singapore. The policies selected will usually be modified to suit the local context. For example, the government has examined the Japanese and French civil services and the Shell system of performance appraisal as part of its efforts to improve personnel management in the SCS.

Obviously, this reliance on "policy diffusion" – that is, the "emulation and borrowing of policy ideas and solutions from other nations"[28] – is not confined to the bureaucracy; the impetus comes from the government itself. Stella Quah has identified three steps in this process which she has described as "pragmatic acculturation":

> (1) after identifying the problem to be solved or the goal to be attained, a team of experts and officials go on a fact-finding tour of relevant technical centers and organizations around the world; (2) internationally recognized experts are invited to Singapore to give their professional opinions; (3) the final plan comes from what has been learned, tailored to the specific needs of Singapore. If ideas and procedures used elsewhere are deemed unsuitable to Singapore, they are not adopted.[29]

Initially after independence, Singapore looked towards such small countries as Israel and Switzerland as role models for defense and other areas. Later, other countries like West Germany (for technical education), the Netherlands (Schiphol airport was the model for Changi airport) and Japan (for quality control circles and crime prevention) were added to the list. In short, policy diffusion is useful as long as there is no blind acceptance and wholesale transplantation of foreign innovations without modification to suit the local environment.

REJECTION OF THE WELFARE STATE

An important advantage of being a young nation is not repeating the mistakes made by others. The best example of this is the government's decision to reject the welfare state in view of the many problems afflicting the developed countries. In June 1976, Goh Keng Swee, then the Deputy Prime Minister and Minister of Defense, identified the negative consequences of welfare state policies thus:

> But nothing is for free in this world and the end result of indiscriminate welfare state policies is bankruptcy. . . . In several West European countries, unemployment benefits have been so generous that some workers are better off unemployed! The money to pay for welfare state expenditure must come either from taxes or from the printing press. Increasing taxes, which mainly affects the rich, reduces the amount of money available for investment, thereby slowing down economic growth. Printing paper money to avoid unpleasant tax increases merely results in more inflation.[30]

The government considered social welfare as a consumption good and feared that "government provision of social welfare" might lead to "an unhealthy dependence on the state and sap individual initiative and enterprise, thereby also undermining growth." Indeed, such "guaranteed social welfare" was expensive and inappropriate for developing countries, as can be seen from the experiences of China, Jamaica, and Sri Lanka, which have abandoned such "welfarist" policies.[31]

Accordingly, the government "has never committed significant government funds to social security for the unemployed, disabled, aged, or indigent."[32] The criteria for public assistance are very strict; "nearly 90 percent of its recipients are single, elderly persons, most of the immigrants who have spent a lifetime at hard labor, never married, and have no family ties, with the remainder being the mentally or physically handicapped, widows and orphans, and abandoned wives and children." Furthermore, the public assistance provided is meager, and there is no system of unemployment compensation. In short, in the words of former Senior Minister S. Rajaratnam, the PAP government's policy is "to reduce welfare to the minimum" and to restrict it to "only those who are handicapped or old."[33]

Instead of providing social welfare to Singaporeans, it relies on the Central Provident Fund (CPF), originally introduced by the colonial government in 1955, to provide social security for the working population. The CPF was attractive for two reasons: the government could not afford welfare as there were other more urgent priorities; and the concept of "pay-as-you-earn" was ideologically appealing. In other words, the continuation of the CPF enabled the government to provide limited social security for the population without becoming a welfare state.[34]

Unlike other countries "which finance their social security systems on a pay-as-you-go basis, Singapore finances its social security system through a publicly managed, mandatory program of private saving" viz., the CPF. It began as a pension fund managed by the government, with compulsory contributions paid by both employers and employees. However, "the CPF has evolved into a much more complicated system than its original, simple saving-withdrawal plan."[35] The first and perhaps most important change was in 1968, when the Approved Housing Scheme allowed members to withdraw CPF savings to purchase HDB apartments. In fact, it was this scheme that increased the public demand for public housing and contributed significantly to the success of the Home Ownership for the People Scheme.[36]

The success of the Approved Housing Scheme in promoting home ownership made the PAP government realize the importance of the CPF as a source of finance and led to the introduction of other schemes. In 1978, Singapore citizens were enabled to buy shares in the Singapore Bus Services through the Share Scheme. In 1986, two other investment schemes were introduced: the Approved Investment Scheme and the Approved

Nonresidential Properties Scheme, which enabled CPF members to invest in the stock exchange and property market respectively.

In 1987, the government re-examined the *raison d'être* of the CPF in view of the aging population and the low birth rate. In 1987, it introduced the Minimum Sum Scheme to provide members with a regular monthly income after retirement. In 1989, the Dependents' Protection Insurance Scheme was begun to provide protection and coverage for the CPF members and their dependents so that the latter can maintain a decent standard of living in the case of the death or disability of the CPF member. Finally, the Medishield Scheme was created in 1990 to supplement the Medisave Scheme introduced in 1984, to provide protection from chronic illness, while Medisave finances hospitalization and other medical expenses.

In her analysis of the changing role of the CPF from 1955–90, Irene Ng concluded that:

> the changing role of [the] CPF does not ... represent a change in the government's philosophy or direction. It is still a national nest-egg to rely on when they retire. *The fundamental belief held by the government is that Singapore is not and should not fall into the category of welfare states. It is well aware of some of the abuses and wastage that are linked to the welfare state as well as the erosion of individual responsibility in such systems.* The concept of pooling risks and dependence on the state must not take root in Singapore.[37]

Rejection of the welfare state, and reliance on the CPF to provide limited social security and a source of development funds, has enabled Singapore to avoid the excesses and problems afflicting the welfare states as well as attract foreign investment and talent because of the low taxes levied on multinational corporations and professionals.

A COMPREHENSIVE APPROACH TO CURBING CRIME

During the colonial period, the Singapore Police Force (SPF) had three major problems: the Chinese secret societies, police corruption, and rioting and internal security.[38] The criminal activities and rivalries of the Chinese secret societies led to crime and frequent outbreaks of violence. Police corruption undermined the SPF's legitimacy and public image and prevented it from performing its functions effectively. The racial riots of the 1950s and 1960s and the underground activities of the Communist Party of Malaya were serious threats to internal security.

The SPF's efficiency and effectiveness today can be attributed to the fact that it is no longer afflicted by these problems. Indeed, Chinese secret societies are no longer a problem now as a result of the SPF's efforts to curb their activities with the help of the Criminal Law (Temporary Provisions) Act (CLTPA) of 1958, which enabled the SPF to detain criminals without trial. In July 1984, the then Minister for Home Affairs, Chua Sian Chin, justified in Parliament the extension of the CLTPA for another five years because of its effectiveness in curbing secret society and drug trafficking activities in Singapore. He said:

> Without invoking the powers of this Act [CLTPA] it would not have been possible for us to suppress secret society and drug trafficking activities in Singapore. It is not possible to successfully prosecute secret society elements in open court because potential witnesses are intimidated and therefore are unwilling to testify for fear of reprisal. . . . The effectiveness of the Act in curbing secret societies is shown by the significant decrease in the number of secret society incidents. . . . From a peak of 416 such incidents in 1959, the number of incidents dropped to 12 in 1983.[39]

Police corruption was greatly reduced by the methods described above which upgraded the civil service. The SPF's public image has improved and popular misconceptions of how the SPF operates have been corrected. The problem of rioting and internal security is not serious today because economic development and racial harmony have neutralized both the communist and communal threats.

Perhaps, the best manifestation of the tough law enforcement measures is the relatively low crime rate. Writing in 1984, a British expert on terrorist movements, Richard Clutterbuck, observed the linkage between tough laws and the low crime rate in Singapore:

> The law [in Singapore], by West European standards, is very tough in matters great and small. The fine for dropping litter is S$500 (US$250). The death penalty is imposed for murder, kidnapping, and for unlawful possession of weapons, and is mandatory for trafficking in hard drugs. Corporal punishment [caning] is administered for violent crime and is greatly feared. The result is that the rate of robberies and thefts in Singapore is 10 per day compared with 1,800 per day in New York City – a ratio of 1 to 60 in proportion to the population. Singapore society is largely rid of the scourge of the secret societies.[40]

Indeed, an analysis of the crime rate per 100,000 population in Singapore[41] shows that during 1960–90 there was a total of 33,878 seizable offenses and the average annual number of seizable offenses during this period was 1,093. Crime rates for murder, robbery, housebreaking, rape and motor car theft from 1988–90 are lower than those of Tokyo, Hong Kong, and London. Crime rates in Singapore are very much lower than those in Arkansas, Kansas, Mississippi, and Oregon, four states in the United States with approximately the same population size as Singapore.

However, even though crime is not a serious problem in Singapore, it has been increasing in recent years. For example, the annual average crime rate per decade increased from 566 seizable offenses per 100,000 population during 1960–70, to 924 seizable offenses per 100,000 population during 1971–80, to 1,841 seizable offenses per 100,000 population in 1981–90. This is double that for the 1970s and more than three times that for the 1960s.[42]

The most important factor in curbing crime is the SPF's comprehensive approach. Instead of relying only on tough law enforcement measures to deter criminal behavior, the SPF also embarked on community policing in 1981. Its better public image persuaded people to participate in crime prevention activities. Indeed, the underlying assumption for introducing community policing was that it would contribute to the SPF's fight against crime as "the improved police–public relationship should result in a higher level of crime prevention awareness and greater understanding towards and co-operation with the police on the part of the public."[43] To test this assumption, the SPF introduced the Neighborhood Police Post (NPP) System, a modified version of the Japanese *koban* (Police post), in 1983 with the establishment of eight posts. Thus, the SPF learned from Japan and replicated an effective Japanese method of community policing.

An NPP is located in an easily accessible place and is manned by a team of 20 police officers who provide round-the-clock service in three shifts. It is a mini-police station located in the heart of a neighborhood of about 30,000 residents. In addition to providing the conventional services available at any police station, the NPP is also an information center for residents as well as a crime prevention center where exhibitions and talks on crime prevention are held. The NPP officers are required to patrol the constituency and to visit residents' homes. Two officers are assigned to visit 250 households twice a year to enable the officers to develop rapport with the residents and to help the residents to get to know the officers personally and the services provided by them. In short, the NPP brings the SPF closer to the homes of the residents and gives them more opportunities for interacting and cooperating with the public.

The second important element of the SPF's approach to crime prevention focuses on victims and is designed "to educate the public on prevention knowledge and create a population that shares a common concern for security and reprehension of criminal activities."[44]

The positive response of the public to the SPF's crime prevention programs and its success has attracted the attention of the police in Australia, Hong Kong, New Zealand, and even Japan, which was responsible for the original *koban* system.

IS SMD TRANSFERABLE?

Writing in 1887, Woodrow Wilson was perhaps the first scholar in public administration to suggest the usefulness of learning from other countries' experiences and adapting such knowledge for use in the United States. According to him:

it is necessary ... not to be frightened of the idea of looking into foreign systems of administration for instruction and suggestions. ... But why should we not use such parts of foreign contrivances as we want, if they be in anyway serviceable? We are in no danger of using them in a foreign way. We borrowed rice, but we do not eat it with chopsticks. ... We have only to filter it [the science of administration] through our constitutions, only to put it over a slow fire of criticism and distill away its foreign gases. ... If I see a murderous fellow sharpening a knife cleverly, I can borrow his way of sharpening the knife, without borrowing his probable intention to commit murder with it ... we are on perfectly safe ground, and can learn without error what foreign systems have to teach us. ... We can thus scrutinize the anatomy of foreign governments without fear of getting any of the diseases into our veins; dissect alien systems without apprehension of blood-poisoning.[45]

As noted in the introductory section of this chapter, Singapore's economic progress since 1959 and its transformation from a resource-poor developing country into an Asian "dragon" or "tiger" or, to use the World Bank's terminology, a High-performing Asian Economy,[46] have attracted worldwide attention and many political leaders and senior civil servants have visited Singapore to identify the reasons for its success and to consider lessons for their own countries. For example, after his first visit in 1978, Deng Xiaoping indicated that "he wanted to use the Lion City as a model." Consequently, 400 delegations comprising of mayors, governors, and party secretaries from China visited Singapore in 1978 on study missions. In 1992, Deng repeated his call to learn from Singapore in ensuring social order through the exercise of strict management.[47] Indeed, the number of foreign leaders visiting Singapore has increased in recent years from 48 in 1990 to 231 in 1993. In 1995, Singapore was ranked as the second most competitive country in the world, after the United States[48] and, according to *The World Competitiveness Report 1995*, "its record offers a blueprint for other developing countries on how to succeed."[49]

To answer the question of "transferability," we need to define that term more explicitly. Richard Rose has identified five degrees of transferability when drawing lessons from other countries:

1 *Copying*: adoption more or less intact of a program already in effect in another jurisdiction.
2 *Emulation*: adoption, with adjustment for different circumstances, of a program already in effect in another jurisdiction.
3 *Hybridization*: combination of elements of programs from two different places.
4 *Synthesis*: combination of familiar elements from programs in effect in three or more different places.
5 *Inspiration*: programs elsewhere used as intellectual stimulus for developing a novel program without an analog elsewhere.[50]

Using these categories, I argue that it would be difficult to *copy* SMD *in toto* because of Singapore's unique circumstances. In discussing the applicability of Singapore's policy models for reform in urban China, Robert M. Pease has correctly pointed out that:

> The successful policy of country A cannot simply be replanted in the soil of struggling target country B. Instead careful attention must be directed to the wider policy contexts involved as well as to the feasibility of policy transfer. . . . Policies, like garden plants, cannot simply be plucked from one environment to be replanted in another. There are questions of soil type, rainfall, and sunlight just as there are questions of government capacity, efficiency and integrity.[51]

Similarly, hybridization and synthesis are not viable options as the rationale and prerequisites for success of a particular policy vary and might not be combined effectively. With regard to inspiration, SMD can inspire countries afflicted with problems in housing, high crime rates, high taxes to pay for welfare expenditures, corruption, racial conflict, limited opportunities for education, and reliance on patronage in the civil service. However, programs in target countries to solve these problems have not met with much success because of the absence of honest and competent political leaders and senior civil servants, adequate finances, and relevant legislation.

In his analysis of the evolution of policy in the East Asian NICs (Hong Kong, Singapore, South Korea, and Taiwan), Gustav Ranis[52] observed that "their overall success was due primarily to their ability to exploit something they did have: their human resources." He further argued that "the successful policy experience of the East Asian NICs is, in fact, transferable to other open, dualistic, developing economies *if, and only if, economic pragmatism is transferred as well*." Thus, the relevance of Taiwan's experience to other countries would be "dictated by the transferability of its political economy decisions, especially the ability to gradually depoliticize the economic system, so that families are increasingly rewarded by their economic performance rather than by entitlement through political patronage."

In my study of lessons from Japan, Singapore, South Korea, and Taiwan for promoting human resource development in the Commonwealth countries (i.e., those colonized by the British) in Asia and Africa, I concluded that "the message for Commonwealth countries" was clear: "their governments must improve and be committed to economic development and to minimizing corruption; they must also invest in educating and training their populations; and they must introduce comprehensive reforms in personnel management." However, there is no guarantee that governments are prepared to pay to upgrade their human resources; they could also take the easier option of preserving the status quo.[53]

It is difficult to transplant SMD to other countries because of the great costs involved. It is costly to pay civil servants high salaries, invest heavily in education, and build public housing for 86 percent of the population. It is difficult to minimize corruption, introduce meritocracy, reject welfare policies, and adopt tough and comprehensive measures to curb crime without a government that enjoys widespread political support.

Thus, the most suitable option is that of emulation. According to Jean-Louis Margolin,[54] Germany, Japan, and Switzerland were the most important foreign influences on Singapore's development in the 1970s and beyond. The PAP leaders were most impressed with the trade union system and the vocational/technical education in Germany. In Japan, the principal model from the late 1970s until the late 1980s, what was most admired was labor's work ethic and discipline, "the aptitude of both management and unions to work together for the common good of the company; the extensive system of subcontracting;" the low turnover in big companies, quality control circles, and the effectiveness of community policing in curbing crime.

The establishment of the NPP System is a good example of an adaptation to suit the needs of Singapore. The need to avoid *in toto* adoption was emphasized by David H. Bayley, when he visited Singapore to study the NPP System:

> one should not expect the *koban* system to function in Singapore exactly as it has in Japan. Singaporeans are not Japanese and their problems of public safety and crime prevention are not identical. Singapore must learn from Japan. Singapore must adapt Japan's institutions to its own needs.[55]

Switzerland had served as a model because of its multi-ethnic and multilingual society, its small size, its reliance on a citizens' army, and its ability to remain friendly with its neighbors. The PAP leaders' "Vision for 1999", announced in 1984, focused on the target of achieving the Swiss standard of living over that 15-year period. The need to emulate the Swiss because of their wealth was constantly stressed by PAP leaders during the last 12 years.

In short, the answer to the question whether SMD is transferable to other target countries is "no" in view of the differences between Singapore and these countries. However, other countries can emulate and adapt some features of SMD to suit their needs, provided that their political leaders, civil servants, and the population are prepared to make the required changes. If nothing else, SMD can inspire others by demonstrating the paramount importance of honest and competent political leaders and senior civil servants who share the goal of initiating policies that benefit their citizens and the country as a whole.

NOTES

1 See Singapore Department of Statistics, 1983: 7 and 12; Ow, 1971: 1 and 40; and Singapore, Ministry of Trade and Industry, 1986: ix.
2 See Singapore Ministry of Information and the Arts, 1995: 31, 103, and 163; and Ministry of Trade and Industry, 1996: viii.
3 See Singapore International Foundation, 1994: vii–viii.
4 Quah, 1985: 199.
5 Chia, 1986: 205.
6 Quoted in Drysdale, 1984: 327.
7 Gillis *et al.*, 1987: 23–6.
8 Singapore Ministry of Information and the Arts, 1995: 22 and 31.
9 Quah, 1985: 233–38.
10 See Quah, 1987: 87, Table 3; Singapore Ministry of Communications and Information, 1991: 294, Appendix 55; and Singapore Ministry of Information and the Arts, 1995: 163 and 315, Appendix 35.
11 Quah, 1990: 49–50.
12 Quah, 1989: 842.
13 See "PM: Pay well or we pay for it . . .," *Straits Times* (March 23, 1985), pp. 1 and 14–16.
14 Wright and Dwyer, 1990: 6; and information provided by Dr Michael Wood, former Public Service Commissioner for Western Australia.
15 Tai, 1989: 24.
16 Harbison and Myers, 1964: 4.
17 Tai, 1989: 25.
18 Singapore Department of Statistics, 1983: 231, 248; 1994: 283, 306.
19 See S. Quah, 1991: 38–73.
20 Malay Mail (July 9, 1961), quoted in Seah, 1971: 88.
21 Lee, 1961: 18–19, quoted in Drysdale, 1984: 44, emphasis added.
22 Seah, 1971: 147–8.
23 Singapore PSC, 1967–95.
24 Vogel, 1989: 1052–3.
25 See *Sunday Times* (June 3, 10, 17, 24, and July 1, 1984).
26 Lee and Khor, 1984: 20.
27 Maideen, 1989: 105–23, 132–7, 205–15, 223–45, and 269.
28 Leichter, 1979: 42.
29 Quah, 1995: 55. She has defined "pragmatic acculturation" as "the cultural system of behavior and attitudes that allows culture-borrowing or the adoption of aspects of non-native cultures for the purpose of satisfying specific needs." (p. 53).
30 Goh, 1977: 166.
31 Lim, 1989.
32 Ibid.: 186–7.
33 Ibid.: 187.
34 Ng, 1991: 12 and 14.
35 Tay, 1992: 264.
36 Quah, 1975: 124.
37 Ng, 1991: 70, emphasis added.
38 See: Mak, 1981; Phang, 1990: 183–225; and Quah, 1979: 7–43.
39 Quoted in Phang, 1990: 223.
40 Clutterbuck, 1984: 343–4.
41 See Quah, 1992: 168–70 and Table 3; and Yip and Ong, 1992: 87.
42 Quah, 1992: 168 and 170.
43 Quah and Quah, 1987: 4.
44 Seng, 1984: 14.

45 Woodrow Wilson, 1887: 15–16.
46 World Bank, 1993: 1.
47 Kristof, 1992: 4; quoted in Pease, 1996: 1.
48 Zyla, 1995: 76.
49 Quoted in Latif, 1996: 34.
50 Rose, 1991: 19–21.
51 Pease, 1996: 27–8 and 148.
52 Ranis, 1995: 2 and 26, emphasis added.
53 Quah, 1993: 37.
54 Margolin, 1993: 91–3.
55 Bayley, 1983: 44.

REFERENCES

Bayley, David H. (1983) "The Significance of Singapore's Experiment with Neighbourhood Police Posts," *Police Life Annual 83*, Singapore: Singapore Police Force.

Chia, Siow-Yue (1986) "The Economic Development of Singapore: A Selective Review of the Literature," in Basant K. Kapur (ed.) *Singapore Studies: Critical Surveys of the Humanities and Social Sciences,* Singapore: Singapore University Press.

Clutterbuck, Richard (1984) *Conflict and Violence in Singapore and Malaysia 1945–1983*, Singapore: Graham Brash.

Drysdale, John (1984) *Singapore: Struggle for Success*, Singapore: Times Books International.

Gillis, Malcolm *et al.* (1987) *Economics of Development*, 2nd edn, New York: W.W. Norton.

Goh, Keng Swee (1977) *The Practice of Economic Growth*, Singapore: Federal Publications.

Harbison, Frederick and Charles A. Myers (1964) *Education, Manpower and Economic Growth: Strategies of Human Resource Development*, New York: McGraw-Hill.

Kristof, Nicholas D. (1992) "China sees Singapore as a Model for Progress," *New York Times*, Week in Review, August 9, p. 4.

Latif, Asad (1996) "The Singapore Inc. Model: Nothing Succeeds Like Success," *Straits Times* (Singapore), March 16, p. 34.

Lee, Kuan Yew (1961) *The Battle for Merger*, Singapore: Government Printing Office.

Lee, Philip and Christine Khor (1984) "Few Stumble on the Home Stretch," *Sunday Times* (Singapore), July 1, p. 20.

Leichter, Howard M. (1979) *A Comparative Approach to Policy Analysis: Health Care in Four Nations*, Cambridge: Cambridge University Press.

Lim, Chong-Yah and Chwee-Huay Ow (1971) "The Economic Development of Singapore in the Sixties and Beyond," in Poh-Seng You and Chong-Yah Lim (eds) *The Singapore Economy,* Singapore: Eastern Universities Press.

Lim, Linda Y.C. (1989) "Social Welfare," in Kernial S. Sandhu and Paul Wheatley (eds), *Management of Success: The Moulding of Modern Singapore*, Singapore: Institute of Southeast Asian Studies.

Maideen, Haja (1989) *The Nadra Tragedy: The Maria Hertogh Controversy*, Petaling Jaya: Pelanduk Publications.

Mak, Lau-Fong (1981) *The Sociology of Secret Societies: A Study of Chinese Secret Societies in Singapore and Peninsular Malaysia*, Kuala Lumpur: Oxford University Press.

Malay Mail (Singapore), July 9, 1961.

Margolin, Jean-Louis (1993) "Foreign Models in Singapore's Development and the Idea of a Singaporean Model," in Garry Rodan (ed.) *Singapore Changes Guard: Social, Political and Economic Directions in the 1990s*, Melbourne: Longman Cheshire.

Ng, Irene G.M. (1991) "An Analysis of the Changing Role of the Central Provident Fund", B. Soc. Sci. Honours Academic Exercise, Department of Political Science, National University of Singapore.

Pease, Robert M. (1996) "Policy Learning: The Case of Singapore Policy Models for Reform in Urban China", M. Soc. Sci. thesis, Department of Political Science, National University of Singapore.

Phang, Andrew B.L. (1990) *The Development of Singapore Law: Historical and Socio-Legal Perspectives*, Singapore: Butterworths.

PSC Annual Reports 1966–1994 (1967–95) (Singapore: PSC, 1967–1995).

PSC Annual Report 1990 (1991) (Singapore: PSC 1991).

Quah, Jon S.T. (1975) "Singapore's Experience in Public Housing: Some Lessons for Other New States," in Teh-Yao Wu (ed.) *Political and Social Change in Singapore*, Singapore: Institute of Southeast Asian Studies.

—— (1979) "Police Corruption in Singapore: An Analysis of Its Forms, Extent and Causes," *Singapore Police Journal*, vol. 10, no. 1 (January): 7–43.

—— (1982) "The Public Bureaucracy and National Development in Singapore," in Krishna K. Tummala (ed.) *Administrative Systems Abroad*, Washington, DC: University Press of America.

—— (1985a) "Meeting the Twin Threats of Communism and Communalism: The Singapore Response," in Chandran Jeshurun (ed.) *Governments and Rebellions in Southeast Asia*, Singapore: Institute of Southeast Asian Studies.

—— (1985b) "Public Housing," in Jon S.T. Quah, Heng-Chee Chan, and Chee-Meow Seah (eds) *Government and Politics of Singapore*, Singapore: Oxford University Press.

—— (1987) "Public Bureaucracy and Policy Implementation in Singapore," *Southeast Asian Journal of Social Science*, vol. 15, no. 2: 75–94.

—— (1989) "Singapore's Experience in Curbing Corruption," in Arnold J. Heidenheimer, Michael Johnston, and Victor LeVine (eds) *Political Corruption: A Handbook*, New Brunswick, NJ: Transaction Books.

—— (1990) "Government Policies and Nation-Building," in Jon S.T. Quah (ed.) *In Search of Singapore's National Values*, Singapore: Times Academic Press for the Institute of Policy Studies.

—— (1992) "Crime Prevention Singapore Style," *Asian Journal of Public Administration*, vol. 14, no. 2 (December): 168–70.

—— (1993) "Human Resource Development in Four Asian Countries: Some Lessons for the Commonwealth Countries", report prepared for the Commonwealth Secretariat in London, 1993 (reproduced as an annex in *Foundation for the Future: Human Resource Development*), London: Commonwealth Secretariat.

Quah, Stella R. (1991) "Education and Social Class in Singapore," in Stella R. Quah, Seen-Kong Chiew, Yiu-Chung Ko and Meng-Chee Lee, *Social Class in Singapore*, Singapore: Times Academic Press, pp. 38–73.

—— (1995) "Confucianism, Pragmatic Acculturation, Social Discipline, and Productivity: Notes from Singapore," *APO Productivity Journal* (Summer).

—— Quah, Stella R. and Jon S.T. Quah (1987) *Friends in Blue: The Police and the Public in Singapore*, Singapore: Oxford University Press.

Ranis, Gustav (1995) "The Evolution of Policy in a Comparative Perspective, An Introductory Essay," in Kuo-Ting Li, *The Evolution of Policy behind Taiwan's Development Success*, 2nd edn, Singapore: World Scientific Publishing Company.

Rose, Richard (1991) "What is Lesson Drawing?" *Journal of Public Policy*, vol. 11, no. 1 (January–March): 19–21.

Seah, Chee Meow (1971) "Bureaucratic Evolution and Political Change in an Emerging Nation: A Case Study of Singapore," PhD thesis, Faculty of Economic and Social Studies, Victoria University of Manchester.

Seng, Chye Ong (1984) "Crime Trends and Crime Prevention Strategies in Singapore," paper presented at the UNU-UNAFEI International Expert Meeting in Tokyo, May 29–31.

Singapore Department of Statistics (1983) *Economic and Social Statistics Singapore 1960–1982*, Singapore: Department of Statistics.

—— (1994) *Yearbook of Statistics Singapore 1994*, Singapore: Department of Statistics.

Singapore International Foundation (1994) *Can Singapore's Experience be Relevant to Africa?* Singapore: Singapore International Foundation.

Singapore Ministry of Communication and Information (1991) *Singapore 1990*, Singapore: Ministry of Communications and Information.

Singapore Ministry of Information and the Arts (1995) *Singapore 1995*, Singapore: Ministry of Information and the Arts.

Singapore Ministry of Trade and Industry (1986) *Economic Survey of Singapore 1985*, Singapore: Ministry of Trade and Industry.

—— (1996) *Economic Survey of Singapore 1995*, Singapore: Ministry of Trade and Industry.

Singapore National Productivity Board (1987) *Initiatives for Reskilling the Workforce*, Singapore: National Productivity Board.

Straits Times (Singapore) February 25, 1990, November 1, 1990 and March 23, 1985.

Sunday Times (Singapore), June 3, 10, 17, 24, and July 1, 1984.

Tai, Hung-Chao (1989) "The Oriental Alternative: An Hypothesis on Culture and Economy," in Hung-Chao Tai (ed.) *Confucianism and Economic Development: An Oriental Alternative*, Washington, DC: Washington Institute Press.

Tay, Boon-Nga (1992) "The Central Provident Fund: Operation and Schemes," in Linda Low and Mun-Heng Toh (eds) *Public Policies in Singapore: Changes in the 1980s and Future Signposts*, Singapore: Times Academic Press.

Vogel, Ezra, F. (1989) "A Little Dragon Tamed," in Kernial S. Sandhu and Paul Wheatley (eds), *Management of Success: The Moulding of Modern Singapore*, Singapore, Institute of Southeast Asian Studies, pp. 1049–66.

Wilson, Woodrow (1978) "The Study of Administration," *Political Science Quarterly*, vol. 2, no. 1 (June 1887); reprinted in Jay M. Shafritz and Albert C. Hyde (eds) *Classics of Public Administration*, Oak Park: Moore Publishing.

World Bank (1993) *The East Asian Miracle: Economic Growth and Public Policy*, New York: Oxford University Press.

Wright, John W. and Edmund J. Dwyer (1990) *The American Almanac of Jobs and Salaries*, New York: Avon Books.

Yip, Leo and Janet Ong (1992) "How Crime Free is Crime Free Singapore?" *Police Life Annual 1991*, Singapore: Singapore Police Force.

Zyla, Melana K. (1995) "The Right Stuff: Singapore earns Laurels for Competitiveness," *Far Eastern Economic Review*, September 14: 76.

6 Economic reform in Indonesia
The transition from resource dependence to industrial competitiveness

Ali Wardhana

INTRODUCTION

Over the past 30 years, Indonesia's economic structure has undergone a remarkable transition. In 1967, Indonesia was in chaos. Per capita income had declined to a level below that reached five years earlier, the economy was wracked by hyper-inflation, the agriculture sector could not produce enough food, and poverty was the lot of most people.[1] Although the New Order Government moved decisively to establish some degree of economic order, even as recently as 1985 Indonesia showed little evidence of industrialization. The country's exports still consisted largely of oil and gas, with a variety of other primary products making up most of the rest. The agricultural sector still constituted 24 percent of GDP while non-oil/gas manufacturing contributed less than 14 percent. Yet by 1994, real GDP had grown by an average of 7.6 percent per year and non-oil/gas manufacturing had grown to 20 percent of GDP. This performance made Indonesia eligible for inclusion in the World Bank's *East Asian Miracle* volume.

The New Order Government has been committed to the trilogy of development: growth, equity and stability. For the past 30 years, it has sought to improve equity while promoting growth. This led to increased income equality and a reduction in absolute poverty. Moreover, in order to attain growth and equity, the government emphasized developing human, as well as physical, capital.

With a 1995 capita income of US$980, Indonesia cannot yet claim to be a "developed country," but it has clearly demonstrated that rapid growth, combined with an improvement in equity and a reduction in poverty, is possible even in a large and populous country.[2]

Indonesia's policy-makers are often given high marks for focusing on the essential reforms needed to get the economy moving. Yet the question remains why were the specific policy reforms chosen. At one level it could be argued that the reforms are no more than the standard prescription offered to all nations seeking to gain the benefits from global integration. But one must remember that these reform measures seemed much more risky and less obvious in the 1960s and 1980s than they do today. Indeed some of the reforms were considered radical. Why were these policy initiatives politically acceptable in Indonesia when numerous countries, even today, find it difficult to adopt them? Additionally, what reforms are still needed?

THE MAJOR REFORMS

Five main policy actions laid the groundwork for the rapid growth of the past years: the stabilization policies of the late 1960s; tax reform; trade reform; foreign investment reform; and the financial sector reform.[3]

Stabilization reforms

Although the major reforms were undertaken in the 1980s, the seeds of change were planted earlier. The New Order Government that came to power following the 1965 uprising faced a chaotic political and economic situation. The economic situation was so bad as to leave little doubt that stabilization had to be the first order of business. The economic team, formed in March of 1966, moved forcefully to restore some semblance of economic order, realizing that only then, could attention be turned to measures that would allow the economy to grow. The first stabilization program was unveiled in September 1966, after an initial agreement with the Western creditors on debt relief and new loans had been reached. At that time measures were taken that helped establish a semblance of economic equilibrium. The government tightened the money supply, ended subsidies for "key" consumer goods, abolished all quantitative restrictions on imports, and devalued the rupiah. One of the most remarkable aspects of the ensuing period was that not only did the stabilization program reduce inflation, it also led to a real expansion, rather than a contraction, of GDP. This outcome had an important political effect: it established the credentials of the economic team and gave them the necessary support that later allowed them to dismantle other inefficient but politically popular programs and policies.

Two features of macroeconomic management adopted then have been instrumental in guiding the economy ever since. First, the New Order Government constrained its discretion to spend by requiring a balanced budget each and every year. Although foreign borrowing is used to balance the budget, to the extent that the supply of official foreign credits is inelastic, the balanced budget rule serves to enforce a measure of budgetary discipline that protects the economy from inflationary excess. Second, in 1970, the government declared the rupiah to be fully convertible, with no restrictions on the flow of foreign exchange into or out of Indonesia. This move was radical then and would still be considered radical today by some economists. They would argue that such a move is

risky because opening the capital market ahead of a full exchange rate
and tariff reform will bring in such capital inflows that the exchange rate
will appreciate, undermining efforts to promote non-traditional exports.[4]
Despite being warned of the extreme risk, the economic team went ahead
because they realized that an open capital account would put an external
constraint on monetary policy. It does so by ensuring that any monetary
mismanagement will show up almost immediately in an outflow of foreign
exchange. Thus convertibility imposed the discipline needed to deal with
monetary pressures whenever they arose.

These two policy anchors – the balanced budget rule and the open
capital account – left the economic team no choice but to keep macroeconomic balances under close control at all times and strengthened their
hand *vis-à-vis* others whose economic instincts might have been more
expansionary.

Tax reform

In the early 1980s the economy faced a serious crisis. A slowdown in
world economic growth led to a fall in real exports of 9 percent in 1982,
a rise in the current account deficit from 1 to 6 percent of GDP and a
decline of 0.3 percent in real GDP. Various measures were taken to regain
macroeconomic balance. The 1983 budget was austere, allowing for only
a 6 percent nominal increase in government expenditure. Construction of
four major projects was stopped and others were put under review.
Monetary policy was tightened and on March 30, 1983, the rupiah was
devalued by 38 percent, bringing the real exchange rate back to the level
set by the 1978 devaluation.[5] Although these measures were severe, by
this time the economic team had 16 years of experience in managing the
economy through boom and bust and in the process had earned a considerable degree of respect and trust, both domestically and internationally.

Resources were mobilized to reduce pressure on the balance of
payments. Various directed credit programs were discontinued and the
state banks were allowed to set their own interest rates so that they could
compete with the private banks which had already been exempted from
interest rate regulations. But perhaps the most significant reform was the
tax reform of December 1983.

It is often suggested that tax reform was a response to the 1983 decline
in oil prices. While the oil crisis certainly provided a rationale and made
the reform more acceptable than it might otherwise have been, planning
for it had begun a number of years earlier. Thus, the real basis for tax
reform was recognition that over the longer term Indonesia could not
remain dependent on oil and gas revenues for its foreign exchange
earnings and as a source of domestic revenues. The reform introduced a
thoroughly modern tax system, which recognized that a highly complex
system, with high marginal rates, was not only difficult to implement but

Table 6.1 Indonesia: central government revenue, 1982/83–1993/94 (percent of GDP)

	1982/83	1985/86	1986/87	1989/90	1990/91	1991/92	1992/93	1993/94
Revenue (including external grants)	18.2	19.7	15.1	16.6	20.2	17.9	17.1	17.8
Oil and gas	11.9	11.3	5.9	6.4	8.6	6.6	5.8	4.2
Non-oil and gas	5.5	6.7	7.1	8.8	10.2	10.0	10.3	11.2

Source: Indonesian Ministry of Finance

also destroyed economic efficiency. The new tax code reduced the number of tax rates to three – 15, 25, and 35 percent[6] – and moved to a self-reporting income tax system. To ease enforcement, the cutoff point for taxable income was doubled, reducing the proportion of the population subject to income tax from 15 to 10 percent.

In April 1985, this initial reform was followed by the introduction of a value-added tax of 10 percent. Here too Indonesia was a pioneer. It was not only the first developing country to adopt modern tax principles but it was the first one to introduce a value-added tax. These measures eliminated wasteful exemptions, increased government revenues, and ensured that the tax burden was more equitably distributed. These reforms were followed by a new property tax law that made that tax more equitable.

This reform led to a dramatic increase in the revenues from the non-oil and gas sector. Table 6.1 shows that non-oil/gas revenues rose from 5.5 percent of GDP in 1982/83 to 11.2 percent in 1993/94, substantially offsetting the fall in oil and gas revenues.

Trade reform

Although macroeconomic management was generally sound throughout the oil boom period, the oil-generated income hid the cost of substantial microeconomic mismanagement. Domestic industries, flourishing behind high barriers of tariffs and myriad import controls, gave the impression of robust development. In fact, this was no more than the growth many countries experience in the initial stages of import substitution. Rent-seeking behavior was rampant and the customs authority had become corrupt and inefficient, adding more to high import costs, while exchange rate changes were infrequent and abrupt.[7] These inefficiencies, which became known as the "high cost economy," could be tolerated as long as oil revenues provided resources for investment and growth. But with the collapse of oil prices in 1985, Indonesia faced another crisis: the need to stimulate non-traditional exports. In order to do this, the "high cost economy" had to be tackled.

The seriousness of the effort to dismantle, or at least alleviate, the bottlenecks to improve export performance, is exemplified by INPRES (Presidential Instruction) No. 4, of April 1985. This decree drastically reduced and simplified administrative procedures for imports and exports, allowed greater use of foreign shipping, extended port operations to twenty-four hours a day, and brought in a privately-owned Swiss firm, Société Général de Surveillance, to provide customs clearance for all shipments valued in excess of $5,000. Within months the ports became unclogged and tariff revenues rose, while the cost of importing fell noticeably.

In 1986, the first year when the fall in oil prices was reflected in lower oil revenues, there were two further reform measures. In May, the government established a duty drawback facility, P4BM, that enabled export industries to import inputs duty free, and to import directly, regardless of any licensing restrictions. The agency granting these special exporter facilities, BAPEKSTA, part of the Ministry of Finance, quickly and efficiently implemented the duty drawback scheme, substantially reducing exporters' cost of doing business. In September, the rupiah was devalued by 45 percent and a more flexible exchange rate management system was introduced so that, until 1990, the real value of the rupiah, and hence the real incentive to exporters, was maintained.[8]

These trade-related reforms encouraged manufactured exports and gave firms that invested for export, confidence that their profitability would not be impeded by the government. Non-oil exports grew from about US$5.9 billion in 1985 to about US$30.4 billion in 1994 – a more than five-fold increase over nine years. This annual growth rate of 20 percent was more than four times faster than world export growth. It is in the same class as Korea's extraordinary growth in exports of about 23 percent per annum and Taiwan's of about 16 percent per annum between 1970 and 1980. The ratio of non-oil exports to GDP rose from 7 percent in 1985 to about 20 percent in 1994. Including oil and gas exports, the ratio of exports to GDP was 22 percent in 1992, well above the average for all middle income countries (16 percent) and equal to the average for East Asian economies.[9] The composition of non-oil exports also underwent a dramatic change. In 1985, primary products such as rubber, coffee, tea, tin, and aluminum, accounted for close to one-half of total non-oil exports; by 1994 their share had fallen to about one-quarter even though their absolute value had increased. Exports of garments, textiles, footwear and plywood grew rapidly; more recently, furniture, electrical products, and paper products, have further diversified the export structure. By 1994, Indonesia was the third largest footwear exporter in the world (behind Italy and China), the twelfth largest exporter of textile fiber and yarn, the eleventh largest exporter of garments, the thirteenth largest exporter of furniture, and had achieved world market shares in excess of 1 percent in such electronic products as VCRs and sound recording equipment, TV receivers, and radios.[10]

Creating an export-friendly environment depends not only on improving the access by exporters to imported capital and intermediate goods, but also on a general rationalization of tariffs. It is now well understood that tariff protection acts as an indirect tax on exports. The high rates of protection enjoyed by various industries were, in fact, equivalent to a high tax on exports. Beginning in 1986, a series of deregulation packages has lowered tariffs and partially dismantled the non-tariff barriers that supported the "high-cost economy." The impact of these tariff reforms on nominal and effective rates of protection are shown in Table 6.2. It shows a substantial reduction in the protection afforded all tradable goods sectors and a reduction in the anti-export bias of the trade regime. The measured anti-trade bias of the commercial policy regime fell from 41 percent in 1987 to 31 percent in 1994.

In 1995, much remained to be done. While the effective rate of protection for manufacturers had fallen, it was still the highest among the group of East Asian countries, including Malaysia and Korea. The high rate of effective protection not only created an anti-export bias but meant that the protected firms serving the domestic market were not likely to become exporters. In May of 1995 a significant effort was made to resolve this problem. In what is know as PakMei '95, tariffs were reduced on 96 percent of the tariffs in excess of 5 percent; 81 of 269 remaining non-tariff barriers were eliminated. More importantly, a 15-year schedule of tariff reductions will lower nearly all tariffs to 10 percent or less by 2010, with nearly two-thirds of the lines being at 5 percent or less.

Foreign investment reform

While foreign investors responded favorably to the trade and tax provisions of the deregulation packages, reform of investment regulations was needed to take full advantage of heightened investor interest. Until 1989, complex restrictions limited the industries open to new investments and procedures for obtaining approval from the investment agency, BKPM, were cumbersome. In May 1989 these restrictions were substantially scrapped and a much shorter list of restricted industries introduced.[11] This deregulation opened another avenue to a more competitive and more productive economy. In addition the inflow of foreign investment helped transfer technology as well as in the marketing of exports. Foreign investment rose from $0.4 billion in 1987 to $1.7 billion in 1992, with most of the growth in manufacturing investments. Most important perhaps, even in sectors where trade barriers remain high, the freedom to invest has fostered a modicum of domestic competition and generated pressures to reduce costs and maintain productivity.

Since the early 1990s, there has been a progressive loosening of investment restrictions. The list of restricted industries has been substantially reduced and the regulations on domestic ownership and foreign ownership

Table 6.2 Indonesia: protection in broadly-defined economic sectors (percent)

	Nominal rate of protection				Effective rate of protection			
	1987	*1990*	*1992*	*1994*	*1987*	*1990*	*1992*	*1994*
Agriculture	9	8	8	5	16	15	14	9
Mining and quarrying	0	0	0	2	-1	-1	-1	-1
Non-oil manufactures	13	10	9	9	39	34	29	20
All tradables	9	8	7	6	16	14	13	11
Import-competing	17	15	13	11	39	35	22	22
Export-competing	-1	-1	-1	-5	-2	-1	-3	-6
Anti-trade bias of commercial policy	41	36	34	31				

Source: For 1987 and 1990, George Fane, "Agricultural and Agro-Industrial Policy in Indonesia: a Survey" (unpublished manuscript) (Mar. 1991) and for 1992, *An Economic Assessment of the Food, Beverages and Tobacco Sector in Indonesia* (unpublished manuscript) (Dec. 1992). The data for 1987, 1990 and 1992, together with the estimates by Condon and Fane for 1994 are presented in Timothy Condon and George Fane, "Measuring Trade Deregulation in Indonesia" (paper prepared for the conference on "Building on Success: Maximizing the Gains from Deregulation," Jakarta, April 1995)

divestiture have been substantially liberalized. By 1994, foreign investment approvals exceeded $24 billion and in 1995 they reached nearly $40 billion.

Financial sector reform

The economic team recognized that an expanding industrial base required a modern financial system. Without a reasonably competitive financial structure, the investment opportunities opened up by the trade reforms could not be exploited. Before the New Order Government came to power, the Dutch-owned banks that had dominated the financial system had been nationalized and eventually merged into one institution, Bank Negara Indonesia (BNI). This monolithic structure was unworkable. As a first step towards a modern financial system, in 1968 a central bank, Bank Indonesia, was created and BNI was split into five state banks.

These state banks continued to dominate the banking system while interest rates were controlled and credit was directly allocated to various banks and sectors. Bank Indonesia not only gave direct credits to certain enterprises, it also gave "liquidity" credits to the banking system, primarily state banks, to promote targeted activities. As a result, Bank Indonesia and the state-owned banks supplied between 85 to 90 percent of all bank credits.

Credit reforms began in 1983 when restrictions on the allocation of bank credit and on state bank interest rates were eliminated. Bank Indonesia also reduced its role in refinancing bank loans and introduced the Bank Indonesia Certificate (SBI) as a means of improving monetary control. The SBI was a short term liability of the central bank, that was sold periodically by the central bank to the commercial banks and other financial institutions as a means of reducing the supply of reserve money.[12]

An immediate result was substantially increased interest rates paid on deposits and charged for loans, with an improvement in resource allocation, even though the state-owned banks continued to dominate the system.

In October 1988, the government turned its full attention to restructuring the financial markets. "Pakto '88" instituted reforms that removed some of the barriers to entry that had remained in place even after the 1983 reforms. Under Pakto '88, restrictions on foreign banks were eased, procedures for establishing branch banks were simplified, and requirements for becoming a foreign exchange bank were relaxed. Pakto '88 also reduced the special privileges and responsibilities of the state-owned financial institutions and narrowed the differential tax treatment affecting various financial instruments. Finally, bank reserve requirements were lowered to a uniform 2 percent on all deposits, reducing the spread between borrowing and lending rates. Bank Indonesia sterilized most of the expansionary effect of this change by forcing the banks to hold increased quantities of SBIs as secondary reserves, but in mid-1989 and early 1990, monetary policy was loosened and credit growth reached an annualized rate of 70 percent by the middle of 1990. The situation was quickly brought under control by monetary tightening.

The financial reforms led almost immediately to increasing bank deposits and loans although, with the open capital account, it is difficult to disentangle the effect of any financial change from a simple shifting of activity from offshore to onshore and vice versa. Between June 1983 and December 1987 the ratio of total bank assets to GNP rose from 26 to 42 percent. This high rate of growth probably resulted from a combination of increased real savings, increased saving in the form of financial assets, and repatriation of past financial saving from overseas.

Reforms after Pakto '88 were designed to develop a securities market and encourage a variety of other financial institutions and instruments, such as venture capital, leasing, and credit cards. Measures announced in March 1989 strengthened the legal lending limits and a January 1990 measure abolished the bulk of Bank Indonesia's liquidity credit arrangements. Table 6.3 shows how the volume of credit expanded and the share of private banks grew.

As the banking system was expanding, it quickly became apparent that deregulation of banking could not mean *no* regulation. Serious weaknesses developed in the quality of banks' assets; weaknesses that led to the near failure of a major private bank in 1991 and the actual failure of Bank Summa in 1992. These weaknesses contributed to higher risk premia for Indonesian borrowers in foreign markets. In response, the government announced new regulations in February 1991 on loan loss provisioning and Basel Committee capital adequacy guidelines. Although progress has been made in reducing the ratio of non-performing assets to total earning assets, this ratio is still high for the state-owned banks. The loan portfolios of the state-owned banks need to be improved, a difficult task until

Table 6.3 Indonesia: credit volume, 1980–94 (percent)

Item	1980	1982	1984	1986	1988	1990	1991	1992	1993	1994
Total credit as a percentage of GDP	17	21	21	26	31	50	50	47	50	50
Manufacturing credit as a percentage of total credit	28	30	35	34	34	31	29	30	34	32
Total credits by source										
State banks	55	62	71	67	65	55	53	56	48	42
Private banks	9	12	19	21	24	36	37	34	40	46
Foreign banks	5	5	6	5	4	6	7	8	10	10
Bank Indonesia	31	21	5	4	4	1	1	–	–	–

Source: Bank Indonesia

they are privatized.[13] One lesson learned is that it is often easier to deregulate the financial system than it is to ensure that the newly deregulated system operates with prudence that will protect both savers and investors.

The December 1988 reforms opened up private securities markets while also clarifying regulations on insider trading and other unsound and unfair practices. In May 1989, the Minister of Finance issued a decree permitting foreign shareholders to own 49 percent of the shares listed by any company, except commercial banks. These changes, plus the active promotion by BAPEPAM, the capital markets agency, of the stock market has brought new life to the previously moribund Jakarta Stock exchange. At the end of 1988, only 24 stocks were listed and today there are more than 237, while the capitalized value of the exchange has risen from $249 million to over $75 billion. While the revitalized stock market opened up another channel for mobilizing investment resources, the boom also highlighted the need for regulations and procedures consistent with regulatory practices in other countries. Finally, because a critical element of Indonesia's development strategy involves stimulating rural development, rural incomes, and rural employment, the financial reforms were extended to the rural sector. Through the Unit Desas program of Bank Rakyat Indonesia (BRI), a state-owned bank, targeted and subsidized loan programs have been replaced with a rural savings and loan scheme based on market interest rates. Despite some initial skepticism, the BRI rural credit reforms have been remarkably successful. From the end of 1984, the first year of the reforms, through December 1995, the volume of rural credit outstanding from the Unit Desas has expanded 29-fold, while savings deposited with these units have multiplied 143-fold. The Unit Desas now constitute the most profitable of BRI's operations, mobilizing savings while providing small farmers and rural borrowers with needed funds.[14] Here the lesson learned is that reform and deregulation can benefit small farmers and entrepreneurs as much as they support large investments.[15]

THE RESULTS

Growth

Indonesia's economic growth has been strong for two decades, as the data in Table 6.4 show, with an acceleration in the later reform period. In itself this does not justify the deregulation measures; growth can be accelerated by raising investment levels, although the sustainability of such an effort may be called into question. Indeed, Indonesia's fixed capital formation rose from 23 percent of GDP in 1981 to 28 percent by 1994, one of the highest capital formation proportions among developing countries.[16] More important is that total factor productivity increased after 1985, when the deregulation measures began in earnest. This is in contrast to 1979–85, when there was no statistically significant increase in total factor

Table 6.4 Indonesia: Gross Domestic Product, 1974–94

	Values				Annual rates of growth		
	1973	1985	1990	1994	1973–85	1985–90	1990–94
1 Agriculture	28,759.6	44,646.3	53,056.2	59,153.8	3.7	3.5	2.8
(a) Food crops	15,880.7	26,446.3	30,193.1	31,226.9	4.3	2.7	0.8
(b) Other	12,878.9	18,200.0	22,863.1	27,926.9	2.9	4.7	5.1
2 Mining and quarrying	19,115.4	22,638.1	26,627.8	33,172.4	1.4	3.3	5.6
3 Manufacturing	6,753.6	32,144.0	54,210.5	81,690.3	13.9	11.0	10.8
(a) Non-oil/gas	N.A.	25,798.8	45,460.7	71,404.3	12.7†	12.0	11.9
(b) Other	N.A.	6,345.2	8,749.8	10,285.9	24.1†	6.6	4.1
4 Electricity, gas and water	468.4	1,216.1	2,507.6	3,707.4	8.3	15.6	10.3
5 Construction	3,145.4	9,856.4	15,225.6	25,824.6	10.0	9.1	14.1
6 Banking and financial services	1,051.0	5,613.3	10,102.4	15,732.7	15.0	12.5	11.7
7 Other services	30,043.2	72,298.3	101,531.8	134,692.2	7.6	7.0	7.3
GDP	89,336.6	188,412.4	263,261.9	353,973.4	6.4	6.9	7.7

Source: Indonesian Statistical Office

Notes: * Rupiah billions, constant 1993 market prices
† 1978–85

productivity. More specifically: after 1985, GDP grew about 1.1 percentage points per year faster than can be explained by the inputs of capital, labor, and human capital.[17] These results suggest that the increase in total investment and the improvements in resource allocation that occurred after the deregulation process began, led not only to more rapid growth based on applying larger quantities of capital and labor to production but ensured that these factors were more efficiently used. While this result is encouraging, other analysts suggest that total factor productivity growth in Indonesia accounted for a smaller increase in per capita GDP growth than elsewhere in Asia.[18] Although it is difficult to pinpoint a reason, one explanation may be the low levels of learning achievement of Indonesian labor relative to other East Asian countries. Whatever the reason, it is fair to conclude that deregulation contributed to high growth, a contribution that went beyond the increase in investment that followed the opening up of the economy.

Employment and wages

The rapid growth over the past 25 years, and especially over the past decade, has led to a considerable increase in employment and thus reduced poverty. Manufacturing employment grew annually at 5.6 percent from 1971 to 1985 and then at 7.2 percent over the next five years. A major contributor were the jobs created in labor-intensive export industries. While labor force growth is likely to decelerate as the effects of slower population growth are felt, labor will continue to be in ample supply with a continued need for rapid job creation. Wage policy needs also to recognize that higher wages for workers, are in a sense, the ultimate goal of economic development. Increased wages translate directly into higher incomes, reduced poverty, and improved health and welfare. All indicators suggest that wages have risen rapidly in recent years. Indeed during the 1980s, the increase in real wages and other compensation to manufacturing workers has been among the highest in the region. Real earnings grew especially quickly starting in 1988, partly as a result of the strategy that focused on growth and equity, and relied on developing labor-intensive industries.

Improved welfare and reduced poverty

The ultimate goal of economic development is of course an improvement in the general welfare of the population. Rapid growth by itself is insufficient. Indonesia holds that development involves attaining three goals: growth, equity, and stability. Have the deregulation measures contributed to these goals, and to what extent? Deregulation has resulted in a high degree of economic stability and growth, but to what extent has greater equity been achieved?

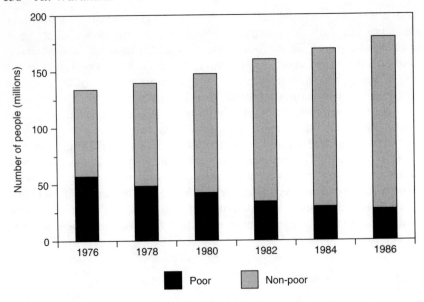

Figure 6.1 Indonesia: poverty incidence, 1976–86
Source: SUSENAS (National Socio-Economic Survey) Biro Pusat Statistik Indonesia
(various years)

Perhaps the most significant achievement has been the reduction in poverty. Only 25 years ago, poverty was widespread. Some estimates suggest that almost 60 percent of the population, nearly 70 million people, were living in absolute poverty in 1970. Since then, poverty has declined steadily and significantly, as shown in Figure 6.1. Indeed, from 1970 to 1987, Indonesia has had the highest annual average reduction in the incidence of poverty among countries studied by the World Bank.[19]

There are several reasons for this success in reducing poverty. Investment in economic and social infrastructure in the 1970s kept the non-oil economy, especially agriculture, viable. Even during periods of financial stringency, a serious attempt was made to protect programs which directly benefited the poor, including the rural poor. For example, modest positive real growth in public investment in the agricultural sector was maintained, while public non-agricultural investment contracted. Among both routine and development expenditures, programs that benefited the poor, were sheltered.[20] In fact, the severest cuts were in the more capital-intensive industrial and mining sector projects.

Human resource development also has received strong emphasis, both as a means of raising living standards and to increase the capacity for growth. From 1960 to 1990, life expectancy increased from 41 to 62 years; infant mortality was reduced from 159/thousand live births to 61/thousand live births; adult illiteracy decreased from 61 percent to 23 percent and the primary school enrollment ratio was raised from 71 to 118. Despite much lower incomes, and starting from a much lower base than many of its East Asian neighbors, Indonesia is catching up to other East Asian countries. More important, the provision of social services has not been limited to urban areas nor to the upper income groups. Indeed access to social services by the poorest 40 percent has been high and has increased during the past 15 years. Improved access of the poor to basic education and health services contributed much to the reduction of poverty.

Equity

Evidence on the distribution of personal income is sparse but the available data point to a gradual reduction in disparities. The share of personal expenditures by the poorest 20 percent of the population increased from 6.9 percent in 1970 to 8.9 percent in 1990.[21] A relatively low and declining level of inequality is also shown by the trend in the Gini coefficient, estimated from the distribution of personal expenditures, which fell from 0.35 in 1970 to 0.32 in 1990. Although the evidence is not conclusive, it does not support the contention by some, that deregulation measures benefited only the upper income groups or the conglomerates.

Despite this evidence, concerns have been expressed that the financial reforms have increased access to financial resources by the conglomerates. However, a recent analysis of the effects of financial liberalization states that "small establishments, which previously lacked access to the financial system, benefited from improved access even at substantially higher interest rates."[22] While there is evidence of a relatively high and growing concentration of ownership and market power in the modern business sector, there is little evidence to suggest that this trend resulted from the deregulation process.

WHY WERE THESE REFORMS ADOPTED? AND WHAT REMAINS TO BE DONE?

Two questions remain to be addressed. What allowed Indonesia to carry out its economic reform process while maintaining a relatively good record on poverty alleviation and agricultural development? And what is the remaining reform agenda?

We have already provided a partial answer on why the reforms were adopted and were successful. First, the economic team won the confidence of the politicians, and indeed of the populace, by successfully stabilizing the economy after the chaos of 1965. Second, the policies maintained a balance between agriculture and industry, and between rural and urban populations. In part this reflected the fact that Indonesia was, and to a large extent still is, a rural, agrarian society. It also reflects the strong agricultural roots to the national leadership, whose concern for the rural poor is deep and genuine. Third, the reform process was carried out over a relatively long period of time. While the current fashion favors a more dramatic "shock" therapy, Indonesia's approach has been one of consistent moderate progress. The argument in favor of a big shock is that rapid and forceful deregulation allows the benefits of such measures to be felt before effective opposition to the reforms can be mounted.[23] Whether a more rapid series of deregulation measures would have been as successful is difficult to say. What is clear is that the impact of the initial deregulations were substantial enough to mobilize support for further measures. Moreover, in the Indonesian social context a gradual approach was more acceptable than a dramatic series of sudden reforms. Finally, some have found it surprising that Indonesia, a resource-rich economy, could successfully deregulate. There is, after all, a growing literature that suggests that the process of adjustment and reform is often less successful in resource-rich countries than in resource-poor ones.[24] It is important to note that Indonesia is not as resource-rich as it seems. On a per capita basis, Indonesia's oil (and gas) reserves rank it among the poorest of the major oil and gas producing countries.[25] While oil exports did form an important part of total exports, the revenues earned from such exports were relatively small in comparison to Indonesia's total population. Given this large population, Indonesia had to rely on more than natural resources.

What is the unfinished agenda? Perhaps most important is the need to ensure that current policies are effectively implemented. This requires further attention to the details of how deregulations affect individual actions. Legal and bureaucratic bottlenecks sometimes frustrate the intent of deregulation measures. Efforts to improve the legal and managerial framework are underway, but these efforts, like all those to strengthen the human capital base, take time. Also, restrictions on market entry and exit, and on equal access to financial and other resources, must be reduced. This is essential if Indonesia is to continue to expand its exports and remain competitive in the global market. In this regard the role of the state-owned enterprises must be further reduced. While public enterprise efficiency can be improved, an accelerated program of privatization, carried out in the domestic stock market, would not only raise public funds but would substantially increase the market's capitalization and trading. Although, as noted, considerable effort has been made to improve the level of education, there is growing evidence that this effort needs to be strengthened. Finally, skilled labor at all levels remains scarce and a substantial effort is needed to increase the supply of scientific and managerial talent. Without such an increase in human capital, the long-term growth prospects are considerably less promising.

The challenge for the near-term is to increase the outward-orientation of the economy and strengthen the role of the private sector, so that rapid growth and poverty reduction can continue. Continued progress depends on further change, carefully planned and effectively implemented.

NOTES

1 See for example, Gillis, 1984, who reports that inflation, measured on the Jakarta consumer price index, reached an annual rate of 636 percent in 1966.

2 All data are in constant 1993 prices and, where appropriate, converted by the author to US dollars at the average 1993 exchange rate.

3 The details of the economic measures that transformed the Indonesian economy have been described in, for example, Woo *et al.*, 1994; and Perkins and Roemer, 1991.

4 See for example Corbo, *et al.*, 1986: 607–40; and Edwards, 1987. While an opening of the capital account obviously can result in a major flow of returning capital that can create exchange rate management problems, Indonesia was not confronted with substantial overseas holdings by domestic residents and so was not threatened with a massive return flow of capital. Moreover capital markets were less integrated in the 1970s that they are today, so that foreign equity capital was not as likely to undermine the exchange rate.

5 Woo, *et al.*, 1994: 33.

6 Tax rates were reduced to 10, 15 and 30 percent in 1995.

7 The rupiah, which is now managed against a basket of currencies, was devalued in 1966 to approximately Rp100/US$ at the time the new rupiah was introduced; devalued again on March 30, 1983 to Rp 909/US$; and again on September 12, 1986 to Rp 1,283/US$.

8 Since 1990 the rupiah real exchange rate against the dollar has appreciated sharply but, given the depreciation of the dollar against most other currencies since 1990, the aggregate real exchange rate of the rupiah had been little changed until mid-1995. After mid-1995 the appreciation of the dollar against other currencies led to an appreciation of the aggregate real exchange rates.

9 See World Bank, 1994.

10 Based on United Nations trade data.

11 Subsequent measures have opened up nearly all sectors to investment and eliminated the rule that foreign investors had to divest controlling interests in investments to local partners.

12 For a more complete description of the financial sector reforms, see Cole and Slade, 1991, as well as Harris, *et al.*, 1994: 17–47.

13 In early 1996, the government announced that BNI, one of the oldest of the state-owned banks, would be privatized.

14 See for example Patten and Rosengard, 1991. Patten and Rosengard note the program's long-term loss ratio is about 3 percent.

15 In order to give further creditability to the stock market, the government in 1995 enacted a new capital market law that codified much of the regulatory innovation that preceded it.

16 Because the stock estimate in the national accounts are a residual in the national income calculations, we restrict ourselves here to the ratio of fixed capital/GDP.

17 Dasgupta *et al.*, 1995.

18 See World Bank, 1993: 64.

19 World Bank, 1990: 45.

20 Ravallion and Huppi, 1991: 52–82, report that ". . . although legitimate doubts can be raised about the size of the changes involved, the analytic techniques adapted allow us to reach the unambiguous conclusion that poverty and under-nutrition in Indonesia continued to decline during the difficult period of the 1980s."

21 This compares to 5.5 percent in the Philippines and to 4.5 percent in Malaysia and Sri Lanka.
22 Harris *et al.*, 1994: 37.
23 For example, Balcerowitz and Gelb (1994: 39) note that "... a radical approach involving forceful stabilization measures and rapid liberalization is almost surely the least risk option."
24 Cf. Gelb *et al.*, 1995.
25 In 1994 Indonesia had oil reserves equal to 33 barrels/per capita; Nigeria had 162 barrels/per capita and Mexico oil reserves equal to 503 barrels/per capita.

REFERENCES

Balcerowitz, L., and Alan Gelb (1994) "Macropolicies in Transition to a Market Economy: A Three-Year Perspective" in *Proceeds of the World Bank Annual Conference on Development: 1994*: 21–44.

Cole, David C., and Betty F. Slade (1991) "Reform of Financial Systems," in Perkins, Dwight H., and Michael Roemer (eds) *Reforming Economic Systems in Developing Countries*, Cambridge, MA: Harvard Institute for International Development.

Corbo, Vittorio, Jamie deMelo, and James Tybout (1986) "What Went Wrong with the Recent Reforms in the Southern Cone," *Economic Development and Cultural Change*, 34: 607–40.

Dasgupta, Dipak, James Hanson, and Edison Hulu (1995) "The Rise in Total Factor Productivity During Deregulation: Indonesia 1985–1992," *Building on Success: Maximizing the Gains from Deregulation*, paper presented at the conference commemorating the Golden Jubilee of the Republic of Indonesia, Jakarta, Indonesia, Apr. 26–28.

Edwards, Sebastian (1987) "Sequencing Economic Liberalization in Developing Countries," *Finance and Development* (March): 26–9.

Gelb, Alan, *et al.*, (1988) *Oil Windfalls: Blessing or Curse?* New York: Oxford University Press.

Gillis, Malcolm (1984) "Episodes in Indonesian Economic Growth," in Harberger, Arnold C. (ed.) *World Economic Growth*, San Francisco: Institute for Contemporary Studies.

Harris, John R., Fabio Schiantarelli, and Miranda G. Siregar (1994) "The Effect of Financial Liberalization, Capital Structure and Investment decisions of Indonesian Manufacturing Establishments," *World Bank Economic Review* (Jan) 8: 17–47.

Patten, Richard H., and Jay K. Rosengard (1991) *Progress with Profits: The Development of Rural Banking in Indonesia*, San Francisco: International Center for Economic Growth.

Perkins, Dwight H., and Michael Roemer (eds) (1991) *Reforming Economic Systems in Developing Countries*, Cambridge, MA: Harvard Institute for International Development.

Ravallion, Martin and Monka Huppi (1991) "Measuring Changes in Poverty: A Methodological Case Study of Indonesia During an Adjustment Period," *World Bank Economic Review*, 5.

Sachs, Jeffrey D., and Andrew Warner (1995) "Natural Resource Abundance and Economic Growth," National Bureau of Economic Research Working Paper No. 5398, December.

Woo, Wing Thye, Bruce Glassburner, and Anwar Nasution (1994) *Macroeconomic Policies, Crisis, and Long-Term Growth in Indonesia, 1965–90*, Washington, DC: World Bank, Comparative Macroeconomic Studies.

World Bank (1990) *World Development Report: 1990*, New York: Oxford University Press.
—— (1993) *The East Asian Miracle: Economic Growth and Public Policy*, New York: Oxford University Press.
—— (1994) *World Development Report 1994*, New York: Oxford University Press.

Part II

Achieving and learning societies

Development requires learning many things. This comes in many ways: through schooling, by making things, by exporting to foreign lands, by buying technology from others, and by inviting foreigners to invest. Many developing countries failed to pursue these routes vigorously and even put barriers in their way. But most East Asian societies did not do this, while some of them are quintessentially learning societies. And, not least, they have learned from each other.

7 Human capital: how the East excels

Harold W. Stevenson

One of the most important accomplishments of the East Asian nations has been the creation of a skilled, knowledgeable work force. In the past, only a small percentage of people attended high schools and universities. However, in the transformation of many East Asian nations from agricultural to industrial societies, it became apparent that a well-educated work force would be needed if the demands of complex industrial and manufacturing economies were to be met. Their governments instituted universal, compulsory education of high quality for all citizens and discontinued the tradition of elite education, at least through the junior high school years. The degree to which this has been accomplished varies, of course, with China still striving to attain the goal and Japan, Taiwan, South Korea and several other nations having accomplished it some time ago.

The success of these efforts is evident, not only in their remarkably rapid economic progress, but also in measures of the academic achievement of East Asian students. Students from East Asia have been among the top scorers in international comparative studies of academic achievement since the 1960s. Typical are the results of the Third International Mathematics and Science Study reported in 1996, where, for example, eighth graders from Singapore, Korea, Japan and Hong Kong were the four top-scoring participants in mathematics among the 41 nations participating in the study. The four top-scoring nations in science included Singapore, Japan, and Korea. Other studies, including the First and Second International Mathematics Study, confirmed these extraordinary accomplishments, thus attesting to the broad level of excellence of East Asian students.

Some critics have challenged the results of these studies, citing, for example, a presumed lack of comparable or representative samples of students in the different countries or an alleged failure to use tests that were relevant for all of the cultures being compared. Their criticisms are ill-informed, primarily because the critics have lacked first-hand knowledge and experience in conducting comparative studies themselves. We can use examples from the studies we have conducted to illustrate the

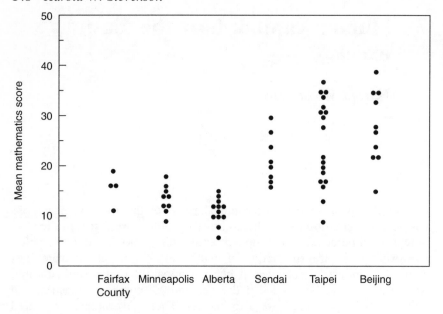

Figure 7.1 Average scores for schools included in the study comparing mathematics performance of eleventh graders in North America and East Asia

kinds of findings that have been reported and to clarify why the criticisms of such studies are without a sound basis.

We have compared the performance of students residing in cities in Western countries with that of students in cities in Japan (Sendai), Taiwan (Taipei), and China (Beijing). Specifically, we have chosen American cities that are among the most successful in terms of students' levels of academic achievement (Minneapolis and Fairfax County, Virginia) and several cities in Alberta, Canada. We were careful at each step of the sampling process not to introduce bias into the sampling of students. We relied on local educational authorities and researchers to provide us with information about the schools in each city, and on the basis of their suggestions we were able to select representative samples that included schools in neighborhoods of high, average, and low socio-economic status. We then randomly chose classrooms within each school and tested all students – in the present case, eleventh graders – in these classrooms. A larger number of schools in Taipei and Beijing was necessary because of the need to sample vocational as well as academic high schools.

We responded to the question of fairness by devising our own tests. Our research group, which included colleagues in China, Japan, Taiwan, and the United States, constructed the tests used in the studies. We undertook this demanding and time-consuming task because we

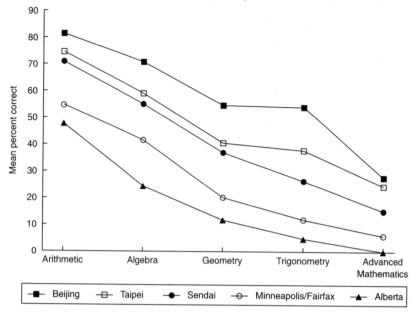

Figure 7.2 Average number of correct responses of students according to domain of mathematics in North America and East Asia

wanted to be sure that the tests were fair and that they covered the knowledge and skills to which the children in each of the cultures had been exposed. Our first step was to analyze the textbooks used in the three cities in East Asia and in the United States. We categorized each concept and skill according to the semester and grade in which it was introduced. We were then able to devise a single test that contained items that had appeared in the analyses of all four sets of textbooks and that therefore contained items that should have been equally familiar to students in all the participating cultures. The results of the mathematics test are presented in terms of the average score obtained in each of the schools sampled (see Figure 7.1).

Some critics have suggested that average scores for the whole test obscure the possibility that American students may have strengths in mathematics that differ from those of the East Asian students. Specifically, it has been suggested that American students may be more effective in problem solving and the strength of East Asian students may lie in their greater grasp of routine mathematical operations. This possibility is easily tested. Items in the mathematics test were divided into different domains of mathematics, ranging from arithmetic to advanced mathematics. The results of this analysis indicate that the North American compared to the East Asian students are deficient in all domains included in the test (see Figure 7.2).

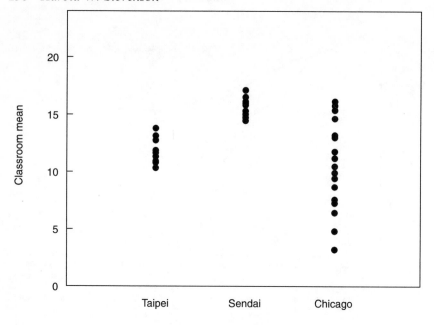

Figure 7.3 Average scores on reading comprehension test by fifth graders in Taipei, Sendai and Chicago

Other studies confirm the extraordinary accomplishments in mathematics and attest to the broad level of excellence of East Asian students in other academic subjects as well. Students in Japan and Taiwan, for example, excel in reading. Despite the difficulties of learning to read the Chinese characters used in both written languages, students from Taiwan and Japan surpass their American counterparts in tests of reading vocabulary and comprehension (see Figure 7.3).

OVERVIEW

This chapter presents an overview of East Asian education, and describes the aspects of East Asian cultures that foster academic achievement and that are frequently included in accounts of the rise of East Asian countries. Japan is emphasized because it has played a central role in East Asia, especially in education, and because more information is available about Japan than about the others. The educational systems of China, Taiwan, and South Korea are discussed briefly.

In general, schooling in East Asia is divided according to a 6-3-3 pattern. Six years of compulsory elementary school are followed by three years of junior high school and three years of high school. Depending upon the country, middle school attendance may or may not be compulsory, but there is a growing tendency in all the countries for students to continue their education at least through this level. Attendance at high school may range from fewer than half to nearly all of the yearly cohort of students.

JAPAN

The organization of education

Prior to the Meiji Restoration in 1868, education was limited to families privileged by economic or social status in society. Following this period, education was modeled after the elitist European systems where ordinary citizens were, at best, likely to obtain no more than a few years of schooling. By 1919, when Japan had become established as a world power, the government realized it was necessary to make education open to all citizens, and it assumed responsibility for major educational expenses for the six years of elementary school. The only persons pursuing education beyond that level were typically the children of the social and economic elite.

This system continued until after World War II, when, with the adoption of the postwar Constitution, the Japanese people pursued the equality they understood to be part of democracy and, to an extent, abandoned old types of social privilege. As a consequence, education underwent dramatic changes. Egalitarian education displaced the elitist system, the number of years of schooling was increased, nine years of education became compulsory, programs of vocational education were expanded, and entrance to a college or university became possible for excellent students. Even with the new emphasis on universal education, the principal goal was to expand and improve primary and secondary education; funding for colleges and universities did not receive top priority.

Currently, over 99 percent of Japanese children and young people are enrolled in elementary and junior high schools. While access to these levels has become easier, entrance to the best high schools and colleges has remained intensely competitive. Even so, 96 percent of Japanese students go on to secondary school and nearly a third of high school graduates enroll in some form of higher education.

During the nine years of compulsory schooling, great efforts are made toward egalitarianism. The guiding principle today is that students throughout Japan should have equal access to a comparable quality of education. They provide national guidelines for education, thereby guaranteeing a comparable curriculum in all schools; avoid tracking of students, either within classrooms or between schools; and provide equal access to outstanding teachers by requiring teachers (and administrators) to change schools at least once every seven years. To further ensure equal access, the national government covers half of the cost of teachers' salaries and teaching materials and one-third of the cost for maintaining buildings. The remaining support comes from the local and prefectural governments, and from fees paid by high school and college students.

High schools are organized in a very hierarchical fashion. Although elementary and junior high schools enroll students from the neighborhoods in which the school is located, high schools serve the whole cities or metropolitan areas. Moreover, high schools are ranked according to the excellence of their students, staff, and facilities, and admission is determined by the score in an entrance examination. Students with the highest scores are admitted to the city's top high schools and those with the lowest are admitted only to vocational schools. The needs of students of a wide range of ability and interests are met by this dual system of academic and vocational high schools.

Coupled with the high value placed by the culture on education, the opportunity to obtain an education suitable to the students' interests and needs results in very low dropout rates. For example, according to the Ministry of Education, the data for 1992 indicate that 96 percent of the junior high school graduates continued to high school, 2 percent joined the work force, and the remaining 2 percent entered other types of special schooling.[1]

A clear ranking system also exists for universities, and, as with high schools, admission depends on the entrance examination. Intense competition exists for the top-ranked schools, and the all-powerful role played by the college entrance examination has led to the well-known "examination hell". Admission to universities has depended solely on entrance examination scores.

According to the Monbusho (1993), 32 percent of high school graduates continued to college or junior college, 30 percent went to various specialty schools, 32 percent found employment, and 5 percent were unemployed or not in school. University education in Japan is predominantly male, following the tradition of preparing males to become the financial providers for their households and women to remain at home to care for the family. In 1992, for example, 71 percent of the students attending four-year universities were male.[2] The discrepancy is even greater at the graduate school level, where 82 percent of the students were male. Young women primarily attend the nations' numerous junior colleges, where they constitute over 90 percent of the enrollment.

The curriculum

Administration is highly centralized in East Asia. Central governments define the content of textbooks and provide curriculum guidelines or in some cases, detailed curricula. As a result, there is great uniformity in subject matter and skills taught throughout the nation. The argument commonly made in support is that students, regardless of the region of the country in which they live, need to have the basic skills for success in contemporary society.

The Japanese elementary school curriculum places strong emphasis on basic subjects such as reading, arithmetic, Japanese language, and social studies. Moral education is also included as part of the curriculum. The Ministry of Education publishes a *Course of Study* that describes in general terms the accomplishments that are expected during each grade. With the exception of specifying which of the Chinese characters (*kanji*) are to be taught at each grade, the *Course of Study* does not provide a precisely delineated curriculum.

The Ministry also establishes standards for education and approves textbooks. Nonetheless, teachers still have authority over how a lesson will be taught and when it will be introduced. The government does not publish textbooks but relegates this task to private publishers who can interpret the curriculum in a manner that they believe to be appropriate. Thus, the image of the Japanese curriculum often portrayed in the Western media is inaccurate. Students at a particular grade level are not all studying the same lesson at the same time throughout the country, nor are they being taught in the same manner.

The high school curriculum allows students some freedom in the choice of subjects, but the Ministry defines the basic curriculum. Academic high schools offer humanities and science tracks. All students in each track must enroll in a set of basic courses, no matter how familiar they are with the content.

The Ministry has tried to introduce more flexibility by reducing the number of required high school courses and allowing students to pursue their own interests. Teachers are also encouraged to form classes composed of students of about the same levels of ability. This means that tracking, avoided during the earlier years of school, exists during high school not only in the type of school and the curriculum studied, but also in the rate at which the curriculum is presented. The tracks are not inflexible, for if a slower student's work improves, he or she moves up to a higher level. This is possible because the basic content of the curriculum is the same in all tracks and conforms to the national curriculum; only the speed with which it is taught varies.

Special classes for gifted students do not exist and special treatment, such as being allowed to skip a grade, is extremely rare. Both practices violate the egalitarian philosophy of education and would be considered by both parents and teachers as displaying unfair favoritism.

Supplementary schooling at school

Special opportunities exist in Japanese public schools for students to enrich their education. After-school clubs and classes offer extracurricular activities that are open to all students. In fact, after the fourth grade all students must enroll in at least one of these activities.

The programs serve diverse purposes. Some primarily promote health and leisure-time and include lessons at school that would be privately taught in other societies, such as martial arts and music. Others cover aspects of culture that are not part of the regular curriculum, such as calligraphy, use of the abacus, flower arrangement, and the tea ceremony. Still others give students the opportunity for types of training that are not available in the regular curriculum, such as computer programming. The range of activities available depends on the size of the school; in high school it may include such topics as sports, orchestra, calligraphy, literature, geology, biology, and journal writing.

During elementary school, students remain for an hour or more after their regular classes to participate in the extracurricular activities; during high school they may participate in several activities and remain at school for several hours. Thus, the image of East Asian students returning home late in the afternoon or early evening after having spent long hours in classes is a misunderstanding. The times spent in academic classes during elementary school are very similar to those in Western countries and even high school academic classes seldom require more than an hour more than they do in the West.

The longer school day in East Asia can be understood, therefore, in terms of the dual function of school in the lives of East Asian students. School is not only a place for learning, it also offers many opportunities for social interaction. Adding to the time spent in extracurricular activities are frequent breaks between classes (totalling about 50 minutes a day), a long lunch hour (typically at least an hour), and the time many students spend at school studying with their friends. The formal activities, plus large amounts of free time, make it possible for students to spend significant amounts of time in social interaction. It is not surprising, therefore, that students' attitudes about attending school are generally positive.

Supplementary schooling outside of school

The intense competition for admission to a college or university and the nearly total reliance placed on the entrance examination have led to the increasing popularity of supplementary forms of schooling. the *juku* of Japan and the *buxiban* of Taiwan serve this purpose. These are privately owned, supplementary forms of schooling outside the jurisdiction of the ministries of education.

Despite the common impression of *juku* as "cram schools," there actually are several types of *juku*. Some, especially those serving younger students, aim at self-improvement. Two additional types of *juku* exist for older students: *shingaku juku*, whose primary purpose is to prepare students for the college entrance examination, and *hoshu juku*, which provide remedial instruction for students encountering difficulty with their school work. *Juku*, like regular schools, serve both academic and social needs of students. When asked why they attend *juku* many students explain that it is to be with their friends as well as to benefit from the academic and cultural programs.

Although the Western press characterizes every student in Japan as spending long hours in *juku*, this description primarily fits large cities, like Tokyo, Nagoya, and Osaka. It falls off notably in more remote cities or smaller communities. Attendance also depends on the student's grade; the highest frequencies occur during the junior high school years, when students are preparing for the high school entrance examinations.

It is difficult to obtain reliable data concerning *juku* attendance because private owners are reluctant to reveal clues about their successes, but some current data are available from a poll conducted by Monbusho (1996). A rise in attendance by students at *shingaku juku* from 12 to 42 percent was found between first and sixth grades. Attendance increased to a high of 67 percent during junior high school, but dropped off to a low of 32 percent during the high school years. Because *juku* are expensive and therefore are not available to all students and also because of the burden of what many consider to be too much time devoted to study, these supplementary forms of schooling have increasingly come under criticism. Teachers are especially critical in cities where there are no *juku* or where few students can afford their high tuition. In such cases, it devolves upon the teachers to provide extra classes and to offer special help to students in picking future schools. Without this help, it would be difficult for the students to compete effectively for places in highly ranked high schools and colleges.

A second form of supplementary schooling available to Japanese students is the *yobiko*. *Yobiko* serve students who believe they may have difficulty in passing the college entrance examinations or who have already failed them, and students who want to take some time off between graduating from high school and entering a university. Classes offered by *yobiko* are much like those of *juku*, except that *yobiko* are full-time, year-long efforts aimed solely at preparing students for the college entrance examination.

Vocational and technical education

Japanese policy-makers, recognizing the need for middle-level technicians, give strong support to vocational education. Two types of programs exist: technical and vocational programs. The first is the more demanding, for it requires five years of enrollment, during which students complete the equivalent of a high school education and two years of specialized classes in areas such as mechanical and electrical engineering. Technical schools enroll no more than 1 percent of junior high school graduates. Vocational schools, in contrast, enroll 20 percent of high school students.

Vocational high schools require satisfactory performance in both academic and vocational classes and in out-of-school work placements. Because of the many opportunities for employment after graduation, some students who qualify for academic high schools choose, instead, to attend vocational ones. Still others choose not to attend vocational high schools because they believe it would be difficult to go to a university after attending the less demanding academic program in vocational schools. The growing desire over the past several decades to enter universities has led to a decline in the prestige of vocational schools, with an accompanying decline in the percentage of students choosing them.

Problems

The rapid growth of knowledge and technology requires constant modification and improvement of educational systems to remain effective. Japanese parents, teachers, administrators, and government officials, show awareness of problems in their educational system and have pressed for rapid changes in a number of areas. Some problems have already begun to be solved; for others, discussions are just beginning.

The most frequently mentioned problems are: funding for education and research; college admissions; the quality of college education; individual differences in learning ability; the rigidity perceived to characterize the Japanese high school curriculum; and the large amounts of time students spend studying.

Research funds and physical plants

Two of the most immediate and obvious problems facing Japan are the lack of funds for research and the poor physical plants of the nation's schools and research laboratories.

The Japanese lament what they consider to be a lack of creativity among Japanese researchers and point to the small number of Japanese who have been awarded Nobel prizes or who have made other internationally acclaimed scientific discoveries. It is apparent, however, that the basis of this lag in scientific advances may be less a matter of creativity than of inadequate funds for research and modern facilities. Japanese schools, universities, and research laboratories are generally housed in austere, crowded buildings that lack many of the most basic amenities, such as heating and cooling systems.

In response, the Council of Science and Technology, headed by Japan's Prime Minister, proposed in July 1996 that the national government spend about $37 billion over the next five years on science and technology – twice the current allocation. An additional $37 billion was estimated for upgrading the physical facilities for education.[3] The government currently provides only 20 percent of the amount spent on research in Japan, with the remainder coming primarily from industry whose interest lies in developing new products rather than basic research.

College entrance examinations

Most Japanese acknowledge that too much emphasis has been placed on the prestige of the university and the role of college entrance examinations in determining admissions. Part of the emphasis on prestige comes from the fact that the kinds of jobs available are linked to the university. Those graduating from one of the former imperial universities, such as Tokyo University or Kyoto University or some of the private universities, are privileged in their search for important positions. As a result, the demand to enter these institutions vastly exceeds the number of students who can be accommodated. Because admission to any university has depended solely on the college entrance examination score, there has been an overemphasis on doing well on this test.

Students begin their arduous preparations for the college entrance examinations well before their third year of high school, when the tests are administered. Because the best high schools are more likely to provide the quality of education needed for doing well on the college entrance examination, it becomes important to do well on the high school entrance examinations. In turn, students strive to attend one of the best junior high schools. Even elementary school students are made aware of the importance of doing well in school so that they will be ready for the entrance examinations that lie ahead of them.

One proposal that has met with some success is that other criteria be adopted for admission to universities. For the past several years, about 20 percent of admissions have been based on recommendations made by the students' teachers. Also, a small number of places in each university department are reserved for students with unusual qualifications, including outstanding academic achievement or some type of exceptional experience, such as living overseas or winning some important award. University faculty members then interview recommended students and decide which ones to accept. Admission to these programs is competitive, but reliance on recommendations rather than test scores has the potential of significantly modifying the way in which Japanese students prepare for universities.

The college years

The quality of education of Japanese colleges and universities has also been criticized. Once admitted, students relax, fail to attend classes frequently, and generally consider the college years as a pleasant break between the grueling years of high school and the demanding years of working for a company. It has been suggested that it should be easier to be admitted to college, but harder to graduate. This, it is proposed, would lessen the fierce competition for university entrance while strengthening the incentive to study in order to graduate from college.

Individualized education

Japanese classes are large and prior to high school are intentionally composed of groups of students who are heterogeneous in abilities and levels of achievement. It is a challenge for the teacher to provide lessons at the appropriate level of difficulty for all students. Some slow learners may fail to understand the lesson and fall behind, while rapid learners may quickly become bored.

Teachers attempt to meet these different needs through various teaching strategies, but the failure to provide appropriate opportunities for gifted students is often criticized because it limits the possibility of the nation's benefiting from exceptional individuals. This inability is perceived to be due to the rigidity of the system, especially at the high school level.

A proposed solution is to individualize education. Currently, the discussion focuses on the high school years. This is an attempt to make their curricula more flexible so that the schools can do a better job of meeting the students' individual interests, abilities and needs. How this would be extended downward to elementary and middle school students is unclear. Educational leaders continue to struggle with the concept of individualized education and how to put it into practice, but what is notable about the effort is that it is being considered at all.

Studying

There has been criticism from parents and teachers that students spend too much time on academics and too little on socialization. To remedy this problem, the school week has been reduced; classes have been canceled on two Saturdays each month and it is expected that classes on the remaining two Saturdays will be eliminated within the next few years. There has been pressure, too, to reduce the amount of homework assigned to students to enable them to spend more of their after-school hours in social activities.

Thus, despite worldwide interest in the successes of East Asian education, there obviously remain important problems. Trying to deal with them will take time and dedication, but Japanese educators, as well as those in other East Asian countries, recognize that they need to do this to provide the educated and skilled work force for an expanding, competitive economy.

Before turning to some of the explanations that have been offered for the remarkable successes of the Japanese educational system and for the intense efforts that continue to be made to improve it, brief descriptions of the educational systems of China, Taiwan, and South Korea will help to extend the discussion beyond a single country.

CHINA

The Chinese educational system is very similar to that of Japan. Elementary and secondary education follows the 6-3-3-year pattern and the control of the curriculum and textbooks lies with members of the central government. Nearly all school-aged children complete six years of elementary school, but only three-quarters go on to junior high school. Admission to junior high school and to all high levels depends on the student's score on entrance examinations. Of those who finish junior high school, fewer than 40 percent continue their education in high school and admission to universities is possible for only one-fourth of high school graduates. This means that fewer than 10 percent of each age cohort qualifies for admission to any form of university or college education. Because of this, college entrance examinations are even more important than in Japan.

The intensity of the competition for admission to colleges and universities has been relieved somewhat during recent years by the introduction of a market economy because, paradoxically, opportunities spawned by the market have reduced the value of higher levels of education. Graduates of even elementary or junior high schools may engage in entrepreneurial activities that yield higher incomes than are available to many graduates of universities, especially in coastal cities and new economic development zones. In inland cities and rural regions, where opportunities for entrepreneurial activities are less favorable, economic and social advancement still lies primarily in a person's education.

Government policy continues to be aimed at improving the quality of primary and secondary education rather than expanding universities. Vocational and other types of schools offering specialized training are growing rapidly in popularity. Currently, 58 percent of Chinese secondary school students are enrolled in vocational schools of varying quality, but many are turning out persons with high skills.[4] For example, the better vocational schools seek to train chefs, clothing designers, and electricians rather than cooks, seamstresses, and repair persons. Graduates are assured of good positions, for they possess skills in high demand in China's rapidly developing economy.

As in Japan, there are many opportunities for China's students to participate in extracurricular activities. Some activities, such as calligraphy, arts and crafts, and paper cutting, are open to all students. Others are attended by those recommended on the basis of their academic performance or special talents. These include such activities as playing in an orchestra, choir singing, soccer, gymnastics, public speaking, and Red Cross. Opportunities for secondary school students are often more academically oriented, and include clubs devoted to mathematics, physics, chemistry, calligraphy, drawing, choir singing, photography, computers, and sports.

Four types of junior high and high schools exist in China. In addition to academic and vocational high schools, "skilled worker" schools train graduates of junior high school for three additional years. Specialized secondary schools enroll graduates of high schools and require only two years of additional training. The latter are aimed at training persons for a wide variety of skilled occupations, ranging from kindergarten teacher to electrician or auto mechanic.

TAIWAN

For the past several decades, Taiwan has undergone a transition from an agricultural to an industrial economy and high priority has been given to the development of its educational system. Education is compulsory during the first nine years of the twelve-year program of primary and secondary education. At the end of nine years, students have several alternatives. Most enter high school; others enroll in vocational or technical schools; some go to work. Currently, over 99 percent of the students graduate from elementary and junior high school; 85 percent of the graduates of junior high schools attend academic or vocational high schools; and nearly half of the high school students go on to colleges or universities.

SOUTH KOREA

The education system of South Korea, like Taiwan shares many of the characteristics found in the Japanese system – a product of the colonial era. Schedules, course offerings, and school organization are very similar to those of Japan. South Koreans have a passionate involvement in education; almost 70 percent of South Korean students attend academic high schools to prepare for college entrance examinations; but only one-fourth of the students who take the examinations are admitted. As elsewhere in East Asia, exclusive reliance on standardized testing encourages rote learning and memorization. Because of the demand for a college education there has been little impetus to alter any aspects of the system that might reduce a student's chances of higher education.

THE CONTRIBUTION TO EAST ASIAN SUCCESS

Westerners have held stereotyped views of the characteristics that have enabled East Asian students to attain high levels of academic achievement. In addition to being described as uncreative, they are often depicted as willing to spend long hours in dull, repetitive tasks, subjected to the demands of authoritarian teachers and required to memorize large portions of their lessons. These negative images lead Western parents to ask if the cost of academic success is not too high in terms of stress and loss of individuality. But these views prove to be invalid upon observation and interaction. There are other, more accurate explanations.

If we accept the importance of education in the outstanding success of East Asians, we are still faced with the need to explain why so much emphasis has been placed on education and why the educational systems have been so successful. What possible biological, familial, educational, and cultural factors are involved in these explanations? Several of the most common interpretations are these.

Biological factors

A commonly heard explanation of the East Asian success is that East Asians possess superior intellectual ability. This explanation has, to say the least, been controversial, primarily because it has been impossible to find convincing evidence in support. For example, in a study of the intellectual abilities of elementary school children in Japan, Taiwan, and the United States, we found no clear advantage of one group over the others. Although students in each culture excelled in some tasks, the overall scores of the students from the three locations did not differ significantly.[5]

Value of education

For centuries, East Asians have believed in the value of education for the nation's well-being as well as for personal advancement. Many centuries ago, well educated young men in China were recruited as civil servants through a system of national examinations. This procedure was designed to promote administrative competence, and as a result young people found that a good education was a means of gaining upward mobility. Inculcated with the belief in education as a means of advancement, most Chinese children and youths came to perceive getting a good education as a central goal in their lives. This belief continues and families mobilize their resources to support children in obtaining the best possible education.

Value of hard work

Another cultural value that characterizes East Asians is the importance placed on hard work. Confucian teachings emphasize the malleability of human beings. They believe that achievement is possible if they work hard – regardless of their level of ability. They do not deny the existence of differences in innate endowments, but they de-emphasize its importance as a controlling factor in people's lives. Innate abilities may determine the rate at which one acquires knowledge, but effort is believed to be the factor that differentiates the level of achievement individuals can attain.

From ancient sayings, such as "The slow bird must start out early," to Chairman Mao's more recent exhortations to students to "Study hard and make progress every day," great reliance has been placed on effort as the key factor in human accomplishment.

This is an optimistic belief, and underlies the expectation common in East Asia that all children are capable of performing effectively in school. Success depends on having devoted teachers and supportive parents – but even more importantly on the hard work of students. Chinese and Japanese believe that stressing the importance of innate abilities is self-defeating, and potentially limits the achievement of students of all levels of ability. Average students and slow learners may begin to doubt that they can succeed even if they do work hard, and gifted students may come to believe that their high abilities are sufficient for success.

Teaching techniques

Many East Asian teachers are remarkably effective in guiding their students through the curriculum. Rather than relying on lectures, they have an interactive style of teaching. During each lesson they attempt to elicit information from students on alternative interpretations and solutions to a problem, and then call on other students to evaluate the correctness and utility of the alternatives that have been offered. This style of teaching departs notably from the stereotyped image that portrays intense, highly pressured children learning under the control of a rigid teacher who seeks conformity and stresses memorization and rote learning. Some of these attributes may still be present, especially in some high school classrooms, but they are an out-of-date portrayal of the dynamic quality of teaching in most elementary and junior high schools.

Another technique is the emphasis on whole-class instruction. The need for whole-class instruction is partly determined by the cramped space and the large number of students in most East Asian classrooms. It is also influenced by the belief that the whole-class approach gives the largest number of students the greatest amount of their teacher's time. We know that children *can* learn on their own or in small groups. The question is whether learning occurs as effectively under those conditions, and whether organizing the classroom into small groups serves to limit the opportunities that each student has for benefiting from a skilled, knowledgeable teacher. With effectively managed whole-class instruction, it is argued, all students receive the same amount of guidance and instruction during every lesson.

Family involvement

Schools by themselves bear only part of the burden of education and success is very difficult unless parents are involved. Parents in East Asia are intensely involved in all aspects of the education of their children.

They set high standards for students, spend large amounts of time supervising school work, and try to provide a home environment conducive to studying.

Healthy attitudes

Visitors to schools in East Asia come away with stories about the students' remarkable attentiveness and responsiveness in class and about their generally calm demeanor. They are also surprised when they see the same children become vigorous and noisy when class is over and recess begins. Especially impressive to most visitors is the lack of indications of tension among the students, a lack that parents, teachers, and students all report. Contrary to what might be expected of students who work hard at their studies and are so intent on improvement, Japanese and Chinese high school students exhibit low rates of psychosomatic disorders, anxiety, stress and aggression.[6] The incidence of teenage suicide in East Asia is low.

The most reasonable interpretation is that stress comes from conflict and that for most students there is little conflict about education. They know that social activities, dating, working at an outside job, and doing household chores are secondary to their main mission: to get a good education and to do well in school. The belief in academic achievement is so pervasive and so well accepted by the students' parents, teachers, and peers that most students seldom experience conflict in deciding whether or not to study hard.

CONCLUSION

Over the past 40 or 50 years, East Asians have developed educational systems that are providing their countries with the well educated and highly trained workers needed by industry and society at large. The emphasis has been on primary and secondary education, and dual systems of academic and vocational programs in high schools have generally been successful in meeting these needs.

This does not mean that they are without problems. Some, such as reducing the importance of college entrance examinations, lessening the rigidity of the educational system, and reducing the time students spend studying, are not especially difficult to solve. Others, such as improving the quality of college education and increasing the funds available for physical facilities and research may be more difficult. The small number of well-trained college graduates and graduate students has not impeded development thus far, but it is questionable whether reliance on secondary school graduates will meet the needs for innovation in the future.

The formula is neither exotic nor surprising; rather, it appears to be straightforward: develop an awareness in the culture of the importance of education, persuade students to study effectively, provide schools with well-trained, responsive teachers, make school an enjoyable place to be, and maintain strong cultural interest and family support in education. These characteristics are not new to anyone who has thought about the relation of education to productivity and innovation. It is a matter now of trying to understand whether and how cultures outside of East Asia can put them into practice so effectively.

NOTES

1   Monbusho, 1993.
2   Ibid.
3   Pollack, 1996.
4   Li Wang, 1996.
5   Stevenson *et al.*, 1985.
6   Crystal *et al.*, 1994.

REFERENCES

Crystal, D.S., C. Chen, A.J. Fuligni, H.W. Stevenson, C.C. Hsu, H.J. Ko, S. Kitamura, and S. Kimura (1994) "Psychological maladjustment and academic achievement: A cross-cultural study of Japanese, Chinese, and American high school students," *Child Development*, 65, 738–53.
Li Wang (1996) "National meeting on vocational education held in Beijing," *People's Daily Overseas Edition*, June 18, p. 1.
Monbusho (1993) *Gakko kihon chosa hokokusho* [Report of the basic statistics related to schools] Tokyo: Okurasho Insatsukyoku.
Monbusho (1996) *Gakushu juku to ni kansuru jissai chosa* [A report on academic *juku*] Tokyo: Government Printing Office.
Peak, L. (1996) *Pursuing excellence: A study of U.S. eighth grade mathematics and science teaching, learning, curriculum, and achievement in international context*, Washington, DC: US Department of Education.
Pollack, A. (1996) "Japan is planning a large increase in its science research budget," *New York Times*, July 2, p. B9.
Stevenson, H.W. (1995) "Mathematics achievement of American students: First in the world by Year 2000?" in C.A. Nelson (ed.) *Minnesota Symposia on Child Psychology*, 131–149. Hillsdale, NJ: Erlbaum.
Stevenson, H.W., J.W. Stigler, S.Y. Lee, G.W. Lucker, S. Kitamura, and C.C. Hsu (1985) "Cognitive performance and academic achievement of Japanese, Chinese, and American children," *Child Development*, 56: 718–34.

8 Education in Korea and Malaysia

Donald R. Snodgrass

EDUCATION AND ECONOMIC DEVELOPMENT

How East Asia was able to do much better than everyone else, and most spectacularly, accelerate its growth during the "lost decade" (as seen from Africa and Latin America) of the 1980s, has been the subject of voluminous discussion, in which education has featured prominently. We begin by comparing some measurable features of education with similar data for other regions of the world. When this is done, East Asia looks surprisingly ordinary in some respects, but extraordinary in others.

According to the World Bank:

> The East Asian economies had a head start in terms of human capital and have widened their lead over other developing economies. In the 1960s, levels of human capital were already higher in the HPAEs[1] than in other low- and middle-income economies. Governments built on this base by focusing education spending on the lower grades: first, by providing universal primary education, later by increasing the availability of secondary education. Rapid demographic transitions facilitated these efforts by slowing the growth in the number of school-age children and in some cases causing an absolute decline. Declining fertility and rapid economic growth meant that, even when education investment as a share of GDP remained constant, more resources were available per child. Limited public funding of post-secondary education focused on technical skills, and some HPAEs imported educational services on a large scale, particularly in vocationally and technologically sophisticated disciplines. The result of these policies has been a broad, technically inclined human capital base well-suited to rapid economic development.
>
> World Bank, 1993

Although this line of argument is basically correct, aspects of it require correction or qualification.[2] Available data make East Asia look somewhat less different from other regions in terms of educational achievements than the World Bank would have us believe. Looking first at "initial

Table 8.1 Average years of schooling by region, 1960–85 (population age 25+)

Region	Number of countries	1960	1965	1970	1975	1980	1985
Middle East & North Africa	12	1.0	1.2	1.6	2.2	2.8	3.5
Sub-Saharan Africa	21	1.5	1.6	1.9	2.0	2.3	2.7
Latin America & Caribbean	23	3.0	3.2	3.5	3.7	4.0	4.5
East Asia & Pacific	10	2.3	2.8	3.4	3.8	4.4	5.2
South Asia	7	1.3	1.5	1.8	2.2	2.5	2.8
All developing countries	73	1.8	2.0	2.4	2.7	3.1	3.6
OECD	23	6.7	7.0	7.4	7.9	8.7	8.9
Centrally-planned economies	10	6.8	7.3	8.0	8.3	8.8	9.2

Source: Robert J. Barro and Jong-Wha Lee, "International Comparisons of Educational Attainment," *Journal of Monetary Economics* 32 (1993), pp. 383–4.

endowments" of educational capital, East Asia was not the most educated Third World region in 1960; Latin America was (Table 8.1). The average adult (age 25+) in Latin America and the Caribbean had 3.0 years of schooling in 1960, compared to an average of 2.3 years in East Asia and the Pacific. Similarly, 61 percent of adults had not completed primary schooling in East Asia and the Pacific in 1960, compared to only 42 percent in Latin America and the Caribbean. In truth, educational attainments in East Asia and the Pacific in 1960 were not much better than the average for all developing countries. For all developing countries, the average adult had 1.8 years of schooling, while 68 percent of adults had not completed primary school.[3] But it is true that East Asian countries had higher than average enrollment ratios at both the primary and secondary levels in the 1960s for their incomes; in short, the region was preparing to supply its future needs for educated workers.[4]

East Asia was also doing more to build a broad-based educational pyramid, in which near-universal primary-level enrollment was attained before large-scale expansion of secondary and higher education.[5] Enrollment ratios at the primary level in all regions are rapidly converging on something close to 100 percent.[6] At the secondary and tertiary levels inter-regional differences are greater, but again convergence is occurring. By 1992, East Asian countries (not just the high-performing ones) had lower secondary-level enrollment ratios than Middle Eastern countries and lower tertiary-level enrollments than either the Middle East and North Africa or Latin America and the Caribbean (Table 8.2).

Data on central government expenditure on education suggest that East Asian countries, with the possible exception of China, were not spending

Table 8.2 Average gross enrollment ratios by region, 1960, 1980 and 1992 (total enrollment as percent of population in the relevant age range)

Region	Primary			Secondary			Tertiary		
	1960	*1980*	*1992*	*1960*	*1980*	*1992*	*1960*	*1980*	*1992*
Middle East & North Africa	51	81	97	11	42	56	2	10	15
Sub-Saharan Africa	40	85	67	7	15	18	0	1	4
Latin America & Caribbean	88	105	106	14	40	45	3	15	18
East Asia & Pacific	101	116	117	19	36	52	1	4	5
(excluding China)	77	101	108	14	41	43	3	10	13
South Asia	56	74	94	18	26	39	3	7	n.a.
(excluding India)	39	66	67	10	18	25	1	34	
All developing countries	77	97	102	19	34	42	1	6	n.a.

Source: World Bank, *World Development Report*, New York, Oxford University Press for the World Bank, various years. Some averages have been calculated by the author.

Note: The gross enrollment ratio expresses enrollment in a particular level of schooling as a percentage of the total population of children in the age range that normally attends that level of school. It can exceed 100 when significant numbers of under-age or over-age children are enrolled.

Table 8.3 Central government expenditure on education by region, 1980 and 1993

Region	*1980*		*1993*	
	Percentage of government budget	*Percentage of GNP*	*Percentage of government budget*	*Percentage of GNP*
Middle East and North Africa	13.7	4.5	16.4	4.8
Sub-Saharan Africa	15.2	3.7	n.a.	n.a.
Latin America and Caribbean	13.5	2.2	9.7	1.8
East Asia and Pacific	17.3	n.a.	n.a.	n.a.
(excluding China)	12.4	2.4	14.3	2.7
South Asia	3.2	0.5	3.2	0.6
(excluding India)	7.4	1.0	11.4	1.2

Source: World Bank, *World Development Report 1995*, New York, Oxford University Press for the World Bank, 1995, pp. 216–17. Averages compiled by the author.

unusual amounts in 1980 (Table 8.3). East Asia (excluding China) did, however, increase public educational outlays relative to both the total government budget and GNP between 1980 and 1993, while Latin America and Africa retreated during this period.[7] These statistics include only central government expenditure; they exclude spending both by sub-national governments and by individuals. Although expenditure by sub-national governments is not particularly large in East Asia, private spending is very high in some of these countries.[8]

Beyond this, however, as Nancy Birdsall *et al.*, have shown, East Asia's combination of shrinking school-age populations and rapidly rising GNP enabled spending per student to rise steadily, even as public spending remained a constant share of GNP.[9] Moreover, the increased supply of educated people in East Asia caused teachers' salaries to decline (relative to GNP per capita), making it easier to finance education and reduce class size.[10] This contrasts dramatically with Africa, where GNP is stagnant, the school-age population is still growing rapidly, and teachers' salaries are relatively high because people with secondary or tertiary schooling are still in scarce supply.

Birdsall *et al.* suggest that higher primary enrollments are by far the largest single contributor to the difference in economic growth rates between East Asia and other regions between 1960 and 1985. Higher secondary enrollment ratios made smaller contributions (or, in Dani Rodrik's recalculations, none at all).[11] Investment in physical capital ranks second to primary education as an important contributor to higher growth rates in East Asia, according to World Bank calculations.

In short, while education is not a sufficient condition for economic growth to occur, it may be a necessary one.[12] Birdsall *et al.* further argued that an increase in schooling reflects, strictly speaking, only an increase in the *supply* of educated labor.[13] For education to boost growth, they say, *demand* for educated labor must also rise. Macroeconomic, agricultural, and especially export promotion policies in East Asia have been strongly labor-demanding. Their analysis suggests that export of manufactures increases the contribution that a given educational endowment makes to economic growth.[14] In the early stages, this demand is likely to be concentrated on low-skilled labor, but as more sophisticated goods are affected the demand grows for workers with more education. If ever there was a region where development succeeded in raising the demand for educated labor, it is East Asia.[15] There, education contributed to economic growth, both in ways that the econometricians can capture and in ways that they cannot.

This topic is explored through parallel analytical histories of two high-performing East Asian countries: South Korea and Malaysia. The *Miracle* study accepted the model of the "flying geese," according to which East Asian countries followed Japanese leadership and example. After the lead goose (Japan), the next phalanx consisted of the Newly Industrializing

Economies (South Korea, Taiwan, Hong Kong, and Singapore), and the one after that included Thailand, Malaysia, and Indonesia. There are, however, significant differences between the Northeast Asian countries, which resemble Japan in many ways, and those of Southeast Asia, which differ considerably, and do so in ways that make them more like other developing countries in other regions of the world.

EDUCATION AND DEVELOPMENT IN SOUTH KOREA

Scholarship in traditional Korea had high prestige as the means of entry into the civil service; however, the opportunity was open only to members of the aristocratic *yangban* class. After Japan assumed control in 1905, public education strongly favored resident Japanese. Koreans who obtained education were taught Japanese values, social patterns, and language, and were discouraged from striving for high-level jobs. This colonial experience left a residue of bitterness. With independence in 1948 after a brief period of US military rule, six years of free compulsory education and equal opportunity to advance to higher levels were guaranteed for all citizens. New educational goals stressed patriotism and sought to blend traditional values such as the cultivation of harmony in body and spirit with modern ideals such as freedom, rationality, and scientific inquiry. However, the Korean War soon disrupted all aspects of normal life and eventually destroyed nearly three-quarters of all the classrooms. After the war, a new start was made with the help of massive international assistance, mainly American. By the late 1950s, all levels of education were expanding rapidly, but the government's efforts at this time emphasized primary schooling. During the 1950s, about 70 percent of central government expenditure on education was devoted to this level.[16]

South Korea's emergence as a star economic performer is often dated from the *coup d'état* of 1961, which brought General Park Chung Hee to power. Increasingly during the "development decade" of the 1960s, education came to be seen as crucial, as reflected in slogans such as "nation-building through education" and "education for economic development." Enrollments followed a cascading pattern, with the achievement of high enrollment ratios at one level pushing up enrollments at the next higher level. Although the Six-Year Plan for Completion of Compulsory Education (1954–59), which targeted a 96 percent net enrollment ratio,[17] achieved only 80 percent enrollment, strong public demand and a willingness to crowd students into classrooms caused universal primary schooling to be achieved by 1965. Despite packed schools and high pupil–teacher ratios, Korean children achieved basic literacy and numeracy. Literacy classes for adults were also offered from the mid-1950s on. After 1970, crowding in elementary schools began to ease and enrollments declined absolutely under the influence of a sharply falling birth rate.

Universal enrollment in primary school led inevitably to escalating demand for higher levels of schooling. Middle school enrollment rose rapidly through the 1960s and 1970s, peaking at about 2.5 million around 1980. At the high school level, the fastest expansion occurred in the 1970s when the number of students jumped from 590,000 to 2.7 million. Higher education has expanded rapidly since the 1950s. Like secondary enrollments, the number of third-level students grew rapidly during the 1970s (from 201,000 students to 602,000), but it continued to climb in the 1980s with enrollment reaching 1.5 million by 1990. By the early 1990s, South Korea had achieved the widest educational coverage of any developing country. Not only were virtually all primary-age children enrolled, the gross enrollment for high school had reached 90 percent. At the tertiary level, once a sharp peak at the top of the education pyramid, enrollment hit 42 percent of the age group by 1992, a larger share than in most European countries.[18]

Educational policy provided for automatic promotion at the elementary level, permitting all pupils to complete the cycle. In 1968, the entry examination for middle school was abolished. Although a lottery system had to be instituted to allocate limited school capacity, more schools were built. At the elementary level, the pupil–teacher ratio was 69 in 1945 and was still 59 in 1960. It did not fall significantly until the 1970s, and even in 1990 it was 36 : 1, higher than in most other countries. In the middle schools and high schools, initial student–teacher ratios were lower than in elementary ones, but they were forced up during the period of fastest enrollment expansion. That in the middle schools rose from 40 students per teacher in 1960 to 45 in 1980; by 1990, this number had been reduced to 25, closer to international norms. The student–teacher ratio in high schools shot up from 30 to 53 during the 1970s, but by 1990, this ratio was down to 28 through an 82 percent augmentation of the teaching force.

The government was far less enthusiastic about expanding tertiary education. In the early days, there was much concern about graduate employment. Both then and later, Korean governments have worried about the participation of university students in protests, often violent, against government policies. But there was no suppressing the demand for this level of education, so the private sector took up the slack. The number of universities, colleges, and other tertiary-level institutions (teachers' colleges, junior colleges, etc.) soared from 19 in 1945 to 85 in 1960 to 556 by 1990. More than four-fifths of them were private. None the less, many high school graduates cannot obtain admission to a university or college. In 1990, out of more than 900,000 high school graduates who applied (37 percent reapplying after being rejected in previous years), fewer than 200,000 were accepted, an acceptance rate of 22 percent.[19] As in Japan, severe competition for places (and especially in Seoul National University and a few other prestigious institutions) has led to heavy emphasis on examinations and large expenditures on private tutoring.

The Ministry of Education has tried to raise the quality by requiring private universities to maintain science faculties and encouraging reductions in class size as well as faculty development and the hiring of more PhDs.

Many efforts have been made to satisfy the skill needs for development. The greatest achievement of the 1950s and 1960s was the attainment of basic literacy and numeracy by virtually all children and many adults. Literacy classes served the many adults who had missed out on schooling when they were young. During this decade, there was a focus on technical education at the secondary level under the slogan, "one skill for one person." This campaign failed because of the low pay and prestige that blue-collar work still commanded. Parents and teachers preferred to prepare children for better-paid, more prestigious white-collar work, if possible in the professions. By the early 1960s, there was a surplus of college graduates and a shortage of skilled middle-level technicians, and this led to renewed efforts to expand vocational education at the secondary level, on the one hand, and to reduce the number of colleges and universities, on the other. Nevertheless, it proved impossible to prevent the continued expansion of both general secondary schooling and higher education. In the late 1960s, the government bowed to popular demand and decided to increase the promotion rates both from elementary to middle school and from middle to high school. School construction was accelerated to reduce crowding and double-shifting. Admission to middle school became automatic in 1968.

In 1972 an assessment by the Korean Educational Development Institute (KEDI) led to curriculum reform, a new system emphasizing learner-centered instruction, and other changes. Only in 1977, however, was an effort made to relate secondary and tertiary eduction to economic needs. In 1980, technical and trade schools were upgraded to two-year junior colleges in an attempt to improve middle-level skills. A standardized examination was also introduced for university admittance and an attempt was made to prohibit private tutoring except for art and music.

By the 1980s, concern over growing social inequality had become strong as earnings differentials widened; this was reflected in compulsory free middle school education and the expansion of pre-school education and "head-start" programs for rural areas and disadvantaged groups. Educational management was decentralized to local governments. The most recent emphases are twenty-first century concerns such as widespread computer education, "the teacher as a researcher," increased spending on instructional materials, better instruction in basic and advanced science, expansion of research and library facilities in higher education, and closer ties between industry and universities.[20] The government also continues to try to reduce the buoyant demand for higher education by shifting high school enrollment from academic to vocational courses and expanding vocation counseling.

In sum, while government officials from the 1960s on recognized that education could make an important contribution to development, there were competing considerations and the public's interests often differed from those of policy-makers. Especially during the early period, political goals such as national defense and loyalty to the government competed successfully with economic goals in official minds. While the government kept trying to channel more secondary students into vocational schools and to limit the expansion of the universities, students and parents preferred arts education and struggled to climb as far as possible up the educational ladder. That private preferences won is unsurprising given that government has consistently devoted meager resources to education, leaving the private sector to pay most of the bills. Central government spending on education as a percentage of GDP climbed during the 1960s, reaching 3.2 percent by 1972. Thereafter, this percentage was essentially flat at around 3 percent, making South Korea one of the lower government-share proportionate spenders among developing countries. Since the country has consistently been top-rank in economic growth, however, the absolute amount of public spending on education yielded by a low and constant share of GDP has increased continuously and rapidly.

Despite education's relatively low claims on public sector resources, educational outcomes have been among the best.[21] There appear to be two major reasons: (1) there was strong family support for education, including willingness to make substantial financial outlays; and (2) the educational system was efficient. During the 1960s and 1970s, students' families covered approximately two-thirds of educational expenditures, including both in-school and other costs.[22] While comprehensive data are not available for later periods, this proportion clearly remained high. In the late 1980s, the public sector covered 98 percent of in-school costs in elementary schools, but only 59 percent in middle schools, 27 percent in high schools, 17 percent in junior colleges, and 28 percent in colleges and universities.[23] Private tutoring and supplementary instructional materials help children succeed in the heated competition for advancement to higher levels. As elsewhere, this demand is partly explained by the pay and prestige that more highly educated people command, but education-related earnings differentials have been smaller in Korea than in many other countries, and many scholars have cited the influence of Confucian tradition.

Pre-pupil costs have been lower in Korea than in other developing countries at similar levels of income.[24] Large class sizes and intensive use of facilities have helped, as have low relative teacher salaries. These seem to have little effect on student learning, compared to libraries, longer periods of instructional time, more frequent and demanding homework assignments, and more textbooks.[25] The cost-effectiveness of Korean education has been high.

Earlier, income and wealth were unusually equally distributed. This resulted from the general poverty of the society, the redistribution of previously dominant Japanese assets, war losses suffered by the few rich Koreans, and land reforms. As a result, the local elite was small and did not lobby for large public expenditures on secondary and higher education as did their counterparts in many other countries. The export-oriented pattern was employment-creating and supported a relatively egalitarian distribution of income. Later, as the country grew richer and large business conglomerates (*chaebol*) came to dominate the economy, inequalities increased. This accentuated already-present concerns about the effects of education on inequality, particularly at the secondary level, where continued advancement through the system requires increasing spending, especially at the top, where there are sharp perceived differences among educational institutions.

In 1973, the Ministry of Education launched a High School Equalization Policy, which aimed to reduce differences among schools. This was implemented in Seoul and Pusan in 1974 and in 18 other cities by 1981, but it was then halted because of "fiscal and possibly other constraints."[26] Nevertheless, all regions seem to have remarkably similar transition ratios from elementary school on. The traditionally strong bias against girls has been reduced at the secondary level, but the growth of female enrollment in tertiary institutions fell behind after 1970.[27] Nevertheless, it seems likely that distributive inequality remains lower in South Korea than in most other countries and that education contributed to it. At a minimum, universal primary education, near-universal secondary schooling, and massive expansion of higher education ensured that differences in enrollment rates among regions, social classes, and even genders were held in check. In 1980, McGinn *et al.*, characterized Korean education as "general at the bottom of the pyramid, comparatively restrictive at the top."[28] Today, the restrictiveness at the top is greatly reduced, although qualitative differences among institutions remain considerable, at least in popular perception.

Because education-related earnings differentials are relatively small while private spending is larger than usual, estimates of private returns to investment in education have generally yielded relatively low rates of return.[29] This is contrary to the widely shared intuitive (and doubtless correct) view that education has made enormous contributions to development.

EDUCATION AND DEVELOPMENT IN MALAYSIA

While Korea was colonized by Japan, Malaysia's last colonial ruler (after earlier experiences with Portugal and the Netherlands) was Great Britain. The British entered the region in the late eighteenth century and finally established control over all the territories now incorporated in Malaysia in 1909.[30] Malaya became one of the most prosperous colonies after the mid-nineteenth century, occupying an important niche as a producer, first of tin and later of natural rubber grown on plantations and indigenous smallholdings. Following the severe disruptions of the Depression of the 1930s and the Japanese occupation of 1942–45, the economy was rebuilt through measures such as replanting rubber trees, settling poor farmers on previously uncultivated lands, planting oil palm, and opening up the forests to timber harvesting. Industrialization began in the late 1950s and accelerated after measures in the early 1970s to encourage investment in labor-intensive export industries. The economy grew well in the 1970s as industrial growth received strong support from oil and gas discoveries and favorable commodity prices. In the early 1980s, however, prices slumped and a recession ensued. In 1986, policies regarding foreign ownership were liberalized, leading to rapid recovery and a boom in investment and manufacturing growth that has continued. By 1993, it had become possible to predict with some confidence that Malaysia would achieve the official goal, defined in 1991, of becoming a developed economy by 2020.[31]

The development of education, like much else, has been strongly influenced by the multi-ethnic character of the population. In the mid-nineteenth century, the Malay Peninsula was thinly populated by Muslim Malay peoples closely related to those in Sumatra and other parts of the Malay Archipelago. The development of tin mining brought about large-scale immigration from southern China, while the later opening up of rubber plantations led to contract laborers coming from southern India. Migration from both sources continued until 1930, gradually reducing the indigenous Malays to minority status. This process was halted by the Depression and Japanese occupation, but concern among the Malays about being outnumbered and subordinated "in their own country" continued. As a reassurance, Malays were accorded special protections by the 1957 constitution, which foresaw a country in which the Malays would be politically dominant while the Chinese and Indian immigrants would receive citizenship and freedom to pursue their individual economic interests. This formula failed to prevent the outbreak of race riots after the 1969 general election, which led to the introduction in 1971 of the New Economic Policy (NEP). This defined ambitious goals for achieving "racial economic balance" but gave until 1990 for them to be realized.[32] Its objectives included reduction in poverty among all ethnic groups and increased Malay participation in employment within industries and occupational groups in which they were under-represented, and also, more controversially, in the ownership and control of corporate wealth.[33] These goals were to be reached through economic growth; no one was to be deprived of an existing job or business.

In colonial Malaya, most Malays were farmers, and only a small elite was groomed for eventual leadership as members of the civil service. Few were in private business, which was dominated by the Chinese at the small- and medium-scale levels while the British controlled the banks, shipping companies, and the larger-scale plantations and tin mines. Most

Indians were laborers on plantations or in public bodies, although a few were able to enter professions such as medicine and law. These patterns, traces of which persisted in 1970, in large part reflected differences in educational opportunity related largely to region of residence.[34]

Colonial governments in Malaya provided little education. Most of what happened occurred through private rather than public initiative. Rural Malays often provided their sons with Koranic education and their daughters with no education. Only after 1870 was free public schooling in Malay gradually made available in some parts of the Peninsula. Upward social mobility, which required education in English, was actively discouraged, except (after 1905) for the sons of the nobility and a few future teachers. Similarly, Tamil language elementary schools were opened on plantations, but they led to no secondary or higher education. The Chinese community founded its own schools, which taught in Mandarin after the Chinese Revolution of 1911. English-language schooling was available only in urban areas, and most of the enrollment (80 percent in 1938) was Chinese.[35] Higher education had barely begun to develop by World War II.

The approach of independence in the 1950s launched a gradual process of creating a national system of education. The influential Razak Report of 1956 recommended that primary schooling be offered to all children through a common curriculum that would promote national unity and consciousness, even though four separate languages would continue to be used. Around 1960, a 90 percent net primary level enrollment ratio was reached, with the most rapid expansion in the Malay and English streams. The expansion of secondary schooling followed rapidly. Secondary schools (conducted in English and, to a lesser extent, Chinese) continued to be concentrated in urban areas, to charge fees, and to be entered by means of a competitive examination. In 1960, public support was limited to secondary schools teaching in Malay and in English, which remained an official language until 1967. This crippled the Chinese-medium schools and caused English-medium enrollments to boom. Many Malay students had difficulty gaining admittance to lower secondary school, so in 1964 admission to this level (grades 7–9) was made automatic. Meanwhile, upper secondary education and higher education in the form of public colleges and universities were growing. The University of Malaya, the only university in the 1960s, taught primarily in English to a student body that was about 60 percent Chinese and only 20–25 percent Malay.

Shortly after the 1969 riots, the Minister of Education announced that English-medium schools would be converted to Malay one grade at a time, beginning with Standard One in 1970. Chinese- and Tamil-medium schooling could continue at the primary level, but transfer to Malay would be required for lower secondary schooling and a pass in the Malay language would immediately become a condition for admission to upper secondary school. The change in medium of instruction would gradually move through the system, reaching the universities by 1983.

By the early 1970s, enrollment ratios had been substantially equalized among ethnic groups and gaps between the sexes had been reduced considerably. However, large differentials among social classes persisted within all ethnic groups as children from poorer households were frequently forced to drop out of school before completing nine, or in some cases six, years of education.[36]

During the NEP era (1970–90), rapid expansion continued, particularly at the secondary and tertiary levels. By 1992, gross enrollment ratios were 93 percent in primary school, 58 percent at the secondary level, and still only 7 percent for tertiary education. These were not outstanding rates by regional standards.[37] The primary school gross enrollment had not increased since 1975, while the secondary level increased from roughly 40 percent of the age cohort to 60 percent.[38] The NEP concentrated on tertiary education, the level at which the ethnic composition of the future national elite was being determined. Tertiary enrollment rose from 3 percent of the population age 20–24 to 7 percent, a large increase but from a tiny base.

Strong ethnic quotas were established at public institutions of higher education to correct the imbalances. They severely limited the access of Chinese and Indian students. Since, moreover, there was a strong demand for education in English, unavailable in Malaysia from 1980 on,[39] Chinese and Indian parents who could afford to do so sent their children abroad in large numbers. By the late 1970s, Malaysia had become one of the major suppliers of overseas students to the United States, the United Kingdom, and Australia, as large numbers of private students (mostly Chinese) were joined by smaller numbers of officially sponsored students (mostly Malay). The few places provided for non-Malays in local universities tended to be filled by able students from poorer families. Many less able Chinese and Indian children whose families could not afford to send them abroad to advanced countries were compelled to end their schooling, or to study in Taiwan or India for degrees that were not recognized in Malaysia. Although several new universities were opened, capacity grew too slowly to realize the government's plans for expanding the number of *Bumiputera* graduates.[40] Hence the need for large-scale official sponsorship of overseas education. With economic recession in the early 1980s, foreign universities were invited to conduct programs that would lead to overseas degrees, often through two years of training in Malaysia followed by another two years at the university's home campus. Even so, in 1992 there were still about as many Malaysians studying at foreign colleges and universities as at home.[41]

Largely as a result of this massive effort, dramatic changes in the ethnic mix of employment had taken place by 1990. *Bumiputera* were proportionally represented in many industries and occupational groups where they had been severely under-represented in 1970. Proportionality had not yet been achieved on the highest rungs of occupations, but the remaining imbalance was primarily attributable to the time required to obtain the experience for a professional, technical, or managerial position.

In the early 1970s, the government had begun promoting export-oriented assembly industries to soak up unemployed labor and draw on the labor reserves of low-productivity rural labor and women. The main policy instrument was export processing zones, established first in Penang and then elsewhere. The growth of the electronic component and garment industries in particular employed thousands of people, utilizing basic educational skills and benefiting from widespread knowledge of English. By the late 1970s, the available labor supply was beginning to dry up and immigrant workers began to appear. After the recession, these processes resumed; by 1990 there was essentially full employment and more than one million workers immigrated from Indonesia, the Philippines, and even Burma and Bangladesh.[42] Wages began to rise rapidly in the early 1990s.

Between 1970 and 1995 Malaysia underwent a startling transformation. By 1995 Malaysia was a highly industrialized economy with one-quarter of its labor force in manufacturing and a larger share of GDP (33 percent) originating in that sector than was the case in Germany (27 percent).[43] Manufactures accounted for more than 80 percent of gross exports, which in turn exceeded GNP. A large consumer electronics industry and many other new activities had joined the simple assembly industries of the 1970s, which had themselves been transformed by capital investment, rising skills, and imported technology. Unlike South Korea, where corporatist domestic investment led the way, Malaysia has depended heavily on direct investment by multinational corporations.

Between 1970 and 1990, Malaysian educational policy was dominated by affirmative action considerations, especially at the tertiary level. Success in achieving most of the goals of the NEP, plus full employment, led to changes both in economic strategy and in educational policy.[44] The National Development Policy (NDP), which replaced the NEP in 1991, stressed the 2020 target and downplayed ethnic quotas, yet did not forswear *Bumiputera* preferences. The emphasis shifted to using the education and training systems to supply the skills needed to permit the economy to move up-scale to higher levels of technological sophistication and capital intensity. Skill shortages were perceived to be a major obstacle to national objectives, and this encouraged new educational initiatives that would have been unthinkable earlier.

Rates of return to investment in education in Malaysia are not well documented, especially for recent years. Dipak Mazumdar estimated high private rates of return to secondary and higher education in the late 1970s[45] and there have been indications that Malays in particular have received high private rates of return, not least because their education has been heavily subsidized. What has happened to returns as the supply of educated people has expended rapidly since 1980, and the economy has boomed since 1987, remains to be determined.

The 2020 target entails higher levels of industrialization and greater technological sophistication.[46] Accordingly, there is emphasis on scientific and technical education at the secondary and higher levels. In upper secondary school (grades 10–11), efforts are being made to increase the share of students in the science stream, in preference to the arts stream (although the science stream is traditionally preferred by the stronger students, its share in total enrollment has been declining). Similarly, enrollment in scientific and technical faculties is being promoted in the universities. A six-fold increase in the proportion of engineers in the labor force has been targeted. In 1995–96, the policy reserving higher education for the public sector was finally changed, and private universities will now be permitted, although under restrictions. Efforts have also been made to upgrade secondary vocational education, traditionally not very successful in Malaysia (as in many other countries), and incentives for firms to provide occupational training have been strengthened through a Human Resources Development Fund.

A major issue is finance. Compared to low-spending South Korea and to most other developing countries, the Malaysian government has spent heavily on education. In 1993, for example, federal government spending on education was 5.4 percent of GNP, compared to only 3.7 percent for the central government of South Korea.[47] This spending has been directed primarily toward affirmative action objectives and has not necessarily led to superior educational outcomes. Special facilities have been established to help Malays overcome disadvantages.[48] Yet enrollment ratios in Malaysia are not outstanding and student learning is probably not outstanding by international standards.[49] As US experience indicates, affirmative action often involves tradeoffs with academic achievement. While these were understandable under the NEP, the NDP has different objectives. Large and costly increases are now planned in secondary and tertiary enrollments, and these are to be accompanied by increases in scientific, technical, and vocational education, all higher-cost than the arts education that they are intended to replace. Moreover, more Malays are taking part in these more expensive forms of education. Essentially, education for Malays has been regarded as a financial obligation of the state so far, but with larger numbers of them reaching higher levels, this obligation becomes increasingly difficult to support.[50] Educational policymakers are considering such options as permitting private institutions to operate, increasing cost recovery in public universities, and expanding scholarships and student loan programs. Education's already-substantial claim on the government budget might be permitted to increase. It is unlikely, however, that all these measures will suffice to finance the ambitious program of educational expansion. It remains to be seen how a balance will be struck.

CONCLUSION

Although it can be dangerous to regard investment in human resources as a panacea, that education has been important for the economic development of South Korea, Malaysia, and other East Asian countries is not to be doubted. The fact that educational investments failed to boost growth in other regions clearly has something to do with the absence of buoyant demand for educated labor, unlike South Korea and Malaysia.

These two country cases provide no simply answer to countries seeking to design educational systems to support growth. After doing an excellent job of providing all its youth with basic education, South Korea tried to concentrate on creating middle-level skills for industry. Since, however, it was unwilling to commit large public funds, the preferences of the people who were paying much of the bill became important. Korean society valued higher education and eventually was able to force large-scale expansion on a reluctant government. The popularity of higher education in Korea, one not shared in all cultures, despite apparently modest private rates of return, suggests benefits that are not captured in the economists' equations.

Malaysia is contrasting in two important respects. Its economic take-off came a decade later than South Korea's and coincided with the New Economic Policy, a 20-year program of affirmative action. While the government was willing to spend heavily on secondary and higher education, building on a foundation of primary schooling that was not as solid as South Korea's, the main purpose was redistribution, not growth. Only when the New Development Policy replaced the NPE in the early 1990s did growth assume top priority. Like that in South Korea, the Malaysian government has struggled with the problem of supplying technical and scientific skills at the middle and upper levels. Although more willing to expand tertiary education than South Korea, Malaysia has been unable to meet demand because of the affirmative action quotas in public universities and its refusal to permit private universities. That is now changing, with effects that remain to be learned.

South Korea, at $7,660 per capita in 1993 and with an 8.2 average growth rate of per capita income in 1980–93, will clearly meet the World Bank's definition of a high-income economy (about $10,000 per capita) within the new few years. Malaysia, at $3,140 in 1993 and a 3.5 percent average growth rate in 1980–93 will clearly meet the World Bank's definition of a high-income economy (about $10,000 per capita) within the next few years. Malaysia, at $3,140 in 1993 and a 3.5 percent average growth rate in 1980–93 (but a much higher one since 1987), has much farther to go, but its target for 2020 is plausible. Both countries have put the cheap labor phase of development firmly behind them,[51] so the development of marketable, productivity-raising skills will be critical to achieving their economic goals.

NOTES

1 High Performing Asian economies, meaning Japan, South Korea, Taiwan, Hong Kong, Singapore, Thailand, Malaysia, and Indonesia.
2 See Rodrik, 1994.
3 Barro and Lee, 1993. Note that the World Bank quote refers to the eight HPAEs, while the discussion here includes all of East Asia (ten countries in Barro and Lee's data set).
4 World Bank, 1993: 383–4; Birdsall *et al.*, 1995: 481–2.
5 A notable exception is secondary education in Thailand, which has been slow to expand and still enrolls only about one-third of the age cohort, compared to one-fifth enrolled in tertiary education.
6 Except in Sub-Saharan Africa, where backsliding has occurred since 1980, and the Muslim countries of South Asia, where girls remain unenrolled. Enrollment ratios above 100 signify the presence in school of children either older or younger than the normal age range.
7 The African retreat is inferred, since data for many countries are unavailable for 1993.
8 In South Korea, families covered approximately two-thirds of education costs in the 1960s and early 1970s. See McGinn *et al.*, 1980: 15–27.
9 Birdsall *et al.*, 1995: 477–508.
10 Shultz, 1988.
11 World Bank, 1993: 48–55; Rodrik, 1994: 20–1.
12 Pritchett, 1996.
13 Yet if people have to pay a significant part of the cost of schooling, attainments are unlikely to rise unless earnings differentials in the labor market offer a suitable incentive.
14 Birdsall *et al.*, 1995: 483–9.
15 According to calculations made by Sabot, wage employment in South Korea increased at an average annual rate of 18.7 percent between 1970 and 1990. High rates of employment growth were also recorded by Singapore (11.4 percent, 1970–89) and Indonesia (14.4 percent, 1974–8). Although Malaysia is not included in the table, it also experienced high rates of employment growth. Illustrative lower rates for countries in other regions are 1.8 percent for India (1970–89), 7.7 percent for Kenya (1970–90), and 4.3 percent for Venezuela (1970–84) (see Sabot, 1995).
16 The main sources for this section are McGinn *et al.*, 1980 and Adams and Gottlieb, 1993: 158.
17 The net enrollment ratio measures the percentage of children in the normal age range of a particular level of schooling (in this case elementary school) who are actually enrolled. The more familiar gross enrollment ratio compares total enrollment (including children who are either younger or older than normal) with the number of children in the normal age range. While the net enrollment ratio peaks at 100 percent, the gross enrollment ratio for primary schooling in developing countries often exceeds 100 percent.
18 See World Bank, 1995: 216–17.
19 Adams and Gottlieb, 1993: 65–6.
20 Adams and Gottlieb, 1993: 133–7, 140–1.
21 Evidence on the quality of education in Korea is less systematic, but the high productivity of Korean workers and the success of numerous Korean students in the United States suggest that quality is at least acceptable at the bottom of the system and quite good at the top.
22 McGinn *et al.* (1980): 18–27, 155. Private costs of education include: (1) "voluntary" PTA contributions made at all levels and in all types of schools;

(2) school tuition fees applicable to virtually all post-primary education; (3) special tuition fees paid by many parents to coaches who prepared students for standard exams, and (4) other costs, such as books and instructional materials, extra-curricular activity fees and transport costs.

23 Ministry of Education (Republic of Korea), 1989; Adams and Gottlieb, 1993: 168.

24 McGinn *et al.*, 1980: 66–8.

25 Fuller and Clarke, 1994.

26 Adams and Gottlieb, 1993: 174.

27 Adams and Gottlieb, 1993: 173.

28 McGinn *et al.*, 1980: 175.

29 Psacharopoulos, 1985.

30 Establishment of colonies at Penang (1786), Malacca (1795), and Singapore (1819) was eventually followed by "intervention" in the Malay states of the Peninsula, beginning in 1874. By 1895 the Federated Malay States had been formed, grouping four of the most important states. The four northernmost states were ceded by Thailand in 1909, but the Federation of Malaya was not constituted until 1948, following three and a half years of Japanese occupation and postwar controversy over the form the new government would take. Independence was delayed until 1957 by the Communist uprising of 1948–60. In 1963, Malaysia was formed, merging the Federation of Malaya with the British colonies of Singapore, Sarawak, and North Borneo (Sabah). In 1965, Singapore was expelled from the Federation, leaving the present grouping of 13 states, eleven of which are on the Malay Peninsula with the remaining two on the north coast of Borneo.

31 Mahathir, 1991. See also Snodgrass, 1993.

32 Faaland *et al.*, 1990.

33 Around 1970, Malay incomes averaged only half as much as the incomes of non-Malays and Malays controlled only two percent of corporate wealth. Official statements of NEP objectives include the *Second Malaysia Plan 1971–1975, Mid-Term Review of the Second Malaysia Plan,* and the *Third Malaysia Plan 1976–1980.* (See Malaysia, 1971, 1973, 1976.)

34 Disfavored groups included residents of the unfederated states and all rural residents, see Hirschman, 1972.

35 Snodgrass, 1980: 237–60.

36 For example, among urban Malays 88 percent of 15-year-olds from high-status families were still enrolled at age 15, while comparable rates for middle- and low-status families were 54 and 27 percent respectively. For rural Malays, the respective rates were 67, 28 and 14 percent. Similar patterns applied to Chinese and Indian children, see Ministry of Education (Malaysia), 1973.

37 World Bank, 1995: 110–11. Not only South Korea and the other NICs but also Indonesia, Thailand, and the Philippines had higher gross enrollment ratios than Malaysia at the primary and tertiary levels, and the Philippines also had higher enrollment at the secondary level.

38 Based on World Bank, 1980: 110–11.

39 Chinese pleas to be allowed to establish a private university that would teach in English were repeatedly rejected. However, the International Islamic University, founded in 1983, was permitted to use English as a medium to attract an international clientele, although it also enrolled substantial numbers of Malaysians.

40 *Bumiputera* is a term introduced in the 1970s to encompass all the indigenous peoples, i.e. Malays, Malayan aborigines, and the various native groups of Sabah and Sarawak. In practice, however, preferential policies were directed mainly at the Malays (and later other indigenous Islamic groups).

41 While the tertiary enrollment ratio published by the World Bank was seven percent, another six or seven percent of the age cohort (exact statistics are unavailable) were studying abroad. Even at 13–14 percent, however, Malaysia was providing a smaller share of its youth with tertiary education than were South Korea (42 percent), the Philippines (28 percent) or Thailand (19 percent). (The comparison rates include only domestic enrollment, and all these countries have substantial numbers of students overseas.)

42 Exact numbers are not available, see Pillai, 1992.

43 World Bank, 1995 and Ministry of Finance (Malaysia), 1995.

44 Malaysia, 1991: 4–15, Snodgrass, 1995.

45 Mazumdar, 1981.

46 These assumptions underlie the forthcoming *New Industrial Masterplan.* However, as one who worked in Malaysia in 1970 and therefore knows how imperfectly policy-makers at that time foresaw the changes that had occurred by the mid-1990s, the author feels entitled to skepticism about the accuracy of current perceptions regarding the shape of the economy in the year 2020.

47 Calculated from World Bank 1995: 180–1.

48 An example that caused controversy between the government and the World Bank was the junior science colleges operated in rural areas by MARA, a government agency devoted to economic advancement of the *Bumiputera.* These schools, intended to improve preparation in mathematics and scientific subjects, have much higher unit costs than other schools.

49 This is speculative. Malaysia has not participated in international testing programs such as those conducted by the International Association for Educational Assessment.

50 This has been the case even for Malay children from well-off families.

51 One qualification is necessary for Malaysia: much depends on future immigration policy. Continued liberality toward unskilled immigrants would certainly boost the overall growth rate, but it could retard the transition to a higher-wage, higher-productivity labor force that must ultimately take place. Immigration of skilled and professional labor, on the other hand, may be too tightly restricted at present, in view of the severe shortages of some types of highly skilled labor and the bottlenecks that they are creating.

REFERENCES

Adams, Don and Ester E. Gottlieb (1993) *Education and Social Change in Korea,* New York: Garland.

Barro, Robert J. and Jong-Wha Lee (1993) "International Comparisons of Educational Attainment," *Quarterly Journal of Economics* 32: 363–94.

Birdsall, Nancy, David Ross and Richard Sabot (1995) "Inequality and Growth Reconsidered: Lessons from East Asia," *World Bank Economic Review* 9, no. 3 (September): 477–508.

Chai Hon-Chan (1994) *The Development of British Malaya 1896–1909,* London: Oxford University Press.

Faaland, Just, J.R. Parkinson and Rais Saniman (1990) *Growth and Ethnic Inequality: Malaysia's New Economic Policy,* Kuala Lumpur: Dewan Bahasa dan Pustaka in association with Chr. Michelson Institute, Bergen, Norway.

Fuller, Bruce and P. Clarke (1994) "Raising School Effects while Ignoring Culture? Local Conditions and the Influence of Classroom Tools, Rules and Pedagogy." *Journal of Educational Research* 64, no. 1: 1191–57.

Hirschman, Charles (1972) "Educational Patterns in Colonial Malaya," *Comparative Education Review* 16, no. 3 (October): 486–502.

Koh Eng Kiat (1965) "American Educational Policy in the Philippines and the British Policy in Malaya, 1898–1935," *Comparative Education Review* 9, no. 2 (June): 139–46.

Lindauer, David L. and Michael Roemer (1994) *Asia and Africa: Legacies and Opportunities*, San Francisco: ICS Press for International Center for Economic Growth and Harvard Institute for International Development.

McCune, Shannon (1966) *Korea: Land of Broken Calm*, Princeton, NJ: Van Nostrand.

McGinn, Noel, Donald R. Snodgrass, Yung Bong Kim, Shin-Bok Kim and Quee-Young Kim (1980) *Education and Development in South Korea*, Cambridge, MA: Council on East Asian Studies, Harvard University.

Mahathir bin Mohamad (1991) "Malaysia: The Way Forward (Vision 2020)", Kuala Lumpur: National Printing Department.

Malaysia (1971) *Second Malaysia Plan 1971–1975*, Kuala Lumpur: Government Press.

—— (1973) *Mid-Term Review of the Second Malaysia Plan 1971–1975*, Kuala Lumpur: Government Press.

—— *Third Malaysia Plan 1976–1980*, Kuala Lumpur: Government Press.

—— (1991) Sixth Malaysian Plan 1991–1995, Kuala Lumpur: Government Press.

Mazumdar, Dipak (1981) *The Urban Labor Market and Income Distribution: A Study of Malaysia*, New York: Oxford University Press for the World Bank.

Ministry of Education (Republic of Korea) (1989) *Statistical Yearbook of Education 1989*, Seoul: Ministry of Education.

Ministry of Education (Malaysia) (1973) *Laporan Kawatankuasa Pendapat mengenai Pelajaran dan Masyarakat (Lapuran Keciciran)* [Dropout Report], Kuala Lumpur: Government Printing Office.

Ministry of Finance (Malaysia) (1995) *Economic Report 1995–96*, Kuala Lumpur: Government Printing Office.

Pillai, Patrick (1992) "People on the Move: An Overview of Recent Immigration and Migration in Malaysia," ISIS Issue Paper, Kuala Lumpur: Institute of Strategic and International Studies.

Pritchett, Lant (1996) "Where Has All the Education Gone?" Policy Research Workings Paper No. 1581 (March). Washington, DC: World Bank.

Psacharopoulos, George (1985) "Returns to Education: A Further International Update and Implications," *Journal of Human Resources* 20, no. 4: 583–604.

Puthucheary, James J. (1960) *Ownership and Control in the Malayan Economy*, Singapore: Eastern Universities Press.

Rodrik, Dani (1994) "King Kong Meets Godzilla: The World Bank and *The East Asian Miracle*," in *Miracle or Design: Lessons from the East Asian Experience*, Washington, DC: Overseas Development Council.

Sabot, Richard (1995) "Human Capital Accumulation and Development Strategy" paper delivered to United Nations High Level Group on Development Strategy and Management of the Market Economy, Laxenburg, Austria, April 20–22.

Schultz, T. Paul (1988) "Expansion of Public School Expenditures and Enrollments: Intercountry Evidence on the Effects of Income, Prices, and Population Growth," *Economics of Education Review* 7, no. 2: 167–83.

Snodgrass, Donald R. (1980) *Inequality and Economic Development in Malaysia*, Kuala Lumpur: Oxford University Press.

—— (1993) "Malaysia: The Next NIC?" *International Economic Insights* 4, no. 3 (May/June): 8–11.

—— (1995) "Successful Economic Development in a Multi-Ethnic Society: The

Malaysian Case," Development Discussion Paper No. 503, Cambridge, MA: Harvard Institute for International Development, March.

World Bank (1993) *The East Asian Miracle: Economic Growth and Public Policy*, New York: Oxford University Press for the World Bank.

World Bank, *World Development Report*, New York: Oxford University Press for the World Bank, various years.

9 Science and technology policy and its influence on economic development in Taiwan

Otto C.C. Lin

1 INTRODUCTION

In the period since the early 1970s, the Republic of China in Taiwan has made remarkable economic achievements despite formidable difficulties. This success can be attributed to many factors, of which progress in technology has been crucial. Supporting this remarkable progress was an early national commitment in developing science and technology.

The advances in science and technology of Taiwan, and of other East Asian newly emerging economies – Korea, Singapore and Hong Kong – illustrate one of the main themes of this book: the high learning capacity of the peoples in the area with deep Chinese culture. The speed of their technological advances during this period is perhaps the most rapid in history. The various ways in which this was accomplished provide important lessons for developing countries throughout the world.

These countries had what, paradoxically, has come to be seen increasingly as an advantage: a lack of land and raw materials. They were compelled to develop other vehicles to achieve prosperity. Science and technology became a logical choice. Unlike other production factors such as land, minerals or labor, science and technology is an acquired resource. It is markedly different from natural resources in the ability of regeneration and accumulation. Countries with limited natural resources such as Japan, the Netherlands and Switzerland have become prominent economic players owing largely to the motivation to use technology to upgrade the values of their goods and services.

This chapter focuses on the role of science and technology in Taiwan's industrialization, especially in the last two decades. The key question addressed is how Taiwan, under extremely difficult circumstances, was able to use science and technology to achieve economic growth.

2 TAIWAN'S PERFORMANCE: FROM LABOR-INTENSIVE TO TECHNOLOGY-INTENSIVE OUTPUT

Taiwan's industrial growth in this period can be characterized as a "take off". In 1972, the GNP was approximately US$7.9 billion, in current

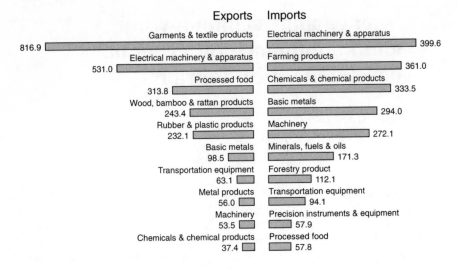

Figure 9.1 Taiwan: major goods traded, 1972 (US$ million)
Source: Monthly Statistics of Exports and Imports, Taiwan Area, R.O.C.

dollars, and the per capita income was $522. In 1992, the GNP had increased to US$210.7 billion, with per capita income reaching a landmark at $10,202. Industrial output had soared from a meager US$2.7 billion to $69.3 billion, and manufacturing industry had become increasingly high-technology. In 1972, for example, the exports of labor-intensive industries, including clothing and textiles, food processing and bamboo and wood products, totaled US$1.4 billion, while exports of machinery and electrical products, as well as plastic products, were only US$760 million. By 1992, the former was US$9 billion and the latter had jumped to US$35 billion. The shift of Taiwan's industries from labor-intensive to technology-intensive can also be shown by the composition of imports and exports during the period 1972–92 (see Figures 9.1 and 9.2).

Industrialization was realized in two parts: the establishment of new hi-tech industries and the upgrading of traditional industries. These reinforced each other and transformed Taiwan's industrial structure.

3 THE EARLY STRATEGIC PROBLEM: HOW TO MAKE RAPID TECHNOLOGICAL PROGRESS

Taiwan, and the other East Asian NICs, had many liabilities and certain assets in the early days, i.e., the period after the stabilization of power by the ruling parties. All four had achieved stability by the mid-1960s – although much earlier for Taiwan. But their liabilities were numerous. One was poverty. The average per capita income of Taiwan was only

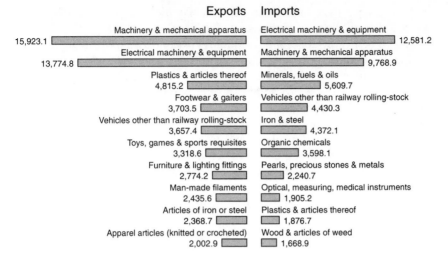

Figure 9.2 Taiwan: major goods traded, 1992 (US$ million)
Source: EURO-ASIA Trade Organization

US$202 in 1964. Its industrial products were far behind those of the United States, Japan, and West Germany in performance, quality, and technical sophistication. Although the workforce was educated by the standards of the developing world, and school enrollments were high, the educational level lagged behind that of the advanced countries. Taiwan also faced competitive pressure from the low labor costs of other emerging countries, such as South Korea, Thailand, and the Philippines. And Taiwan had to import over 90 percent of its raw materials and energy.

Later on, Taiwan suffered an experience the others did not: the breaking of diplomatic relations by the US in 1979. Previously, Taiwan had lived under a US security umbrella. The unilateral action by the Carter Administration made painfully clear to the people of Taiwan that they had to depend on themselves for survival. The sense of crisis precipitated efforts in many sectors; it became an important impetus for the development of science and technology.

All through the 1980s Taiwan had other important assets besides the motivation to survive. The society was peaceful and the government was effective in supplying basic services. Its education effort was rapidly building human resources. The talented young graduates, of all levels, were increasing skills and productivity on the job. Equally important, the Chinese cultural tradition had created a strong work ethic. This disciplined and energetic labor was inexpensive compared with that in the advanced countries. After the end of the military turmoil in the Taiwan Strait in the 1950s, and in the relatively tranquil post-Korean War environment, Taiwan was at peace; it was not involved in the Vietnam conflict. On the Chinese mainland, the Cultural Revolution had distracted the leadership and largely paralyzed the economy. The People's Republic of China was weak in international commerce at that time.

The challenge in upgrading technology was how to move from a condition of little know-how, inadequate institutions (private and public), and an under-supply of trained scientists and engineers. After post-war reconstruction, Taiwan had proceeded through a phase, common in the developing world, of import substitution. Given its low technological level and low-cost labor, it concentrated on such products as textiles, toys, and hand tools, a familiar phase in the international product cycle, in which labor-intensive products migrate among countries driven by relative wages. Taiwan could not live long making such products; their production would migrate sooner or later to Thailand, Indonesia, and beyond. The key problem was how to keep upgrading the technological content of the country's products.

There were four key components to the overall strategy:

- Building human resources;
- Acquiring technology from the more advanced countries;
- Creating science and technology capacities;
- Converting research results to commercial products.

4 BUILDING HUMAN RESOURCES

The human resource is Taiwan's most valued asset. The emphasis on learning and education is a deep tradition of the Chinese culture, perhaps the most profound influence of Confucius' teachings. It is expressed in the Constitution of the Republic of China, Article 164, which proclaims that no less than 15 percent of the national budget shall be appropriated for education, culture and science; and so shall be 20 percent of the provincial budget and 25 percent of the county budget. Article 18 of the Second Constitution Amendment in 1993 has further outlined the roles of science and technology in national developments.

The building of human resources had several elements. The education system is the foundation. Since the early 1960s, strengthening education has been a national priority. By the 1990s, over 99 percent of school-aged children received primary education and over 85 percent of the students advanced to senior high, technical and vocational schools. Today there are almost 5.3 million students, about 25 percent of the total population, enrolled in various levels and types of education (see Table 9.1).

This has resulted in a large pool of well-trained university and technical college graduates. The number of science and engineering degree holders also increased significantly over the years. Table 9.2 shows the achievement of Taiwan and other NICs in training engineers by the late 1980s. Along with Japan, Korea and Singapore, Taiwan had more engineering

Table 9.1 School enrollments in Taiwan: historical

	Percent of school-aged children in elementary schools	Percent of elementary school graduates in junior high schools	Percent of junior high school graduates in senior high schools	Percent of senior high school graduates in schols of higher education
1960–61	95.59	52.24	75.88	43.41
1970–71	98.01	78.59	82.66	41.92
1973–74	98.09	83.71	67.90	37.92
1980–81	99.72	96.14	65.16	44.64
1983–84	99.81	97.95	69.55	46.40
1990–91	99.89	99.77	84.70	48.58
1992–94	99.89	99.53	87.78	65.48

Source: Ministry of Education

Table 9.2 Engineering graduates per 10,000 population (bachelor degree level), 1989

South Korea	6.70
Japan	6.62
Singapore	4.84
Taiwan	4.00
Mexico	3.32
France	2.97
US	2.70
West Germany	1.55
China (1992)	1.30
India	0.34

Source: UNESCO, Statistical Yearbook 1994

graduates than other advanced industrial countries, such as the US and West Germany or developing countries such as China and India.

Recognizing the need to learn from the outside world, the government encouraged students to go abroad for post-graduate studies. Government programs were set up for the selection of candidates and for their financial support. During this period, various scholarships, fellowships, assistantships and loans by major US universities were extremely helpful; most Chinese students could not otherwise have afforded such education. After the 1970s, the number of students going abroad, mostly to the US, increased steadily, and with increased affluence in the 1980s, more of them were supported on family or personal resources. Furthermore, the easing of travel restrictions has enabled students to go out of Taiwan through many non-education channels. After 1990, government statistics covered mainly students supported by government scholarships. This is shown in Figure 9.3, Curve A.

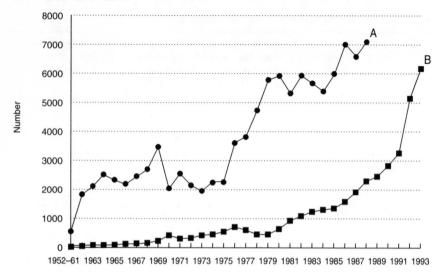

Figure 9.3 Students studying abroad (A) and students returning to Taiwan (B)

After finishing post-graduate studies, many students found jobs abroad, mostly in the US, since opportunity in Taiwan was limited. Not until the late 1980s did the number of returning students start to climb (Figure 9.3, Curve B). The contribution of these expatriate scholars to development in Taiwan is a factor unmatched in most other developing countries. The Industrial Technology Research Institute (ITRI) was an important channel for returning experts because of its early engagement in cutting edge technology. With technology transfers from ITRI to industries, some of these professionals also moved with them. As the development of hi-tech industries progresses, more returning professionals are going directly into industry.

After the mid-1980s, science education, scientific instrumentation, and general research in universities greatly increased. Academic departments involved with national research and development (R&D) projects received additional funding. The government set up a "key research institute" and "center of excellence" at each of the four national universities: National Taiwan, National Tsing-Hua, National Chiao-Tung, and National Cheng-Kung, in the fields of applied mechanics, materials science, information technology, and aviation and aerospace technology, respectively. Technical presentations at international conferences and publications in refereed journals numbered in the thousands every year. In the 1990s, technical contributions from researchers in Taiwan were listed among the top 20 countries in the world (Table 9.3), ahead of Singapore, South Korea, and Hong Kong.

Table 9.3 Scientific publications in several East Asian countries, 1988 and 1993

| | *1988* | | *1993* | |
	Number	*Rank*	*Number*	*Rank*
Sciences				
Taiwan	2001	30	5164	21
South Korea	1683	33	2431	32
Hong Kong	904	38	1632	34
Singapore	653	40	1435	36
Engineering				
Taiwan	918	16	2399	11
South Korea	380	28	1249	16
Hong Kong	153	37	383	33
Singapore	208	36	651	22

Source: Scientific Citation Index and Engineering Index, as reported by National Science Council, Republic of China.

5 ACQUIRING TECHNOLOGY FROM THE MORE ADVANCED COUNTRIES

The industrial structure of Taiwan has a large number of small- and medium-sized firms and a few large ones. In the 1950s over half of Taiwan's industrial output was from the relatively large state-owned firms, but this proportion rapidly shrank with the expansion of the private sector. These small firms are family-run and remarkably nimble in the marketplace. Thus it has a very different structure from that of Korea, with large conglomerate firms, or that of Singapore, with many multinational corporations. Because these small firms find it difficult to be expert in a wide range of technologies, cooperation between them and their suppliers and customers, and between them and government laboratories, is very important for acquiring needed technologies.

Taiwan's technologies originally came mostly from Japan and the US. By establishing linkages backward with materials and technology suppliers, domestic and foreign, and forward with buyers and customers, most of them foreign corporations, the industry slowly developed niches of advantage. This strategy succeeded in developing a strong position in consumer electronics, small machineries, footwear and textiles, bicycles and other sporting goods, and other fast-growing industries.

Progress in information products illustrates the process. Taiwan began by making simple transistor radios and black-and-white TVs in the 1950s and 1960s, moved to color TVs in the 1970s, and in the 1980s to monitors, VCRs, and computers. By the early 1990s, much of Taiwan's consumer goods and other lower technology products had moved on to the Mainland and elsewhere. Although some firms, such as Ta Tung and Acer became large (each achieving sales of over $1 billion by 1990), in 1985 the average electronics firm had only 24 employees, even less than in Hong Kong.

In 1989, there were 3,700 exporters of computers, of whom 650 were manufacturers and most of the rest were companies dealing with parts, components and trades.

In the late 1950s and early 1960s, multinational firms from Japan and the US found Taiwan's good and low-cost labor force to be attractive. Early firms included Sanyo, Sony, Sharp, Matsushita, Philips, NCR, DEC, General Instruments and Texas Instruments. In the long run, the financing they supplied was far less important than the technology they brought. The pattern became one of the Japanese firms forming joint ventures, initially to supply the local market and later exporting, while American firms produced for export to the US. Local firms in Taiwan relied heavily on licensing agreements and improvements by reverse engineering. And, as noted above, many experienced ethnic Chinese from the US and elsewhere brought valuable technical, management and marketing skills.

The government increasingly began to influence this process by, on the one hand, discouraging further labor-intensive investments by foreign multinationals and, on the other, by supporting Taiwan's own science and technology buildup. Increasingly, local firms were making more sophisticated products. In doing so they increased their technology inputs, offered more advanced designs, and moved into higher value-added niche markets. They became innovators. The development of high definition television (HDTV) using digital image processing technology is a good example. The project was formed by a consortium which consisted of ITRI and domestic manufacturers such as Proton, Ta Tung, Sam Po and others. Although the targeted HDTV will not be in the market until 1997–98, its intermediary technologies have contributed to the manufacturing of camcorders, projection TV and other high value consumer electronics.

6 CREATING SCIENCE AND TECHNOLOGY CAPACITIES: ORGANIZATIONS

The science and technology system has three principal parts: basic research, industrial technology, and manufacturing and marketing. Basic research covers all the academic institutes and universities, as well as the Academia Sinica. Funding of the institutes and universities comes from the Ministry of Education and National Science Council. The Ministry of Education funds training of students at all levels and the National Science Council supports basic research.

The organization for applied research and industrial technology is more complicated. Since applied research and technology development requires more funds, closer coordination with government policies is needed. In telecommunication, for example, the Ministry of Communication has direct supervision of the Telecommunication Laboratory. In agriculture, the Council of Agriculture directs the operation of the Taiwan Swine-Raising Experimental Station and various fishery laboratories. In manufacturing, the Ministry of Economic Affairs supports about 14 to 15 non-profit R & D organizations such as ITRI, the Institute for Information Industry (III), the Metal Industry Development Center (MIDC), the Center for Biotechnology Development (CBD) and the China Productivity Center (CPC), etc. The backbone of R&D for the manufacturing industry is formed by ITRI and its 11 research laboratories and centers.

Commercial manufacturing comprises both state-owned and private firms. In the 1970s, government-owned enterprises, such as China Steel, Chinese Petroleum, China Petrochemical Development, Taiwan Power and Taiwan Sugar accounted for about 15 percent of national industrial output. Private enterprises were mostly medium- and small-sized. Among them, Formosa Plastics, Far Eastern and Ta Tung were among the leading groups.

In the early 1970s, little R&D was done. In basic research, researchers were few, funds were limited and projects scattered loosely. A similar situation existed in the manufacturing industry. Overall R&D expenditure by industry was less than 0.4 percent of revenue, far below that in the industrialized countries; in the US it was common for R&D expense to account for 3 percent of sales revenue. By comparison, Taiwan's total R&D spending, public and private in 1985, was about at the level of Digital Equipment Company, which then ranked number ten among US companies for R&D investment. Shown in Table 9.4 is a summary of total R&D expenditure expressed as a percentage of business revenue in Taiwan in the decade 1982–92.

When ITRI was founded in 1973, it had about 450 employees; it grew slowly in the first decade. But, with the inception of major R&D projects, it grew rapidly in the 1980s. By 1994, ITRI had about 6,000 employees, of whom 4,250 had bachelor's or higher degrees, and 560 held doctorates. Its research scope covered semiconductors, computers and communications, opto-electronics, advanced materials, machinery, chemicals, energy and resources, industrial measurements and standards, pollution prevention, industrial safety, and, civil aviation and aerospace.

ITRI is now the largest industry-oriented research institution in Taiwan. It has established technology relations with more than 20,000 manufacturing companies. It receives contracts from the government to develop

Table 9.4 Taiwan: R&D expenditure as a percentage of business revenue

Industry	1982	1986	1990	1992
Total manufacturing industry	0.56	0.47	0.92	0.95
Textile	0.21	0.23	0.52	0.40
Chemicals and Materials	0.38	0.16	0.88	1.08
Plastic Products	1.53	1.07	0.86	1.24
Machinery and Equipment	2.08	0.36	0.44	0.60
Electric and Electronic	1.14	0.86	2.53	2.05
Precision Instrument	0.50	0.48	0.39	1.27

Source: Indicators of Science and Technology, National Science Council, Taiwan

generic technologies and transfer the results to industry in a non-exclusive manner. It conducts short-term R&D projects in cooperation with private sponsoring organizations, generally to improve product performance and process efficiency. Adhering to the principle of fairness and openness, it transfers technology to industrial companies through many channels. It has systems for strategic planning, performance evaluation, human resource development and total quality management. ITRI's mode of operation has become a model for similar organizations in the world.

7 CREATING SCIENCE AND TECHNOLOGY CAPACITIES: SCIENCE AND TECHNOLOGY POLICY

Developing science and technology has been a major national effort since 1980 (see Figure 9.4).

In 1968, the National Advisory Committee on Long-Term Science Development outlined a 12-year "National Science Development Plan" with two key elements. One was strengthening science education and personnel training at college and university levels; the second was outlining the need for research and development in all fields of science and technology.

The First National Science and Technology Conference in 1978 named energy, materials, information technology and industrial automation as national thrust R&D objectives. (It was also at this time that diplomatic relations between Taiwan and the United States were severed; this sent shocks across Taiwan and quickened the pace of science and technology development.)

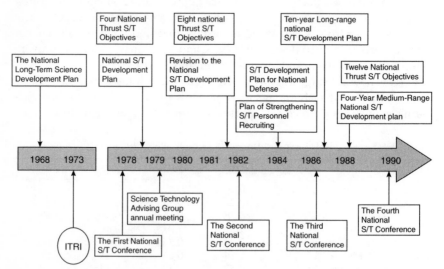

Figure 9.4 Taiwan: schematic diagram showing the key milestones in science and technology development

The second such conference in 1982 raised R&D expenditures from 0.6 percent to 1.0 percent of GNP and added four more objectives: bio-technology, opto-electronics, food science and hepatitis prevention. Together they became known as the "Eight Thrust Objectives of Science and Technology." The "Plan of Strengthening Technical Personnel and Recruiting Senior Professionals" and "Science and Technology Development Plan for National Defense" also took shape. Science and technology development grew rapidly after 1984, with Government spending on R&D, excluding national defense, moving from NT$7.8 billion in 1984, to $32.9 billion in 1993, an average growth rate of 17.3 percent for the decade.

The third conference in 1986 adopted a ten-year plan with a R&D investment target of NT$90 billion for 1996 (making it 2.2 percent of GNP), with 12 percent of the total R&D expenditures earmarked for basic research. It also set a target of 60 percent of all R&D to be performed in the private sector by 1996. It called for the continued development of Hsin-Chu Science Based Industrial Park, as well as of ITRI's hi-tech R&D projects.

In 1988, the government put forth a "Four-Year Medium Range Plan for Science and Technology Development." Natural disaster prevention, synchrotron radiation, ocean science and technology, and environmental science and technology were added to form a total of twelve "Thrust Science and Technology Objectives."

These twelve thrust projects are mixed in nature. Some are designed to strengthen basic national competencies, such as energy and materials. Some are related to timely issues such as hepatitis prevention and environmental and other disaster prevention. Others are related to economic development such as automation, opto-electronics and information technology. Still others are futuristic such as bio-tech, synchrotron radiation, ocean science and technology. Over half of them were targeted to support hi-tech industry.

The fourth conference in 1991 increased the GNP percentage of R&D expenditure, from 1.32 in 1989 to a goal of 2.8 in the year 2002. It also proposed to strengthen the protection of intellectual property rights.

Overall R&D spending by the central government increased significantly between 1984 and 1994 (see Figure 9.5), but in recent years the growth rate has declined. For fiscal year 1993 and 1994, it was 6.6 percent and 4.4 percent, respectively. In 1995, the central government R&D spending saw no real growth.

Many private organizations have also been active. For instance, the Modern Engineering Technology Seminar sponsored by the Chinese Institute of Engineers, held alternatively in Taiwan and in the United States annually, has become an important forum for information and personnel exchanges.

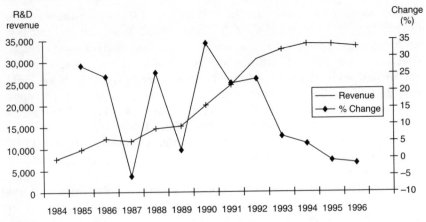

Figure 9.5 Taiwan: government (non-defense) R&D budget, 1984–96
(NT$ million)

8 CONVERTING RESEARCH RESULTS TO COMMERCIAL PRODUCTS: THE GROWTH OF HI-TECH INDUSTRY

The beginning of high-tech industry in Taiwan can be traced back to the 1970s when the China Steel Corporation (CSC), Chinese Petroleum Corporation and China Petrochemicals Development Corporation (CPDC) were part of the Ten National Construction Projects under President Chiang Ching-Kuo. China Steel built its fully integrated production line and became an important factor of the national infrastructure. It now has a 5.5 million-ton per year capacity of carbon steel. CSC has branched out recently to form a joint venture with US partners to make silicon semi-conductors. The naphtha-cracking plants of CPC, along with CPDC's acrylonitrile and terephthalic acid plants, have supported Taiwan's petrol-chemical, plastic, and synthetic fiber industries. The polymers produced by private enterprises such as FPG, China General and Chi Mei are highly regarded in the world market.

Taiwan's participation in the emerging hi-tech industries progressed rapidly after the mid-1980s. There are three major contributing elements.

The establishment of the Hsin-Chu Science Based Industrial Park

This was set up by the National Science Council, under the leadership of Dr S. S. Shu, Chairman of the NSC, in 1978. It started operations in 1983 with about 35 participating companies and has attracted hi-tech companies and seasoned scientists and engineers from overseas. By 1993, the number of companies had reached 150, providing employment for 30,000 and had a total business revenue of NT$130 billion, accounting for 2 percent of

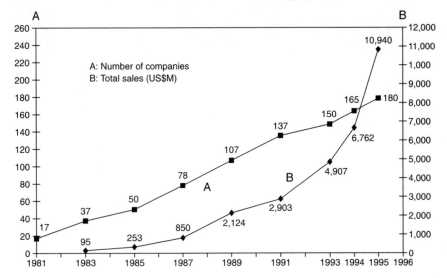

Figure 9.6 Taiwan: growth of the Hsin-Chu Science-Based Industrial Park
Source: SIPA

that year's GNP (see Figure 9.6). Presently its most difficult problem lies in acquiring more land for expansion at the Hsinchu site. Thus, a similar park is being planned in Taiwan.

Technological assistance offered by industrial research institutes and academic circles

Among the eight national thrust projects, five having direct impacts on hi-tech industry were managed by ITRI. Between 1983 and 1994, about 25 percent of the central government's non-defense projects were carried out by ITRI contributing to the commercialization of many hi-tech products. During this period, intellectual property rights and their protection were emphasized. Patents awarded to ITRI, both domestic and international, increased rapidly in the decade (see Figure 9.7).

In 1993, ITRI transferred 209 technologies to 297 companies. Several major companies in the Hsin-Chu Park are ITRI spin-offs, including UMC (1980), TSMC (1987), MIRLE Automation (1988), the Taiwan Mask Co. (1989), as well as the recently-founded VSIC (1994), which will manufacture 16 megabyte DRAM and other sub-micron devices. About 50 percent of the companies in the Park have established technical relationships such as joint R&D, technology transfer, and technical services, with ITRI. Many universities have also taken active parts in various R&D and training projects of the Park's companies and ITRI.

Hi-tech industries have, in recent years, increased their R&D spending to about 5 percent of sales revenue, about 5 times the average R&D

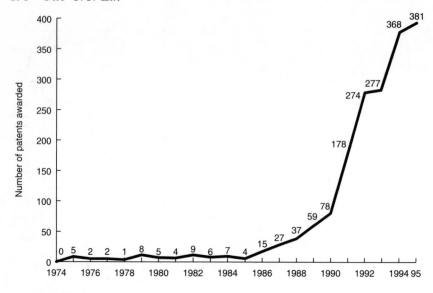

Figure 9.7 Taiwan: patents awarded to ITRI

expenditure of the manufacturing industry. Many companies outside the industrial park, in areas such as specialty alloy, stainless steel, super-fine fiber, optical fiber, light emitting diodes, fine ceramics and bio-tech, are also engaged actively in product R&D as well as in marketing development.

Entrepreneurship

Taking advantage of government support, many start-up companies prospered. Firms found synergies with each other and with R&D institutions, forming an integrated network, as is shown most clearly in the information industry. As a result, Taiwan passed Britain as the world's fifth largest producer of semiconductors by 1993. The total output value of information industry products in 1995 was nearly US$20 billion, making Taiwan one of the top three exporting countries of information products. Personal computers made in Taiwan, for instance those made by Acer, Mitac and Ta Tung, are now competitive with those made in the US and Japan. Many peripheral products have gained top market shares in the world, such as monitors (57 percent), computer mouse devices (70 percent), and printed circuit boards (65 percent). In addition, the satellite communication products of MTI and consumer electronics of TECO and Taiwan Philips are well-received in the world market. The software industry, although smaller than the hardware industry, is also developing rapidly.

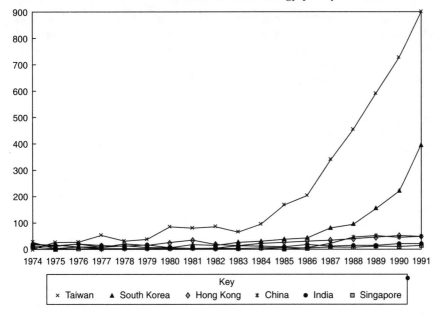

Figure 9.8 US patents granted to inventors from emerging East Asian economies

A measure of technology progress is the number of US patents awarded to Taiwan inventors: individuals, institutions and industries. These have increased rapidly in the last decade and outnumbered all other East Asian emerging economies, including South Korea, Singapore and Hong Kong (see Figure 9.8).

Hi-tech advances have not been limited to electronics and information products, they included such areas as chemicals, speciality materials and machinery. For example, advances in high-speed fiber spinning and ultra-fine fibers technologies have made possible the development of high-value textile products. Structural and functional ceramics have contributed to the development of electro-mechanical end-uses. Another important development was the establishment of the China Engine Corporation in 1995 for manufacturing of a common automotive power train, the result of a R&D consortium consisting of ITRI, four domestic manufacturers – Yue Loong, Chung Hwa, San Yang and Yu Tien – and the British Lotus Engineering Co. This was a pioneering effort in establishing an indigenous automobile engine manufacturing capacity.

While there is uncertainty, Taiwan's hi-tech sector basically has a bright future. In 1990, the Executive Yuan put forward a Six-Year National Development Plan, which identified ten emerging industries and eight key high technologies. These are sectors with demonstrated technology foundation, manufacturing capability and sales experience. If successfully implemented, total sales could reach US$60 billion by the late 1990s, about 25.5 percent of all manufacturing. The added value will be 40 percent, and export value will total US$34 billion, accounting for 32 percent of the total export value of manufacturing. This was the vision for the economic development of Taiwan.

9 CONVERTING RESEARCH RESULTS TO PRODUCT COMMERCIALIZATION: THE UPGRADING OF TRADITIONAL INDUSTRY

Traditional enterprises are the mainstay of manufacturing. They consist mainly of small and medium-sized companies with assets under NT$40 million and account for 98 percent of all manufacturing firms. The number of employees of a typical small company may be as few as ten, or as many as hundreds. In total, they account for approximately 75 percent of Taiwan's industrial employment. Restricted by limited capital and production scale, they are susceptible to such disturbances as labor shortages, skyrocketing land prices, energy shortages, environmental protection laws, labor–management disputes, exchange rate fluctuations, tariff changes, and criminal underworld threats.

The government tries to help these firms through the Bureau of Industrial Development and the Medium and Small Enterprises Service. The state-owned Chiao Tung Bank has established funds for industrial automation and for improving pollution controls. Besides various ITRI laboratories, the China Productivity Center helps to improve management quality. The Metal Industry Development Center, Textile Research Development Center, Food Industry Research and Development Institute, and Bio-tech Development Center, etc., all have responsibilities for technical support.

There are four fundamental elements of industrial technology: design, material, processing, and quality. By improving these elements, the product value and manufacturing cost can be significantly upgraded. One example is the use of carbon fiber composite materials in bicycles and other sports equipment. In the 1970s, the average price of a Taiwan-made bicycle was under US$50. In 1984, ITRI, working with Giant Manufacturing Corporation, started to develop a carbon fiber/epoxy resin system for bicycle frames. After four years, the designed carbon fiber bicycles were introduced and rapidly became popular all over the world market, with a 20–30 fold increase in unit price. Similar composite materials technology has also been used in tennis rackets, golf clubs, and other sporting goods. Taiwan has become the largest exporter in the world of these products.

Other examples of upgraded traditional industries include programmable logic control, precision mould design, optimized materials layout, electroless plating of plastics, chemical process improvement, processing and recycling of metals and plastics, chemical and bio-chemical treatment of waste water, dehumidifying air conditioning, loss control, risk analysis and management, total quality improvement, industrial metrology and ISO-9000 certification, etc.

In 1991, ITRI began to develop the technology for making components and parts for aircraft, with the aim of helping small- and medium-sized companies enter the aviation and aerospace markets. More that 30 enterprises have since received certifications and become qualified suppliers.

In the national quality contests in 1992 and 1993, over 70 percent of the silver and gold prize winners had technical cooperative relations with ITRI. These winners were awarded the "Made-in-Taiwan" and "Mark of excellence" emblems. Thus increasingly more traditional enterprises have recognized the importance of improving technology and have regarded R&D as a crucial means for strengthening competivity in the world market.

10 A REVIEW OF SOCIAL AND CULTURAL FACTORS

Success factors

(A) Rich human resources

Both the quantity and quality of human resources have been crucial. The commitment to achievement through learning and hard work has been at the base of these accomplishments.

(B) Clear and Compelling Missions

All along, it has been evident that Taiwan had to succeed. In the late 1970s, various diplomatic setbacks raised the sense of crisis and provided further motivation for developing science and technology for national survival.

(C) Good Organizational Structure

The R&D establishment supporting the industrial growth has operated satisfactorily. Each R&D organization has largely focused on a defined area of responsibility in basic research, applied research, or commercial manufacturing. A small but healthy overlap among institutions provides channels of communication and creates a good competitive spirit. The role each plays is also subject to adjustment at different stages of industrial growth and technological development.

(D) Delivering on Key Projects

The eight thrust science and technology projects have set specific goals, with good market orientations, and have been analyzed for economic feasibilities. And most have been well managed. In the early stages the government was aggressive in providing the needed resources. A case in point is information technology. Since the early 1980s, about 45 percent of the government R&D expenditure has been dedicated to electronics and information-related projects. This has helped in nurturing technology, cultivating personnel and building infrastructure. The results as shown by the phenomenal growth of the information industries in Taiwan, were impressive. Recently, the introduction of more thrust projects has diluted national focus and distorted resource allocation and project management. Since 1995, R&D expenditure from the Central Government has declined and development has suffered. It is worth noting that most advanced countries have continuously budgeted 2–3 percent of GNP as R&D expenditure over several decades. Consistency and perseverance in R&D investment is very important for long-term results.

(E) Technology Diffusion

Diffusion of the technology is as important as its development. There are numerous ways to do this, including direct technology transfer, technical consulting, technical services, cooperative R&D, personnel training, strategic alliances, seminars and exhibits, and spin-off companies. As an example, ITRI makes several hundred technological transfers yearly (see Table 9.5).

(F) Cooperation among Enterprises

Since the 1970s, Taiwan's industry has accumulated much marketing and management experiences. Firms have gradually built up foreign distribution and sales channels, and, up- and down-stream cooperation. Supply networks have formed, especially in electronics-related industries. When a new technology is developed by a research organization, the business community can readily follow up by manufacturing the product and marketing it worldwide.

Table 9.5 Taiwan: technology diffusion of ITRI

		1992	*1995*
Technology transfers	Projects	143	280
	Companies	262	418
Contracted research/joint R&D	Cases	411	1,004
Conferences and Exhibitions	Sessions	643	880
Patents approved	Cases	274	368
Seminars/workshops/technical training programs	Attendees	40,150	59,492
	Cases	37,141	50,944
Technology services	Companies	21,943	27,061

(G) Establishing the Hsin-Chu Science Based Industrial Park

The Park had remarkable successes in nurturing hi-tech start-up companies.

(H) Professionalism of Entrepreneurs and Researchers

Taiwan's industries have encountered severe pressure in natural resources, technical capacities, environmental restrictions, and foreign competition, but entrepreneurs have carried on business successfully, opened up new markets and have created new lines of business. Researchers in Taiwan, often somewhat isolated due to adverse political circumstances in the scientific community worldwide, have maintained high professionalism and dedication. This has resulted in a gradual narrowing of the gap between Taiwan and advanced countries in many fields of science and technology.

(2) Negative factors

In the 1990s, Taiwan's political and social environment has seen major changes, some of which have been negative for science and technology development.

(A) Resistance from environmental activists

Earlier, economic growth and employment opportunities were regarded as high priority. Because environmental protection and industrial safety issues were not adequately addressed, heavy pollution and industrial hazards have created adverse public reactions. The skepticism and caution of environmental activists today are, by and large, justifiable. But constructive criticism should not be confused with negative resistance and misused with political motives. The ten-year delay for the construction of the fourth nuclear power station of TPC is a classic case.

(B) Weakening of Government Functions

Changes in the political and social environment have taken their toll on policy priorities and governmental efficiency. Land profiteering, traffic jams, labor shortages, illegal underground influence, and erosion of public powers have confronted the business community. A deterioration of the infrastructure, in both hardware and software, has surfaced. As a result, the momentum of rapid industrial development has slowed. The commitment of the government to science and technology has been hurt.

(C) Excessive Speculation of the Stock Market

A properly functioning stock market increases the efficiency of an economy by bringing together investors and entrepreneurs. In recent years, however, the stock market in Taiwan has seen excessive speculative activity. This has created undue tensions, heightened risks and uncertainties and has dampened the entrepreneurism of industrialists.

(D) Disorderly Outflow of Businesses

Recently, owing to the changes of the business environment, many manufacturers have reacted by moving investments abroad. Under normal circumstances, business moves offshore to lower manufacturing cost or to better serve the marketplace. This type of globalization is appropriate. However, if Taiwan's firms fail to upgrade their technical capability as they globalize, they are likely to have troubles at both ends.

(E) Outdated Regulations for Science and Technology

There have been alarming signals that some government agencies were losing efficiency and policy focus. The Legislature, on the other hand, was often paralyzed by excessive politicking. Many laws and codes have failed to keep pace with the advancements of science and technology and the impacts they have shown on the society at large. In the hands of bureaucrats who would insist on enforcing outdated regulations, the consequences can be grave with innovation smothered. The Fourth National Science-Technology Conference in 1990 resolved to submit draft legislation to help science and technology; however, some agencies fumbled and stumbled on actions.

11 CONCLUDING REMARKS

The rise to international prominence of Taiwan in economic development from the early 1970s is a remarkable story. Many cultural, social and organizational factors have contributed. Technologically, the Taiwan story illustrates the progress from a low level of skills through multiple paths of learning to high achievements. Two components have been key: the development of industrial technology and the nurturing of the business environment, both bolstered by an increasingly competent scientific and technological establishment.

Industrial technology is the bridge connecting scientific research to product commercialization. It consists of many linkages: applied research, product development, process development, technology diffusion and pilot trials. Strengthening these components is the responsibility of the R&D establishment.

Creating a favorable environment is the responsibility of the government. This includes a system of laws, tax and monetary measures, the supply of land, labor, energy and transportation, rational environmental protection regulations, work safety rules and a safe and orderly society. It is understandably difficult to achieve complete control of these components.

In Taiwan, after an initial period of import substitution, the government adopted a strategy of acquiring technology from foreign sources followed by building domestic competencies. Government R&D policy bet on certain broad sectors, but much of the implementation was left to professionals, technocrats and the private sector. The government created ITRI and the Hsin-Chu Science-Based Industrial Park complex, as a mini-environment, to nurture hi-tech industries. As the start-ups and the spin-offs grew, they were encouraged to move and to multiply outside the fence; hopefully, a maxi-environment conducive to the growth of high-tech business can be generated throughout. This approach has proven successful and has served as a model throughout the Asia/Pacific region. However, there is no guarantee of success if the ingredients are not adjusted for time and place. It should be noted that success brings changes in the environment which, in turn, require changes in future actions.

In the national comparisons conducted by the International Management Development Institute/World Economic Forum (IMD/WEF), Taiwan has been ranked high since the turn of the 1990s, with science and technology recognized as a competitive strength. Among the emerging Asian economies, Taiwan and Singapore have alternated in being number 1 in science and technology in the study. For 1995, Taiwan was ranked number 5 in science and technology worldwide in the IMD/WEF competitiveness report. Although the policy and practices of the NIC East Asian economies – South Korea, China, Hong Kong, Taiwan, and Singapore – in science and technology have differed, all have succeeded in varying degrees. Overall, the ability to synchronize business, government, and technology circles will continue to be the key to reaching national goals.

ACKNOWLEDGMENTS

In the course of preparing this chapter, I received valuable information, references, and suggestions from Mr Hsu Chi-sheng and Ms Hou Yu-chen of the Industrial Technology Research Institute. During the final stages of preparation, Mr George Wilson, Ms Nancy Wong and especially, Ms Betty Hsieh have offered valuable assistance in finalizing the manuscript. I extend my sincere thanks to them.

REFERENCES

Chinese-language sources

Council for Economic Planning and Development, *Summary of the Income Statistics of the Taiwan Region*, Taipei, 1992.

Hsiao F.S., *Industrial Policy and Industrial Developments in R.O.C.*, Far Eastern Economics Research Publisher, Taipei, 1994.

Industrial Technology Research Institute, *A Synopsis of Twenty Years' Research and Development at ITRI*, 1993.

Industrial Technology Research Institute, *1993 Annual Report*, 1994.

Lin, Otto C.C., *Twelve Fleeting Years of R&D*, The Central Daily News, Taipei, April 18, 1994.

Lin, Otto C.C., in *The Taiwan Experience: Past and Future*, Kao and Lee, eds, Chapter 7, Commonwealth Publishing Co., Taipei, 1995.

Ministry of Economic Affairs, *Synopsis of the Industrial Science and Technology Development of R.O.C.*, 1992.

National Science Council, *Science and Technology Development Yearbook of the Republic of China*, Taipei, 1992.

National Science Council, *Guidelines of Scientific and Technological Statistics*, Taipei, 1993.

English-language sources

Hobday, M., *Innovation in East Asia: The Challenge to Japan*, Brookfield, Vt, Edward Elgar, 1995.

IMD/DEF, World Competitiveness Reports, 1992–95.

Lin, Otto C.C., in *Development and Transfer of Industrial Technology*, in Lin, Shih and Yang, eds, *Advances in Industrial Engineering*, vol. 20, Elsevier Science, 1994.

UNESCO, Statistical Yearbook 1994, UNESCO, 1994.

US National Science Foundation Report No. 95–309, 1995.

Part III

Growth with equality

The East Asians have had the least inequality in incomes of any developing region. The full significance of this observation has only become evident in recent decades. It is that societies that share the fruits of growth systematically do better than those that do not. However, there is an important qualification: it is that relative equality be brought about through the wide distribution of opportunities and not through redistribution of income and wealth. The former is the course followed in this region.

10 Poverty reduction in Indonesia

Dipak Dasgupta[1]

> Poverty is man's most powerful and massive affliction. It is the pro-
> genitor of much further pain – from hunger and disease on to civil
> conflict and war. ... There are two broad lines of action ... The first
> is to combat accommodation. It is by universal education – literacy and
> its employment – that individuals gain access to the world outside the
> culture of poverty and its controlling equilibrium. The second is to facil-
> itate that escape ... Economic development consists in enlarging the
> opportunity ... to escape the equilibrium and culture of poverty.
>
> (Galbraith, 1979)

A. INTRODUCTION

During the past two decades or so (1970–93), the proportion of the population in Indonesia with expenditures below the official poverty line is
estimated by the national statistical agency (Biro Pusat Statistik – BPS)
to have fallen from about 60 percent to about 14 percent, and the absolute
numbers of poor from about 67 million to about 24 million. This is an
extraordinary achievement.

The BPS uses a minimum daily caloric intake of 2,100 calories (and
a scaling-up of food expenditures to include non-food expenditures) as a
cut-off for estimating poverty-incidence. The 2,100 calorie intake is
derived from the Recommended Daily Dietary Intake of the 1978
Workshop on Food and Nutrition. This is reasonably close to the FAO
norm of a minimum of 2,150 calories per person per day. Other studies
(Sayogyo, 1975) have used a minimum amount of consumption equivalent to 25 kg of rice per person per month – which also yields poverty
lines similar to that derived from a caloric approach. The estimation
of poverty from different approaches is, however, less sensitive to these
kinds of cut-offs, than to the choice of appropriate prices (since prices of
rice or other essential consumer items vary greatly between rural and
urban areas, and between different provinces) and to the measurement
of essential non-food expenditures (especially between urban and rural
areas).

The official poverty-lines in Indonesia are low. But there can be little doubt that poverty has fallen sharply: "All the available studies (on the extensive literature on poverty in Indonesia) show a decline in poverty at the national level ... whatever the poverty line used and whatever the means adopted to adjust it for inflation".[2] This progress is supported by other evidence: gains in life expectancy, nutrition, health and other social indicators as well as accounts of improving social and economic conditions.

What factors led to the reduction of poverty in Indonesia? In Section B of this paper, we first describe the transition from mass to increasingly localized poverty. We then analyze the factors that contributed to this change. In Section C, we discuss how broadly-based economic growth was a decisive factor. In Section D, we analyze the roles of labor-demanding growth, strengthening of rural–urban links, and labor-migration in pulling people out of poverty. In Section E, we analyze the importance of public investment and human capital gains in both enhancing overall economic growth, and reducing poverty. The concluding section, Section F, conjectures on the social basis for equity-enhancing public policies in Indonesia and possible connections to a similar pattern throughout East Asia.

B. THE TRANSITION

Java

In the 1960s, much of rural Java (over 67 percent of the population) was desperately poor.[3] In the words of one demographer, it was "asphyxiating for want of land" (with some 40 percent of all farm households completely landless); in the words of another, to the extent that fertility rates were starting to fall, it reflected a feeling among the poor that "they no longer wished to bring another beggar into the world."[4] Rice was a staple food only for the relatively well-off, while the poor ate maize and cassava for much of the year.[5] A regional survey of the then predominantly rural Yogyakarta district, where the poverty incidence was among the highest in Indonesia, found the prospects "rather disheartening."[6]

In urban areas, the situation was only slightly better. About 56 percent of the urban population were poor. There were many temporary migrants from rural areas, their principal sources of earnings being daily labor, scavenging, *becak* (a trishaw, three-wheeled bicycle) driving, and petty trading. Groups of people often shared a room of no more than six square meters, with no sewerage, water, or lighting, and working 12 hours a day for 6 or 7 days a week.[7] More permanent poor city dwellers were no better-off, living on illegally situated, easily flooded land, and often working in illegal petty trading subject to risks of confiscation by municipal authorities.

Whilst that may still apply to the still substantial numbers of poor, the overall situation has changed dramatically – marked by the transition from mass to localized poverty. In rural Java today, although incomes remain low, there is a shortage of agricultural workers, unemployment of land-less people is not a serious problem, and rice is a cheap staple for virtually all.[8] Rural poverty has fallen to about 24 percent. In the cities, the poverty incidence has fallen to about 12 percent. Unskilled workers can find jobs relatively easily, such as in the booming construction industry which pays daily wages that are higher than the equivalent for public school-teachers, most poor urban settlements (*kampungs*) now have some sewers, drainage and electricity, with water served by vendors and stand-pipes; petty urban trading faces lower risks from municipal authorities, and incomes of the bottom 20 percent of urban households are at least twice that of rural households. These changes are reflected in the declining trends in poverty shown in Figures 10.1 and 10.2 below.

Changes in the Outer Islands

In the Outer Islands, the starting levels of poverty were much less severe than on Java. The main reasons were the lower density of population, less than 80 persons per square kilometer, about one-twentieth of that in Java, and a surplus in agricultural production in many of the major populated provinces – e.g., North, South and West Sumatra, and North and South

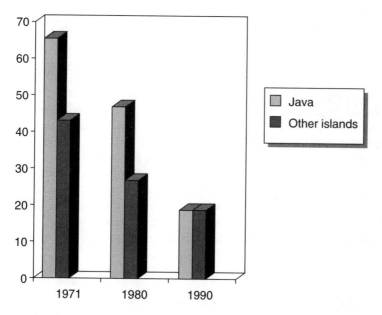

Figure 10.1 Indonesia: trends in poverty, 1971–90 (percentage of population classified as poor)
Source: BPS, World Bank, 1994

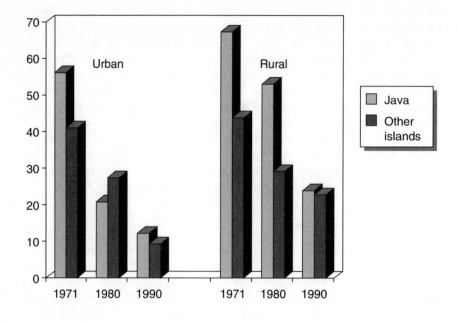

Figure 10.2 Indonesia: trends in poverty, by urban and rural regions
(percentage of population classified as poor)
Source: BPS, World Bank, 1994

Sulawesi. Smallholders had relatively large (over one hectare) land holdings, and cash crop cultivation was well-developed. Still, rural poverty was
significant, at over 40 percent in 1970. During the decade of the 1970s, it
fell greatly; by 1980 overall poverty in the Outer Islands had fallen to
about 28 percent, about one-half that in Java.

In the 1980s, however, the rate of decline in poverty in the Outer Islands
appears to have slowed relative to Java. Growth in Java was in manufacturing and services; this was less true in the Outer Islands. Poverty in
parts of the remote, resource-poor Eastern Islands was especially deep-
seated. Nevertheless, poverty in the Outer Islands continued to fall, to
less than 20 percent by 1990, a level now about the same as on Java (and
much lower than that in most developing countries).

How did 40 million poor people manage to escape acute poverty within
a generation? We discuss three principal reasons: broadly-based economic
growth, growth in jobs, and human capital gains.

Table 10.1   Indonesia: GDP growth by sector, 1975–95 (percent per annum)

	Agriculture	Manufacturing	Services	Total
1975–85	4.6	11.0	8.4	6.1
1985–95	3.2	12.5	10.0	8.0

Source: BPS data and own estimates
Note: Agriculture excludes forestry; manufacturing refers to non-oil manufacturing; services include power and utilities.

C. THE IMPORTANCE OF BROADLY-BASED ECONOMIC GROWTH

During the past two decades, Indonesia's economic growth averaged over 6 percent per annum (Table 10.1), and over 4 percent per annum per capita. More importantly, this growth was also broadly-based, with an improvement in living standards for all. Three factors were important:

- First, the Government placed consistent emphasis on the agricultural sector, on which the livelihood of the greatest number of people, especially the poor depended.
- Second, there was a marked shift to outward-oriented, export-led industrialization after the mid-1980s (after a crisis caused by a fall in oil revenues); hence a more labor-intensive path of industrialization.
- Third, these processes multiplied service-sector jobs, in non-farm activities, and in urban trade, construction, finances and other services.

Agriculture and poverty reduction

Much of the early success in poverty reduction came from improving agriculture. Between 1971–83, the average annual production of rice, the most important crop, increased by 5.3 percent per annum, nearly three times as fast as population growth. This was a decisive break from the past (Table 10.2). The effects were improved rural incomes, employment and

Table 10.2 Indonesia: production, imports and per capita rice consumption, 1956–84

	Average annual Level production (mmt)*	Imports (mmt)	Per capita consumption (kgs)	% increase in production
1955–60	8.3	0.8	93	–
1961–65	9.8	0.9	97	17
1966–70	11.6	0.6	99	19
1971–75	14.4	0.9	110	19
1976–80	17.5	1.8	122	21
1980–84	23.5	0.6	142	35

Source: L. Mears, 1984, "Rice and food self-sufficiency in Indonesia," *Bulletin of Indonesian Economic Studies.*
Note: *million metric tonnes

Table 10.3 Indonesia: apparent per capita food consumption, 1968–88 (kg/year)

	Rice	Maize	Wheat	Cassava	Sweet potatoes	Soybeans	Peanuts	Fruit	Vegetable	Fish	Meat	Calories
1968–70	99.7	20.0	3.4	70.1	18.4	3.3	2.1	26.2	16.7	10.0	3.4	1947
1978–80	122.4	23.4	6.5	63.3	13.6	4.8	2.9	27.1	15.6	11.3	3.5	2341
1986–88	141.7	29.8	9.8	54.3	11.3	7.4	3.0	34.1	21.4	14.1	5.8	2675
Percentage increase	42.1	49.0	188.2	-22.5	-38.6	124.3	42.8	30.1	28.1	41.0	70.6	37.4

Notes

Daily Calorie Supply Index (1965 = 100) 1990

- Indonesia 149
- High Human Development Countries 115
- Medium Human Development Countries 130
- Low Human Development Countries 110
- All Developing Countries 119

Source: FAO AgroStat, 1992; and UNDP, *Human Development Report*, 1993

Table 10.4 Indonesia: trends in food consumption by different income groups, 1965–90 (per capita kg/month)

Percentage of population	Rice			Vegetables			Fish			Meat		
	1965	1984	1990	1965	1984	1990	1965	1984	1990	1965	1984	1990
Bottom 15%	0.5	6.1	7.8	0.36	2.9	3.5	0.03	0.4	0.5	0.01	0.02	0.03
Next 15%	1.0	8.2	9.5	0.43	3.6	4.6	0.05	0.6	0.7	0.01	0.04	0.06
Next 30%	1.9	9.5	10.5	0.5	4.9	6.1	0.09	1.0	1.2	0.02	0.08	0.14
Next 40%	2.8	10.9	10.8	0.65	8.5	9.5	0.25	2.1	2.1	0.06	0.5	0.6
Ratio: bottom 15%/top 40%	0.17	0.56	0.72	0.55	0.34	0.37	0.12	0.19	0.24	0.16	0.04	0.05

Source: SUSENAS

Note: Derived by using average national prices; since lower income-groups will be expected to buy lower-priced food items, the differential between average consumption by income-classes is expected to be narrower than shown in the table.

consumption, country-wide. In the relatively land-abundant Outer Islands, an added impetus came from rapid growth in high-value tree-crops production, which increased by over 6 percent per annum. In Java, where nearly 40 percent of the rural population were landless and where typical landholdings were small (0.25 hectares), the effects of agricultural growth on rural poverty were less pronounced, but still sizeable. Multiple cropping and increased yields raised labor demand. Rice shortages were eliminated, and with improving real wages (relative to the price of rice), the most basic problem of enough income to buy food was addressed.

Indonesia registered the highest increase in apparent per capita food consumption among comparative countries between 1968–88 (Table 10.3). As the rich have low income-elasticities for food, most consumption gains were by the lowest-income groups, especially for basic staples such as rice (Table 10.4).

Policies

Achieving rice self-sufficiency was a key policy aim of the government of one of the world's most densely populated countries (one with endemic food shortages). In the late 1960s, recourse to large-scale rice imports successfully stabilized rice prices. Subsequently, the combination of the rice-intensification programs (e.g., the BIMAS and INMAS programs), the rapid spread of irrigation, the subsidization of key inputs (e.g., fertilizers, seeds, credit), and the spread of high-yielding varieties ensured success. Development spending emphasized agriculture, including irrigation rehabilitation and development. The oil-price booms (in 1973 and 1978) allowed massive increases in agriculture spending and there was a strong political commitment that encouraged innovation in the delivery of services. A notable policy success was avoiding the "Dutch disease" problem (in sharp contrast to other oil-exporting countries) by keeping the exchange rate competitive and protecting agriculture's terms of trade – as evidenced by the 50 percent devaluation in 1978 even though international reserves were at record levels and there were no compelling balance of payments reasons for a devaluation.

Two questions related to the agricultural success remained: what was the relative gain to the poor and what role would agriculture play in the future? On the first question, many commentators at the time were uncertain whether the poor would gain as much as the non-poor, i.e., the income-distribution might worsen in favor of the larger/irrigated landowners and the urban middle-classes, and against landless labor. These doubts were misplaced.[9] Labor demand grew sharply, with high labor-intensities, high rates of female labor use, and a high share of hired labor, even on small plots.[10] The introduction of high-yield varieties and irrigation caused the demand for hired labor to grow faster than total labor supply on Java (as in virtually all other rice economies throughout Asia); this produced a rapid growth in real wages.[11] The gini-coefficients of expenditure distribution improved in rural areas.[12]

On the second question, some commentators at the time were agnostic that a strategy focused on increasing rice and agricultural production could achieve much poverty alleviation (especially if the oil windfall dried up) without greater redistribution, including land reforms.[13] However, given the already very small size of landholdings, and the large number of landless on Java (as well as the political difficulty in redistribution), the gains from land redistribution would have been small. As we shall see below, the biggest gains in poverty reduction in the 1980s were to come, not from agriculture and not from redistributive policies, but from broadly-based growth and human capital gains.

Shift to labor-intensive industrial growth

In the late 1980s, agricultural growth in Indonesia slowed to about 3 percent per annum; agricultural incomes were also hit by the slump in international prices of many commodities. In the Outer Islands, this was a factor in the slowdown in poverty reduction. On Java, a different process started as reforms led to dramatic growth in labor-intensive export industries. Manufacturing output growth accelerated to over 12 percent per annum, while manufacturing employment increased by over 7 percent per annum. Nearly 80 percent of manufacturing value-added originated in Java. There was a large increased in non-agricultural employment and incomes and a corresponding fall in poverty.

Given the historical background, this was a large and difficult shift in strategy. At independence in 1948, the Indonesian economy was characterized by large colonial enterprises. These were then nationalized; combined with a highly interventionist state, a very regulated and protected, inward-looking, state-dominated economy resulted. The New Order Government initially promoted an outward oriented economy in the late 1960s; then, the oil-boom of 1973–83 brought a return to heavy reliance on public investment and import and investment restrictions. The incentive structure became biased towards supplying the domestic market, resulting in an uncompetitive industrial sector and economy, almost wholly dependent on oil and a few primary commodities for export earnings and state revenues.

These problems were brought into sharp focus when external shocks hit the economy starting in 1983. A declining oil price drastically reduced both export earnings and budget revenues. The Government responded with a wide-ranging adjustment program, reforms that have been documented elsewhere.[14] The main elements included: (a) two large devaluations, in 1983 and again in 1986; (b) successive trade reform deregulation packages after 1985, dismantling a number of non-tariff barriers to imports and reducing the levels and dispersion of tariffs; (c) reform of the export

Table 10.5 Indonesia: the shift to outward-oriented industrialization

Non-oil export growth (% p.a.)		Share of non-oil exports (%)		Share of non-oil exports in GDP (%)		Non-oil GDP growth (%)	
1975–83	1983–93	1983	1993	1983	1993	1973–83	1983–93
9.5	25.0	23.0	71.5	7.5	20.0	6.5	8.7

Source: BPS

regime, including establishing duty-exemption and drawback facilities, and deregulating customs, ports and shipping; (d) reforms and deregulating investment restrictions, opening virtually all sectors to private investment and competition, eliminating the investment licensing framework, and removing most barriers to foreign direct investment; and (e) liberalizing the financial sector, including market-determined interest rates, entry and expansion of private banks and non-bank financial institutions, and rapid growth in capital-market activities.

Most important was altering incentives away from inefficient import-substitution to outward-oriented, export-led industrialization.[15] After several years of stagnation in the early 1980s, private investment, both domestic and foreign, grew rapidly, especially after 1988. Non-oil exports grew from only $5.9 billion in 1985, to $26.6 billion 1993. Growth in non-oil exports accelerated (to about 25 percent per annum), the share of non-oil exports increased from less than one-quarter to nearly three-quarters of total export earnings, non-oil exports in GDP increased nearly three times (to a level comparable to the East Asian NICs). In response, non-oil GDP growth accelerated (Table 10.5).

Labor-intensive manufacturing grew fastest, including garments and textiles, plywood and furniture, footwear, handicrafts, processed food and fisheries, and electrical products. The manufacturing sector changed, with a higher share of output in products based on the relatively abundant factor – unskilled labor. The number of jobs created in new sub-sectors in manufacturing outpaced those leaving agriculture.

Acceleration in services sector growth

The earlier agricultural and manufacturing growth had both direct and indirect impacts on the service sector. The direct effect was that trade, transport and other services activities associated with growth in agriculture and industry increased by at least the same high pace as these production sectors. Liberalization provided an additional impetus. For example, as the number of activities of private banks, listed companies, stock market capitalization and market volumes grew manifold, the number of jobs created in the financial sector also grew phenomenally. The indirect impact was that growing incomes and earnings provided strong consumption demand for services – e.g., in retail trade, housing and construction. The construction sector grew at an average rate of over 15 percent per annum after 1988 – one of the fastest in the world – generating large numbers of jobs. Services sector growth accelerated to over 10 percent per annum in the early 1980s and early 1990s.

Deregulation and poverty reduction

Deregulation after the mid-1980s created many jobs and raised incomes of workers in new sectors. Moreover, economy-wide efficiency (i.e., total factor productivity) improved, permitting output to grow much faster than it would have from simply the additions to capital stock and labor.[16] However, as in the case of the previous agricultural growth episode, an important question remains: did the poor benefit from deregulation, or did a narrower section of society benefit more (e.g., as in Mexico, Brazil)?

That the head-count of numbers of poor (i.e., those with expenditures below a defined poverty line) declined because of the employment and income effects of growth is clear. But there is some controversy with regard to the issue of distributional changes. Measuring poverty trends reliably, through household expenditure surveys, is difficult. Measuring inequality – the gap between the rich and poor – is even more complicated. One reason is the significant under-reporting of spending, especially at the upper-tails of the distribution. If we assume that the scale of such under-reporting has not worsened, the measured inequality of the distribution of spending provides some clues. Its gini-coefficient has fallen steadily, from about 0.35 in 1970 to 0.34 in 1980, 0.32 in 1990, and 0.31 in 1992.[17] Similarly, the ratio of spending of the bottom 20 percent of the population to the total covered by household expenditure surveys has been rising steadily, from about 6.9 percent in 1970, to 7.7 percent in 1980, 8.9 percent in 1990 and about 9.5 percent in 1992. These figures imply reduced inequality, unless the undercoverage of the better-off has worsened.

The growth process appears to have raised average expenditures of the lowest groups substantially, and this contributed most to the fall in poverty. Distributional gains, i.e., proportionately larger gains in consumption of the poor than of all groups, helped to reduce poverty further. An analysis suggests that distributionally-neutral growth accounted for most observed change in poverty between 1984–87; to the extent that inequality in expenditure was also improving, the poor benefited further.[18]

Despite these observations, the inequality of overall incomes and wealth might not have fallen because inequality in spending in major *urban* areas appears to have risen in recent years, and as urbanization increases, urban inequality might become more important. For example, the gini-coefficient for expenditure distribution in Jakarta apparently worsened from 0.29 in 1987 to 0.42 in 1993; some worsening is also noted for provinces in

Sumatra. Second, income (rather than expenditure) inequality may be an issue. However, given under-reporting and problems in measuring unearned incomes and capital gains from wealth, the measurement of income inequality remains controversial. Third, the growing importance of large corporate groups, or "conglomerates," which control a substantial part of non-agricultural activities in Indonesia (as in Korea), increases the perception of inequality.

D. JOBS AND POVERTY

Labor market change – i.e., demand for workers rising faster than the growth in labor supply – was probably the single-most important factor in the decline in poverty over the past two decades. Given a large pool of under-employed labor force in low-productivity occupations, and few restrictions on the mobility of labor, the most important effect was more jobs. As labor markets tightened, real wages rose.

Slowing labor supply

Although fertility rates had started to fall in Indonesia in the 1960s, the lag in the effect on labor supply meant that growth in the potential labor force (the population aged 10 years and over) in the 1970s was still high, about 2.9 percent per annum. Each year, the potential labor force increased by about 2.7 million people.

Indonesian society was also educating its children, and traditional household activities kept a sizable number of females out of the labor market. As a consequence, the actual increase in those looking for work in the 1970s was much smaller. In the 1980s, despite a slight slowing in labor supply, 1.8 million still entered annually. This is about the same as in all of Europe, USA and Japan combined a century ago when these countries were industrializing rapidly.[19]

Rising labor demand

Table 10.6 shows employment growth for males, females and total between 1971–90, using adjusted population census numbers.[20] Total employment growth was about nearly 4 percent a year in the 1970s, and 3 percent a year in the 1980s, a faster rate than in the labor force, resulting in rising employment participation rates, from 49 percent in 1971 to 54 percent in 1990. There was a larger rise in female employment participation rates, from 32 percent in 1971 to 40 percent in 1990. Finally, earning-employed participation rates (i.e., excluding unpaid family workers) improved from 36 percent in 1971 to 42 percent in 1990.

Table 10.6 Indonesia: labor force and employment growth, 1970–90 (millions, unless indicated otherwise)

	1971 Male	Female	Total	1980 Male	Female	Total	1990 Male	Female	Total
Population (10 years and above)	39.0	41.4	80.4	51.3	53.0	104.3	66.7	68.3	135.0
Employed	26.2	13.0	39.2	35.6	19.6	55.2	46.1	27.5	73.6
Employment Participation Rate (%)	67%	32%	49%	69%	37%	53%	69%	40%	54%
Family workers	4.7	5.3	10.0	5.1	7.7	12.8	5.2	11.1	16.3
Non-family earning employment	21.5	7.7	29.2	30.5	11.9	42.4	40.9	16.5	57.3
Earning employed participation rate	55%	19%	36%	59%	22%	41%	61%	24%	42%
Employment growth	3.4	4.5	3.8	2.6	3.4	2.9			
Population growth (10 years & above)	3.1	2.8	2.9	2.6	2.6	2.6			

Source: CENSUS, SAKERNAS, BPS; Mayling Oey-Gardiner (1993); World Bank (1993)

Table 10.7 Indonesia: employment distribution by sector, 1980–93

	Distribution of incremental employment (%)					Growth in wage and formal employment (% per annum)	
	Agriculture	Industry	(Manufacturing)	Services	All	Wage employment	Formal employment*
1980–85	53.5	16.7	12.3	29.8	100.0	n.a.	n.a.
1985–90	17.1	41.5	29.3	41.5	100.0	4.6	6.5
1990–93	-67.6	61.8	32.4	105.9	100.0	3.6	8.2

Source: SAKERNAS, and World Bank, 1996

Note:* Non-agricultural wage employment

The shift to better paying jobs

Not only did aggregate employment growth exceed that of the labor force, but the jobs became higher-productivity ones, and more of them involved wage and formal sector employment. Table 10.7 shows that by the early 1990s the agricultural sector was losing jobs to the fast-growing industrial and service sectors. The table also shows the growth in formal sector employment.

Rising real wages

These changes led to large gains in wages and incomes. Between 1976–88, agricultural real wages improved by about 3.7 percent per annum in Indonesia, one of the fastest in the world; and between 1970–91, average manufacturing wages improved by about 5.5 percent per annum.[21] There was a slow-down in wage growth in the 1980s, which led some observers to infer that the country had not made a clear transition; however, real wages have grown rapidly since 1989[22] (see Figure 10.3 for manufacturing wage trends, which are similar for other sub-sectors).

Labor mobility

When people move in large numbers from low-income and under-employment situations to higher income and more productive jobs,

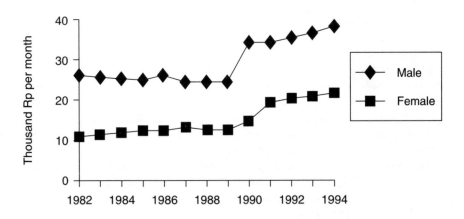

Figure 10.3 Indonesia: real wage trends in manufacturing, 1982–94 (at 1983 constant prices)
Source: Sakernas

Table 10.8 Indonesia: estimated migration from rural to urban areas, and by the main islands, 1980–90 (millions of people)

	Java			Sumatra			Other islands		
	Rural	*Urban*	*Total*	*Rural*	*Urban*	*Total*	*Rural*	*Urban*	*Total*
Net Migration	–14.1	11.6	–2.5	–1.5	2.6	1.2	–0.7	2.0	1.3
As % of population	–21.0%	30%	–3%	–5%	27%	3%	–3%	29%	4%

Source: CENSUS, BPS.
Note: Negative numbers denote out-migration, and positive numbers denote in-migration.

poverty reduction can be dramatic. The generation of jobs for millions of new entrants to the labor force in urban areas decisively reduced poverty in rural Java over the past two decades, especially in the 1980s. In contrast, in the Outer Islands, the impact of such migration and growth in rural–urban links has been much less significant.

Table 10.8 below estimates migration from rural to urban areas, and by the main island groups, between 1980–90. (See also the Appendix to this chapter.)

The table shows that in Java, there was an out-migration from the rural areas estimated at about 14 million (i.e., 21 percent of the rural population) in the 1980s. A statistical analysis corroborates that "pull" factors, rather than "push" factors were predominant in the relative decline in agriculture.[23] The expansion of non-agricultural opportunities, rather than a "failure" in agricultural growth, was the reason for labor movement (unlike the experience of most other developing countries).

The numbers in the table are only suggestive. More careful analysis is necessary. For example, some areas classified as rural in 1980 were reclassified as being urban in 1990, and this may exaggerate the migration out of rural areas on Java. However, the broader picture remains valid: the rural population on Java remained virtually unchanged at about 68 million between 1980–90, only slightly more than the 62 million in 1970; during these two decades, agriculture growth was high and non-agricultural rural activity also improved. Rural incomes improved rapidly. At the same time, the links between rural and urban areas, in terms of movement of goods and services and daily and more permanent migration of labor became prominent, as portrayed by 25 years of village studies of changes in rural Java.[24] None of these factors were at work on the same scale in the Outer Islands, especially outside Sumatra, partly because of their dispersed population and remoteness.

E. HUMAN RESOURCES AND POVERTY

Growth benefited the majority, because people also became better schooled and were healthier. Birdsall *et al.* (1995) suggest that rapid growth and reduced inequality were promoted in East Asia because of the emphasis on education. Education contributed to economic growth, which in turn, stimulated more investment in education, setting up a virtuous cycle; increased levels of education reduced inequality of incomes. These processes were central to the Indonesian experience.

Pro-poor public spending

The oil-boom years after 1973 provided the Government with the where-withal to expand public infrastructure and social services dramatically. A series of special programs, the INPRES (or Presidential Instruction) programs, covered the countryside with roads, primary schools and public health facilities. Primary schooling was made compulsory, free textbooks provided, health facilities expanded, and rural roads built and maintained. Regional financial transfers increased from about 14 percent of total consolidated central government expenditures in the mid-1970s, to about 22 percent by the early 1980s. Since total central expenditures also increased from about 17 percent of GDP to about 25 percent of GDP, with GDP increasing by about 6.5 percent per annum during the period, real central transfers on these infrastructure and social services increased about three-fold between 1975–83.

Public expenditure decisions were biased towards basic services. In the education sector, Indonesia allocated more than 80 percent of total public spending to basic (primary and secondary level) education, while in the health sector, about 60 percent of total public spending was allocated to rural health centers and sub-centers, family planning and maternal and child health, and disease control activities – services likely to be more intensively used by the bottom half of the income distribution.[25] During and after the oil-price decline of the mid-1980s (1985–87), public expenditures were reduced heavily, to restore the macroeconomic balance, but those on social services were protected.[26]

The spatial spending patterns and placement of Government programs were not random either. They favored areas and regions that had higher poverty and lower human resources. Pitt *et al.* (1993) estimated the effects of schools and health and family clinics on basic human capital indicators – school attendance, fertility and mortality. They conclude that the presence of primary schools, and to a lesser extent, lower secondary schools, significantly affected school attendance rates. Similarly, the presence of health clinics in villages positively affected the schooling of females. The study also found evidence that the placement of primary schools significantly increased the attendance of children whose mothers had little or no schooling. They conclude that program support was higher for areas which were relatively undeserved; moreover, the spatial distribution of programs became more equal over time.

Human capital gains

As a result, Indonesia achieved one of the fastest rates of educational transition in the world. Gross primary enrollment rates rose from 75 percent to over 100 percent between 1970–early 1980s, and the numbers of children attending primary schools doubled from 13 million to over 26 million. Near-universal primary education was attained by the early 1980s, a feat that virtually no low-income country and very few middle-income countries then matched. In secondary education, gross enrollment rates rose from 16 percent to about 40 percent, and the numbers enrolled from 1.5 million to 5.6 million. Cross-country comparisons suggest that Indonesia's primary and secondary school enrollment rates by 1987 were nearly twice what would be otherwise expected, given its per capita incomes. Gender differences in access to schooling were remarkably small. Along with formal schooling, Indonesia also conducted one of the most successful adult literacy programs in the world, raising overall adult literacy levels to about 80 percent.

This effort entailed a large increase in services for the poor. Between 1978–87, primary school enrollments among the bottom 40 percent of all expenditure groups rose from 78 percent to 90 percent, lower secondary enrollments jumped from 42 percent to 65 percent, and the utilization of health services by the poor doubled (World Bank, 1994b).

Human capital contribution to growth

Cross-country studies (e.g. World Bank, 1993; Birdsall *et al.*, 1995; Barro, 1996) suggest that education (primary and secondary enrollment rates) contribute significantly to growth. There are also important spill-over benefits, such as lower fertility rates and population growth.[27] Examination of Indonesia suggests similar results.[28] The increase in human capital per worker is estimated to have raised GDP growth per worker by about 0.5 percent per annum between 1978–92.

However, this contribution is smaller than expected, given the fact that the average years of schooling per worker expanded by about 4 percent per annum. One reason could be that education gains did not show their full effects during the period under study; another is that the quality of education was low. Per pupil expenditures, which are sometimes used as a proxy for educational quality, are low in Indonesia compared to other countries. Student cognitive tests also suggest lower quality. Still, the large quantitative gains in schooling had a significant cumulative impact on per capita incomes (e.g., about 12 percent higher, cumulated over 20 years).

Table 10.9 Indonesia: narrowing wage differentials by schooling, 1977–90

	Male				*Female*			
	1977	*1982*	*1987*	*1990*	*1977*	*1982*	*1987*	*1990*
Less than primary	100	100	100	100	100	100	100	100
Primary	151	142	128	122	149	151	128	126
Junior secondary	275	203	170	158	396	290	225	203
Senior secondary	245	249	212	214	380	368	304	287
Tertiary	1033	410	372	366	1428	582	551	508

Source: SAKERNAS; Agrawal, 1996

Contribution to poverty reduction

Rapidly rising student enrollments did much to reduce income inequalities for two principal reasons. First, wage differentials, the scarcity rents to education, fell as rapid increases were made at all education levels (see Table 10.9) – as in Korea.[29] Second, the poor still gained by moving from no or little formal education, to at least a completed primary education; average annual earnings for primary school graduates were 22 percent to 26 percent higher than those with less than completed primary schooling in 1990. Third, there were lower fertility rates, better health and better child nutrition.

F. THE SOCIAL BASIS OF PUBLIC POLICIES, AND A REGIONAL COMMONALITY

Three basic public policy choices appear to account for much of the success: (a) an early emphasis on developing agricultural and rural sectors; (b) a shift to a labor-demanding and outward-oriented growth strategy; and (c) public investments in basic education and other services, with a pro-poor bias. Why did the Government adopt these policies?

To answer that question, we turn to the "Trilogy of Development" framework, often invoked to explain Indonesian public policy choices: that economic policies were guided by the need to achieve stability, growth and equity.

The imperative of stability

The achievement of economic stability has been an important objective of the Government. It based its early credentials on having restored stability out of the chaos of the early 1960s. Any source of potential crisis was perceived as a threat to that stability and policies deemed necessary to resolve that crisis overrode other interests.

Rice, agriculture and rural development

The imperative of stability helps to explain why rice self-sufficiency (and agricultural development) was important in the Government's early strategy. Rice self-sufficiency was a goal of all Indonesian governments after independence, since rice was the most important commodity and since its import was a major drain on the resources of the state. The failure of successive governments in the first 15 years of independence, especially in the period 1958–65 to control rice prices – which soared more than twenty-fold between March 1965–66 – was a factor in the eventual collapse of the guided democracy government.[30] Given that background, rice-agriculture received close attention in the New Order Government's agenda. It also helped that the political leadership saw the country as a nation of small (rice) farmers first, and shared much in common with these interests in the early stages. The rice self-sufficiency program involved import-substitution, but it was an efficient choice because the country had a comparative advantage in the production of rice and domestic prices remained at or below comparable world prices.

The imperative of growth

The achievement of sustained growth was a second source of credibility. The Government successfully restored growth in the late 1960s and in the 1970s, with the help of the booming oil sector, growth accelerated. But in 1983, when oil prices started to fall, and especially by 1986, when oil prices dipped to below $10 a barrel (or one-third the level in 1981), the prospects were for a sharp decline in growth. Between 1983–86, a deep recession in the non-agricultural sectors was evident (accompanied by small urban riots as joblessness increased). This led the Government to shift to an outward-oriented and private sector-led strategy. Orthodox stabilization policies would probably have achieved short-run macro-economic stability (at some cost to consumption). But there was a near-certainty of a drastic slowdown in long-run growth, the second plank of the Government's development trilogy. The Government therefore decided to deregulate and open the economy, going much further than it might have, to spur non-oil exports and other newer sources of economic growth. The oil crisis thus spurred policy-makers to undertake deeper reforms than they probably otherwise would have.

The basis for equity

There were underlying pressures, given the history of the country, for the Government to pursue socially equitable policies, but it resisted ex-plicitly redistributive policies. "From the very onset we realized that equitable distribution without growth will only mean sharing poverty.

Growth without equitable distribution means sharing injustice" (President Soeharto, 1992). If deliberately redistributive policies were not to be pursued, but the outcome of growth was to be equitable, the only policy choice was making public investment in basic services that benefited a broad section of society.

Such reasoning helps explain both the marked absence of income transfer programs on the one hand, and broadly-based public investment (Presidential Instruction) programs on the other. The allocation of public investments – e.g., roads, schools, health centers – followed equity rules (e.g., using formulas based on factors such as equality by province, equality in per capita allocations, and adjustments for relative per capita incomes). Public officials at the center also generally had a sense of a social mission to ensure equitable distribution of the oil-boom resources, and to prevent waste by: (a) centralizing revenue collections; (b) setting "technocratic" rules for allocating resources; and (c) setting detailed physical and program indicators (e.g., enrollment rates, teacher–student ratios, immunization rates, family-planning acceptance rates, staffing ratios in health centers, etc.) by which to judge performance and achievements.

The heavy investment in human resources is explained by the long history of neglect of education and health services by the Dutch colonial government, and resentment against colonial elite-based systems (i.e., special schools, higher education only for a very few, and education in the Dutch language). It also helped that the leadership in the Government shared strong personal commitment to basic services in rural areas.

In addition, the Government faced a continuous assessment of its equity record, by both inside and outside analysts, a scrutiny to which it was more sensitive than otherwise, given the weaknesses in representative politics.

A regional commonality?

In addition to domestic policy factors for explaining poverty reduction, there are possible foreign ones. Other neighboring countries – notably, Korea, Taiwan, Hong Kong, Singapore, Thailand and Malaysia – also achieved a remarkable record of growth with more equality. What were the connections, if any, between Indonesia's success in poverty reduction, and those in other East Asian neighboring countries? We examine two possible sources for the regional convergence (as hypotheses that need to be tested by further research).

I. Learning from regional models: growth with equity

The *ideas* spread on how successful neighbors have functioned – and prospered – seem to have been important in East Asia, including Indonesia.[31] The successful spread of an idea – i.e., the adoption of a superior economic model – can be presumed to be hastened by geographical proximity and learning by observation.

Regional proximity seems to matter. It is easier for countries to learn from each other when they are neighbors because they share broadly similar social settings and it is easier for ideas to travel. The size of the region of the Industrial Revolution in Europe between the late sixteenth and eighteenth centuries was also relatively small, with rapid advances in technology and economic growth occurring among a neigboring group of countries.[32] The diffusion of the Green Revolution in Asia, between the mid-1960s and 1980s, was also based on similar processes of innovation, role-models, and learning by observation and emulation.[33]

In Indonesia, learning by observation and emulation of neighbors' successes – e.g., Japan, Korea, Hong Kong and Taiwan in the first instance, and Singapore, Thailand and Malaysia in the second and more immediate instance – appears to have been important.[34] The main idea was that *rapid growth with widely shared benefits* was possible and necessary, and that the key lay in *an efficient state based on an implicit "social contract"* (see further below).

Japan's post-war economic success (and, to no small extent, its pre-war success) exemplified this possibility. It was this success that other East Asian countries, and Indonesia, were trying to emulate in achieving rapid growth through trade and exporting, spreading the benefits of growth, educating their population and building a cohesive society that was capable of achieving clear long-term economic goals. A measure of the importance of this in Indonesia was the policy emphasis on macroeconomic stability, growth and equity. These elements were also prominent in Korea, Taiwan, Singapore, Thailand and Malaysia.

II. A different role of the state

Many observers have pointed to a shared attribute of East Asian countries: their relatively authoritarian governments, characterized by strong executive powers, weak representative politics, limited freedom of the Press, and limited rights of labor and other groups to organize. Yet, perhaps there was (at least temporarily) an implicit contract between people and governments towards achieving rapid growth with widespread benefits.[35] Even without formal mechanisms, the "climate of common opinion" in East Asian countries exercised a strong influence on the policies of the state. If governments did not perform, especially on equity, they remained vulnerable (and usually reacted quickly) to the climate of public opinion.

In Indonesia, one of the five basic principles of the state – one most directly related to a notion of such a contract – deals with the idea that its role is to ensure "a just and prosperous society" that benefited all its citizens, and not just reconciling competing demands of different sections of society.[36] The appropriate job of a body such as the People's Assembly was to ensure that this contract was fulfilled by the government, and not the running of the affairs of the state itself. This notion of "economic democracy," rather than political democracy, remains a key element in the Indonesian setting. In different forms, this principle was followed in Singapore, Malaysia, Thailand, Korea and Taiwan.[37,38,39]

Even if there was an implicit "contract," how did the East Asian contract with governments differ from – and work better than – those in other developing countries? Two distinguishing characteristics appear to have been important.

First, economic performance benchmarks were more important than elsewhere. The rate of economic growth promised and achieved was a measurable performance yardstick used by all East Asian governments. These governments also used benchmarks not just for GDP growth but for virtually all other areas of economic performance (such as export growth, children immunized, school enrollments, adult literacy, etc.) to underline their achievements.[40] In contrast, many governments in other countries also frequently set targets, but there was limited accountability for results, in practice. A large gap between rhetoric and reality could be blamed on competing parties, interests, or external events.

Second, the East Asian "contracts" afforded governments, and their bureaucracy, relative insulation from outside pressures. But because this also limited channels for redress, governments were under an obligation to ensure that economic decisions and development were seen to be broadly-based, whereas elsewhere, the role of the state was often diverted towards short-term populism, and meeting the needs of the politically more powerful urban middle classes and elites. The results in East Asia were a bias towards equity in public expenditures (e.g., extending primary education and basic health, rather than higher education or urban hospitals) and a bias in public investment towards basic services (such as physical infrastructure), rather than transfers and subsidies and (inefficient) state-led investments in commercial activities.

APPENDIX

Since there are no official data on such migration (i.e., from rural to urban areas), it is estimated by the following method: (a) population numbers from the 1980 Census are multipled by an assumed rate of natural population growth, to derive an expected population in 1990; (b) the assumed rate of natural population growth is differentiated by Java and the Outer Islands, and by rural and urban areas (i.e., higher population growth in the Outer Islands, lower in Java; and higher in rural areas, lower in urban areas) using differences in total fertility rates reported in the Demographic and Health Survey, BPS 1992; and (c) this expected population is then subtracted from the actual 1990 Census reported population to derive estimated in-migration or estimated out-migration (i.e., if the actual reported Census population is higher than expected from calculated expected natural population, then there is in-migration, and vice-versa).

NOTES

1 The views expressed in this paper are strictly the author's alone, and should not be attributed to any organization with which the author may be associated.
2 Booth, 1993.
3 Sayogo, 1975.
4 Penny and Singarimbun, 1973.
5 Booth and Damanik, 1990.
6 Mubyarto and Partideraja, 1968.
7 Jellinek, 1977.
8 W. Collier *et al.*, 1993.
9 Manning, 1987.
10 Naylor, 1992.
11 Ibid.
12 Booth and Sundrum, 1979.
13 Ibid.
14 Woo *et al.*, 1994; World Bank, 1994.
15 Dasgupta, *et al.*, 1995a.
16 Dasgupta *et al.*, 1995b.
17 World Bank, 1994a.
18 Ravallion and Huppi, 1991.
19 Manning, 1993.
20 Oey-Gardiner, 1993.
21 World Bank, 1995b.
22 Manning, 1993.
23 Martin and Warr, 1993.
24 Collier *et al.*, 1993.
25 World Bank, 1994c.
26 World Bank, 1993.
27 D. Dasgupta, 1993.
28 Dasgupta *et al.*, 1995.
29 Birdsall *et al.*, 1995.
30 Manning, 1987.
31 D. Dasgupta, 1993.
32 The notable differences between the Industrial Revolution in Europe and the more recent growth processes in East Asia are two: (a) the time-horizon was much shorter in East Asia (one generation, rather than several generations in Europe); and (b) the equity impacts were far better (workers benefited fairly immediately, rather than from the third generation or so in Western Europe). More generally, the commonalities between the two processes appear to be: (a) a leading role-model played by a major country(ies) in the region (Britain in Europe, and Japan in East Asia); (b) rapid learning and diffusion – fostered by technology diffusion, trade, and education (the Scientific Revolution in Western Europe, and gains in broad-based education in East Asia).
33 The commonalities between the European Industrial Evolution and Asian Green Revolution (in the Punjab or in Java) were, again: (a) the role-model provided by other countries adopting new technologies, and (b) the rapidity of learning – supported by the market, and the state (research, varietal improvements, extension, credit, irrigation and fertilizers).

34 Even in Japan, the first East Asian role-model, when it emerged out of its historical isolation around the turn of the 20th century, it was the deliberate emulation and adoption of Western social and economic models (e.g., the formation of joint-stock companies), rather than Confucianism, that provided the springboard for its subsequent successful drive towards modernization and change.

35 The mirror of this argument is the need for legitimization. East Asian governments were also under pressure to perform better economically, especially on equity.

36 Sukarno, 1969.

37 Tilman, 1969.

38 The Philippines, in contrast, experimented with liberal democratic principles, and ended up with a very different system in the 1970s.

39 A more specific example of the contractarian nature of the East Asian states was their publicly announced emphasis on economic stability. In Indonesia, this took the specific form of the balanced budget law (as well as an open capital account and free convertibility of the currency), which were among the early economic acts of the government.

40 Performance contract arrangements are now becoming popular in more liberal democratic settings (e.g. New Zealand), to measure and improve public administration, and introduce greater accountability.

REFERENCES

Agrawal, N. (1996) "The Benefits of Growth for Indonesian Workers," Conference Paper, Indonesian Workers in the 21st Century, Jakarta.

Barro, R.J. (1996) "Determinants of Economic Growth: A Cross-Country Empirical Study," National Bureau of Economic Research Working Paper Series No. 5698: 1.

Bhattacharya, A. and M. Pengestu (1993) *The Lessons of East Asia: Indonesia: Development Transformation and Public Policy*, World Bank, Washington DC.

Birdsall, N., D. Ross, and R. Sabot (1995) "Inequality and Growth Reconsidered: Lessons from East Asia," *World Bank Economic Review*, vol. 9, no. 3: 508.

Booth, A. (1993) "Counting The Poor in Indonesia," *Bulletin of Indonesian Economic Studies*, vol. 29, no. 1.

Booth, A. and Konta Damanik (1990) "Central Java and Yogyakarta: Malthus Overcome?" in Hal Hill (ed.) *Unity and Diversity: Regional Development in Indonesia Since 1970*, Oxford University Press, pp. 285–305.

Booth, A. and R.M. Sundrum (1979) "Trends and Determinants of Income Distribution in Indonesia," mimeo.

Collier, W., Kabul Santoso, Soentoro, and Rudi Wibowo (1993) "A New Approach to Rural Development in Java: Twenty-Five Years of Village Studies," Report prepared for the ILO Project, Jakarta.

Dasgupta, D. (1993) "Why Some Regions Do Better Than Others," in *Amex Bank Review Essays in International Economics and Finance*, London, Oxford University Press.

Dasgupta, D., J. Hanson and E. Hulu (1995b) "The Rise in Total Factor Productivity During Deregulation: Indonesia 1985–92," Conference Paper, "Building on Success: Maximizing the Gains from Deregulation," Indonesian Economic Association and the World Bank, Jakarta.

Dasgupta, D., E. Hulu, and B. Dasgupta (1995a) "The Determinants of Indonesia's Exports, 1985–93," Conference Paper, "Building on Success: Maximizing the Gains from Deregulation," Indonesian Economic Association and the World Bank, Jakarta.

Dasgupta, P. (1993) *An Enquiry into Well-Being and Destitution*, London, Oxford University Press.

Galbraith, J.K. (1979) *The Nature of Mass Poverty*, Cambridge, MA: Harvard University Press.

Gardiner, P. (1994) "Urbanization, Urban Growth and Poverty Reduction in Indonesia," mimeo, World Bank, Jakarta.

Gertler, P., C.A. Serrato, E. Frankenberg, J. Molyneaux and L. Kohn (1994) "Poverty Analysis and Policy Formulation: Targeting Poverty with Economic and Non-Monetary Measures From the 1992 SUSENAS," RAND Corporation, report prepared for the Government of Indonesia, Jakarta.

Jellinek, L. (1973) *The Life of A Jakarta Street Trader*, Clayton, Victoria (Australia): Centre of Southeast Asian Studies, Monash University.

―― (1977) "The Pondok System and Circular Migration," in Jellinek *et al.* (eds) *The Life of the Poor in Indonesian Cities*, Clayton, Victoria: Centre of Southeast Asian Studies, Monash University.

Keyfitz, N. (1965) "Indonesian Population and The European Industrial Revolution," Asian Survey 10.

Lipton, M. (1988) *The Poor and The Poorest – Some Interim Findings*, World Bank, Washington DC.

Manning, C. (1987) "Public Policy, Rice Production and Income Distribution: A Review of Indonesia's Rice Self-Sufficiency Program," *Southeast Asian Journal of Social Science*, vol. 15, no 1.

―― (1993) "Examining Both Sides of the Ledger: Economic Growth and Labor Welfare under Soeharto," in C. Manning and J. Hardjono (eds) *Indonesia Assessment 1993: Labor: Sharing in the Benefits of Growth*, Research School of Pacific Studies, Australian National University, Canberra.

Martin, W. and P.G. Warr (1993) "Explaining the Relative Decline of Agriculture: A Supply-Side Analysis," *World Bank Economic Review*, September.

Mears, L. (1984) "Rice and Food Self-Sufficiency in Indonesia," *Bulletin of Indonesian Economic Studies*, vol. 20, no. 2: 123–38.

Mubyarto and A. Partideraja (1968) "An Economic Survey of the Special Region of Jogjakarta," *Bulletin of Indonesian Economic Studies*, vol. II: 29–47.

Naylor, R. (1992) "Labor-Saving Technologies in the Javanese Rice Economy: Recent Developments and A Look into the 1990s," *Bulletin of Indonesian Economic Studies*, vol. 28, no. 3.

Oey-Gardiner, Mayling (1993) "A Study of Women's Issues in Agricultural Transformation," report for the World Bank, Jakarta.

Penny, D.H. and M. Singarimbun (1973) "Population and Poverty in Rural Java: Some Economic Arithmetic from Srijarjo," Cornell International Agricultural Development Mimeo, Cornell University.

Pitt, M.M., M. Rosenzweig and D.M. Gibbons (1993) "The Determinants and Consequences of the Placement of Government Programs in Indonesia", mimeo.

Ravallion, M. and M. Huppi (1991) "Measuring Changes in Poverty: A Methodological Case-Study of Indonesia During an Adjustment Period," *World Bank Economic Review*, vol. 5, no. 3.

Sayogyo (1975) Usaha Perbaikan Gizi Keluarga [ANP Evaluation Study], Institut Pertanian Bogor, Bogor.

President Soeharto (1991) Budget Speech, 1991/92, Government of Indonesia, Jakarta.

Sukarno (1961) "The Birth of Pantja Sila", in R.O. Tilman (ed.) *Man, State, and Society in Contemporary Southeast Asia*, Praeger, New York.

Tilman, R.O. (ed.) (1969) *Man, State, and Society in Contemporary Southeast Asia*, Praeger, New York.

Woo, W.T., B. Glassburner, and A. Nasution (1994) *Macroeconomic Policies, Crises and Long-Term Growth in Indonesia, 1965–90*, World Bank, Washington DC.

World Bank (1990) *Indonesia: Poverty Assessment and Strategy Report*, A World Bank Country Report, Washington, DC.

—— (1993) *The East Asian Miracle: Economic Growth and Public Policy*, New York: Oxford University Press.

—— (1994a) *Indonesia: Stability, Growth and Equity in Repelita VI*, A World Bank Country Report, Washington, DC.

—— (1994b) *Indonesia: Sustaining Development*, A World Bank Country Report, Washington, DC.

—— (1994c) *Indonesia: Public Expenditures, Prices and the Poor*, A World Bank Country Report, Washington, DC.

—— (1995a) *Indonesia: Improving Efficiency and Equity: Changes in the Public Sector's Role*, A Country Economic Report, Washington, DC.

—— (1995b) *World Development Report*, World Bank, Washington, DC.

—— (1996) *Indonesia: Dimensions of Growth*, A Country Economic Report, Washington, DC.

11 Demographic transition, education and economic growth in East Asian countries

Sung-Yeal Koo

1 INTRODUCTION

An important contribution to East Asia's remarkable growth was its early and strong demographic transition. The demographic transition is a shift from higher fertility–mortality to lower fertility–mortality. One implication is the substitution of higher quality of the population for larger numbers. This implies a more rapid increase in educational attainment and in human capital more broadly.

The fact that the East Asian countries had enrollment levels above the norm for their incomes initially and had faster increases in educational attainment is associated with their high performance.[1] The demographic transition, a phenomenon related to education, is a good candidate as a contribution to this performance. This analysis supports that observation.

One mechanism is that more education leads to fewer but higher quality members; then slower population growth implies more capital per worker. Also, an increase in the quality of workers implies greater technical progress, either through absorption of existing technology or the creation of new technology. Both lead to higher incomes.

This chapter links demographic transitions to East Asia's growth. We first examine demographic trends in these countries and link them to the rise of school enrollment. We then connect the rise in educational attainment to more rapid economic growth.

We divide the region into three groups. First is North East Asia, including Korea, Japan, Taiwan, Hong Kong and Singapore (as an honorary member of this group). They have much in common: culture, ethnicity and historical experiences. Second is South East Asia, including Thailand, Malaysia, Indonesia, and the Philippines. They are more diverse in culture and ethnicity. Third is China, a country enormous in size and in economic diversity.

II THE DEMOGRAPHIC TRANSITION

1. Trends of population growth

Trends of population growth are shown in Figures 11.1 (a), (b) and (c), where crude birth rate (CBR), crude death rate (CDR) and natural increase rate (NIR) are presented separately.

a. Birth rates

As shown in Figure 11.1(a), birth rates – CBR – in North East Asian (NEA) countries, with the exception of Japan, started to decline from 36–46 per thousand in the late 1950s. The pace of decline was rapid, reached 11–16 per thousand by the late 1980s, and stayed there. Korea started at a higher level in the late 1950s and, with a similar decline, ended up with higher birth rates than did other NEA countries. Japan is exceptional, maintaining a constant, and relatively low, birth rate since the late 1950s.

Birth rates in China and South East Asian (SEA) countries started to decline from slightly higher levels, 43–49 per thousand in the early 1950s. Their decline was slower than those in NEA, reaching 19–30 per thousand in the early 1990s when they were still going down. China and Thailand started earlier, declined faster and reached levels much lower than others in the group – near those of NEA. The Philippines stands out; it started higher and declined less than the others.

b. Death rates

CDRs – crude death rates – in NEA countries (see Figure 11.1(b)) show, except for Korea, a very gradual decline from around 7–10 per thousand in the late 1950s to around 6 per thousand in the 1990s. That in Korea started much higher than others in the group but converged on them by the 1990s. The crude death rate in Japan, on the other hand, has been increasing since the late 1980s because of aging.

Crude death rates in SEA countries were higher than those in NEA in the early 1950s at 19–26 per thousand, but their pace of decline has been so much faster that their rates came close to those in NEA in the 1990s. The Philippines, Malaysia and Thailand had declines like that of Korea. On the other hand, death rates in Indonesia and China started higher and have declined faster, approaching other SEA countries in the 1990s.

c. Natural increase rates

As a result of rapidly declining birth rates and stagnant death rates, NIRs – natural increase rates – in Northeast Asia (Figure 11.1(c)), except for

Northeast Asian Countries

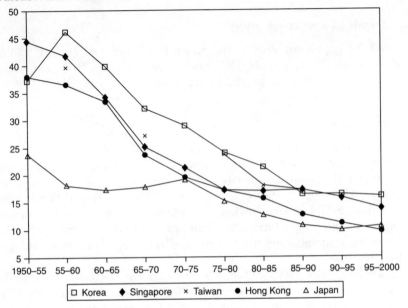

Southeast Asian Countries and China

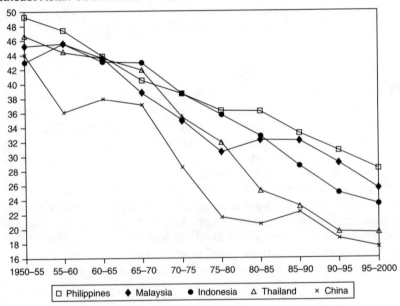

Figure 11.1(a) Trends in crude birth rate in East Asian countries (rate per thousand population, available data)

Northeast Asian Countries

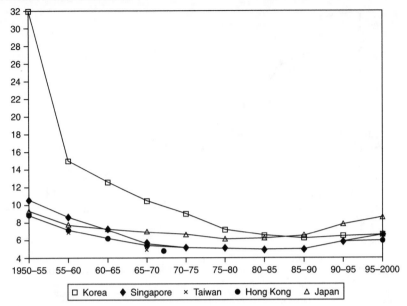

Southeast Asian Countries and China

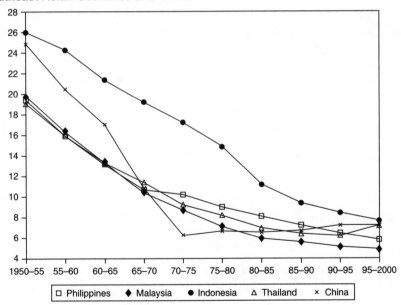

Figure 11.1(b) Trends in crude death rate in East Asian countries (rate per thousand population, available data)

Northeast Asian Countries

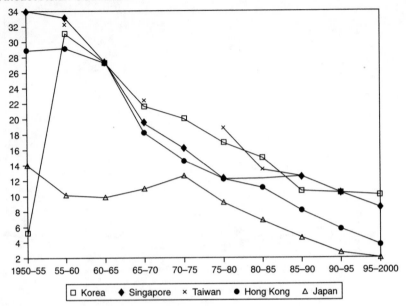

Southeast Asian Countries and China

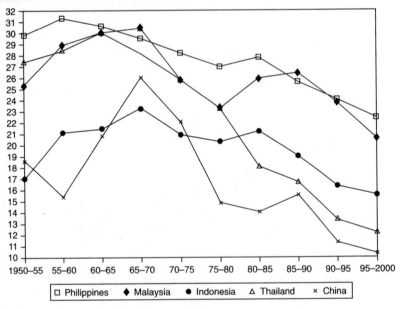

Figure 11.1(c) Trends in natural increase rate in East Asian countries (rate per thousand population, available data)

Japan, rapidly fell from the 30s per thousand in the 1950s to the 10s per thousand in the 1990s. Japan's stayed high until the early 1970s around 12 per thousand, but then began to decline to nearly zero.

With birth and death rates both declining, population increases in Southeast Asia stayed high until the early 1970s and then began to fall. Increases in Philippines and Malaysia were as high as those in Northeast Asia in the 1950s and remained at over 20 per thousand even to the early 1990s. Indonesia and China are substantially lower, with China in the 1990s approaching the very low rates of the Northeast Asians. Thailand started at a high level similar to the Philippines and Malaysia but ended up at a level between China and Indonesia in the 1990s; it had the most rapid transition among the SEA countries.

The demographic transitions in NEA preceded those in China and SEA countries by 10 to 20 years. The result is that annual population growth rates in NEA are 1 percent in the 1990s; those in SEA countries and China are still above 1 percent; and the Philippines and Malaysia are above 2 percent.

2. FERTILITY AND MORTALITY

Change in birth rates results from changes in both age-specific fertility and in the age composition of the population. Figure 11.2(a) shows trends in total fertility rates – TFR – defined as the summation over age of age-specific fertility rates – and the proportion of women 15–49 years of age.

The total fertility rate in NEA countries (Figure 11.2(a)), excluding Japan, declined rapidly from 4.7–6.1 per woman in the late 1950s to a below-replacement level of 1.3–1.7 per woman in the late 1980s. By the late 1950s, Japan was already below the replacement level of 2.1, 20 years ahead of Singapore. Korea was the last among the group to reach replacement level fertility, in the late 1980s. This is the most rapid known decline in total fertility for so many countries.

Total fertility rates in China and SEA countries started to decline before 1965 but remained around 5.6–6.1 per woman in the late 1960s. China and Thailand reached near replacement levels in the early 1990s, while Malaysia and the Philippines lagged behind at around 3.6–3.8 per woman, and Indonesia stayed in the middle.

Total fertility rates in these countries reached replacement levels in the following order:

Japan	Late 1950s
Singapore	Late 1970s
Hong Kong, Taiwan	Early 1980s
Korea	Late 1980s
China, Thailand	Early 1990s
Indonesia	15 years behind China and Thailand

Northeast Asian Countries

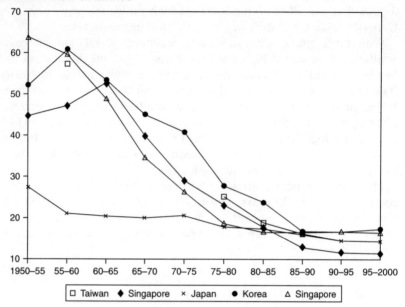

Southeast Asian Countries and China

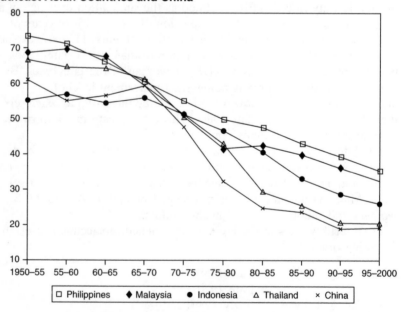

Figure 11.2(a) Trends of total fertility rate in East Asian countries (available data)

Northeast Asian Countries

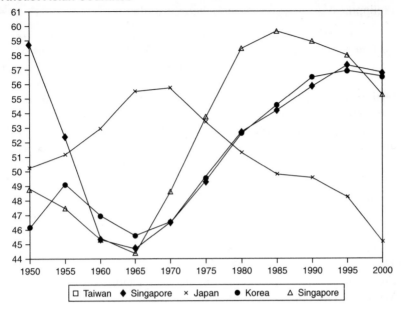

Southeast Asian Countries and China

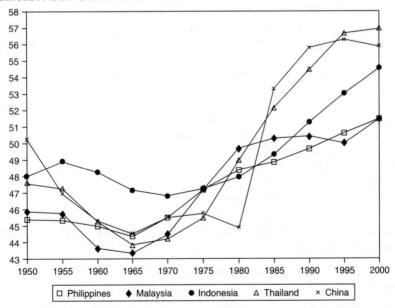

Figure 11.2(b) Trends of proportion of women aged 15–49 in East Asian countries (available data)

| Malaysia | 10 years behind Indonesia |
| Philippines | 5 years behind Malaysia |

Figure 11.2(b) shows the trends in the ratio of fecund age women to all females. In all these countries, except for Japan, this ratio began to increase in the 1960s and reaches a maximum after one generation or so. Although the proportion of the fecund age women is a function of the fertility trend itself, it shows that declines in all of these countries' birth rates occurred despite an increasingly "unfavorable" age structure.

The shape of the curves in Figure 11.2(b) shows the sequence of demographic transitions. The order of the countries and the years when the proportion of fecund age women reached, or will reach, a maximum is as follows:

Japan	1970
Singapore	1985
Hong Kong, Korea	1995
China	1995
Thailand	2000
Indonesia	behind China and Thailand
Malaysia, Philippines	behind Indonesia

This order is, naturally, the same as that of total fertility rates. Trends of life expectancy and infant mortality are shown in Figures 11.3 (a) and (b). The ordering in NEA is nearly the same as fertility except that Hong Kong was ahead of Singapore in life expectancy at birth. However, the mortality pattern of China and SEA countries differs from the ordering of fertility. Malaysia is ahead of China and Thailand in both life expectancy at birth and infant mortality, and the Philippines is ahead of Indonesia in both indicators.

In all of these countries, the decline in infant mortality is striking, in Korea by ten-fold, over 40 years.

Considering both fertility and mortality, the order of demographic transitions is Japan, followed by Singapore and Hong Kong as a second group, Taiwan and Korea as the third one, China and Thailand fourth, Malaysia and Indonesia fifth, and the Philippines bringing up the rear.

3. CHANGE IN AGE COMPOSITION OF POPULATION AND DEPENDENCY

Although the age composition of a population is affected by both mortality and fertility, fertility is more significant because it directly influences the number of young people, whereas mortality's influence on the age structure can be negligible. The different parts of Figures 11.4 and 11.5 show the age composition of these countries for younger and older age groups respectively.

Northeast Asian Countries

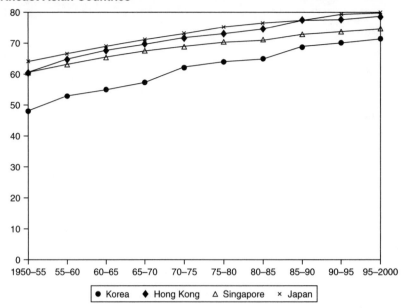

Southeast Asian Countries and China

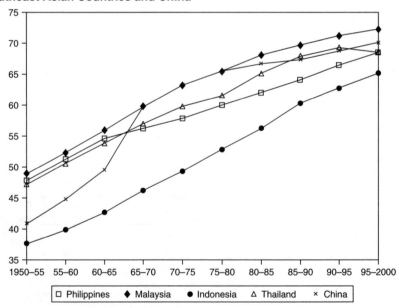

Figure 11.3(a) Trends in life expectancy at birth in East Asian countries (years, available data)

Northeast Asian Countries

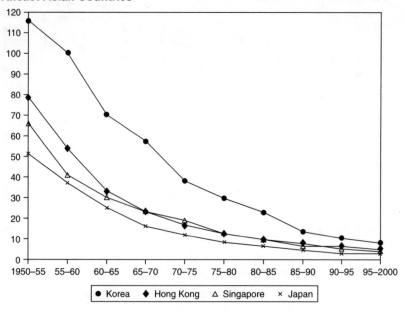

Southeast Asian Countries and China

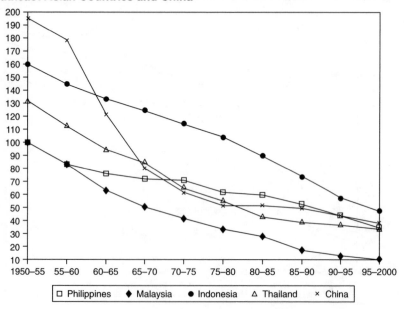

Figure 11.3(b) Trends in infant mortality rates in East Asian countries (rate per thousand population, available data)

Northeast Asian Countries

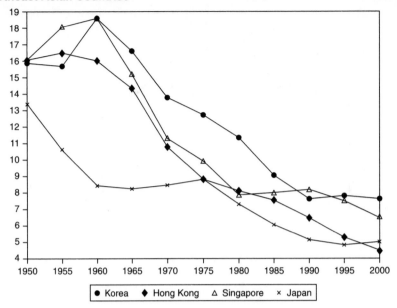

Southeast Asian Countries and China

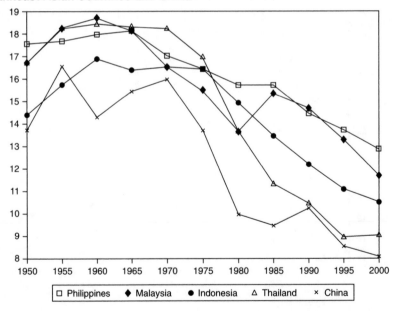

Figure 11.4(a) 0–4 age group in East Asian countries as percentage of total population

Source: *World and Korea in Statistical Perspectives*, Statistical Office of Korea, 1995

Northeast Asian Countries

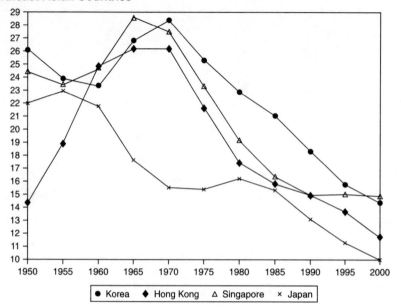

Southeast Asian Countries and China

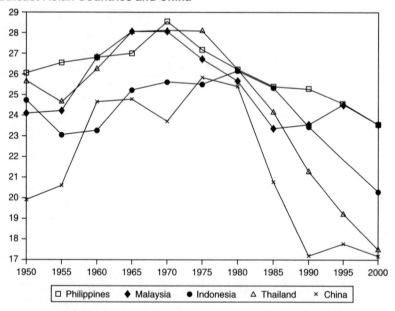

Figure 11.4(b) 5–14 age group in East Asian countries as percentage of total population

Northeast Asian Countries

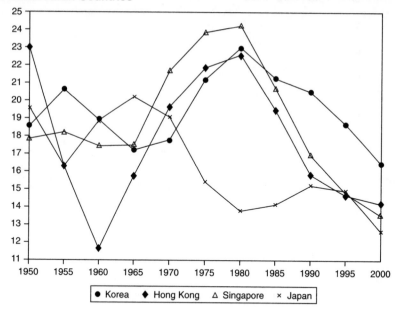

Southeast Asian Countries and China

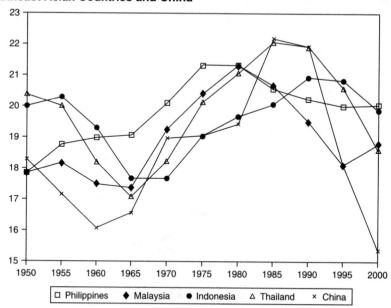

Figure 11.4(c) 15–24 age group in East Asian countries as percentage of total population

Northeast Asian Countries

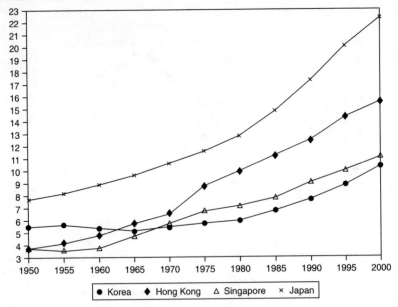

Southeast Asian Countries and China

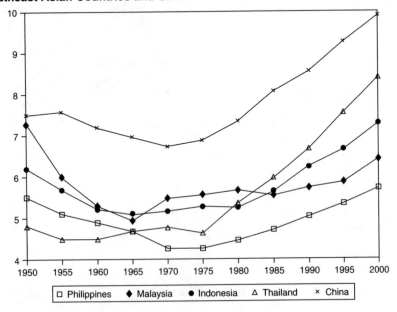

Figure 11.5 60-and-above age group in East Asian countries as percentage of total population

Except for Japan, the burden posed by young dependents peaked in 1960 for the 0–4 age group, in 1965–70 for the 5–14 age group, and in 1980 for the 15–24 age group. Hong Kong peaked slightly ahead of Singapore and Singapore ahead of Korea (Figure 11.4(a)). The ordering is, naturally, similar to that for crude birth rates.

On the other hand, the young dependent burden for China and SEA countries (Figure 11.4(b)) peaked later: in 1955–1970 for the 0–4 age group, in 1970–75 for the 5–14 age group, and in 1980–90 for the 15–24 age group.

Figure 11.5 shows that the proportions of older age dependents began to rise in 1955–60 in NEA and in 1960–70 in SEA countries. It will continue rising beyond 2000.

III EXPLANATORY FACTORS

Why did the demographic transition occur so early and strongly in these countries? We will examine their age-specific fertility rates (ASFR); this is the purest indicator of fertility net of age composition. The determinants of fertility are then discussed.

1. Trends of age specific fertility rate

Figures 11.6(a) and (b) show the ASFRs in East Asian countries. In general, the SEA countries have higher ASFRs than those in NEA, and Malaysia and the Philippines have higher ones than any other countries in the East Asia region. Thailand is exceptional with ASFRs for the 25–34 age group even lower than most NEA countries.

2. Determinants of fertility decline

What factors lie behind these fertility declines? In the so-called new household economics, fertility depends on the demand for children. The relevant parameters that determine the number of children are (1) the quality (or investment in) per child; (2) the consumption of goods and quality not related to children; (3) the price of these other goods; and (4) family income (and some other variables). The relation among these factors is taken to be as follows:

- As family income rises both the number and quality of children demanded rise at first, but, because quality is more income elastic, the number of children grows less.
- The number of children and their quality depends on their relative prices; they are substitutes. If quality increases more than number, then having more children is relatively more costly and people will have fewer of them. The overall result is that higher incomes can reduce the number of children wanted.

ASFR of NEA Countries, 1965

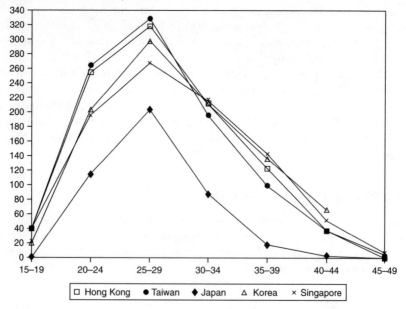

ASFR in EA countries, 1990

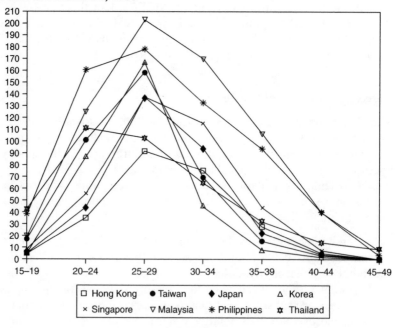

Figure 11.6(a) Age-specific fertility rates (ASFR) in East Asian countries (available data)

Sources: United Nations, *Demographic Yearbook 1992*; United Nations, *Patterns of Fertility in Low Fertility Settings*, New York, 1992; Korea Institute for Health and Social Affairs, *Low Fertility in East and Southeast Asia: Issues and Policies*, August 1994, p. 274

Drop of ASFR during 1965–90 in NEA countries

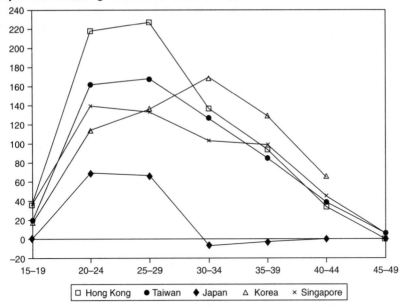

Drop of ASFR in EA countries during 1980s

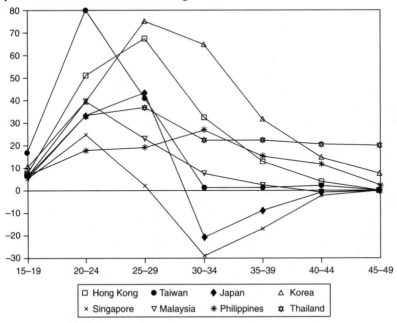

Figure 11.6(b) Drop of age-specific fertility rates (ASFR) in East Asian countries (available data)

- If people consume more other goods and services they will tend to have fewer children but invest more in them, since the quality of children and other goods are complements while the number of children and other goods are substitutes.

However, empirical analyses, both by economists and by demographers, show that economic variables play only partial roles.[2] Effects of income are not always significant if other variables are not properly controlled. Non-economic variables which need to be included in an analysis are in two categories. One is a set of demographic variables which directly affect individual behavior, desired or not. The most important are infant mortality and fertility control. A change in infant mortality leads to a change in desired fertility. Even though having more surviving children implies higher fertility through more survival, it ultimately leads to a lower level, as shown by the evidence on demographic transitions. Although infant mortality is a function of income, a substantial portion of its change is independent of income, especially in developing countries where mortality is influenced by aid from developed countries. The prevalence of fertility control is independent of the level of income in developing countries.

The environmental variables are population policy, density and homogeneity of population, religion and culture, etc. These are related, one way or another, to fertility norms and behavior.

Another variable is the status of women, with their educational attainment and labor force participation rates being especially salient. These variables are not only observable from international cross-section data but are also related to the cost of children, which in turn, depends on the cost of women's time relative to price of other commodities. The effect on fertility of women's educational attainment level however, is not only limited through the cost of children.[3] For one thing, having more educated women may lead to lower fertility via lower infant mortality or better fertility control. For another, it may induce late marriage or a lower proportion of women being married and so lead directly to lower fertility.

3. Factors behind rapid demographic transition in East Asian countries.

A statistical analysis was used to estimate TFR on three kinds of variables: economic, demographic, and environmental. The economic variables were income per capita, female labor force participation and the illiteracy rate of women. The demographic ones were infant mortality and family planning. The environmental one was population density. The results are these.

First, the rapid decline of TFR in Korea, China, Hong Kong and Singapore is due mainly to the demographic factors. In China, family planning rather than infant mortality lies behind the below-the-norm TFR of the country.

Second, in SEA, economic factors in Thailand and Malaysia seem to explain TFRs in these countries better than the other factors, although demographic ones are not far behind. Incomes and labor force participation seem to be important. Malaysia's TFR is higher than that predicted, possibly from pronatalist population policies in the mid-1980s.[4] For Thailand, labor force participation, higher than any other country in the region, seems to be important.

Third, TFR in Indonesia is lower than predicted. One possible candidate is the effectiveness of the family planning program. Indonesia, like China, has an administrative structure that operates at the grass-roots level with a wide range of development activities, including family planning.[5] The family planning program reached into remote and backward communities so that contraceptive use rates for the poorest people were not lower than those for the richest.

Fourth, in the Philippines, the low prevalence of family planning practice is responsible for the lagging fertility decline, behind economic development.

In sum, in NEA except Japan, the fertility decline preceded strong economic development; in China and Indonesia family planning programs may have been responsible. For Thailand and Malaysia, economic factors seem to have dominated. For the Philippines, the demographic transition is far behind the economic development, due perhaps to Catholicism which is opposed to abortion and artificial control of fertility.

IV THE ROLE OF SCHOOL ENROLLMENT

During the demographic transition, all of the East Asian countries increased school enrollments. The demographic transition and the rise in enrollments seem to have been closely related.

1. School enrollment trends

School enrollments are shown in the separate parts of Figure 11.7 by three broad educational categories. Figure 11.7(a) shows primary school enrollments. These have remained about 100 percent since 1965 for all NEA countries and for China and the Philippines. Among the other three SEA countries, Indonesia experienced a dramatic increase in primary enrollments, from below 70 percent to above 100 percent by 1985. Those for Thailand and Malaysia also rose to near 100 percent by 1985.

Secondary school enrollments are shown in Figure 11.7(b). The NEA countries, except Japan, increased their secondary school enrollments after 1965 to reach plateaus in the latter half of the 1980s. Korea shows a remarkable change in the secondary school enrollment rate, rising from 34 percent in 1965 to 90 percent by 1985, far exceeding Hong Kong and Singapore and coming close to Japan.

Northeast Asian Countries

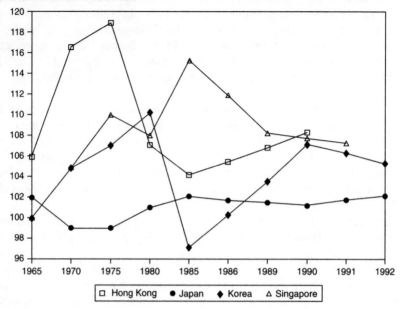

Southeast Asian Countries and China

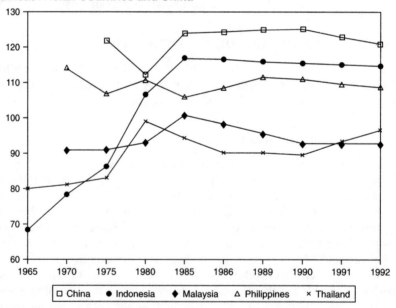

Figure 11.7(a) Primary school enrollment in East Asian countries as percentage of age cohort

Source: World and Korea in Statistical Perspectives, Statistical Office of Korea, 1995

Northeast Asian Countries

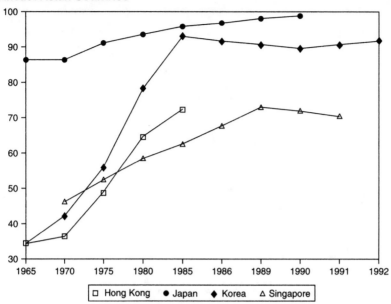

Southeast Asian Countries and China

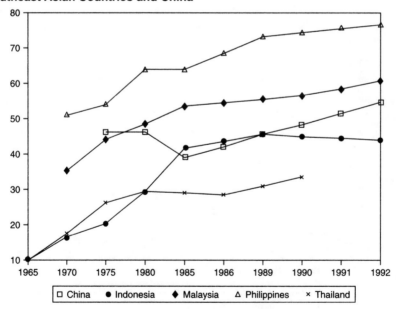

Figure 11.7(b) Secondary school enrollment in East Asian countries as percentage of age cohort (available data)

Source: *World and Korea in Statistical Perspectives*, Statistical Office of Korea, 1995

Northeast Asian Countries

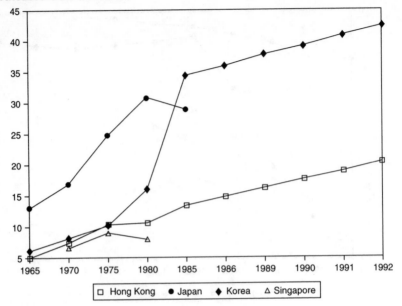

Southeast Asian Countries and China

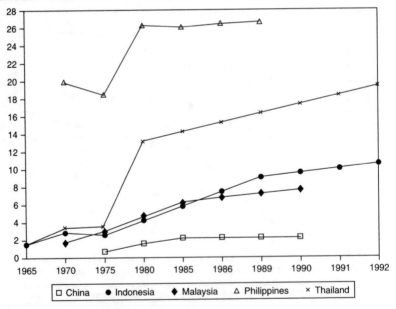

Figure 11.7(c) Tertiary school enrollment in East Asian countries as percentage of age cohort (available data)

Source: *World and Korea in Statistical Perspectives*, Statistical Office of Korea, 1995

Indonesia aside, enrollments in the SEA countries and China increased less dramatically than in NEA. Among them, the Philippines had the highest secondary school enrollments, rising from 50 percent in 1970 to 70 percent by 1989. Malaysia shows a similar trend but it has stayed behind the Philippines. China, unusually, reported a drop, from near 50 percent in secondary school enrollments during the 1975–85 period, but recovered to reach 50 percent again by 1992. Indonesia had the most remarkable increase in secondary school enrollments in SEA, moving from 10 percent in 1965 to 40 percent in 1985. Thailand has lagged, reaching only 30 percent by 1990. These two countries have had slow increases since 1985.

Changes in tertiary school enrollment have been less dramatic, as shown in Figure 11.7(c) – except for Korea. It had a huge increase in tertiary school enrollment, from 6 percent in 1965 to 35 percent in 1985. It exceeded even Japan in the middle of 1980s.

In SEA, tertiary enrollments in the Philippines has been consistently higher than other countries. Those in Malaysia and Indonesia remain low, reaching 10 percent in 1990. China shows no increase, staying below 2 percent to 1990.

2. The linkage of school enrollment to demographic transition

The demographic transition characteristically involves a shift from quantity to quality of population. As incomes rise, both quantity and quality tend to rise at first, but since quality is more income-elastic than quantity and higher quality implies a higher price for raising children, quantity tends to be substituted by quality. The result is that we observe decreasing fertility and higher school enrollments.

The NEA countries, with earlier and more rapid demographic transitions than in SEA and China, not only started with higher enrollments in the mid-1960s but then also had larger increases in them. Although starting points may be affected by varying country-specific factors, such as educational aspirations and initial socio-economic conditions, the enrollment increases might have been more influenced by the demographic transition in each country.

Statistical regressions show that both primary and tertiary level enrollments were largely unaffected by the demographic transition. This is because primary education was compulsory and near universal; tertiary was tightly limited by governments. However, the analysis shows a negative relationship between enrollments and the percentage of secondary school age children; i.e. the larger the cohort, the lower the percentage in school. There were, of course, differences among countries. Japan, Korea and the Philippines had relatively high secondary enrollments whereas China, Thailand and Indonesia had lower ones. Singapore, Hong Kong and Malaysia were in the middle.

3. School enrollment in East Asia compared to the world

Might other factors than demographic transitions explain school enroll-ments? To explore this possibility we have estimated a regression equation that relates school enrollments to explanatory variables observable from world cross-section data. We can then assess the relative position of East Asia, and the probable contribution of demographic transitions, via changes in age composition, on school enrollment.

In sum, school enrollments in East Asian countries are generally higher than the normal levels for their stage of economic development, with Singapore being the only important exception. Secondary school enroll-ments in East Asian countries are rising fast, and are associated with rapid demographic transitions, which seem to be a significant factor in the rise.

V EDUCATION AND ECONOMIC GROWTH IN EAST ASIAN COUNTRIES

It might seem surprising that Singapore's school enrollment rate is lower than the norm while the Philippines' is higher, since the economic perfor-mances of these two countries suggest the opposite if economic develop-ment depends on education. However, the supply of human resources does not necessarily mean better performance unless it is linked to their efficient use. In other words, the supply of human resources is a necessary but not sufficient condition for development. We will consider the mech-anism through which human resources are related to economic develop-ment; consider human resources utilization policies in some of the countries, and try to explain the abnormality in enrollments in Singapore and the Philippines in relation to their development.

1. Intermediate factors between the supply of human resources and its use

The supply of human resources may depend on factors other than economics and demographics. Cultural and institutional factors can affect school enrollments. For instance, Confucian culture has a very high regard for education and the US influence in the Philippines seems to have been positive for higher education.

International migration, both inward and outward, can also be a factor. Immigration of highly skilled manpower from abroad can add human capital. Also, studying abroad is a good substitute for domestic education and affects statistics of tertiary enrollment. Singapore and Hong Kong seem to belong to this category.

The many factors that link education and other aspects of the supply of human resources to their use can be classified into four categories. The first is quality, which includes the intensity as well as the content of education. An example is the ratio of vocational to general education; there is great diversity in this aspect among countries. The second is the efficiency or competitiveness of the labor market and the role of government in linking human resources to firms; countries also differ in these respects. The third is on-the-job training by firms; there are also great differences among countries in the size and structure of firms and their job training activities. The fourth is the growth of markets. Since the demand for labor is derived from the demand for products, the latter ultimately determines the extent to which human resources, no matter how supplied, are used. Whether the country is outward looking (export oriented) or not and how much its major export products are demanded in world markets are important variables.

2. Human resource use

Most of these countries restrict immigration. Singapore is an exception with quite liberal policies on immigration of foreign workers. The NEA countries have many students going abroad for advanced studies because of limited domestic opportunities. Through government effort and with prosperous economies, Korea and Singapore enjoy a high rate of return of these students. In contrast, the SEA countries, especially the Philippines and Indonesia, have low return rates. The leakage or "brain drain" creates a gap between the supply of human resources and that available for economic development.

Countries that share a Confucian culture seem to have higher educational aspirations, with education being both in formal schooling and in off-school tutoring. The intensity of education can be measured by educational expense (not by public educational expense only).[6] The NEA countries and Singapore do not report spending larger proportions of GNP for public education; some SEA countries, i.e., Malaysia and Thailand, allocate about the same shares. However, data on private spending are sparse.

One measure of the intensity of the value attached to education in the NEA countries is the high repetition rate in college entrance examinations and the good performance of students in international contests. For example, in the second "International Assessment of Education Progress" held in 1991, Korea and Taiwan won first and second places respectively both in mathematics and in science for elementary school students (age 9) and middle school students (age 13).[7]

To fully use human resources, the fields chosen and the content of education are no less important than intensity. The NEA countries focused early on technical or vocational education. For example, Korea and Singapore began to pay attention to vocational and technical education from the early 1960s.[8] Although most NEA countries now have shortages of technical and skilled workers, they are better off than those in SEA. Malaysia, Indonesia and Thailand all have shortages of technical manpower that result from their focus on general rather than technical education.[9]

Labor markets resolve such mismatches through competition and wage adjustment. The industrial environment is more competitive and flexible in Korea and Singapore than in SEA. Labor markets in NEA are oriented more to efficiency than to rent-seeking behavior and make more meritocratic allocation of talents in public and private sectors: employment of high-skill laborers is managed through open competition. Also, Singapore tries to solve information asymmetries in the labor market (the so-called "lemons" problem) through standards set by the government.[10]

Firm structure is also important, especially for hi-tech industries. Big business groups in Korea and multinational corporations in Singapore provide internal learning opportunities for their employees to help them adapt to new technologies. Lifetime employment and job-hopping within the group enhances the use of human resources in Korea. SEA has more limited opportunities due either to the limited capacity of domestic business firms or to restrictive labor policies toward foreign direct investment.

The NEA countries have done better than SEA countries in matching the supply and the use of human resources. Singapore pays more attention to this aspect than any other East Asian country; the SEA countries, including the Philippines, have begun to pay attention to it only recently. This helps explain Singapore's fast economic growth with below-the-norm school enrollments and the Philippines' slow economic growth with above-the-norm enrollments.

V CONCLUSIONS

Over the last three decades, most East Asian countries have undergone unprecedentedly rapid demographic transitions. During them, school enrollments rose substantially for all levels. The increase in secondary school enrollments was strong and was closely related to the demographic transition. Since the NEA countries had earlier and more rapid transitions than those in SEA, secondary and tertiary enrollments rose more rapidly for the former than for the latter. Thus there was a positive reinforcement: early high school enrollments contributed to the demographic transition which, in turn, led to a better educated and more productive population later.

The rise in educational attainment ultimately leads to higher output by raising the capacity to absorb new technologies. But between the education of people and the use of their skills, there are labor markets, governments and firms that allocate talent. These intermediary factors work better in NEA than in SEA. Singapore is a case of fast economic growth with relatively low educational attainment while the Philippines represents the opposite case of slow economic growth with relatively high educational attainment.

Education of the population is a necessary condition for economic growth. However, a rise in educational attainment by itself may not produce faster growth, but in combination with well-functioning markets and with advancing technologies, it can have a large effect. The demographic transition has made an important contribution toward fulfilling this condition in East Asia.

NOTES

1 Barro, 1991; Ogawa *et al.*, 1993; World Bank, 1993: 38–60.
2 Simon, 1974; Freedman, 1995; Miro and Potter, 1980: 92.
3 Higher cost of children here may mean higher aspiration for children.
4 Singapore had also taken pronatalist population policy in the middle of the 1980s. While family planning practice, once acquainted, may be still prevalent, the effectiveness of the practice may be affected by the change of policy.
5 Freedman, 1995: 10.
6 Snodgrass, "Education in Korea and Malaysia," Chapter 8 of this volume.
7 Korea Educational Development Institute, 1994: 397; Harold Stevenson, "Human Capital: How the East Excels," Chapter 7 of this volume.
8 Wong and Ng, 1992: ch. 3.
9 Ibid., chs. 4–6.
10 Ibid., ch. 7.

REFERENCES

Barro, Robert J. (1991) "Economic Growth in a Cross Section of Countries", *Quarterly Journal of Economics*, May: 407–444.
Becker, G.S. (1981) *A Treatise on the Family*, Cambridge, MA and London: Harvard University Press.
Freedman, Ronald (1995) "Asia's Recent Fertility Decline and Prospects for Future Demographic Change", *Asia-Pacific Population Research Reports*, Number 1, Program on Population, East-West Center, Honolulu, Hawaii.
Hong, Koon Sik *et al.* (1993) *Population Policies in Low Fertility Countries*, Seoul: Korea Institute of Health and Social Affairs (in Korean).
Korea Education Development Institute (1994) *Educational Indicators in Korea*, Seoul: Korea Education Development Institute.
Korea Institute for Health and Social and Social Affairs (1994) *Low Fertility in East and Southeast Asia: Issues and Policies*, Seoul: Korea Institute for Health and Social Affairs.
Miro, Carmen A. and Joseph E. Potter (1980) *Population Policy: Research Priorities in the Developing World*, Report of the International Review Group of Social Science Research on Population and Development, London: Frances Pinter.
Ogawa, Naohiro, Gavin W. Jones and Jeffrey G. Williamson (eds) (1993) *Human Resources in Development Along the Asia-Pacific Rim*, Oxford, New York: Oxford University Press.
Simon, Julian L. (1974) *The Effects of Income on Fertility*, Carolina Population Center, University of North Carolina at Chapel Hill.

Statistical Office (1995) *World and Korea in Statistical Perspectives*, Seoul: Statistical Office of the Republic of Korea (in Korean).

United Nations (1995) *World Population Prospects, the 1994 Revision*, New York: United Nations.

Willis, R. (1973) "A New Approach to the Economic Theory of Fertility", *Journal of Political Economy*, vol. 81, no. 2, Part II: s14–s69.

Wong, Kam poh and Yuen Chee Ng (eds) (1992) *Human Resource Development and Utilization in the Asia-Pacific: A Social Absorption Capacity Approach*, Singapore: Institute of Southeast Asian Studies.

World Bank (1993) *The East Asian Miracle: Economic Growth and Public Policy*, A World Bank policy Research Report, Oxford University Press, 1993.

Part IV

External influences

Hardly any developing country has been free of invasions, migrations, colonialism, foreign threats and other major external influences. As in other regions, colonialism had a large impact here – although with one significant difference: Japan was a colonial power only in East Asia. The Cold War from the late 1940s to the 1990s was a worldwide phenomenon but it was expressed more strongly in this region than in any other developing one – as was also the influence of the United States.

12 How many models of Japanese growth do we want or need?

James H. Raphael and Thomas P. Rohlen

INTRODUCTION: WHAT KIND OF MODEL?

High growth rates in Japan in the 1955-73 period, the subsequent rapid development of Korea, Taiwan, Singapore and Hong Kong, and then of Thailand, Malaysia, Indonesia and China, have unleashed a deluge of inquiry, speculation and argument on the Asian development pheno-menon. There is keen interest among policy-makers and within academic circles to extract "lessons" or to build "models" based on these experi-ences for possible use in the rest of the developing world. A crucial question is whether the East Asian experience can be reduced to a universal model.

This chapter considers some of the issues one encounters in trying to construct a generalizable model for economic development, based on Japan's experience. Japan holds a special place in the study of development because it was the first non-Western society to industrialize. Other Asian governments have studied Japan closely since the 1960s, and as its economic power and prestige have reached global proportions, countries outside of Asia increasingly have looked to Japan for a formula for success.

We make no claim that the economic systems or sources of growth of other Asian nations are like Japan's. Indeed, the very question we wish to explore is whether or not there is a single Japanese model; more precisely, which aspects of Japan's experience are most salient for other countries today? Earlier scholarship, in the 1960s and 1970s, focused on Japan's industrialization in the context of Western history. While a corpus of solid analysis came from this early work, much of it suffered from weaknesses typical of such comparisons. It was not possible then to dis-entangle what seemed particular to Japan in light of the Western experi-ence from what could be attributable to "late-comer" development as a general phenomenon. There are now much richer data for a truly compar-ative analysis encompassing the West (in its variety), Japan, and the rest of Asia.

Rather than thinking of "a" model of Japanese growth we suggest several different models that one might consider based on three initial questions. First, what is the relevant time frame? Second, what level or how much detail (how many factors, inputs, causal chains, institutional contexts, and so forth) is appropriate? Third, what is the comparative framework? Responses to these questions greatly influence the resulting product. The ingredients – the time frame, the degree of inclusiveness, and the comparative emphases – produce many combinations, more than we want or need; but they highlight the key issues.

What is the relevant time frame?

It has become commonplace to focus on the post-World War II period of Japan's very rapid industrialization, the "miracle" run of historically unprecedented, double-digit, GDP growth from the mid-1950s to the oil shocks of the early 1970s. This period has much to recommend it, particularly because the world had never seen growth rates of over 10 percent for consecutive decades. Accordingly, the institutional arrangements and political economy then in place in Japan are what observers examine first for insights.

But by 1960, Japan was hardly a "developing country." The birth rate had fallen almost to European levels, and educational attainment was rapidly approaching the OECD average. Industrial production had surpassed that of the United Kingdom and France.[1] Moreover, the excellent growth performance after World War II was not entirely without precedent in Japanese history. Japan had enjoyed a similar position, under very different global circumstances, in the prewar period. From 1913 to 1939, Japan's growth rate of 3.9 percent was notably higher than that of either the United States (1.1 percent) or Germany (1.8 percent). Indeed, from 1878–1940, Japan had one of the highest growth rates in the world – around 3.5 percent per year average (rivaling Sweden for first place, depending on the data set used to measure Japan's performance).[2] In any event, Japan's economy had performed well long before the war and the "miracle" surge from the mid-1950s.

Presumably then, one would like a model for Japan that accommodates both its prewar development and that after World War II. Pivotal questions are involved. Was the post-World War II experience qualitatively different from the prewar one, or does the war (and the seemingly low starting point for growth in the late 1940s and early 1950s) simply represent a temporary deviation from a long-term trend of gradually accelerating growth dating back to the 1870s? We shall return to this issue later, but it's worth noting here that the answer is of great relevance in determining whether Japan's experience more closely resembles that of the West historically or of the rest of Asia today.

The time frame is critical because we need to know when key developments occurred (the historical context) and how long it took for them to gestate, mature and then transform (dynamic change). The value of "lessons" gleaned from a snapshot of a short period of time is limited on both accounts. The parameters of time also help us to distinguish the question "what happened?" from the questions "how and why?".

Take human capital development. It took some time to build a modern school system, beginning very early in the Meiji Period. The foundations of Japan's educational system were laid several generations before the results became impressive. This was not only because the policies, infrastructure and teaching personnel (institutional dynamism) took decades to reach the stage where all young people were completing the compulsory nine grades. There was also a changing context: (1) demographic shifts due to advancing education, especially of women, led to smaller families and more household investment in education; (2) official educational standards (not just enrollment rates) were raised incrementally over many decades; and (3) rising levels of parental education proved to be important for the increased capabilities of their children. Change and development are thus slower and more complex for this growth factor than, say, with a very fluid and variable one like direct foreign investment. A similar argument holds for technological progress, where much initial learning involves imitation, borrowing and incremental improvements to imported knowledge. This, too, requires a long-time perspective.

What level of analysis is appropriate?

One is tempted to say that this is a matter of disciplinary taste. But economic development is of such complexity that a single discipline cannot successfully tell the story. In earlier generations, history served as a lead discipline in synthesizing the perspectives of other fields into a single portrait of society. In recent decades, neoclassical economics has moved to the forefront. But the discourse between economists and many, if not most, scholars in other disciplines is fragmented. There is uneven agreement across disciplines on the assumptions about human and institutional behavior undergirding the tools of contemporary economic analysis.[3]

Most economists prefer to consider only variables that are regularly measurable and quantifiable. They also prefer parsimony in their models of causality. The resulting analyses of growth typically use deceptively simple inputs (capital, land, and labor) as proxies for complex realities and treat the remaining story (after that which is explicitly accounted for) as a residual (total factor productivity or TFP). In its most extreme, "macro" form, neoclassical economic growth analysis reduces the human and social dimensions, understates the institutional context, and fails to capture many of the forces that are operating. We learn relationships among a few inputs and outcomes but usually not how or why. Even within the economics profession, there is debate about the cause-and-effect linkages among the factors of production.

For most of us non-economists, much more detail is needed for understanding than is allowed in typical economic modeling. We tend to build our models inductively, from detail to generalization, rather than deductively. We find that economists often tell us too little about the contribution of factors such as the international environment, legal regimes, government policies, sociological patterns and the like. The accidents of history – the emergence of visionary leadership at a critical point or the unintended consequences of certain policies – need to be taken into account. Much of this detail does not lend itself to quantification. As a result, the chains of causal logic become less linear and less statistically demonstrable as detail in the model expands.

Where, then, do we start in thinking about these issues? Nathan Rosenberg, an economic historian whose thinking seems more congenial than most to the non-economist's mind, has written about modeling national growth in terms of specifying a system that combines human, technological, entrepreneurial, and organizational factors within a framework focusing on capital investment. He surveys the broad terrain, noting: "There is now broad agreement that long-term economic growth is more a matter of using resources productively than merely employing more resources. Beyond that, however, there is still no close consensus on the quantitative importance of the separate variables."[4] Rosenberg goes on to explain, "Successful industrialization, where it has occurred, has involved the creation of what might be called a growth *system*, a highly interactive set of forces and institutions that mutually influence one another. Within such a system, it is impossible to separate out the contributions. Rather, within this system changes in any one variable need to be recognized as significantly influencing the "payoff" from other variables."[5]

This can be interpreted to mean a number of important things for constructing a model of Japan. The weighting of any factor needs to take into account that it is part of a system which is neither simple nor static in time. Rosenberg clarifies the implications of this in discussing how technological change must be viewed:

> Thus, the interactions between technological change and capital formation have been central to this growth system. The large size of "the residual" pointed forcefully toward technological change – an unmeasured input – as the critical variable. Yet, technological change, *by itself*, can probably exercise only a very limited impact upon productivity improvement. This is so because most technological changes exercise their impact only when they have been embodied in the form of new and more productive capital equipment. Thus, capital formation is typically the necessary vehicle for determining the speed with which, and the range over which, new technologies generate economic benefits. *Ceteris paribus*, societies that generate high rates of capital formation

will derive the benefits of technological change more rapidly, and to a greater extent, than will societies with lower rates of capital formation.

The economic payoffs to technological change and capital formation have been closely intertwined, with the behavior of each simultaneously determining the value of the other. Similar observations hold, within an industrial system, between the commitment of resources to education and training of the labor force and the rate of technological change. An economy experiencing rapid technological change requires a more highly educated labor force, because such a labor force can more readily make the necessary kinds of adaptations and adjustments. Conversely, in a world of absolutely unchanging technology, the purely economic payoff to further education is likely to be low.[6]

Accordingly, defining a model as a growth system means understanding that all inputs are in dynamic relationship to one another. One must decide whether policies, institutions and historical shifts are to be granted a status comparable to the more measurable, conventional considerations. The same is true for major aspects of the general environment. Is the quality of the bureaucracy, a one-time event like a major land reform, a cultural element like a thirst for learning, or a government policy of targeting industries, important enough to be included as elements of a model? Obviously, the disciplinary preoccupation of the model builder makes an enormous difference in these choices.

What is the appropriate comparative framework?

If we compare Japanese growth after the Meiji Restoration with industrialization in England in the late-eighteenth century certain considerations stand out, such as the transformation of the agrarian sector and the advantages of being a "late comer" (but not too late). If, on the other hand we compare post-World War II Japanese development with recent Korean growth (or for that matter, with Egypt's), very different factors get highlighted. The point is an old, but still important one: that the nature of the comparison shapes our perceptions. The greatest danger is to read history backwards and to compound the problem by doing so for two or more countries whose development occurred at differing times.

JAPANESE GROWTH IN THE 1960s: THE FAMILIAR MODEL

In 1955 – with the economy recently restored to its peak prewar level – per capita income in Japan was thirty-fifth among capitalist countries, and 40 percent of the working population was still employed in agriculture.[7] International economists and business leaders were not looking to Japan as a likely prospect for rapid development; predictions of new centers of growth focused on Latin America and even India, not on Japan.

But by 1965, Japan arguably already had the world's third largest economy,[8] and a decade later the entire world would be talking about the "Japanese miracle."

As spectacular as the 1953–73 growth spurt was, there are good reasons to think of it as continuing the prewar trend. While the physical infrastructure had been ravaged by World War II, the social foundations survived mainly intact. From the individuals who populated executive offices and the corridors of government to the managers and workers on the shop floor, the talent that orchestrated the miracle growth all came from a human resource pool many decades in the making. The ways people organized themselves to work relied heavily on prewar antecedents as well. Finally, postwar growth in the manufacturing sector was especially rapid, more so than for the economy as a whole – again continuing a trend of some 50 years; light manufactures had supplanted agriculture by the early twentieth century as the lead sector and heavy industry emerged as a vital part of the economy in the 1930s as Japan prepared itself for war. Both light and heavy industry continued to expand rapidly in the 1950s and 1960s.

Nonetheless, the idea that postwar growth merely resumed the long-term upward trajectory temporarily disrupted by war is too simplistic. It ignores important institutional adjustments after the war and a more favorable international environment in the 1960s. Growth kept increasing after the economy returned around 1954 to the prewar peak and even after it intersected and surpassed in the early 1960s the trend line one might have expected, extrapolating from the Meiji Period.[9] Postwar growth thus differed from the prewar experience. But the fact that it was launched from a pre-existing high base – the legacy of prior development – partially explains why the postwar era produced such remarkable outcomes.

The mid span of Japan's era of 10 percent average growth was the 1960s, when Prime Minister Hayato Ikeda's trumpeted "income doubling plan" was underway, and it is here where attention typically first focuses. What kind of "growth system" do we find in that decade?

I. Inputs: capital, labor, and technology

Much of early postwar Japan's performance had to do with rapidly increasing inputs – capital, labor and technology – and can be explained at the most general level by standard neoclassical economic theory.[10] Decomposing the double digit growth of the 1960s, it is estimated that approximately 15 percent came from increases in labor inputs (mainly expanding employment and better education), 32 percent from capital accumulation in plant, equipment, and infrastructure, and 53 percent from TFP.[11] The last derives from many processes, such as technology improvements (primarily through adaptation of imported technologies); increasingly efficient labor and capital resource allocation from structural changes in the economy and even industrial policy; and more productive organization and management of the workplace. Much total factor productivity experienced by Japan up to the 1970s, in fact, seems to have come from increasing returns due to economies of scale.

Capital investment grew at 22 percent per year in the 1950s and 1960s; during the decade of the 1960s, gross domestic fixed capital formation (domestic investment) accounted for 30 to 35 percent of Japan's GNP, very high numbers. At the end of the high growth period – in 1973 – Japan's ratio of gross domestic investment to GDP was 38.2 percent compared to the OECD average of 26.2 percent. This capital accumulation came from domestic savings – and not, importantly, from foreign borrowing.

High savings are now widely identified as a key element of Japan's and the Asian NIEs' growth systems, but there is continuing debate over why savings – and notably personal savings – are as robust in Japan as they are. Personal savings rates rose steeply during World War II, plummeted with Japan's defeat and then continued to rise from 1953, peaking in 1974. In 1955, the personal savings rate was about 13 percent and at the end of the high-growth period it had reached 20 percent.[12] There may have been in the traditional world outlook and lifestyles of Japanese citizens something of a culturally-based bias towards frugality, although this historically was insufficient to have substantially affected savings behavior. In prewar Japan, personal (and private) savings episodically were high relative to per capita incomes at the time, but also fell to very low levels with swings in the economy; overall the national savings rate was not impressive.

The growth of savings in postwar Japan suggests instead that the high rates achieved in the 1960s were partially an outcome of optimal institutional arrangements. Policy-determined circumstances both induced savings (by maintaining positive interest rates for savings accounts; providing tax benefits and user convenience through the postal savings system, etc.) and constrained consumption (due to a weak consumer credit system, housing not being principally financed through debt, etc.). Beyond these factors, the postwar structure of salary payments to most employees – featuring large percentages of annual compensation concentrated in semi-annual bonuses – is considered by some to have been an important mechanism for stimulating savings at the household level.[13]

In addition, high savings behavior in Japan closely tracked growth in per capita income. As with all the fast growers in East Asia, increases in Japanese savings rates were partly induced by growth itself. Equally important, income gains – and savings – were broadly distributed through the entire population. As the era of rapid growth progressed, income became more – not less – evenly distributed. By 1970, poverty was all but eliminated in Japan; and from the mid-1970s, over 90 percent of Japanese identified themselves as part of the middle class.

Relative income equality is now widely recognized as an integral part of the Japanese growth model (as well as for Korea and Taiwan).

Broad-based growth directly addresses one of the main purposes of development – making sure that the worst-off members of society have the opportunity to emerge from absolute and then relative poverty.[14] Moreover, a more equal initial distribution of income and an equitable sharing of the subsequent gains of growth can be also important for improving the rate of growth itself.[15]

Growth with equality in Japan had its origins in widely-shared educational attainment, starting in the prewar period and was reinforced by specific policy measures in the immediate postwar period. While inadequate data make analysis of the Meiji era difficult, it is apparent that the income gap in Japan widened from the early twentieth century and especially after World War I; similarly, there were increasing inequalities in land-holding patterns.[16] Occupation reforms imposed by the United States leveled some of these inequalities, notably through land reform and the dissolution of the *zaibatsu*. A relatively flat salary system within firms, extensive consultation with company unions, and an emphasis on seniority in compensation all contributed to income equality.[17]

More importantly, widely-instilled notions of social advancement through ascription, combined with universal literacy and access to education, put enormous weight on human resource development at virtually all levels of society. The 1950s and 1960s saw rapid increases in enrollments at the upper secondary level and in higher education. Standards in education, set by the government, were quite high by 1965, and the result was an educational profile with both a very broad base of educated workers and a rapidly rising level of advanced learning. In 1950, 14 percent of new entrants into the labor force were high school graduates. By 1965, the figure was 47 percent. Similarly, from 1950 to 1965, the percentage of new entrants with some higher education rose from 1 percent to 11 percent. "Education mamas," housewives actively engaged in overseeing their children's progress through their school years, became a widespread social stereotype of the day.

Systemic changes in the postwar labor market dovetailed with the idea of advancement through education. Japanese prewar industrialization developed along the lines of a labor-surplus economy, at least until the 1920s. Growth in the modern sector was first driven by increasing labor inputs at low wages – as seen in light manufacturing and textiles, the lead modern sectors before World War 1. As of 1890, wages for textile workers in Japan were reported to be even lower than in India.[18] With the rise of a heavy industrial sector during and after World War I, wage gaps appeared between large and small firms (and between the agricultural and modern sectors). The differential between large and small companies – often then seen as part of the "dual economy" – persisted through the 1950s, after which it began to close.

By the 1960s, surplus labor and low wages were no longer prominent features of the economy. With full employment and rising wages, small and medium businesses were forced to become more capital intensive (hence, the decline of the dual economy). Demand for higher skilled labor reinforced the importance of education. This tightened the virtuous connection between human and physical capital development and economic growth.

The link between human capital and technological advancement was the other powerful component of the growth system. Japan proved itself to be an astute and very diligent apprentice to Western technology, beginning in the nineteenth century. Circumstances after World War II allowed Japan to continue sourcing technology on the world market – most notably from the United States. Through the 1950s and 1960s, spending on technology licenses was high, and many joint ventures were formed, providing avenues for Japan to acquire foreign know-how.

Human capital and technology interact in mutually reinforcing ways. High human capacity helps technological learning and increases the likely returns from investment in physical capital. The acquisition of new technologies, on the other hand, helps deepen human capital through learning by doing. It is one thing to observe that Japan invested heavily to acquire and adapt foreign technology during this period, but it is quite another to explain why the country did so well in the learning process. The skills needed are many, and they must be accompanied by a strong desire and cultural orientation toward learning.[19] Put another way, Japan was an eager and talented apprentice of Western technology, and this "cultural" aspect of the story cannot be ignored if we are to understand thoroughly the degree of success attained. Here, the comparative question comes into play, for it is only in contrast with less eager and/or talented societies (as far as such learning is concerned) that this aspect stands out as distinctly Japanese or critical to defining "the" Japanese model.

Finally, demand played an integral part in industrial success. The 1950–73 boom period for the world economy and an open trade system, led by the United States, offered an environment particularly favorable to Japan. The Korean War provided an early boost in demand for Japanese goods and services as well. Domestically, reconstruction after World War II – from housing to public infrastructure – was followed by a consumer boom in the 1960s centered on durable goods like refrigerators, televisions and air conditioners. The increasingly even distribution of income (and the accelerating formation of new households due to a young population structure) created a large, middle-class domestic market. Combined with growing exports, sophisticated firms in many sectors achieved economies of scale in production. This, in turn, contributed much to the advance in TFP.

II. The role of government

Acknowledging that rapid growth came from increasing inputs – including technology – there is considerable room to debate the contribution of the state in mobilizing and allocating these factors. Interpretations range from elaborate theories of induced growth from above (the model of the developmental state) to those that portray government intervention in the form of sector-specific industrial policy as of minor consequence in achieving rapid growth. (All sides agree on its positive role in crafting sound macroeconomic policy.) This disagreement is problematic for developing countries seeking to learn from a Japanese model.

A conventional view of latecomer development is that any value from direct government intervention diminishes over time as market forces take hold. From this perspective, the immediate postwar years in Japan present something of an anomaly: government–business relations from the 1950s into the 1970s were closer than they had been in earlier stages of development. Indeed, the level of state intervention in micro-managing the economy was remarkably high compared to the early twentieth century.

History explains much of this. The mobilization of the economy during the Pacific War went far in creating a system with strong bureaucratic influence over the private sector, including national planning to meet strategic objectives and finance for critical industries. The extraordinary measures required to build an economy for war (not the prewar experience) seemed to offer much by way of example for the extraordinary times after defeat. The stage was completed when the Occupation reformers broke the power of the old industrial conglomerates (the *zaibatsu*) but did little to the economic bureaucracies that had guided the wartime effort. Power, for a time, tipped in favor of the bureaucrats.[20]

The system was heavily managed, but with the idea that the domestic market would be competitive. The part of the economy subjected to industrial policy was extensive and included many inefficient industries, as well as those that were proving to be internationally competitive. The government used cartels and sponsored mergers to help firms survive business cycles and to make orderly adjustments; some of these policies were aimed at preventing monopolies and some were anti-competitive. There was a clear government intention that some industries were to be helped in gaining global competitiveness. Furthermore, foreign direct investment was constrained and largely forced into joint ventures with majority Japanese ownership; this helped provide domestic firms with foreign technology. High tariff barriers protected domestic producers. A combination of protection and export promotion helped some firms in achieving economies of scale.

It is difficult to distinguish how much of the resulting economic structure came from the pervasive government interventions as opposed to market forces. Our view is that industrial policy did much to enhance development during the mission-oriented 1950s, when growth and national infrastructure investments were most intimately bound together, but its utility declined steadily from the mid-1960s. The immediate goals were to remove bottlenecks by supporting the reconstruction of critical sectors (electric power, shipping, steel and coal) and to get the country working again.[21] Government intervention was important in stimulating savings and investment, allocating scarce capital to preferred industries, and encouraging competition to attain full employment. Japanese industrial policy during the early part of the high-growth period walked a thin line between promoting infant industries with rapid growth potential and sheltering less efficient sectors with a high capacity to absorb labor.

Success in heavy industry (steel and shipbuilding especially) owed much to government involvement. But in consumer electronics and autos, which emerged in the 1960s, state intervention made little difference or actually hindered exports. Policy failures were also evident, as in efforts at industrial consolidation in the 1960s. What was left at the end of the high growth era was something considerably less than the developmental state model: the government still pursued industrial policies, which had an impact on some sectors, but only marginal – and in some cases negative – consequence for growth as a whole. Industrial policy from the early 1970s was increasingly occupied with ameliorating the unintended consequences of growth, such as pollution and sunset industries; it also shifted to promoting new technologies rather than new sectors.[22]

What lessons can be learned from Japanese industrial policy? It appears to have worked best when goals were concrete and of limited duration (e.g. rebuilding the country's electric power capacity), when the gap with the more advanced countries was largest, when the methods of intervention were indirect and stimulated competition by rewarding successes and penalizing failures (through tax breaks, generous depreciation allowances, export credits, etc.), when *sectors* were targeted for assistance instead of favoring or discouraging *specific companies*, and when financial and labor markets were not yet fully functioning.

But the conditions that made industrial policy optimally effective were particular to the 1950s and early 1960s. The devastation of the war and repudiation of Japan's international geopolitical ambitions provided a unique context for creating a national consensus on a rapid growth strategy. The government could blatantly favor producers over consumers without creating large political problems. Japan also benefited enormously from the openness of the world trade system without having to reciprocate in kind, at least for some years. Foreign exchange controls were tight and capital flows in and out of Japan were strictly limited. Foreign direct investment in the manufacturing Sector was restricted. The banking system was regulated extensively and protected from foreign competition. The percentage of the budget allocated to defense spending was less than 2 percent of GNP.

Finally, industrial policy would not have looked as attractive in hindsight if the government had not gotten macroeconomic policy right and maintained financial stability. Government spending was kept in check by a tight-fisted Ministry of Finance which contained outbreaks of inflation and restrained public expenditures (even at the expense, when necessary, of industrial policy). And a fixed exchange rate added to the overall predictability of the financial environment.

Policies are no better than their execution, and a stable political environment clearly was helpful. The Liberal Democratic Party (LDP), which made high growth the centerpiece of its political program and the basis of its legitimacy, controlled the government throughout the 1955–73 era. With this continuity, policy announcements encompassing long time-horizons could be taken as reliable signals to markets of future trends. Had Japan experienced alternating party control, or political instability, or a ruling party less unambiguously dedicated to growth, investment decisions would have been much more difficult and risk premiums would have been higher.

Considering the consensus for rapid growth, the income distribution pattern, the enthusiasm for education and savings, and greater worker involvement in management, we see a pattern of mass participation or popular mobilization that was both congruent with the overall growth effort and a guarantee that it would be sustained. A sense of a shared economic destiny among Japanese and a common willingness to invest in the future were also aspects of these trends.

III. Trade

International trade has been generally viewed as important to Japan's postwar "growth system." Imports provided raw materials for Japanese industrial production, as well as new technology. Exports were an engine of domestic growth, both in encouraging capital accumulation and in changing the industrial structure toward higher value-added manufacturing. Here, the intersection of industrial policy and private sector initiative were compatible, although the role of government on the export side tends to be over-stated. More generally, competition in international markets set the standards for quality and efficiency by which Japan's major firms benchmarked themselves.

One should not exaggerate, however, the experience of postwar Japan as a model of export-led growth for developing countries today. First, large parts of the Japanese economy were protected from international forces in the 1950s and 1960s in ways that are not feasible to replicate today. Infant industry protection, capital controls, and barriers to entry for foreign direct investment helped shelter large pockets of inefficiency, even as certain Japanese industrial sectors approached and then ultimately surpassed leading world productivity levels. The very low levels of intra-industry trade and generally small imports of manufactures, hallmarks of postwar Japan's trade structure, would be hard politically to sustain today.

Second, the forms of protection practiced by Japan created structural conditions that cannot be reproduced by developing countries in an era of globalization. One characteristic of the Japanese trade system in the pre-war and post-war periods was that nearly all aspects – from local materials sourcing, manufacturing, financing, shipping and handling, to local marketing – were conducted by Japanese firms. Today's world trade system, featuring the ubiquity of multinational corporations, transnational strategic alliances, and international finance, requires a very different approach.

Third, the overall impact of trade needs to be kept in perspective. Trade grew largely because the domestic economy grew. The ratio of Japanese merchandise exports to GDP in 1973 (8.9 percent) was not much different than it had been in 1900 (8.3 percent). Outside the United States, Japan's export ratio in 1973 was lower than every other OECD country (the OECD average being 20.9 percent).[23]

IV. Firm-level developments

The Japanese historically owed much to private entrepreneurship. Businessmen were at the center of the rationalization process that reduced production costs, raised competitiveness, developed products, and incrementally accomplished what was necessary to achieve growth.

It was during the 1960s that many aspects of Japanese corporate management emerged. Zero-defect management was very widely pursued and led to a preoccupation with quality. The QC Circle movement was spreading rapidly by the late 1960s, as was just-in-time inventory systems. That these and other changes contributed to large efficiency gains is clear; they made Japanese exports, such as autos, electronics and machine tools, more competitive. But other sources of productivity gains, largely arising from heavy investment in equipment, arguably had a greater impact over the entire period we are considering.

This should not cause us to remove the role of management from our model, however. A critical aspect of the 1955–73 period was the steady decline in labor problems and the fact that wage increases consistently remained below productivity gains. Lifetime employment and the distinctive salary system in large firms were foundations for company unions, which, in turn, were the institutional basis for moderating labor strife and wage increases. Days lost to labor disputes were very high in the early 1950s, but due to subsequent improvements in labor relations and the employment system, Japanese industries were able to raise productivity, control wage inflation, and increase working hours.

V. The international environment

The world after the Pacific War was a relatively benign place for Japan. Protected by the American security umbrella, Japanese military expenditures could be kept low (in contrast to South Korea or Taiwan where defense spending was heavy). Similarly, world resource prices, especially for oil, were low, a major advantage for a heavy importer of raw materials. Finally, the American market was not only open, but also growing rapidly.

United States–Japan relations at the people-to-people and business-to-business levels similarly expanded, in part because of connections made during the Occupation and the wars fought by the United States in Korea and Vietnam. Honda motorcycles, Japanese cameras and stereo equipment, and much more appear to have gotten their toehold in the American market as a result of initial GI interest. Many of the Japanese who became managers of marketing activities in the United States at this time also got their start by working with Americans in Japan. What Japan's economic performance would have been under differing conditions is impossible to know, but almost certainly there would not have been as export-oriented a pattern of development or as long a period of growth.

In this overview of the high growth era, we have emphasized the many considerations involved and their interrelations. We have left out other explanations, such as the Japanese work ethic, the homogeneity of the population and the harmonious nature of Japanese society, the risk-reducing aspects of *keiretsu* (networks of companies linked by mutual obligation) and main bank systems and the relative efficiency of the central government. The real work of model building is not to create laundry lists, but to specify the key inputs, the system that generates them, and their relationships over time. In order to further examine the dimension of time, we now turn back to the Meiji period, when fundamentals were being established and to wartime Japan, when several more of the postwar characteristics of the Japanese system were created.

PREWAR HISTORY AND "THE" JAPANESE MODEL

Growth systems do not arise overnight; their origins must be sorted out from complex historical circumstances. There is now a consensus that rapid growth in post-World War II Japan was rooted in a trajectory of industrialization over the period from 1868 to 1945 and, furthermore, that the antecedents of modern development, from the mid-nineteenth century, can be traced to the gradual transformation of Japan during the Tokugawa period (1600–1868). Even in 1868, Japan had many of the makings of a modern state: a well-established sense of national identity, relatively strong institutions of governance, a literate bureaucracy, a sophisticated agricultural economy with high productivity levels, a well developed network of markets based on monetary exchange, an incipient division of production (proto-industrialization), a vibrant merchant class and a well-honed curiosity about the outside world. These preconditions did not determine Japan's success, but they made it more likely with the right mix of circumstances and policy. Japanese economic development, in other words, evolved over relatively long periods, not unlike the story in Europe.

Obviously, there have been significant institutional discontinuities, especially from external shocks and/or changes in the international system. But the fabric of the Japanese economy is embedded deeply in history.

In looking at Japan's development before World War II, we emphasize three themes. First, the pattern was not unlike much of the West's – with obvious time lags. That is, there was a protracted but progressive transformation of the economy and society from agriculture to labor-intensive, light industry to heavy industry. The distinctiveness of Japan's case – if there was one aside from the particular historical and cultural context in which it occurred – rests in moderate trend acceleration over this period toward ever-higher rates of inputs and subsequent growth.[24]

A second, related theme is the rapidity and adroitness with which Japan acquired the institutional capacity, in both the public and private sectors, to modernize. Japan's leadership quickly gained the acuity to steer through a maze of policy options at a time when there were no theories of development available and no international institutions to lend a helping hand. The Meiji leaders were not the carefully groomed, foreign educated elite so typical of developing countries today. Rather, they were members of the warrior class of a relatively isolated and politically feudalistic society transformed into statesmen, diplomats and captains of industry. Their only models were the advanced Western countries, and they soon learned to evaluate them astutely and selectively. Their accomplishments – now almost taken for granted – were truly the first "miracle" of modern economic development.

Third, the rule of unintended effects certainly applied. Many of the elements later viewed as beneficial to growth did not originate for the purpose of development and others intended to produce one kind of effect actually produced different ones.

Demographic circumstances

Japan, much like Europe, passed through the demographic transition to moderate and then low population growth with few of the challenges confronting developing countries today. Population growth in the 150 years before 1868 was very low. Between 1720 and 1870, the population grew from 26 million to only 30 to 33 million – annual increases a fraction of the 2.6 percent experienced by East Asia's developing countries in the late 1960s as they entered their rapid economic growth periods. From the 1880s into the early 20th century, Japan's population growth increased to moderately high levels (averaging 1 percent per annum – slightly higher than Europe but significantly lower than the United States over that period). By the 1920s, Japan's fertility rate was already in secular decline; government pro-natalist policies from 1940–45 could only momentarily arrest this trend.

The implications of Japan's population dynamics over time for the course of economic development have been enormous, even though largely unplanned. Japan entered Meiji as a mid-sized state with a population large enough that development could be pursued, wittingly or unwittingly, using the marginal gains from surplus agrarian labor in industry. At the same time, the population was not growing so rapidly as to absorb increases in agricultural output, which were instead a source of industrial capital. Domestic markets were of a size to allow for economies of scale. Moreover, population growth – even in the peak decades – was low enough to accommodate human capital deepening through increased educational spending; productivity was helped through higher capital to worker ratios; and higher incomes led to more savings.

The political economy in historic context

Born out of resistance to the encroachment of Western powers in its immediate environment, the Meiji state viewed economic development as an instrument of national military power. "Fukoku-kyohei" (rich nation, strong army) became the galvanizing slogan for a generation of modernizers – with significant implications for public policy, the relationship of state and society, and mobilization of the populace for change.[25] The importance of these historical circumstances can hardly be exaggerated. Free market liberalism – as imperfectly formed and practiced as it might have been at the time in the West – was not embraced by Meiji Japan. Reflecting both national security imperatives of the day and the Tokugawa political economy from which it emerged, Japan's modern growth instead arose as a hybrid of market competition and government guidance, adjusted with circumstances.[26] Nationalism was the dominant ideology, and unlike twentieth-century nationalisms, neither democracy nor socialism were of much importance; even capitalism was not intellectually well grounded.

Initial development policies

Are there elements of the Meiji experience that can help us identify the contours – if not the details – of a rudimentary development model? The Meiji state was an autocratic regime; in implementing policies, it more closely resembled the authoritarian governments in much of developing Asia 20 or 30 years ago than did the post-World War II Japanese political system. But Japan's leaders had a vision of grander national goals than those of merely perpetuating the regime for their self-centered interests. Early on, the oligarchy carried out a "revolution from above," stripping the former samurai class (from which the Meiji leaders themselves hailed) of its hereditary privileges (impoverishing most ex-samurai in the process) and creating a government and society based on the principle of merit.[27]

It helped that the small collective of oligarchs who guided the Meiji state – the *genro* – were nationalists to the end, putting the interests of the nation above all else, including personal gain.

The Meiji leadership charted an activist role for the state in Japan's mission to catch-up to the West. It mobilized the population to its cause and shaped a modern citizenry through compulsory education, military conscription, and emphasis on the Imperial institution, and it appealed to nationalist sentiment via periodic foreign military ventures. It marshaled and distributed economic resources for physical and social infrastructural development. It created institutions to support modern business (universal commercial codes and property right laws, a national banking and financial system, etc.). It sent its citizens and officials abroad in large numbers to learn about the West – including what made it strong. Finally, it encouraged industrial sectors of strategic importance.

Do these activities constitute a sufficiently robust model to explain Japan's early industrialization? Does Meiji Japan represent a classic case of "growth from above" led by the state? Much of the government's activity in the first decades of Meiji was part of a broader nation-building process, rather than a conscious effort to create a top-down political economy. Nonetheless, there are elements of the Gerschenkronian notion that under conditions of backwardness, where capital, technology and enterprise are in short supply, the state can serve as a mobilizing agent for development.

In the 1870s, for example, the Japanese government built and ran factories related to national defense (machinery, shipbuilding, mining, telegraph lines, etc.) and as models of modern industry (e.g., textiles and glass making), doing what Peter the Great and others had tried before – to generate national power by creating the industrial base for military might. Up to 1880, nearly all the modern sector was government owned. This flurry of early interventions seems natural, given the tremendous task of developing the infrastructure of a modern economy and the fact that few industrial enterprises existed before Meiji.

But few economic historians today would argue that Meiji Japan represents a simple "growth from above" model. Most growth in the first decades of the Meiji Period came from below – from agriculture and agrarian-based industries like sake brewing and sericulture and then from light industry centered around textiles where government involvement was minimal.[28] Development of a modern industrial sector came much later – in the decades after World War I.

Indeed, what is striking in historical context was how quickly the Meiji state backed out of the business of business once a private sector began to emerge. The Meiji leaders found bureaucrats ill-fitted to their tasks as factory managers; the state-owned factories were inefficiently run and increasingly costly to a financially-pressed government. Nearly all were privatized in 1880, after only 12 years, in a wholesale sell-off of assets.

The operations played an important role at that moment as demonstrations for an uninitiated citizenry and to the outside world, but were generally failures as businesses; few survived into the twentieth century.[29]

Aside from these early experiments, the Japanese government played a role in the nineteenth and early twentieth century economy little different from governments in the West. Japan rapidly moved from a command economy to a market-based one. It soon left the creation and management of enterprises – even most of those critical to the military – to the private sector.

There were exceptions, of course, such as the state-run Yawata Iron Works and the national railway system. But nearly all the industrialized countries supplied examples of state intervention. These were features, for example, of the Russian, German and Italian political economies of the late nineteenth century.[30] Even in the United States, the construction of the transcontinental railroad network – perhaps the single most powerful engine of modern American economic growth – was stimulated by government intervention in the form of land grants.[31] There is little in the Meiji initiatives to suggest that the government was trying to create a political economy or system of capitalism outside the range of variations found in the West. This should not be surprising since the frame of reference came almost solely from Japanese observations of the actions of Western governments.[32]

What is remarkable was how quickly the Meiji government moved on many fronts to create the institutions required for modern development. The long European course of institutional evolution that led to innovation and industrialization through market incentives for labor and enterprise[33] was truncated into decades by the Meiji elite. It was, to be sure, a process of trial and error, but the successes greatly outweighed the failures. Perhaps the most valuable lesson from the Meiji experience is that even as the government encouraged development of critical sectors, it opened the economy to market forces, thereby fostering entrepreneurship, competition and broad-based participation in the growth process. The model of development was at once classical, neoclassical, and Gerschenkronian.

The political economy also evolved in idiosyncratic fashion around institutional, political and cultural circumstances specific to Japan. Fallouts from the early government-led industrial experiments, for instance, are still around. For one, bureaucrats have sought ever since to use markets as the principle means to their industrial policy goals. Second, the financial and commercial *zaibatsu* in Japan were converted overnight into diversified conglomerates, acquiring major facilities at low cost, thanks to the government sell-off in 1880. And third, these strategic industries evolved ties between government and business that became the foundation of the post-World War II system (involving frequent consultation, recourse to various instruments supporting entire sectors, industry compliance with "administrative guidance", and so forth).

The state–industry nexus, before the 1930s, centered on government efforts to stimulate technological innovation and to support industries and infrastructural needs with military-strategic implications. The government share of new capital investment from 1870 to 1914 averaged 40 percent per annum.[34] From the early twentieth century, there was an increase in government expenditure as a percentage of GDP, but it did not go beyond levels found at the time in Germany and the United Kingdom.[35] At peak periods (around the time of the Sino-Japanese and Russo-Japanese Wars and in the 1930s through the Pacific War), massive military expenditures helped create a domestic market for heavy industry (especially ship-building and iron and steel). This stimulated growth of certain industries, but the motivation was less economic than political and military. Indeed, it is far from clear whether the economy would not have grown at least as rapidly if demand had been driven by private consumption.[36]

The role of agriculture

Other elements of Meiji development are potentially relevant for constructing an explanatory model of growth. One might be agriculture. Agriculture is at the core of the two-sector development model common to much of the earlier development literature, and it relates to the debate about whether Japan experienced growth from above or below.[37]

Where it was once thought that fast growth in the agricultural sector was the critical foundation of modern Japanese growth (with gains in late nineteenth century agricultural productivity providing the capital input for industrialization through government taxation and redistribution), we now see a more complex interdependence between the agrarian and modern sectors. Productivity appears already to have been high at the beginning of Meiji (Japanese paddy rice yields in 1878–82 were substantially higher than those of Thailand, Indonesia and India in the period 1953–62 and not much lower than those of Korea and Taiwan in the 1950s); the gross value of farm production continued to rise steadily (1.5 percent per annum before 1890 and 1.8 percent up to 1920), allowing for a modest transfer of savings from agriculture to other sectors of the economy.[38] But the more important contribution of agriculture now appears to have been as an incubator of entrepreneurship, commercialization and marketization in the countryside (i.e., growth from below), led by the production of light consumer goods like processed food and sericulture. Out of these early successes emerged the urban-based national merchants and industrialists of the early twentieth century.

The agricultural sector was also significant in other ways. First, the land tax, the initial primary source of government income, was important. As late as the 1880s, it provided 70 percent of all national and local government revenues, although its share of total state revenues dropped steadily thereafter (falling to under 5 percent by the 1930s). Second, as is typical of early developing countries, agricultural products initially dominated Japanese exports (making up nearly two-thirds of total exports in the 1880s), and helped fund the import of needed capital goods and equipment. Finally, a robust agrarian sector had a moderating influence over time on food prices, which helped keep down industrial wages in Meiji.

We can thus see that agriculture played a large role in Japan's early Meiji growth, but this was less directly connected to structural changes than the growth-from-above model suggests. Also, the transformation of agriculture in Japan proceeded slowly compared to many developing countries today. Between 1878 and 1940, the number of gainful workers in agriculture declined from 15.5 to 14 million; agriculture's employment ratio dropped from 82 percent in 1878–82 to 48 percent in 1933–37.[39] Agriculture in prewar Japan remained a large employer of labor.

Other dynamics: human resources and technology, export-led growth, entrepreneurship, and capital formation.

Let us now look at early Japanese development through the lens of a strategic resources model. It was once thought that resource endowment – and the efficient extraction of resources – was the key variable in successful industrialization. (It provided a powerful rationale for both nineteenth-century Western imperialism and Japanese imperialism.) Economists of the day spoke frequently of the advantages of possessing iron, coal, and the other material ingredients of manufacturing, but resources more broadly defined to include agricultural and forestry products generally fit into the model as well.

Japan's industrialization helped undermine and then transform this model, but not until after the fateful era of Japanese expansion and warfare in East Asia aimed at securing a resource "lifeline."[40] By the late 1960s, the question had become: if a country as meagerly blessed with natural resources as Japan could industrialize, what factor endowments account for its success? From this basic reformulation emerged two new models – one that focused on human resources and technology generation as key, strategic resources in the development process and the other that put primacy on the role of foreign trade. Both of these models have been widely employed to explain Japan's post-World War II success. We consider them here in the context of the prewar experience.

(1) The human resource/technology development model

Perhaps no single element of the prewar Japanese experience is more salient for developing countries today than the persistent effort at human resource development. New, endogenous theories of growth link high levels of human capital accumulation to rapid technological advance. The higher the human capital stock, it is now argued, the higher the rate of later physical capital investment and income growth.[41]

About 15 percent of the population was literate at the beginning of Meiji. The new government moved quickly to establish universal elementary education. The emphasis was on primary education, where the social costs are lowest and the payoffs the highest. Enrollments did not immediately reach the goals set but this effort began very early, even by European standards. The elimination of illiteracy typically takes several if not many generations; even at the turn of the century, military conscription data show that between 10 and 20 percent of the young men still had serious limitations in reading and writing. But by 1905, Japan had a 96 percent enrollment rate for primary schooling (grades 1–6). Years of schooling steadily increased from that point. As of 1950, it had an average of 9.11 years of primary and secondary education per person over the age of 15, close to the OECD average of the time of 10.2 years.[42] Equally significant, the concept had been implanted throughout society that education was the best means of social ascent.

The linkage between human resource deepening and technology development is direct and mutually reinforcing. A literate population can more readily learn and use technologies and higher human resource levels become an important source of technological development. While the capacity to create technology was to come later, Meiji Japan proved to be surprisingly adroit at importing and adapting it to local needs in sectors from agriculture to modern manufacturing. Technology was transferred through capital equipment imports and personnel exchanges (both in the form of hiring foreign technicians to come to Japan and sending Japanese to study abroad).

Meiji Japan quickly recognized the importance of technology, both as a substitute for absent natural resources and as a cornerstone of its military–security strategy. Technology was treated as a strategic resource, and the state played an active part in its acquisition and development. Technology gaps with the West came to be narrowed – and some to be closed.

But the "lessons" coming out of Japan's "techno-nationalism" are difficult to isolate because much of the learning was of an incremental, trial-and-error nature. Domestically-produced breakthroughs and technology leap-frogging were rare.[43] These efforts, it must be remembered, centered on technologies moving at slower rates of change than today. Japanese universities, it should also be noted, turn out large numbers of engineers relative to natural scientists in comparison to Western universities, and this has been true since the 1880s. Borrowing and improving, not inventing, has been the national strategy until very recently.

In the prewar era, Japan essentially set the pace and defined conditions for technology acquisition on its own terms. From the start, technology transfer was viewed as an indigenous, learning-by-doing process. Foreign advisors were replaced with Japanese technicians and imported equipment with domestic manufactures as rapidly as possible. Most significantly, foreign direct investment was carefully channeled. This, of course, is a very different situation than we see in much of contemporary Asia (although South Korea's strategy is remarkably like Japan's).

The path toward technological catch-up also was easier for Meiji (and postwar) Japan than for nations today. It benefited from an era when core technologies, even at the state of the art, were more readily available for appropriation, often well below full cost, from the West. Segmented markets, often small, made firms more willing to license their technologies and made trade barriers easier to maintain. Moreover, competition from within the ranks of developing countries was meager; Japan was able, for example, ultimately to dominate sectors like silk and upper-end textiles without new competitors constantly coming on stream.

(2) The export growth model

Models of export-led growth treat international competition as a critical mechanism for getting domestic market signals right, maximizing potential national comparative advantages, and moving up the ladder of value-added manufactures. But Japan's rationale for exporting also hinged on the need to import nearly all its raw materials and many capital goods. Japan usually ran trade deficits up to the 1930s. In many ways, Japanese growth in the prewar period can thus be characterized as import-led, not export-led.[44]

Trade has been an integral part of Japan's modern economic life, but its overall contribution to development before World War II remains a point of controversy. Trade showed impressive growth (between 1878–1938, 7 percent per annum versus a little over 3 percent for GNP), but the trade volume baseline in early Meiji was very low. Even as late as 1913, the value of Japan's exports lagged behind the smaller economies of Europe (e.g., Norway, Finland and Denmark all had higher exports at the time); Japan's exports as a ratio of GDP (13 percent) were unexceptional as late as 1929 (only the United States at 5 percent and Italy at 10.4 percent were lower among the future OECD countries).[45]

More than the direct contribution of trade to growth, Japan's economy from early on was relatively open. The unequal treaty system (and low tariffs) imposed by the West in the late 1850s left Japan's infant industries exposed to foreign competition from the start. Rapid progress in the consumer goods sector became critical in early Meiji as substitutes for imports and to stem the outward flow of currency. From import substitution came export success in labor-intensive industries like textiles and in primary products, such as silk and tea, which helped finance needed imports.

In making this transition, Japan was the beneficiary of a prosperous and liberal world order (especially between 1900–13) and then of the material requirements of the allies in World War 1. But these benefits were not accrued passively: even before the Meiji Restoration, it was recognized that producing for the world market would be critical to the nation's industrialization.[46] This outward orientation resurfaced as a dominant theme in Japan's postwar development.

(3) The enterprise-level or entrepreneurial model

It is worth repeating that private enterprise and market competition have been the driving forces of Japan's economy.[47] The basic agents of growth have been businesses, not the government. So any appropriate development model based on the nineteenth- and early twentieth-century Japanese experience must allow for the emergence of a vibrant business/ management class, the role of politics in enhancing (or at times reducing) firm competitiveness, and the internal characteristics of companies that allowed them to adjust to the changing business environment.

Within the vast literature on Japanese business development, attention has focused on management practices and labor relations (corporate paternalism, permanent employment, the seniority wage system, etc.) and on the structure of enterprise. For the nineteenth and early twentieth century period, Japan's industrial combines, the *zaibatsu*, are generally viewed as exceptional from a Western perspective. Two of the three largest (Mitsui and Sumitomo) pre-date the Meiji Period and are not amenable to an analysis that begins with the period of Western-inspired industrialization.

Today's *keiretsu* (the successors to the *zaibatsu*; more specifically, long-term, stable relationships among many kinds of firms – usually including a bank) have prospered over the many changes of the last one hundred years. The structure of Japanese industrial conglomerates evolved. The *zaibatsu* progressively brought into their subcontracting networks a significant portion of small and medium manufacturers, and because of the centrality of banks to their financial dealings, they established what is today referred to as the "main bank" system. In periods of tight credit and high debt/equity ratios (such as 1955–73), the system has enabled a high level of risk to be managed within a network of corporate financial relations.

Trading companies, another legacy of the prewar *zaibatsu*, were central to Japan's export drives well into the 1960s when the largest manufacturers took over much of their own exporting. That trading companies still handled much of Japan's external transactions during the 1955–73 era was no surprise, given their historic roles as intermediaries between a still insular Japan and a world equally unfamiliar with Japanese language and mores. History shows, however, that the trading firms arose more to import raw materials than to export manufactured ones – another interesting irony – and a reflection of the initial role played by trade.

(4) The macro-growth model

We are left at the end of this exercise with a mixture of explanations for Japan's start on modern growth. No single theory or model of development adequately captures the complexities of the process that led Japan to industrialization. At the end of the day, we are back to basics – namely, the argument that the prewar Japanese economy developed in the usual way: through market mechanisms and increasing capital, labor, and technology inputs. Identifying the essence of the Japanese growth system, one might argue, is as simple and as difficult as identifying the relevant institutional and social variables that mobilized factors of production in a mutually reinforcing, accumulative and efficient manner.

We wish here to only re-state several highlights. Despite wide business cycle swings, there was a long-term movement towards higher levels of capital, labor and human capital inputs, resulting in higher output. The annual growth of physical capital was a robust 5.4 percent from 1889-1938, significantly higher than the growth rate of the economy as a whole. As a result, gross domestic fixed capital expenditures took an ever increasing share of Gross National Expenditures – rising from 9.2 percent in 1888 to 19.3 percent in 1920 and 26.2 percent in 1938.[48] These investments were financed almost exclusively through domestic savings, unlike the United States in the nineteenth century.

Because Japan had a large population on the eve of modern development (its 34 million people in 1870 was second in size to only the United States and France among the countries later to form the OECD) and a dense man-to-land ratio, it came to have a large pool of agrarian labor to draw into industry. The early growth gains came in substantial part from a surplus of labor, which industry used at low wage rates; low-skilled, labor-intensive enterprises dominated the economy (including the export sector) into the 1920s. The crossover point at which labor supply became inelastic is still debated.[49] From World War 1, real wages in heavy manufacturing began to increase, but aspects of a dual economy with substantial wage differentials between the large-scale modern sector and traditional small and medium manufacturers persisted until the 1960s.

At the same time, it is important to recall Japan's slow population growth through the nineteenth and early part of twentieth centuries; the labor supply grew steadily, at 0.5 percent per annum, between 1880–1920. In consequence, the nation did not face the daunting problems of labor absorption or mass unemployment seen in parts of the developing world today.

INSTITUTIONAL CHANGE IN HISTORICAL PERSPECTIVE

Many institutions that have been considered both distinctly Japanese and critical to the growth system of the 1955–73 period were created at the beginning of Meiji, and were based on Western models. The banking system was copied from the United States structure of local and state banks; only gradually did it become centralized. The school system was an amalgam of the French compulsory system, the German university and the American technical institute. The rules of the stock market were largely derived from the Paris Bourse. The regulations governing corporate stock companies, the postal savings system, the economic ministries and so forth all trace their roots to some Western exemplar (rather arbitrarily determined by Meiji officials under considerable time constraints).

The more interesting point, however, is not the origin of Japan's economic institutions, but their transformation over the 80 years from the beginning of Meiji to the outset of the economic boom. The most critical period was World War II when central authority was radically extended over all aspects of the economy. The banking system, for example, was consolidated into a highly regulated set of distinct categories. A number of innovative changes were implemented within firms. Workers were organized into patriotic production organizations at the company level, and management was expected to "consult" extensively with them about working conditions and production goals. These proto-unions became the foundation of labor unions after the War when, under the Occupation, the government legalized such organizations. Thus, the Japanese company union was a product of the convergence of unlikely events.

The financial organization of the postwar *keiretsu*, the subcontracting system between large and small firms, the seniority wage system and the practice of administrative guidance by the economic bureaucrats all trace their origins to wartime mobilization.[50] In other words, many of the postwar institutional elements of the growth model need to be understood as specific products of history, most with origins that had surprisingly little to do with their ultimate functions in the 1955–73 growth era. There was never a grand scheme, and no one could have predicted as late as 1950 what the juxtaposition of the nationalist/planned wartime system with the American-inspired liberal reforms instituted by the Supreme Command Allied Powers (SCAP) would produce.

World War II produced another important contribution to Japan's postwar growth. Military conscription and the industrial mobilization increased the technical skill level in the population. Military training introduced advanced technology in aviation, ship machinery, tool making, vehicle design and telecommunications to a much wider audience than would have received it in peacetime. These skills became available to postwar industries.

Heavy industry, the object of much of early postwar industrial policy, was of increasing interest to prewar and wartime governments. If there were heavily managed sectors, they were in chemicals, shipbuilding, heavy machinery, steel, and the like. Despite their increasingly mutual dependence during this period, the military distrusted the old *zaibatsu* and vice versa; and, as a result, the military encouraged upstart conglomerates in the areas under their control (which included armaments). It is not an exaggeration to characterize elements in the 1930s military establishment as anti-capitalist. After Pearl Harbor, this tendency accelerated. Defeat ended these experiments, but the main point is that as Japan approached World War II, the foundations of Meiji and early 20th century economic growth became less recognizable. Had Japan won the war, the economy would likely have been heavily managed, with extensive constraints on most markets.

Instead, SCAP dissolved the *zaibatsu*, reformed land ownership, legalized labor unions, and to a degree decentralized and democratized government functions. Ironically, the agents of these reforms were central government bureaucracies that were largely holdovers from the wartime ministries which had wielded such administrative power. The liberalization of Japan by the Americans served to perpetuate a governing apparatus whose origins and recent history were of a very contradictory nature. The major difference was that military requirements were no longer the central concern. MITI and MOF (the Ministries of International Trade and Industry and of Finance respectively) were left to focus their efforts on recovery and economic growth. This is not a story of brilliant planning or of a clever bureaucratic conspiracy to achieve world power. The Japanese "model" in its postwar institutional configuration is a complex history full of unintended results.

CONSIDERATION OF SOME LESS TANGIBLE FACTORS

Institutions and data are the ingredients of the conventional models of economic growth, but these may not provide for certain kinds of understanding. We need to know how institutions actually work and why economic relationships take certain forms. Take corruption, which is rampant in some countries and not in others. Similarly, why do things turn confrontational in some nations' labor–management dealings and not in others, or why do some resort easily to legal processes in business transactions and others hardly at all? We need to understand why aggregate behavior in one nation, such as enthusiasm for learning or trust in the government, differs from another. Answers can be found only through extensive immersion into the cultural and social roots of everyday life and thought. This chapter does not pursue such inquiries, but the following are some of the less tangible qualities about Japan in this century that deserve serious consideration:

1 Honest bureaucrats. While politicians have been much involved with the flow of money under the table, there has been remarkably little bureaucratic corruption. No account of this phenomenon is adequate without mention of the ideals of the key ministries, their socialization

of new recruits, the elite education and status of bureaucrats, and the many checks and balances involved. Without such honesty, the economic policy mechanisms would have had little integrity.

2 A general conviction in the population and among parties in economic relationships that trust is justified, that reciprocity will ultimately be balanced, and that all parties share many interests. This "in the same boat" mentality, a transformed version of Meiji economic nationalism, is evident throughout society in the postwar years, and leaders defended and reinforced it. The presumption that the benefits of economic growth would be shared fairly lies at the foundation of many kinds of transactions among economic actors. In many other countries, there is strong evidence of lower levels of trust (and trustworthiness).

3 A broad enthusiasm for learning and little resistance to the humble status of apprenticing the nation, the firm, and oneself to foreign knowledge. Typically it is cheaper (and more reliable) to borrow than to invent. Japan stands out in this regard.

4 The lack of natural resources and Japan's geographical and cultural isolation have often been suggested as barriers to development, especially by Japanese. However, under modern conditions, the opposite may be more plausible – that such disadvantages caused the Japanese to pull together, to do many things right (e.g., emphasize human resource development, technology and trade) and to take a longer-term view of the growth effort.

5 The idea that national strength and pride would be achieved via economic development has been pervasive. The ability to see one's country in an international context and to score the game in this way is a condition of public discourse much in evidence in Japan.

6 The Japanese are conscientious about the quality of information, and there is much information sharing, as in the government–business and union–management relationships. Trustworthy information makes for more effective coordination among companies and between companies, unions, and bureaucrats.

CONCLUDING REMARKS

This chapter has illustrated the many complex issues involved in modeling Japanese growth. We have sought to highlight the various relationships that arise when we expand time frames, introduce several levels of analysis (and thus detail), and ask about the comparative perspective being applied.

The notion that inputs are not discreet but interrelated, as suggested by Rosenberg, was our starting point. While predictably this has not led to a single, conclusive model, it has highlighted the problems of model building in the rich Japanese experience. We summarize the most significant analytic points here.

Any growth system evolves, and yet when we seek to model it in terms of a particular subset, we can easily fall into the trap of relying on a static picture of its institutions or an assumed direction of connection among its elements.

To understand how inputs such as capital and human resources interact, one needs to examine key institutions in historical perspective and to ask how they evolved. Why bureaucrats are relatively free of corruption or why schools set high standards or why companies are particularly adept at technological borrowing, are questions that do not have simple answers, but comparative analysis will reveal many essential points.

When we look for elements of a growth system that are of special salience, we should be aware that our search is guided by a host of assumptions that derive from our comparative starting point. If we start from the perspective of the developed West for example, it is not difficult to see that such things as "late developer" industrial policy and cultural distinctiveness will be of great interest. If, on the other hand, we examine Japan from the perspective of the East Asian NICs, different issues arise, including a shared Confucian tradition, the role of military threats during formative periods of many institutions, and a high proclivity to save. They differ in other ways, such as experiences of colonialism, early demographic changes, the pattern of democratization, and the role of the military in the post-war period. If we view Japan from a Southeast Asian perspective, the role of agriculture looms large, as do questions about institutions and governance in multi-ethnic states; education also assumes greater saliency. The point is simply that we need to find ways to use many perspectives when evaluating the Japanese growth system.

Perhaps the most revealing insights have been those that come from looking farther back in history. We find, for example, that institutions now credited with being essential (e.g., Japan's industrial policy) arose in very different circumstances and for very different reasons.

We also have highlighted the importance of special historical circumstances. The impact of both World War II and the American Occupation, when joined together, defined a society, a government and a system of management that evolved into the "model" we observed with such favor in the 1960s and have since made into a conventional understanding of the Japanese growth system.

There have been distinct eras in Japan's economic history, but the institutions and the policies that shaped them did not change in a uniform or discreet manner. We find continuity in the midst of rapid transformation. Changes in human capital, savings behavior and government supervision of the economy evolved over long periods. It makes sense to try to discover a means of modeling institutions and their change over time in a larger historical framework. How they evolve depends on earlier interactions, but there is much room for new outcomes.

Idiosyncratic events like wars can play a central role in shaping the system.

Even when planning was an important part of the economy, the planners could not correctly anticipate how the system would actually evolve. Much more seems accidental in history than rationalist considerations normally acknowledge.

In sum, as economists attempt to fine-tune their models, the exercise often becomes increasingly esoteric and removed from historically-grounded analysis. In much modeling there is little concern with such details as how savings or education or labor markets actually expanded or the role of government or other factors in these processes. The questions this approach begs often are far more important than the answers it provides.

The chapter has also underscored the importance of both the international and temporal contexts; these have substantial bearings on the model's relevance to other countries operating under different circumstances. Consider industrial policy. It remains uncertain whether one can extract from Japan's prewar or postwar experiences a model of a political economy that specifies how state intervention consistently stimulated development without also stipulating numerous other conditions. For example, the urge for development in much of the world arises out of domestic circumstances – poverty, ethnic strife, and revolutionary movements which threatened to topple fragile states and regimes unless livelihoods were drastically improved. Modernizing Japan of the Meiji Period, in contrast, was a classic model of a "hard" state bent on accomplishing nationalistic goals in the face of a perceived external threat without the constant tug of domestic interest groups to detract it. It had a homogeneous population which shared a strong sense of national identity; personal motivations to get ahead were reinforced by greater community goals and patriotic ambitions.[51] Few countries today operate in a similar milieu.

Finally, in our description of Japanese development, there is little to suggest the spread of a uniform type of capitalism from Japan to the rest of Asia. The range of business structures and practices, political economies, and underlying ethos are too varied to suggest a simple West-versus-Asia divide of the capitalist world. This is not to argue that Japan or any other East Asian country has no lessons to offer – quite the contrary. It is rather to underscore the need to dig deeper to discover actual institutional processes and their relationship to an overall growth system. In doing this, it is important to apply a multiplicity of perspectives rather than to be the prisoner of a single, abstract model.

NOTES

1 Uchino, 1978: 154.
2 Ito, 1992: 16–17.

3   See, for example, Heilbroner and Milberg, 1995: especially 97–128.
4   Rosenberg, 1993: 129.
5   Ibid., pp. 129–30.
6   Ibid., pp. 129–30.
7   Uchino, 1978: 86.
8   Denison and Chung, 1976: 8.
9   Minami, 1994: 33–55.
10 It is important to keep Japan's performance in international perspective. 1950–73 was a time of unparalleled world prosperity, one with high levels of demand, trade, and capital and labor inputs in developed and developing countries alike. A satisfactory growth model, therefore, needs to account for the differential between Japan and strong performers elsewhere. Maddison, 1989: 65–84.
11 Estimates are from Shinohara, 1986, as cited in Ito, 1992: 49.
12 Horioka, 1993.
13 Nakamura, 1981: 95–100.
14 Chuubachi and Taira, 1976: 391–437.
15 On this issue generally, see Fields, 1995: 75–107.
16 Ono and Watanabe, 1976: 363–89.
17 We must also keep in mind that in addition to land reform under the US occupation, the war itself caused massive destruction of real property and private assets. The much-admired Gini coefficients for Japan, in other words, would seem to rest importantly on historical forces rather unique to Japan. Property income, which was 23 percent of all income in 1935, dropped to 3 percent after the war. Reflecting on this, it appears that Japanese salaried work is generally inclined to a relatively egalitarian pattern, but the ownership of property and productive assets has no such structure. When Japan was largely agricultural, it may have been no more egalitarian than other East Asian societies. It was only when a large proportion of the population entered into salaried work that the present egalitarian qualities became dominant.
18 Nafziger, 1995: 104.
19 Rohlen, 1993.
20 See Nakamura, 1981: 3–20; and Johnson, 1990.
21 Nakamura, 1994: 173–96.
22 Vestal, 1993: 219–32.
23 Maddison, 1989: 143.
24 Ohkawa and Rosovsky, 1973.
25 Samuels, 1994: 33–48.
26 Morris-Suzuki, 1989: 44–70.
27 Smith, 1961.
28 In fact, until the 1930s, manufacturing output was dominated by foodstuffs and textiles (Macpherson, 1987: 18).
29 The classic study of this topic is Smith, 1955.
30 Morris and Adelman, 1988: 106–10.
31 Atack and Passell, 1994: chs. 6 and 16. The same was true of the early nineteenth-century canal system, which was built both with state and federal land grants and capital.
32 It is also worth noting that first-hand observers of late nineteenth-century Japan from the West commented frequently on the "uniqueness" of the culture and society but seldom described efforts to develop the modern economy in those terms.
33 See, for example, North, 1981.
34 Macpherson, 1987: 33.
35 Maddison, 1989: 71.

36 It has been argued that the rate of Japan's GNP growth in late Meiji would have been even more rapid if military expenditures had not ballooned between 1895–1905 (Kelley and Williamson, 1974: 106–27).
37 For a good summary of the debate on the role of agriculture in Japanese development, see Tomlinson, 1985.
38 Francks, 1992: 101–11. It is now generally agreed that most of the capital accumulation for the industrial sector came from manufacturing itself, not from agriculture.
39 Ito, 1992: 23.
40 In fact, the model continues to carry explanatory power in the case of the United States; see Wright, 1990. Sachs and Warner (1995) have shown that possessing abundant natural resources is associated with poor growth.
41 Ogawa *et al.*, 1993.
42 Maddison, 1989: 78.
43 Morris-Suzuki, 1994: 71–104.
44 Ohkawa and Ranis, 1985.
45 Maddison, 1989: 138–44.
46 For an extended discussion of this argument, see Sugiyama, 1988.
47 This is a major theme of Lockwood, 1954.
48 Minami, 1994: 127–42.
49 See Macpherson, 1987: 63–70; and, Nafziger, 1995: 103–18.
50 Nakamura, 1981: 14–20.
51 On this point, see Dore, 1971.

REFERENCES

Atack, Jeremy and Peter Passell (1994) *A New Economic View of American History*, New York: W.W. Norton.
Chuubachi, Masayoshi and Koji Taira (1976) "Poverty in Modern Japan: Perceptions and Realities," in Patrick, Hugh (ed.) *Japanese Industrialization and Its Social Consequences*, Berkeley: University of California Press.
Denison, Edward F. and William K. Chung (1976) *How Japan's Economy Grew So Fast*, Washington, DC: Brookings Institution.
Dore, Ronald P. (1971) "Japanese Industrialization and the Developing Countries: Model, Warning or Source of Healthy Doubts?" *Institute of Southeast Asian Studies* Occasional Paper, no. 8.
Fields, Gary S. (1995) "Income Distribution in Developing Economies: Conceptual Data, and Policy Issues in Broad-Based Growth," in Quibria, M.G. (ed.) *Critical Issues In Asian Development: Theories, Experiences and Policies*, Hong Kong: Oxford University Press.
Francks, Penelope (1992) *Japanese Economic Development: Theory and Practice*, London: Routledge.
Heilbroner, Robert and William Milbert (1995) *The Crisis of Vision in Modern Economic Thought*, Cambridge: Cambridge University Press.
Horioka, Charles Yuji (1993) "Consuming and Saving," in Gordon, Andrew (ed.) *Postwar Japan as History*, Berkeley: University of California Press.
Ito, Takatoshi (1992) *The Japanese Economy*, Cambridge, MA: MIT Press.
Johnson, Chalmers (1990) "The People Who Invented the Mechanical Nightingale," *Daedalus* (Summer) 119: 71–90.
Kelley, Allen C. and Jeffrey G. Williamson (1974) *Lessons from Japanese Development: An Analytical Economic History*, Chicago: University of Chicago Press.
Lockwood, William W. (1954) *The Economic Development of Japan: Growth and Structural Change, 1868–1938*, Princeton, NJ: Princeton University Press.

MacPherson, W.J. (1987) *The Economic Development of Japan c. 1868–1941*, Basingstoke: Macmillan.

Maddison, Angus (1989) *The World Economy in the 20th Century*, Paris: OECD.

Minami, Ryoshin (1994) *The Economic Development of Japan: A Quantitative Study*, New York: St Martin's Press.

Morris, Cynthia Taft and Irma Adelman (1988) *Comparative Patterns of Economic Development 1850–1914*, Baltimore: Johns Hopkins University Press.

Morris-Suzuki, Tessa (1989) *A History of Japanese Economic Thought*, London: Routledge.

—— (1994) *The Technological Transformation of Japan*, Cambridge: Cambridge University Press.

Nafziger, E. Wayne (1995) *Learning From the Japanese: Japan's Pre-War Development and the Third World*, Armonk, NY: M.E. Sharpe.

Nakamura, Takafusa (1981) *The Postwar Japanese Economy: Its Development and Structure*, Tokyo: University of Tokyo Press.

—— (1994) *Lectures on Modern Japanese Economic History, 1926–1994*, Tokyo: LTCB International Library Foundation.

North, Douglass C. (1981) *Structure and Change in Economic History*, New York: W.W. Norton.

Ogawa, Naohiro, Gavin Jones, and Jeffrey Williamson (1993) *Human Resources in Development Along the Asia-Pacific Rim*, New York: Oxford University Press.

Ohkawa, Kazushi and Gustov Ranis (1985) *Japan and the Developing Countries*, Oxford: Blackwell.

Ohkawa, Kazushi and Henry Rosovsky (1973) *Japanese Economic Growth: Trend Acceleration in the Twentieth Century*, Stanford: Stanford University Press.

Ono, Akira and Tsunehiko Watanabe (1976) "Changes in Income Inequality in the Japanese Economy," in Patrick, Hugh (ed.) *Japanese Industrialization and Its Social Consequences*, Berkeley: University of California Press.

Rohlen, Thomas P. (1993) "Learning: The Mobilization of Knowledge in the Japanese Political Economy," in Kumon, Shumpei and Henry Rosovsky (eds) *The Japanese Political Economy: Social and Cultural Dynamics*, Stanford, CA: Stanford University Press.

Rosenberg, Nathan (1993) "How the Developed Countries Became Rich," *Daedalus* (Fall) 123: 127–34.

Sachs, Jeffrey D. and Andrew M. Warner (1995) "National Resource Abundance and Economic Growth," Harvard Institute for International Development, Development Discussion Paper No. 517a (Oct).

Samuels, Richard J. (1994) *"Rich Nation Strong Army:" National Security and The Technological Transformation of Japan*, Ithaca, NY: Cornell University Press.

Smith, Thomas C. (1955) *Political Change and Industrial Development in Japan: Government Enterprise, 1868–1880*, Stanford, CA: Stanford University Press.

—— (1961) "Japan's Aristocratic Revolution," *Yale Review* 50: 370–83.

Sugiyama, Shinya (1988) *Japan's Industrialization in the World Economy, 1859–99; Export Trade and Overseas Competition*, London: Athlone Press.

Tomlinson, B.R. (1985) "Writing History Sideways: Lessons For Indian Economic Historians From Meiji Japan," *Modern Asian Studies* (July) 19: 669–98.

Uchino, Tatsuro (1978) *Japan's Postwar Economy: An Insider's View of Its History and Its Future*, Tokyo: Kodansha.

Vestal, James (1993) *Planning for Change: Industrial Policy and Japanese Economic Development, 1945–1990*, Oxford: Clarendon Press.

Wright, Gavin (1990) "The Origins of American Industrial Success, 1879–1940," *American Economic Review* (September): 651–68.

13 Japan's influence on the East Asian economies

Yutaka Kosai and Fumihide Takeuchi

1. INTRODUCTION

This chapter examines the factors behind the East Asian model of development and compares them with the experience of Japan,[1] the first of the East Asian economies to develop. East Asian economies are sometimes described as following a "flying geese" model, whose economies take off successively after absorbing advanced technologies from the industrialized countries. On this perception, a comparison of development in Japan, "the lead goose," and other East Asian economies should unveil some underlying factors. The Japanese pattern is also helpful in putting in perspective the structural adjustment policies that the IMF and World Bank recommend to economies in transition and other developing nations. In many cases, macro-based, one-shot therapies have not established conditions for sustainable, long-term growth. Thus, the gradual reform of Japan seems to be particularly relevant for those economies.

However, the Japanese model does not warrant a claim to universality because each country differs in its initial conditions. The transfer of one nation's entire system for growth to any other country could easily be counterproductive.

2. HOW JAPAN DEVELOPED

Here, we focus on the following three points: (1) the sequence of steps, given the initial conditions; (2) the role of social systems and industrial organizations, especially private sector activities; and (3) human and physical capital and other system infrastructures as fundamentals for growth. Figure 13.1 illustrates the relationship among them for Japan.

Earlier studies have focused mainly on government institutions and industrial policies. The usual inference is that industrial policies played a major role in Japan's spectacular economic performance and was responsible for it becoming the first of the East Asian "geese" to take off. The conventional prescription links political institutions and economic development in a cause-and-effect relationship, without any thought to the

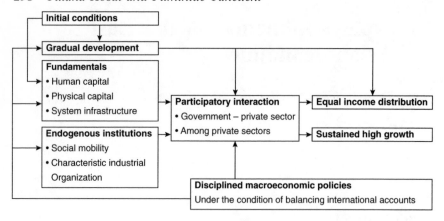

Figure 13.1 The mechanism of Japanese development (1868–1970)

ability of economic agents to react to policies and to benefit from or adapt to them; we call this their "responsive capacity." Figure 13.1 shows that the "participatory interaction" (the working relationship) between the government and the private sector, and within private sectors as well, was nurtured by favorable fundamentals, endogenous institutions and a gradual pattern of development. This interaction produced relatively equal income distribution and high growth.

We pay more attention to a wide variety of causal relationships: the quality of human capital, the organizational and institutional arrangements at the firm and industry level, and the way policies are implemented rather than the policies *per se* in building capacities in Japanese and East Asian economies. Our method is largely historical; we find significant points for analysis, including social and political issues unique to each country, in the history of each one.

Initial economic conditions conducive to growth

Table 13.1 summarizes the economic performance of some industrialized countries including Japan, and Table 13.2, that of East Asian countries, also including Japan.

As shown in Table 13.1, the most noticeable feature of Japan's growth is its low initial level and its long-sustained high growth. This may be Japan's most prominent characteristic, one in which many developing countries are keenly interested. Many conditions conducive to growth were inherited from the past. These included human and physical infrastructures, the existence of highly competitive small businesses, and an already high level of technical knowledge. The combination of a low early income level and such favorable conditions seems to be due to the fact that these strengths were geographically "scattered" in the feudal period

Table 13.1 Modern economic growth rates of advanced nations

Start of modernization (year)	GNP per capita of the start year	Growth rate to 1965		Average annual growth rate		Income per capita
		GNP	GNP per capita	1965–80	1980–90	(1990)
Japan 1886	136	3.6	2.5	6.4	4.1	18,970
United States 1834–43	474	3.6	1.6	2.7	3.4	17,319
Germany 1850–59	302	2.7	1.7	3.3	2.1	13,555
England 1765–85	227	2.2	1.2	2.3	2.1	12,856

Sources:
(a) GNP per capita at start of modernization (1965 US$): Ryoshin Minami, *The Economic Development of Japan*, Table 1–1
(b) GNP per capita to 1965, Ryoshin Minami, *The Economic Development of Japan*, Table 3–1
(c) GNP per capita for 1065–90 and average income per capita in 1990: World Bank, *World Development Report 1992*

Notes: Growth rate = percent; GNP per capita and income per capita = US$

Table 13.2 Average annual growth rates of real GDP in East Asia (1955–93) (%)

	1955–70	1965–80	1980–93
Japan	9.7	6.4	4.1
Singapore	–	10.0	6.4
Hong Kong	9.6	8.6	7.1
South Korea	6.7	9.9	9.7
Malaysia	5.3	7.4	5.2
Thailand	6.9	7.3	7.6
Indonesia	3.6	7.0	5.5
China	–	6.8	9.5

Sources:
(a) World Bank, *World Development Reports 1992 & 1995* for 1065–80, 1980–93
(b) IMF, *International Financial Statistics 1960/89* for 1955–70

and not combined on a national scale. Not until transportation and communication infrastructures helped the flow of information and integrated the economy, could Japan take advantage of these inherited fundamentals.

The evolution of Japanese economic development is shown in Figures 13.2, 13.3 and 13.4. The 100 years or so from the start of the Meiji Restoration in 1868 to Japan becoming a mature, industrialized nation in 1970, can be broadly classified into three stages based on its industrial

Systems and policies
(The era starts with substantial accumulation of fundamentals)

Human resources	⇨	• Spread of compulsory education to masses, establishment of universities • Establishment of technical, agricultural, and vocational schools to train workers for the industrial age • Establishment of healthcare system, preventative measures for communicable diseases
Capital accumulation	⇨	• Abolition of inherited stipend for royal familes and samurai class • Land tax reform • Promotion of industry • Expansion of trade • Adoption of gold standard, issuance of foreign debt • Matsukata deflation policy (increased taxes, curtailment of expenses, revaluation of paper currency) • Subsequent tax levy system in favor of business at expense of individuals (Income tax becomes primary revenue source, replacing land tax; expansion of consumption tax)
Technology	⇨	• Transplantation of Western technology through promotion of industry • Spread of traditional technology
Infrastructure	⇨	• Establishment of post office and telephone and telegraph network • Establishment of railway network • Nationwide distribution of electric power • Adoption and widespread expansion of company and banking system

⇩

Industrial structure	⇨	• High agricultural productivity • Growth of native industries • Rapid emergence of business
Industry organization	⇨	• Rapid emergence of business
Labor market	⇨	• Labor surplus re-emerges especially in farm villages and ultra-small businesses
Income distribution	⇨	• Disparity gradually widens
Trade structure	⇨	• Shift from production of substitutes for primary imports to primary exports (Textile exports)
International accounts	⇨	• Trade deficit

Figure 13.2 The Meiji Restoration and the period of industrialization (1868–1920)

structure and the changing role of government. The first is the Meiji Restoration and the period of industrialization, 1868–1920, characterized by a relatively *laissez faire* economy and the growth of traditional industries.[2] The second stage is the era of militarism and tight economic controls, 1920–45. The third stage, 1945–70, is that of postwar recovery followed by the high economic growth era, when major economic and social reforms accelerated growth.[3]

Systems and policies

Human resources	⇨ • Increased enrollment into middle school and high school • Population control measures; administration of sanitation measures • Protection of labor force with health insurance system
Capital accumulation	⇨ • Industry controls, fostering of heavy chemical industry, formation of *zaibatsus* (financial combines) • Centralization of banks, monetary controls, indirect financing • Went off gold standard, devaluation of exchange rate, tariff increases, expansion of exports • Mobilization of household savings, forced savings, expansion of post office savings • Swelling of public debt
Technology	⇨ • Rationalization of industry • Expansion of education and research system and facilities • Better production technology with introduction of foreign capital • Agricultural technology stagnated
Infrastructure	⇨ • Electricity causes shift from price competition to price controls • Expansion of telephone network • Expansion of railways, construction of highways • Urbanization and formation of industrial zone • Rural relief programs

⇩

Industrial structure	Fostering of heavy chemical industry Stagnation of agriculture
Industry organization	Expansion of old and new *zaibatsus*, business diversification, expansion of business groupings Expansion of small business, estalishment of sub-contractor system
Labor market	Separation of skilled and unskilled labor market Labor surplus re-emerges with shift from primary industries to non-modern sectors (farm villages and ultra-small businesses)
Income distribution	Expansion of dual structure
Trade structure	Production of substitutes for secondary imports (Rapid decrease in import reliance of producer goods)
International accounts	Trade imbalance (Extreme fluctuations from deficit to surplus)

Figure 13.3 Militarism and the war years (1920–45)

The top parts of Figures 13.2, 13.3 and 13.4, describe systems and policies on human resources, capital accumulation, technology, and infrastructure. The resulting industrial structure, industrial organization, labor market, income distribution, trade structure, and the state of the international balance of payments are summarized at the bottom.

Systems and policies
(Succession from pre-war years)

Human resources	⇨ • Education reforms (equal opportunity, integration of systems, extension of compulsory education) • Increased recruitment of science students, establishment of high schools and vocational schools • Training of personnel for technical revolution • Democratization of labor • Establishment of healthcare system
Capital accumulation	⇨ • Agricultural land reform leads to income equality • Dissolution of *zaibatsus*, decentralization • Priority production • Industry rationalization plans • Monetary controls, low-interest financing • Indirect financing, main bank system • Treasury investments and loans, policy finance • Preferential tax measures • Fiscal imbalance
Technology	⇨ • Foreign investment controls • Establishment of national research institutions • Unionization of researchers, system of commendation • Subsidies, preferential tax measures, low-interest financing • Introduction of foreign technology • Organization and greater sophistication of small business, formation of *keiretsu* (sub-contractor systems)
Infrastructure	⇨ • Construction of freeways and bullet trains becomes big business • Energy conversion from coal to oil • Pacific rim industrial zones

⇩

Industrial structure	• Advancement of heavy chemical industry • Technical revolution from basic industries to related industries, increasing market competition
Industry organization	• Formation of keiretsu, cross-shareholdings • Promition by seniority, lifetime employment, unionization by business
Labor market	• Full employment
Income distribution	• Narrowing of wage gap
Trade structure	• Shift from production of substitutes for secondary imports to secondary exports
International accounts	• Shift from fluctuating state to constant surplus

Figure 13.4 Recovery and high growth phase (1945–70)

When examining the initial conditions before development, there are actually two "starting points" to be considered – Japan really "developed" twice. One was at the beginning of modernization in 1868, and the other was after World War II.

Regarding human resources, a good education system was already in place when modernization began because private elementary education had spread throughout rural and urban areas; it is said that Japan already had the highest literacy rate in the world in the nineteenth century. Japan concentrated on primary education and within a short period of time caught up with advanced nations in school enrollment rates. The postwar heavy and chemical industries were direct beneficiaries of this human capital, for it was the vast pool of skilled labor that supported this industry.

Small businesses were crucial in creating the unique Japanese industrial organization. They played a large role in the country's development and have maintained a fixed share of all employment since the start of industrialization early in this century. In some developing countries, capital-intensive industries were introduced in an early stage, leaving traditional ones isolated and losing linkages with modern sectors. In Japan, however, large and diverse industrial bases developed through the gradual modernization of traditional, craft sectors. After 1930, in particular, many small and medium-sized businesses sprang up to support the heavy chemical industry and the postwar industrial structure has been characterized by its expansion into the sub-contractor (or *keiretsu*) system. This grouping into *keiretsu*, or "participatory interaction" in Japanese industry, had already built its foundation in the early postwar period (although it was also much strengthened by postwar industrial policy). "Participating interaction" as used here implies mutual adjustments among government, businesses, and individuals; these three units were not in a one-way, director–subordinate relationship, but formed a network of mutual influences.

As for technology, agriculture was fairly sophisticated even before the Restoration. Then, as part of its policy to promote industry, the Meiji government introduced some Western farming methods, including large-scale ones. However, most failed and traditional methods, including the methods practiced in regional Japan, spread throughout the country and built modern agriculture. The same trend was evident in traditional, craft industries; Western techniques in the textile industry did not replace Japanese methods, but rather coexisted with them. In the spinning industry, for example, technology transfer was essentially a refinement of an indigenous spinning technology, with the result being the birth of an exceptional domestic spinning industry whose products could compete internationally.

Agriculture, forestry, and fishery were the biggest industries during the period of industrialization (1868–1920). Including these primary industries, traditional industries formed most of the industrial base. Thus, a substantial part of the foundation for industrial growth was present from the start of the Meiji Restoration.

The *laissez faire* industrial policy of government in the industrial age was dictated by these stable infrastructures, as described, and the improvement of traditional industries. Moreover, the capital accumulation of agriculture and traditional industries contributed to public investment.

The external environment for the gradual development in Japan

One of the significant characteristics of Japan's development strategy was "gradualism" – the country's step-by-step approach to growth. Japan adapted to a changing domestic and foreign environment while maintaining its traditions and order. The social and political chaos that often accompanies rapid economic growth was minimized while traditions were zealously protected to avoid being undermined and forgotten. Gradualism was supported by the high initial social capabilities described above. Given a well-maintained infrastructure and steady productivity growth in industries, a government does not need to use drastic measures.

An industrial structure based on comparative advantage

Japan's industrial structure evolved along with changes in its comparative advantage. Traditional industries and modern industries grew side-by-side. In trade, exports of products from traditional industries such as tea, coal and silk expanded, and then modern labor intensive industries such as cotton yarn and cotton fabrics, were added to this list. Imports included machinery from the West and raw cotton and other raw materials from less-developed areas.

Japan first imported manufactured products from advanced countries and exported raw materials. Later, it imported raw materials and capital goods and exported light industrial products. Finally it shifted to the import of crude fuel and foodstuffs and exported heavy industrial products and processed and assembled products. In recent years, foreign direct investment from Japan has created a division of labor, resulting in a higher proportion of manufactured imports. The Japanese trade structure evolved within the limits of domestic resources; its pattern follows the principle of comparative advantage.

This natural progression in imports and exports was also required for economic growth, while maintaining the country's international balance of payments, because Japan chose not to rely on foreign capital. Therefore, it had to maximize its domestic savings in order to support high investments.

This analysis of Japan's industrial structure aids us greatly in evaluating its industrial policies. If its industrial structure was narrowly based on comparative advantage, the government's industrial policies would not have been discretionary but "passive" in character. In some developing economies in East Asia, however, industrial structures have been determined by foreign capital rather than by governments' industrial policies. Industrial policy and capital markets are almost identical in their function: they decide the dynamic allocation of resources over time.

Table 13.3 Ratio of household savings to disposable income, 1955–65 (%)

Japan	16.5
Finland	10.2
West Germany	13.5
Netherlands	2.7
Switzerland	9.5
Australia	9.0
Austria	8.6
Denmark	10.2
France	7.8
Canada	7.3
Belgium	10.4
UK	4.2
United States	6.0
South Korea	0.8

Source: United Nations, *Yearbook of National Accounts Statistics, 1966*

Conservative spending habits

Related to gradualism in development were conservative spending habits, which led to extraordinary levels of savings. Table 13.3 summarizes household savings as a percentage of disposable income in various countries, and shows that during the period of high growth from the mid-1950s to the mid-1960s Japan had the highest ratio of all the advanced countries.

No matter how eager the Japanese were to ingest all the latest in technology and culture from abroad, their habits as consumers, strongly influenced by traditional values, were not Westernized as quickly, and consumption did not increase linearly with disposable income.[4] This was another example of gradualism – taking time to respond to changes in the environment – and is directly linked to the higher savings rate. These moderate income elasticities for foreign consumption goods are also economically rational. In an early stage of development, the real exchange rate (defined as the relative price of tradables to non-tradables) is generally depreciated in comparison with that in a more advanced stage.

Role of government institutions in developing endogenous institutions

There are two contrasting views on the relationship between Japan's rapid growth and the role of the government. One view emphasizes government intervention, while the other attaches importance to institutions in the private sector.[5] The actual relationship was not a causal one but one where government and domestic institutions interacted.

Here, we analyze more closely the policies for various kinds of infrastructure, including physical and human capital and other systems vital to economic growth. Then we comment on Japanese industrial policy, touching on the previous two viewpoints.

Infrastructure developed in early stages of development

Infrastructure is an essential base for social and production activity to develop smoothly. However, developing an infrastructure takes huge amounts of capital, time, and technology. How to do this efficiently is a crucial problem for sustained growth.

Human capital

We have pointed out that a fairly good education system was in place when modernization began. Recent work in development economics recognizes the importance of investing in human capital, and the Japanese experience is consistent with this view. Most important is to supply primary education to the general population at an early stage. Primary education was made compulsory as early as 1900, and by 1909, school enrollment nationwide had reached 98 percent.

At the same time, good education is linked to social mobility, which increases the effectiveness of education. With the abolition of feudalism during the Meiji Restoration and the adoption of the merit system, a person coming from any class could, provided he was capable, find employment of his choice. High social mobility was linked to the fast growth of the education system.

Transportation and communications

From the very beginning, the government emphasized public transportation, communications, and other means of linking the nation. A nation-wide network was rapidly built up, with total railway lines expanding from 6,206 km in 1900 to 13,636 km in 1920, and 25,000 km in 1932. Telephone, telegraph, and post office networks were laid down at the same time, bringing people even closer together. These networks, partly established for political and military reasons, spurred the development of production, distribution systems and consumer markets and narrowed the psychological distance among regions. This was a major force in making the break from a feudalistic society to a nation state.

Systems infrastructure

The legal system of modern Western Europe was transferred to Japan by the Meiji government. In 1873, the Meiji government enacted land reforms to establish property rights and in 1876 it ended feudalistic privileges by abolishing inherited stipends to the nobility and samurai class. Along with such measures, the government made sweeping fiscal changes, thereby laying the foundation for tax reform.

The new tax system was especially important. Its early enactment strengthened the authority of the government and played a major role in establishing Japan as a modern nation state. In many developing countries today, governments cannot propose and execute vital policies due to the lack of an adequate tax system to support them.

The stock company system was another important system introduced early. From the start of the Meiji era, the government, and various intellectuals, translated materials concerning the establishment of companies, and worked to expand the company system. The diffusion of the stock company system was fairly rapid; within a mere three years after the Commercial Code was put into force in 1893, stock companies constituted 56.2 percent of all companies, and accounted for 89.9 percent of the paid-in capital of all companies.

Industrial policies and participatory interaction

A noteworthy feature of Japan's modernization as a latecomer was that it took off as a relatively *laissez-faire* system (although a few state industries were created, they were soon privatized). In contrast, most developing countries have modernized under heavy government intervention. This discrepancy arises because – whereas Japan took advantage of a significant, preexisting level of human and physical infrastructure, technology and enterprises, and highly productive agricultural and traditional industries – most developing countries have had relatively weak bases on which to build. Their governments have been forced to play a major role in development; the system is often labeled as bureaucratic authoritarianism.

In Japan, the nature of the interaction between government and the private sector changed dramatically during the war years, when government economic controls were increased. However, even the shift to wartime controls was not instantaneous; the private sector resisted it. Contrary to a widely held view, government intervention in industrial policy was not great even during the "post-war economic miracle". Industrial policy, industrial targeting, indicative planning, subsidies and so forth, were well coordinated with endogenous institutions largely characterized by the Japanese *keiretsu* (sub-contractor) system, the main bank system, and the lifetime employment system. The deliberative councils and industrial associations that linked government and the private sector were specific institutions for interaction between the two sectors and not institutions for one-way directives from government to the private sector. Nor, conversely, were they organizations to lobby the government for benefits. Rather, businesses used these forums to transmit information to government in order to make the policies more practical.

Japan's industrial policy was not conducted by discretion, but more by rules. Going back again to the Meiji period, the government was instrumental in laying the foundations, but once that was well under way, its attitude became more classically liberal. There were only a few state-owned enterprises. In trade, tariffs were kept relatively low without tariff autonomy, with the result that competitive pressures from imports raised domestic productivity. In the high growth era after World War II, with controls on foreign investments, and minimal capital movements, the government had to balance its international accounts. Macroeconomic policies were also managed by rules rather than discretion. We can say that industrial structures followed resource endowments and industrial policies encouraged structural changes. For example, the heavy and chemical industries were direct beneficiaries of the vast pool of skilled labor and the miles of Pacific coast line were ideally suited to these industries. They also benefited from advances in transportation technologies that helped to make them competitive worldwide.

Overall, with aggressive competition among industries, the government's industrial policy was a trial-and-error process aimed at predicting future trends in global markets, at shedding light on conditions under which Japanese industries labored, and at adapting to these trends.

3 EAST ASIAN DEVELOPMENT COMPARED WITH THE JAPANESE EXPERIENCE

Drawing generalizations from varied East Asian development experiences is difficult, because there are many countries with very different economic and social structures. However, there have been common features in how initial conditions have contributed to growth and in development strategies. The successful East Asian governments adopted export-push industrial policies for efficiency-generating benefits through competing internationally. This section looks at similarities as well as differences with Japan.

Fundamentals and gradualism

What were the fundamentals and development strategies in East Asia? According to the World Bank,[6] the fundamentals of the rapid growth in East Asia have been: macroeconomic stability, investment in human capital, an effective and secure financial system, the ability to limit price distortions, the ability to absorb foreign technology and a limited bias against agriculture.

As for human capital, East Asian countries invested vigorously in primary education. This also contributed to relatively equal income distribution. Table 13.4 shows correlation coefficients between GNP per capita growth (1960–90), literacy rates, and rates of primary and secondary education attendance in 1960 in low to high income developing countries. The literacy and primary schooling coefficients are higher in the low-income economies than in the higher level ones, and the most significant correlation for secondary education enrollment is in lower-middle-income

Table 13.4 Correlation coefficients between human capital levels and economic growth in developing economies

	GNP per capita average annual growth rate (1960–90)			
Income level	Low	Lower-middle	Upper-middle	High
Literacy rate (1960)	0.565**	0.458**	–0.033	–
Primary education enrollment (1960)	0.555**	0.502**	0.019	0.135
Secondary education enrollment (1960)	0.306*	0.692**	0.361*	0.040

**Statistically significant at the 0.01 level
* Statistically significant at the 0.1 level

Source: World Bank, *World Development Reports* (various years)

economies. This suggests building the primary education system at an early stage, followed by secondary education at the next stage. This sequencing was characteristic of East Asia. However, in some developing economies, higher education is given priority, with primary education enrollment decreasing or stagnating at low levels.

Gradual development and equal distribution of income

Harry Oshima has emphasized the importance of gradual development – including the gradual introduction of capital-intensive industry.[7] In the rice-paddy agriculture of monsoon Asia where the work is very labor-intensive, the introduction of capital intensive industries at an early stage would make full employment difficult to attain, resulting in income inequality and social instability.

Also, domestic industries need time to gain experience, scale, and external economies before venturing into world markets. (This is the famous "infant industry" argument for protection.) It is also important to point out the fact that an ambitious industrialization program at the early stages of development is likely to result in heavy reliance on government protection, regulation, subsidies, and so on.

The most remarkable effect of gradual development is relatively equal income distribution,[8] one of the significant characteristics of East Asian economies. Table 13.5 shows the income distribution in developing countries for major regions and income groups; it shows that the income distribution of Asian countries is relatively equal compared with the other two regions. In Latin America, with higher levels of income inequality, resources allocated through government policies produced a decline in the standard of living in the agricultural sector as well as growth of the urban "informal" sector. Moreover, the concomitant trend of growing consumption, with high rates of time preference, was responsible for low domestic

Table 13.5 Distribution of income in developing countries, by major region and income group (the share of income accruing to the richest 20% and real GDP per capita)

Group 1: GDP per capita <1,000 dollars – inter-regional average income share of richest 20% = 49.5%

AFRICA	Year	*Highest GDP* 20%	*per capita*	ASIA	Year	*Highest GDP* 20%	*per capita*	LATIN AMERICA	Year	*Highest GDP* 20%	*per capita*
Ethiopia	81–82	41.3	322	Nepal	84–85						
Tanzania	914	62.7	534								
Uganda	89–90	41.9	554								
Guinea-Bissau	91	58.9	593								
Zambia	91	49.7	699								
Rwanda	83–85	38.9	776								
Mauritania	87–88	46.3	788								
Ghana	88–89	44.1	821								
Kenya	92	61.8	914								
Lesotho	86–87	60	949								
Nigeria	92	49	978								
Average		50.4									

Table 13.5 Continued

Group 2: GDP per capita 1,000–4,000 dollars – inter-regional average income share of richest 20% = 51.7%

AFRICA

	Year	Highest 20%	GDP per capita
Senegal	91–92	58.6	1,120
Zimbabwe	90–91	62.3	1,248
Botswana	85–86	58.9	2,662
South Africa	93	63.3	3,068
Average		60.8	

ASIA

	Year	Highest 20%	GDP per capita
India	89–90	41.3	1,264
China	90	41.8	1,324
Bangladesh	88–89	38.6	1,375
Pakistan	91	39.7	1,394
Philippines	88	47.8	1,676
Indonesia	90	42.3	1,974
Sri Lanka	90	39.3	2,096
Thailand	88	50.7	2,972
Average		42.7	

LATIN AMERICA

	Year	Highest 20%	GDP per capita
Nicaragua	93	55.3	1,294
Honduras	89	63.5	1,432
Bolivia	90–91	48.2	1,696
Guatemala	89	63	2,137
Dominican Republic	89	55.6	2,430
Jamaica	90	48.4	2,545
Panama	89	59.8	2,785
Peru	85–86	51.4	2,838
Columbia	91	55.8	3,297
Costa Rica	89	50.8	3,451
Average		55.2	

Group 3: GDP per capita >4,000 dollars – inter-regional average income share of richest 20% = 53.1%

ASIA

	Year	Highest 20%	GDP per capita
Malaysia	89	53.7	4,674
Korea	88	42.2	5,607
Singapore	82–83	48.9	8,360
Hong Kong	80	47	8,719
Average		48.0	

LATIN AMERICA

	Year	Highest 20%	GDP per capita
Brazil	89	67.5	4,271
Chile	92	60.4	4,890
Mexico	84	55.9	5,524
Venezuela	89	49.5	5,907
Average		58.3	

Sources: Distribution of income: World Bank, *World Development Report 1995*
Real GDP per capita (1985 international prices): *The Penn World Tables (Mark 5,6)*

Table 13.6 Consumption and saving (as a percentage of GDP)

	1965	1970	1980	1985	1990	1993
East Asia						
Consumption	78	72	69	69	65	65
Saving	22	28	30	30	35	35
South Asia						
Consumption	88	85	85	81	81	79
Saving	12	15	15	18	19	21
Latin America						
Consumption	76	79	77	78	78	–
Saving	21	20	20	17	22	19
Africa						
Consumption	84	82	79	88	83	85
Saving	14	18	18	9	16	15
Japan						
Consumption	72	59	69	68	66	68
Saving	28	40	31	32	34	33

Source: World Bank, *World Development Reports* (various years)

savings and too much foreign borrowing; it resulted in the debt crisis of the 1980s. In East Asia, the resource shift occurred mainly through the market and not by policy intervention.[9]

The conservative spending habits of Japan have been shared to some extent by other East Asians. In East Asia, the share of consumption to GDP fell and became the lowest of all regions (Table 13.6). The more moderate income-elasticities-of-demand in Asia for foreign consumption goods gave technocrats greater leeway to pursue a developmentally rational sequencing of industries to be promoted, as opposed to the import-biased Latin American case.[10] Moreover, relatively high income-elasticities for indigenously designed, traditional, consumption goods contributed to the emergence of many small- and medium-size enterprises that became large, craft-based industrial sectors.

Consumers have behaved very differently in the developing economies. One sees widespread, "explosive" consumer booms with an unprece-dentedly fast diversification of consumer goods. This phenomenon is partly due to the infusion of foreign capital, which promotes domestic consump-tion at an early stage of development despite low savings. In Japan, which chose not to rely on foreign capital, the ratio of net resource flow to gross domestic investment (GDI) was low in the postwar high growth era (1950s–1960s) and even in the 1970s; many other East Asian countries arguably relied too heavily on foreign capital – although it must be acknowledged that they invested the borrowed money instead of consuming it, as has happened all too often in Latin America (Table 13.7).

Table 13.7 Ratio of net resource flow to gross domestic investment (%)

	Japan	Korea	Malaysia	Indonesia	Thailand	Philippines
1885–1900	0.4	–	–	–	–	–
1901–10	19.2	–	–	–	–	–
1911–20	–5.9	–	–	–	–	–
1921–30	4.2	–	–	–	–	–
1931–40	–5.1	–	–	–	–	–
1952–60	–0.1	–	–	–	–	–
1961–70*	–0.2	23.4	–9.3	37.9	8.0	6.1
1971–80	–1.5	19.5	2.3	5.7	14.3	12.4
1981–90	–7.7	–2.1	7.3	11.2	15.6	16.6

Sources: Japan: Minami, 1994, Tables 6–9; Korea, Malaysia, Thailand, Philippines,
Indonesia – World Bank, *World Tables*; IMF, *International Financial Statistics* (1960/89)

Note: Net resource flow = – (current account balance)
    1966–1970 for Korea,Malaysia, Thailand, Indonesia, Philippines

Gradual liberalization

Gradualism in policies is another important characteristic of East Asian development. Many governments have not imposed general import restrictions, as such measures have hurt exporters who depend too much on imported materials and capital goods. However, we wonder how countries with trade deficits can develop without imposing these restrictions. The East Asian answer has been a "gradual liberalization" strategy that took a long time and did not incur serious current account deficits.

Many observers stress that East Asia adopted an "export-push" policy, but the undeniable fact is that each country had varying periods of import-substitution before, or accompanying, the export-orientation policy. Historically, in some East Asian countries, including Japan, indigenous technology was advanced in an import-substitution policy regime, and then countries ventured into world markets with some internationally competitive exports. This sequencing of policies was one of the very important factors for development in East Asia.

Industrial policies based on this kind of gradualism may protect some unproductive domestic industries, but they also contribute to a stable regime shift if managed well.

The "flying geese model" as part of the shift in external environment

The East Asian economies have revealed a common pattern with intra-regional trade and investment and information exchange growing and promoted by social, cultural and close location. In the flying geese model, latecomers use technologies and institutions of the economies that took off first. In this sense, the flying geese model can be understood as an external factor in East Asia.

Why is it that only East Asian geese have taken off successively? The answer is that these countries have evolved along a dynamic comparative advantage path in which intra-regional trade and investment has led to a vertical as well as a horizontal division of labor. The model sustains a linked kind of development. By contrast, the development pattern within Latin America hindered backward linkages among members, as trade and investment there were shaped primarily by the desire for a relatively complete market in each country.

Northeast Asian capitalism vs. Southeast Asian capitalism

There is much diversity in economic growth within East Asia. These countries have different resource endowments and historical, social, and cultural backgrounds, all of which affect institutions and policies in different ways.

Industrial policies affected by national characteristics

Their industrial policies have attracted attention because they have worked. There is, however, a danger in grouping them, since they differ in how resources are allocated, in sequencing, and in degrees of government intervention.

Generally, industrial policies correspond to natural resource endowments.[11] The ASEAN countries, with many natural resources, tend to rely on exporting them, and stick to import substitution. On the other hand, the newly industrializing economies (NIEs – South Korea, Taiwan, Hong Kong, and Singapore), relatively scant in natural resources, have ventured aggressively into export markets free from import substitution policies from an early stage.

Not only natural resources but also domestic market size and the level of development influence industrial policies; Singapore, for example, has a small domestic market and thus was forced to be outward-oriented.

Countries in the rest of East Asia focused more on inter-industry allocation of resources, and less on industrial organization than did Japan. In Japan, industrial organization has been an essential element of policy attention. The *keiretsu* system and the substantial role of small- and medium-sized enterprises are now on the agenda for developing countries, as their interest in Japanese industrial organizations and in transplanting Japan's system into their own has grown.

FDI-induced development: a different growth model

There are two development models in East Asia. One is the Northeast Asian model developed by Japan, the leading goose, then South Korea, and Taiwan; the other is that of the Southeast Asians, the later geese.[12]

The most important difference between the two models is dependency on foreign direct investment (FDI). In general, the Southeast Asian economies are much more open to foreign direct investment.

The management of foreign direct investment is crucial for a successful industrial policy. FDI and industrial policies have almost the same function in shaping the industrial structure. Because FDI is a strategically important instrument in developing a domestic industry, it can play a larger role than government industrial policies. Moreover, because the demand for FDI by developing countries, particularly in East Asia, is growing, and competition among them for strategically important FDI is intensifying, governments can come to play a passive role. If they want FDI, it is essential for them to have a domestic financial market to acquire FDI as increasing numbers of overseas affiliates raise capital through domestic stock and bond markets.[13]

FDI contributes to economic growth. Especially in Southeast Asia, many such investments are classified as the out-sourcing type, with the objective of exporting products to the investing country or to a third one and contributing to earning foreign exchange. Moreover, manufacturing technologies and marketing techniques are embodied in FDI and are expected to be transferred to the recipients.

As to technology transfer, however, there are many views, ranging from positive to negative.[14] In Japan, as analyzed above, highly competitive, small enterprises were developed through the *keiretsu* system. As a result, inter- and intra-industry links were formed as typical Japanese organizations. On the other hand, it is doubtful if the East Asian economies can accumulate technologies as did Japan. Each participates in the international production network, one in which a participant has a part in the division of labor and tends to hold a complementary, not competitive, relation to others.

In countries with a large inflow of FDI it may be difficult – and not always meaningful – to classify as domestic versus foreign embodied within FDI, and to specify the mechanics of technology transfer. Nonetheless, developing countries need to create domestic technologies, lest they suffer from de-industrialization or outflow of domestic investments even in early stages as the result of rapidly changing comparative advantages in international trade. With an open and competitive international trade system (quite different from when Japan was first modernizing), the transition from having a comparative advantage in labor-intensive production to losing it takes less and less time.

4. CONCLUDING REMARKS

This chapter has compared the basic characteristics of Japanese and East Asian economic growth. We have focused on the fundamentals for growth, endogenous institutions and sequencing in development policies rather than the content of the policies themselves. These factors are necessary conditions to form the responsive capacity of businesses and individuals to policy changes. Each developing economy needs to develop the capacity to implement policies effectively.

In Japan, industrial structures and related policies and institutions changed gradually in accordance with shifts in its comparative advantage. We see similar changes in East Asia. Even allowing for today's rapidly moving external conditions, gradualism as a development strategy may have major virtues for other developing countries.

In that connection, this chapter has emphasized balanced growth. Intra- and inter-industry resource shifts have occurred mainly through market mechanisms without serious government failures through heavy interventions. One important result is a relatively equal income distribution.

Surely, economic growth and social stability through equal income distribution are related. There have been many studies of Kuznets' observation that income inequality at first increases during the process of development, and then diminishes once a certain level has been reached. However, the level of development is not the only factor responsible for the large difference in income inequality between East Asia and Latin America. Institutions, policies and the process have contributed.

Finally, it should be said once again that lessons from Japan and East Asia need to be interpreted in light of different institutions and external conditions. We have described various contributions to the Japanese high growth era, such as favorable fundamentals and industrial organization. However, some of these now have become the subject of structural reform in a sluggish economy. This fact underscores the message that different stages need different prescriptions.

NOTES

1 The Japan Center for Economic Research conducted a research project entitled "The Role of Systems and Policies in Japan's Modern Economic Growth and Their Applicability to Developing Counties in 1993–94," commissioned by the Economic Planning Agency. Both of the authors of this paper were participants in the project. The section in this chapter dealing with Japanese development analysis draws on the research project.

2 Traditional industries are roughly defined here as industries of traditional commodities inherited from the premodern period and their related services. The companies are often managed by families or small businesses. They include agriculture, forestry and fishery in their broad senses. Takafusa Nakamura analyzed quantitatively the development of these traditional industries and found the following: (1) The share of all employment (excluding those of agriculture and forestry) increased from 28 percent (1991–85) to 42 percent (1931–35), while in the modern sector, the share was only 12 percent even in 1931–35. The share of output by family businesses in the manufacturing sector dropped from 95 percent (1892) to 26 percent (1930), but Nakamura emphasized that the absolute value of the output kept growing to more than double the previous amount, see Nakamura, 1983.

3 There are many different views on how these stages should be divided. The controversy lies in whether the militarism and war years (1920–1945) and the following postwar high growth era (1945–1970) should be viewed as the same era. This depends on how the various postwar economic reforms are evaluated. There is no doubt that these reforms have attained their primary objective of democratizing Japanese society, but their effects on economic efficiency and economic growth are rather controversial. With respect to the manufacturing sector, for instance, some argue that the current competitive structure of the industry is not primarily a result of postwar decentralization policies, but their origin lies in the establishment of the *keiretsu* system in the militarism and war years. See Teranishi and Kosai, 1993.

4 Ragnar Nurkse pointed out conservative spending habits can prevent the excessive permeation of the "demonstration effect," thereby allowing greater savings, see Nurkse, 1953.

5 As to the contrasting views on the role of government in Japanese industrialization, see Minami, 1994: 120–4.

6 World Bank, 1993: 347–52.

7 Oshima, 1987.

8 For the survey of income distribution studies, see International Labor Office, 1984.

9 Teranishi, 1995.

10 Felix, 1994.

11 Mutoh, 1986.

12 *The Economist* (June 24–30, 1995), p.13.

13 Research Institute for International Investment and Development, The Export-Import Bank of Japan, 1995.

14 Krugman, 1994: 62–78.

REFERENCES

Felix, David (1994) "International Development in East Asia: What are the lessons for Latin America?," *UNCTAD Review 1994*, pp. 123–42.

International Labor Office (1984) *Income Distribution and Economic Development, An Analytical Survey*, Geneva: ILO.

Krugman, Paul (1994) "The Myth of Asia's Miracle," *Foreign Affairs* (Nov.–Dec.) 73: 62–78.

Minami, Ryoshin (1994) *The Economic Development of Japan*, 2nd edn, New York: Macmillan.

Mutoh, Hiromichi (1986) "Industrial Policy in the Age of the Pacific", *NIRA Report* 3.

Nakamura, Takafusa (1983) *Economic Growth in Prewar Japan*, New Haven, CT: Yale University Press (originally published in Japanese: *Senzenhi Nihon Keizai Seicho No Bunseki* [An Analysis of Economic Growth in Prewar Japan], Tokyo: Iwanami Shoten, 1971).

Nurkse, Ragnar (1953) *Problems of Capital Formation in Underdeveloped Countries*, Oxford: Basil Blackwell.

Oshima, Harry T. (1987) *Economic Growth in Monsoon Asia: A Comparative Survey*, Tokyo: University of Tokyo Press.

Research Institute for International Investment and Development, The Export-Import Bank of Japan (1995) *EXIM Review*, 15.

Teranishi, Juro (1995) *Keizaikaihatsu to tojokokusaimu* [*Debt and Development: An Analysis of LDC Debt Problems*], Tokyo: University of Tokyo Press.

Teranishi, Juro and Yutaka Kosai (eds) (1993) *The Japanese Experience of Economic Reforms*, New York: St Martin's Press.

World Bank (1993) *The East Asian Miracle: Economic Growth and Public Policy*, New York: Oxford University Press.

Yotopoulos, Pan A. (1995) *Exchange Rate Parity for Trade and Development*, Cambridge: Cambridge University Press.

14 National security and the rise of the developmental state in South Korea and Taiwan

Meredith Jung-En Woo-Cumings

The concept of the state presupposes the concept of the political. . . . In contrast to the various relatively independent endeavors of human thought and action, particularly the moral, aesthetic, and economic, the political has its own criteria which express themselves in a character-istic way. . . . The specific political distinction to which political actions and motives can be reduced is that *between friend and enemy*.

(Schmitt, 1976)

Looking back at the days of the Cold War, we find that the question of national security was much simpler and easier then. Among the nations within the free world, a broad relationship of credibility and fraternity existed. In times of emergency, friends could be counted upon. Not so any more.

(Park, 1979)

EAST ASIA: UNDER WESTERN EYES

An insight that has long eluded the American literature on South Korea and Taiwan, one often absent also in their own literatures, is a simple one: that these states were born of civil wars that have not ended, and that this fact continues to shape state actions. Specifically, social and economic policies are much affected by the issue of national survival. The cold war in East Asia and American decisions connected to it have had strong influences on the industrial strategies of South Korea and Taiwan. This is the principal argument of this chapter: security made a huge difference, if not the *whole* difference. The related topic that also made a big difference is more commonplace: the state-led nature of the developmental process.

The American discourse on the political economy of South Korea and Taiwan has gone through periodic and predictable cycles, depending on American relations with the two countries. Thus in the late 1960s the (unanticipated) economic success of South Korea and Taiwan, coupled with their (especially Korea's) steadfast support of the American effort in Vietnam, led American academics to portray the South Korean and Taiwanese economies as liberal and open, a vindication of reforms enacted under American supervision. In the 1980s much of that changed, amid deep anxiety about Japan's skyrocketing trade surplus and the loss of what came to be called American "competitiveness." As more American scholars and trade negotiators discovered Japanese industrial policies, similar practices in South Korea and Taiwan came under scrutiny: suddenly the latter countries were seen not as the microcosms of liberal America but of illiberal Japan. Some ill feeling may have been assuaged in the 1990s as they reduced their trade surpluses with the United States. In a much publicized assessment, the World Bank concluded that the governments of South Korea and Taiwan were interventionist in a "market-friendly" way, thus splitting the difference between the two earlier views.

Such periodic reversals of opinion highlight the absence of a basic intellectual framework within which East Asia's performance can be understood. Such a framework should draw on history and theory, thereby providing a context for understanding how things actually have worked there. American history, and the social science theories that reflect it, however, are by and large inadequate for understanding East Asia. Furthermore scholars from these countries possess a much more intuitive understanding of national security and the structure of political economy in their home bases, and so their analysis of this linkage has been more sporadic than systematic.

The extraordinary involvement of Korea and Taiwan in the communist–non-communist competition concentrated the minds of leaders. It led to cultivation of the arts of deflecting international pressures, an incessant search for autonomy, and a shrewd exploitation of their positions as wards of a hegemonic power so economically munificent as the United States. It also provided greater social cohesion than otherwise would probably have existed. Although Taiwan was a relatively insignificant island off the Chinese coast, its survival came to be a major issue in American domestic politics in the 1950s. And, although South Korea had, regrettably, not been publicly identified as within the American defense perimeter before June 25, 1950, it became so within hours after the North attacked.

If American history and analysis was bereft of precedents and theories that could have anticipated East Asian developmental trajectories, where might one turn for comparative insights? I have argued that the developmental experience of East Asia is similar to that of late-developing continental Europe, particularly Germany in the late nineteenth century (Woo, 1991).

Theories of economic development that grew out of the history of continental Europe provide useful reference points – all the more so in that the Meiji oligarchs copied Prussian state institutions, and planted them in the colonies they were soon to acquire – Taiwan and Korea. Among specialists it is well known that Japanese leaders found an economist they liked a lot better than Adam Smith: Germany's Friedrich List, who, incidentally had studied Alexander Hamilton's ideas on political economy. Perhaps less well known is the influence of Joseph Schumpeter, an Austrian who came of age in *fin de siècle* Vienna, whose unorthodox ideas on technology, innovation, entrepreneurs, the role of banks, monopoly and economic development seem to find in Japan perfect practitioners. Akamatsu, the great Japanese economist who in the 1930s developed the flying geese thesis, a variant of the product cycle theory that anticipated that of Raymond Vernon, may have gotten the notion from Schumpeter (who visited Japan in the early 1930s as a minor celebrity).

In his Theory of Economic Development, Schumpeter made his famous argument about the irrelevance of neoclassical theory for understanding capitalism. He argued that economic development was an endogenous process, spurred by innovation in the industrial and commercial sectors (i.e., not via the sovereign consumer), and that innovation occurred discontinuously, displacing old equilibria and creating radically new conditions. He believed (as Marx did) that economics was essentially historical, and more specifically, cyclical: this is because innovations appear discontinuously in swarms. His observations were based partly on a cyclical wave in the 1890s with a "swarm-like" series of trail-blazing innovations. In the course of this upswing, in which Austria was a passive "partaker" first and later an active contributor, Vienna's commercial banks came to hold a key position, providing not only the financial wherewithal but fostering the emergence of large-scale enterprises by promoting mergers (Marz, 1991: 129).

For Schumpeter, entrepreneurs and bankers were *dramatis personae* of socio-economic development, the agents of social change. The important insight here for the East Asian admirers of Schumpeter was not so much the emphasis on entrepreneurs and bankers *per se*, but the idea that economic development was an act of will that could be orchestrated in a purposeful manner, to overcome certain historical predicaments that faced the Austria of young Schumpeter's days: namely, lagging behind Western Europe; the challenge of mass democracy and socialism, which robbed capitalism of its aura of heroism; and the need for a stable political order in the face of war, imperialism, and the explosive appeals of Marxism to the intellectuals of his time (Marz, 1991: 31).

If entrepreneurs and banks could not on their own lead development, the state was the obvious candidate. Schumpeter was silent on such a role for the state (List, of course, was not), but another Austrian economist, Alexander Gerschenkron, eventually formulated the idea of "late-development," arguing that in some instances, the state can substitute for the missing private requisites of development.

Much of the debate in the United States over the role of the state in East Asia reflects a liberal ideological view: namely, how important state interventions have been and their net effects. The question of how it has intervened in a socially positive manner, unlike the pattern in the rest of the developing world, is rarely asked, perhaps because the notion that state elites would choose to enhance collective welfare rather than their own seems irrational. But the question of collective motivation, and specifically state motivation, *is* an important one, as Henry Rowen makes clear in the introductory chapter to this volume, even if it is rarely discussed or is merely assumed away.

Albert Hirschman said this about motivation: if instead of thinking in terms of the missing prerequisites for development we were to concentrate "on the need for a 'binding agent' which is to bring together various scattered or hidden elements, the task becomes vaguer, to say the least, and may well turn out to be more complex ... By focusing on determination, we are grasping an essential characteristic of the development in today's underdeveloped countries, namely the fact that they are latecomers. This condition is bound to make their development a less spontaneous and more deliberate process than was the case in the countries where the process first occurred" (Hirschman, 1958). Hirschman's "binding agent" for development remains elusive, however. This is because his reference area is Latin America, which had started the industrialization process earlier than either South Korea or Taiwan, led by entrepreneurs and not the state, at least initially; furthermore its international position was very different.

A suggested "binding element" for Taiwan and Korea, however, might be the determination of the people to organize themselves for development. Late-development in East Asia was fundamentally different from that of Latin America. The "determination of a nation" in East Asia did not reside primarily in the economic but in the political sphere, with economic growth often viewed as indispensable for military security. This should not be surprising because South Korea and Taiwan are still engaged in civil wars and still highly armed. Security concerns have been central state concerns in both for most of this century, in the colonial period and afterwards. The overwhelming aim of these states has been the survival of their sovereign entities, achievable in the end only through the disappearance – somehow – of the communist enemy.

The political economy of South Korea and Taiwan is thus inexplicable without the logic of a continuing mobilization for war. Economic and political theories have not captured this phenomenon. It also remains uncaptured by theorizing about Latin American "bureaucratic-authoritarianism", or totalitarianism of both communist or fascist variants. Perhaps the term Harold Lasswell gave to the national security apparatus, the *garrison state*, comes close, but the garrison state is a far cry from the phenomenon we wish to explain here. To understand anti-communist security states, and to grasp the notion of the political, to which the spheres of economy and culture are subsumed, we might turn to another contemporary of Schumpeter: Carl Schmitt.

The concern behind *The Concept of the Political* was the viability of Germany after its defeat in World War I. He did so by addressing the politics of the Weimar Republic, which in itself is not relevant for my argument. His theory of the state is, however. For Schmitt, the Weberian understanding of the state – an entity with a monopoly of violence within a given territory – was essentially a useless concept that ignored the political and emotional tension that defined *raison d'état* and the power that derived from it. That tension at its simplest and most concrete level, for Schmitt, was the distinction between friend and enemy that undergirded the power of the state.

By enemy he meant a hostile entity that invokes concrete antagonism expressed in everyday language, defining the collective "we" against the alien "other." "The political enemy need not be morally evil or aesthetically ugly," Schmitt argued; "he needs not appear as an economic competitor, and it may even be advantageous to do business with him. But he is, nevertheless, the other, the stranger ... conflicts with him are possible" (Schmitt, 1976: 27). The latent potential conflict with the enemy explained for Schmitt the position of the state as the highest and most decisive entity, with ultimate authority to shape the economy and society in order to preserve the integrity of the collectivity against the existentially-opposed enemy. War, Schmitt argued, was neither the aim nor the purpose nor even the very content of politics. But as an ever-present possibility it was the leading presupposition which created a specifically political behavior (Schmitt, 1976: 35, 37).

Pluralism assumes that an individual is a member of many human associations of equal weight – including the state itself. The essential fact of political life for Schmitt, as a Catholic organicist thinker, was that pluralism, left unchecked, would destroy the politics of Weimar Germany, and it would succumb to enemies from within and without, sooner or later. This dangerous argument could have justified the pathological extremes of the Third Reich (although later Schmitt was roundly criticized by the Nazis, perhaps for his Church-oriented and anti-capitalist views). Schmitt captures the orientation of states engaged in perpetual conflict, and explains not only the logic and the manner of state intervention in the economy, but why for so long the policies of the state, even when they were grotesquely ill-conceived and executed, were suffered and tolerated by the citizens.

The mobilizational and state-oriented aspects of East Asian economic development were associated with a siege mentality – the binary "we" vs. "they" in internationalized civil conflicts in Taiwan and South Korea. In short, societal compliance had more to do with insecurity and authoritarian controls than with cultural habits (as is so often argued these days). From this perspective, the behavior of South Korea and Taiwan makes little sense without attention to their threatened status and promontory position in the Cold War, for the global security structure affected their economic programs. Well before that, however, their experiences of colonialism and war had also left indelible marks.

THE PRECEDENT: THE STATE IN WAR-MOBILIZED KOREA AND TAIWAN

The intellectual link between *fin de siècle* continental Europe and postwar East Asia is this: the essence of the modern European state emerged in full splendor in Meiji Japan – a state which perceived its external environment to be life-threatening. The Meiji oligarchs, including Ito Hirubumi as the first resident-general of Korea, were assiduous students of the Prussian military state. Ito had traveled extensively in Europe and came away fascinated by Prussian military and bureaucracy, which he saw as a route to Western rationality and modernity, but also an alternative to Anglo-Saxon liberalism. He was largely responsible for making the Prussian-style bureaucracy the absolute unassailable base and center of political power (Woo-Cumings, 1995: 439). What Otto Hintze said about Prussia applies to the state structure that emerged in East Asia in the first half of the twentieth century: "The absolutist military developed into the tutelary police state, which understood the *salus publica* inscribed on its banner, not in the sense of the individual felicity of its subjects but in the sense of the preservation and strengthening of the state as a whole. ... This was particularly evident in Prussia, the classic example of the militarist state" (Hintze, 1975: 201).

The militarization of administration was even more evident in colonial Korea than in Japan. The Korean Governor-General always came from the army, and after the Manchurian Incident, Korean society was mobilized for war to a greater degree than Japan's. In the industrial sphere, Korea, as an entrepôt between Manchuria and Japan and as a supplier of mineral resources, cheap labor, and hydroelectricity, was a logical location for a crash industrialization program: hence such slogans as "Chosen as a base of war supplies," and "Chosen as a base of penetration" (Woo, 1991: 31). Japanese colonialism left three imprints that are relevant to us. The first is the political machinery imposed on agrarian economies in Taiwan and later in Korea. From the 1880s, the Japanese interest in Taiwan and Korea sprang from regional security concerns, broadly conceived. In the words of Marius Jansen (1968: 182), the compass of Japan's strategy concern was in concentric circles radiating from the homelands: the "cordon of sovereignty" encompassed territory vital to the nation's survival and under formal occupation, the "cordon of advantages," was an outer limit of informal Japanese domination, seen as necessary to protect the inner line. The territorial contiguity of Japanese imperialism, combined with the fact that Japan was still a developing country, meant that its colonial policies would be significantly different from those of, say, Britain. Japanese control and use of the colonies were much more extensive, thorough, and systematic; the economic structure of the colonies had to undergo radical and brutal transformation tied to the needs of a rapidly-growing Japan.

The colonial state was not accountable to its domestic constituents, nor subject to the supervisional scrutiny of cabinet or parliament. (It reported to the Ministry of Colonies in Tokyo, which tended to ratify colonial government proposals.) This separation both from colonized societies and from superordinate Japanese influence was reinforced by the well-organized and militarized nature of the state machinery, replete with "thought police," and a "spy system," to buttress the civil and police bureaucracy that was probably better developed in Korea than anywhere in the world. Perhaps, but the original architect of colonial police structures was Goto Shimpei, who devised for Taiwan essentially the same system, some years before Korea was colonized. Both colonies got a ubiquitous, centrally-controlled bureaucratic system of top-to-bottom surveillance.

Post-1949 Taiwan had another experience to draw on: the civil war on the mainland, and the heavy militarization of the Kuomintang apparatus, both with major implications for economic policy. The disciplined Kuomintang party-state structure has a long pedigree, going back to the late 1920s when Chiang Kai-shek came to dominate the party, primarily through his military struggle to establish control over China. The KMT was Leninist in character with "a residual effect of military penetration," one that was also influenced by the German military (and later, Soviet advice, with an independent military council that controlled military operations as well as political and industrial programs). Not only were the weapons German-made, but many of the officers were German-trained, and the whole military organization and industrial development was German inspired. The KMT adopted the German tradition of keeping the military independent of legislative interference and the military command apart from administrative functions (Lewis, 1993: 83). Chiang Ching-kuo was also trained by the German military. The military character of the KMT increased with the war against Japan, and then in a full blown civil war with the communists (Lewis, 1993: 81). To the extent that Taiwan's post-1949 economic program was predicated on genuine security needs, it was built on an earlier pattern.

The second important aspect of the Japanese colonial legacy is the relationship between the state and business, especially the prewar *zaibatsu* that came to invest in the colonies. The colonial state offered big business two attractions: political stability and state investment in infrastructure; political and social overhead, so to speak. But most critical in the Japanese private sector's investment decisions was finance: the government's willingness to share the risk should the investment turn unprofitable. This socialization of financial risks foretells the postwar Korean government strategy of "financial repression," a four-decade-long policy of shifting resources from savers to heavily-leveraged, eventually gigantic enterprises, creating in the end a constellation of native industrialists.

The most useful lesson from the colonial political economy for the latter-day industrializers was that it *worked*; and that its success was based on close collaboration between the state and the *zaibatsu*. The colonial state's role in the channeling of capital to target industries was a precedent for a similar mobilization in the 1970s in both Taiwan and South Korea, especially the mid-to-late 1930s "big push" that brought new industries to Korea (steel, chemicals) and Taiwan (aluminium), along with very high growth rates. If a "growth perspective" can best be grasped when one has experienced it, then one can say that the colonial political economy provided such a perspective in the postwar years.

True, the Japanese pattern also devastated the class that carried all before it in the modern world, the entrepreneurial one. Certainly there were Koreans and Taiwanese who did quite well under the Japanese, then parleyed their capital and entrepreneurial skill into fortunes in the post-colonial era. But the Japanese presence was too overbearing for entre-preneurial continuity. It was mainly bureaucrats who "continued" into the postwar period, armed now with a concept of state-guided development.

The suppression of local entrepreneurial talent, combined with revolu-tionary upheavals that bedeviled both countries (further destroying entre-preneurial continuity), had another influence on later development: bereft of powerful local business interests, the new states were also less hamstrung by entrenched interests closely tied to the metropole.

The defeat of the Kuomintang did not have the effect of transplanting a cluster of businessmen to Taiwan. Few leading capitalists followed Chiang Kai-shek to his island redoubt, preferring instead to go to the United States or Hong Kong: and the few that went to Taiwan thought it was a temporary sojourn, and eschewed significant commitments of capital until a bilateral treaty between Washington and Taipei guaranteed the island's security. This also reinforced the state's role in postwar Taiwan – or what Robert Wade has called "governing the market" (Wade, 1990).

The third point is the relationship between the state and the rural sector. Unlike European colonialists in Latin America – or for that matter, else-where in Southeast Asia – the Japanese did not drive the peasants off their land to establish plantations (although it did not redistribute land, either). Instead it used police and administrative methods to root the land-lords firmly in the countryside, for a reliable extraction of agricultural outputs and taxes, and to keep the lid on peasant unrest. Korea and Taiwan differed here: Korea's landed class was of centuries' duration whereas Taiwan never had deeply developed landlordism. Instead it had a significant group of "rich peasants," another reason why Japan could extract resources in Taiwan through incentives, while often having to use coercion in Korea. By 1945, both countries did have wealthy landlords by virtue of strong agricultural growth. But the landlords in post-colonial

Taiwan and Korea did not have long to enjoy their privileges, unlike the latifundia owners in Latin America.

As the historian Bruce Cumings argued, the defeat of imperial Japan burst asunder the "pressure cooker" that was colonial Korea, leading eventually to war and instability (Cumings, 1981). In the midst of this chaos, even the conservative South Korean state quickly enacted a thorough and extensive land reform, at the prodding of the United States, lest the revolution in the north spill over. Likewise in Taiwan, land reform in 1950 was swift and decisive, enacted by the Kuomintang with a lot of help from American advisors, nervously looking over their shoulders to the revolutionary mainland – thus to stave off peasant upheaval.

How then do we sum up the colonial legacy? One is by noting the weakness of entrenched interests, both industrial and agricultural – either because local entrepreneurial talents were not nurtured in the smothering intensity of Japanese imperialism, or because they were shattered when the colonial pressure-cooker blew up in their faces, as with the agrarian interests. This discontinuity had a powerful leveling effect, equalizing incomes more than in most developing countries and providing a fertile ground for an interventionist state, which had a relatively free hand to forge a developmental coalition. It helped that the resources for this coalition had the support of a big power: the United States. But this gets us ahead of our story. If there were useful absences, so there were salutary presences and continuities. The bureaucratic structure imposed on colonial Korea and Taiwan was a modern, meritocratic, and authoritative one, with much of it (all the offices, and substantial personnel) carried forward to independence. The classic colonizer was a careful administrator like Goto Shimpei, who worked in Taiwan and Korea, and helped rebuild modern Tokyo after the 1923 earthquake. In many ways he was an early exemplar of the Japanese practice of "administrative guidance," in this case, colonial-style.

So, the state structure was there and so was the know-how to engineer industrial policy. The disruption caused by colonialism and war, with the wiping out of the entrepreneurial and land-owning class, meant that state-led industrialization was both natural and easier. The state task was then to construct from the vacuum left by colonialism and war, a social class that could carry out industrialization. They went about this in different ways, however; there is a sharp divergence in how these countries dealt with colonial legacies.

Korea essentially replicated the Japanese pattern of nurturing large conglomerates, at least under Park Chung Hee and Chun Doo Hwan (1961–88), whereas Taiwan nurtured only a couple of big firms, while emphasizing small business. What accounts for the difference? The reasons are primarily historical. Because of Korea's mainland connection to Manchuria and North China, Japanese colonizers and *zaibatsu* corporations developed heavy industries and spent huge amounts on social overhead, especially in northern Korea, creating a large marketing, communications and transportation infrastructure in northeast Asia, tied into the mother country. Taiwan did have some heavy industries like aluminium and electric generating by the end of the colonial period, but it was much more a light industrial and agricultural part of the Japanese empire, with much of that exported (sending sugar in great amounts to Japan, for example). History bequeathed bigness to Korea, small-scale practices to Taiwan.

As Thomas Gold and others have shown, Nationalist rule on Taiwan also brought with it Nationalist methods in the economy – a state-centered rather than firm-centered pattern, often called "bureaucratic capitalism" in the literature. Personal connections in the Kuomintang party were often the avenue to upward economic mobility. An additional Chinese pattern, drawn from the practices of the Chinese diaspora, in what Ralph Clough has aptly called "island China," has the family as the prime economic unit, specializing in small business. (The stereotypical Chinese laundry and Chinese restaurant in the US are examples of a widespread pattern in Southeast Asia.) This promoted small business in Taiwan. Taiwan also sought niches in the world economy, quite like Singapore but quite unlike Korea, the leaders of which always wanted a fully-developed industrial structure. For Taiwan, this was something to be accomplished when the mainland was retaken, but not on an island.

All this tended toward a divergence in Korean and Taiwan economic practices by the 1980s, but there is great similarity on something economists do not pay much attention to: security. Here there is also a vast difference from Latin America; the relation of these two "NICs" to the world was much affected by their relations to the United States in the context of the Cold War.

THE POLITICAL ECONOMY OF SECURITY IN EAST ASIA

The aspect of the Cold War in East Asia's development that has received most attention has been the role of foreign aid (Cumings, 1984; Woo, 1991). After the Korean War, both Taiwan and South Korea were seen by the US as important bulwarks against communism: their survival warranted a massive infusion of capital – especially relative to their small economies. In Taiwan over the 1950s, economic aid equaled about 6 percent of GNP and nearly 40 percent of gross investment, and military aid was still bigger than economic aid (Wade, 1990: 82). From 1946 to 1976, the United States provided $12.6 billion in American economic and military aid to South Korea, and $5.6 billion to Taiwan; combined with additional contributions from Japan and international financial institutions, the total gave South Korea in the midpoint year of 1960 a per capita assistance figure of $600 over three decades, and $425 for Taiwan (Woo, 1991: 44). To put these figures in perspective, South Korean and Taiwanese per capita GNPs in 1965 were about $100 (in current dollars).

This aid went far toward rehabilitating these countries and helped to stabilize their economies, societies and regimes; it boosted investor confidence and financial extensive land reforms and other social reforms. It also helped domestic capitalists who got their start through non-competitive allocation of import quotas and licenses, access to bank loans, aid funds and materials, and the non-competitive award of government and US military contracts for reconstruction. Unquestionably, there was much corruption and political chicanery in the use of foreign aid, but that did not interfere with rapid growth rates.

When the Cold War turned into a regional conflagration in Indochina, US aid to South Korea and Taiwan reversed its early 1960s decline. Much as Japan had started its postwar take-off with the Korean War, so Taiwan and South Korea were helped by the Vietnam War. Taiwan was seen as a strategic asset maintaining pressure on China and a useful source of logistical support for US forces in Southeast Asia. As a part of the island chain that surrounds China, Taiwan was an important link in US containment policy and Taiwan, in turn, benefited from American purchases of agricultural and industrial commodities, the use of military facilities and depots for repair of equipment, its use as a site for rest and recreation, and contract work for and in Vietnam (Lewis, 1993: 262).

South Korean involvement in Vietnam was more direct, having sent in rotation more than 300,000 troops by the time the war was over; this was more men per capita than any other nation, including the United States. The total cost to the United States of equipping and paying for these was "peanuts compared to what it would be for a comparable number of Americans," but those "peanuts" went a long way to finance Korea's take-off. The total economic and military aid that Korea received as payment for partaking in the Vietnam War came to more than one billion dollars (Woo, 1991).

Less well studied than the direct impact of this money is that of foreign aid on economic policy. To the extent that this is studied, it focuses on the impact of American advisors in prodding Taiwan and South Korea toward liberalization and export orientation, celebrated as "the most dramatic and vivid change in any developing countries since World War II" (Krueger, 1979: 82). That, of course, is true: the Economic Cooperation Administration (ECA) had its biggest operation in South Korea, and in Taiwan, the US government had close to 14,000 permanent personnel and their dependents in positions with the embassy, USAID and the military forces (Lewis, 1993: 185). USAID also shipped off the best and brightest of economic experts to Seoul and Taipei to forge new economic orders.

In the end, though, the American role had less to do with technicalities than with its ability to manipulate economic actions. The three major policy decisions in postwar South Korea and Taiwan – import-substitution industrialization (ISI), in the 1950s, export-orientation in the late 1950s in Taiwan and early 1960s in South Korea, and, finally, the defense-related industrial deepening in both countries in the late 1960s and early 1970s – were, in essential ways, predictable responses to America's changing geopolitical actions.

The early phase of ISI in South Korea for much of the 1950s was not an ill-thought product of home-grown economists (or even a well-thought policy in a period when ISI was a developmental norm) but a catch-as-catch-can method to absorb foreign aid dollars in infrastructural and industrial projects and to keep the foreign aid spigot open. Of course, infrastructural spending at this stage was quite rational, as was import substitution for simple, low-technology goods. In South Korea, open trade, or even an export orientation to earn foreign currency, was fiercely resisted, especially because it involved an American effort to create a regional market to help the Japanese economy to revive. Syngman Rhee was well aware of the American plan to solve two intractable problems at once – the revival of the Japanese economy, and the maintenance of viability in the two Cold War wards – by linking them in a regional market, which meant recycling US aid dollars through Taiwan and South Korea to buy goods from Japan. This was the spectre of another Co-Prosperity Sphere. Rhee called the scheme of regional integration "the American policy to secure two dollars of benefit – one for Japan and one for Korea – from every dollar expended" (Woo, 1991: 56). What this mercantilist wanted instead was all dollar benefits for Korea alone, to nurture Korean industries with US aid in a zero-sum game. Rhee thought expansion of Korean industry should have its counterpart in suppression of Japan's. In short, he refused to play a part in the global solution to the "dollar gap," which, to rectify the massive structural disequilibrium in world trade, required rebuilding the economies of Europe and Japan. This resistance worked, as did the resulting program of ISI (at least for some years).

The situation was different for Chiang Kai-shek. After the Korean war, the United States was committed to staying in Korea, which only increased the political clout – and recalcitrance – of Syngman Rhee. This was not a luxury that Chiang enjoyed. (In 1960, although the largest MAAG operation in the world was in Taiwan, this was nothing like having many American troops present as in South Korea, a tripwire to ensure an instant American involvement in the event of war.) Of the three states to enjoy strong support by the American right – Taiwan, South Korea and South Vietnam – Chiang was to suffer the deepest penetration by American aid agencies and to implement therefore the most far-reaching economic and social reforms.

In 1950, the relatively weak hand of Chiang – compared to Rhee – led to a quick capitulation on the issue of restoring trade ties with Japan, leading to a Japan–Taiwan trade agreement engineered by American aid officials and the SCAP (Supreme Command, Allied Powers). By 1953,

Japan absorbed one-half of Taiwan's exports of rice, salt and sugar, and exported to Taiwan almost as much in textiles, fertilizers and machinery (Lewis, 1993: 207). Periodically Chiang would enjoy upsurges of American military and economic aid, as he did during offshore island crises, in 1954–55 and 1958. But in general Taiwan was more subject than South Korea to cuts in foreign aid.

To the extent that Taiwan's policy in the 1950s was ISI, it did not stem from Chiang's refusal to earn foreign exchange from Japan. Rather it came from the need for more state revenues, through tariffs and other duties associated with ISI, in order to support a huge military force. By the late 1950s, the ROC possessed the seventh largest land army in the world and the fifth largest among the non-communist countries. Over 6 percent of the population actively served in the armed services, plus there were enormous reserves, making it the most militarized of the non-communist countries.

ISI in Taiwan also had to deal with the legacy of its colonial industrial and infrastructural enterprises. Unlike South Korea, where some government enterprises were sold to the private sector, their Taiwanese counterparts passed onto the state sector rewards to the mainlanders, who became the mainstay of the KMT. The state enterprises were often in infrastructure and heavy industries, and ISI became a way to channel resources to enterprises controlled by the KMT.

In the end, however, both the South Korean policy of making Korea "another Japan" while keeping the real Japan at bay (all of it supported by America), and the Taiwanese policy of concentrating national resources to beef up the KMT-controlled public sector while increasing defense expenditure (which rose more than six-fold between 1951 and 1961), could not stand. The Decade of Mutual Security was coming to an end, and with it a precipitous reduction in aid; Taiwan was forced to turn outward at the end of 1950s, and South Korea by the beginning of the 1960s. (The share of output of the state-owned sector in Taiwan declined sharply in the 1960s; this did not happen as quickly in South Korea probably because of the uncertainty caused by the *coup d'état* in 1961.)

The export-led program in the 1960s, then, was less the result of the American technical advice than a function of declining US aid. This is a point missed in the American political science literature on the East Asian NICs, which prefers to interpret the export-oriented reforms either as emanating from USAID to insulate the native technocracy from political pressures of the Nationalist leadership in Taiwan, or as the result of a reform-oriented coalition in South Korea (Haggard, 1990).

If the first phase of ISI in the 1950s was, in part, politically motivated, that in the 1970s was no less so, and coincided with another shift in US policy. The fulcrum of the new economic program was the need for military self-sufficiency and thus defense-related heavy industrialization, occasioned by declining American fortunes in Vietnam, increasing North

Korean guerrilla infiltration of South Korea, the Pueblo incident, the downing of the American EC-121 by the North Koreans, and, to top it all, the Nixon Doctrine.

The year 1968 was particularly trying for Korea. It still had two divisions in Vietnam, and just as the war in Indochina was escalating, so was North Korean infiltration into the south, possibly in coordination with the Tet Offensive designed to demolish the American position in Vietnam. Of some 629 guerrilla-related incidents reported for 1968 alone, the most noteworthy was a North Korean commando attack on the presidential residence that claimed some 100 casualties and was a near miss on Park Chung Hee's life. But American hackles were raised only when an American spy ship was captured by the North Koreans in the very same month. Park deeply resented all the Pueblo-related brouhaha and the subsequent US negotiations with North Korea, which put the latter in the international limelight. Fearing South Korean expendability, Park let it be known that South Korea would have to "go it alone" to defend itself if Americans were reluctant to do the job. He called for a militia of 2.5 million men, with units even in the smallest villages, to be armed with Korean-made weapons. South Korea embarked on making small arms and ammunitions, both through joint ventures with American firms and through international loans. This was the starting point for a defense industry.

Notwithstanding heightened vigilance, North Korean infiltration increased in frequency, in mimicry of the Viet Cong operations in South Vietnam in the late 1950s. Then, in what Henry Kissinger called the first major crisis in the Nixon administration, in early 1969 North Korea downed an unarmed American reconnaissance plane, the EC-121, in the Sea of Japan. Despite Kissinger's urging that several North Korean airfields be bombed in retaliation, Nixon, on the advice of Secretary Laird, refrained from a tit-for-tat with the North. Kissinger was to complain later that the handling of EC-121 incident was "weak, indecisive, and disorganized," that "it showed major flaws in the [US] decision making – [The administration] made no strategic assessment; no strong leadership; no significant political move; lacked both machinery and conception; made no demands that North Korea could either accept or reject" (Kissinger, 1979: 321). This was one more incident that weakened Korean confidence in America, and was a harbinger of still greater conflicts in store.

Nixon's new foreign policy design, first unveiled to the Congress in early 1970, revealed a switch from what was hitherto known as a two-and-a-half war strategy, to a one-and-a-half one. The former had meant initial defense of Western Europe against Soviet attack *and* a sustained defense against an all-out Chinese attack on Southeast Asia or Korea, plus meeting a contingency elsewhere. In the new strategy, the second category was simply dropped. This revision was a logical, if belated, response to the Sino-Soviet split, to the fact that one-third of the Soviet and one-half of the Chinese military forces were now stationed on the Sino-Soviet frontier. If the Sino-Soviet bloc was no more, there was no reason – beyond bureaucratic pork-barreling – to fund military programs in East Asia based on old Cold War assumptions.

The first place (besides Indochina) where the axe of the Nixon Doctrine fell was South Korea. During the Johnson presidency, the National Security Council had recommended reducing the US troop commitment to South Korea in five or more years depending on the Korean pace of military modernization, but the Nixon administration accelerated the withdrawal out of budgetary pressure. Some 20,000 American soldiers were removed from South Korea by the middle of 1971, with the rest to be phased out in the next five years. Seoul had little to say in the decision, having lost its trump card once the United States had determined upon Vietnam disengagement (Woo, 1991: 123). This was followed by the opening to China, in 1971 and 1972.

In what were perceived to be the waning days of the Pax Americana, the first goal in South Korea was to purge all uncertainties from the body politic by tightening the grip of authoritarian politics, and with the steering mechanism thus made predictable, to make a Big Push with massive investments in steel, shipbuilding, machine building, chemicals and metals. The development of heavy industries implied a strong defense industry, thus ending dependence on American largess in weaponry and various political prices that came with it. In the South Korean context, this meant a partial departure from the export-oriented, sectorally unbiased strategy of the 1960s.

Taiwan's response to Nixon's policies was as determined and swift as that in South Korea. As early as 1967, Nixon intimated in the journal *Foreign Affairs* his view that China should be included in the family of nations, and by 1970, Taiwan was aware of US overtures to the mainland. As in South Korea, Taiwan intensified crackdowns on domestic dissent, raised military preparedness, and tightened the state's control over the economy. But Taiwan's regime was not subject to the same kind of international scrutiny as that of South Korea. This was in part because Park Chung Hee had created a strong authoritarian system through his KCIA (founded in 1961), the 1972 Constitution ushered in a ruthlessly authoritarian regime, and there were periodic declarations of martial law. The KMT always had a well-structured Leninist organization, and had ruled Taiwan through martial law ever since 1949. In other words the intensification of martial law in Taiwan was a much better-orchestrated affair and faced less concerted opposition than in South Korea.

In the late 1960s, Chiang Ching-kuo strengthened his hold over the armed forces, secret police, China youth corps, retired servicemen's association and vital sections of the bureaucracy (Lewis, 1993: 272). He also concentrated power in the newly formed National Security Council, made up of the regime's military and political administrative elites. Chiang

Ching-kuo began focusing on a comprehensive program of economic development with the aim of increasing national self-sufficiency by reorganizing the military and becoming one of the world's major arms importers and a major manufacturer. He also emphasized air and naval power rather than ground troops and shifted from an offensive posture to a defensive one.

This shift required forging links among industrial, research and defense sectors. It was helped by state control of finance, education, and most large-scale manufacturing. Many state enterprises made goods to serve dual functions (commercial and military). Examples included Taiwan Machinery Manufacturing, China Shipbuilding, Taiwan Aluminium, China Petroleum, Taiwan Metal Mining, BES Engineering, China Petrochemical Development, China Steel, Chung-Tai Chemical Engineering, the Aero-Industry Development Center, etc. (Lewis, 1993: 309).

In 1971 Chiang Ching-kuo became Premier, and called for a gigantic investment program centering on the development of heavy industry and chemicals, especially plastics and resins, machinery, shipbuilding, electrical equipment and steel – exactly the foundations of defense industry. Of course, the fastest-growing sector was still the private, small business firms. The Taiwanese agents of heavy industrialization were state-owned enterprises, but they were private ones in South Korea; the huge conglomerates known as the *chaebol*, nurtured by the state. This was done largely through selective application of "financial repression," provisioning capital to big business at rates much lower than what the market would have dictated, as well as through preferential access to imports. This financial policy had a profound impact on the class structure in South Korea, giving a boost to a constellation of domestic enterprises, marking their birth as world-class conglomerates. It also altered the state's relationship to big business, eliminating any possible arms-length relationship.

The policy of credit allocation and low interest rates meant that bank loans (in the context of virtually absent equity markets) became subsidies for the chosen: the entrepreneurs who had proven their mettle through good export records, the risk-takers who entered into heavy and chemical industries, and the faithful who plunged into the untried sea of international competition with new products – relying on the state to rescue them if they got into trouble. These entrepreneurs made the defense-oriented program possible, and thus the drive for overall industrial strength.

To join the chosen few, enterprises had to be big; but to remain chosen, they had to be gigantic: size was an effective guard against default, one which would have forced the government into the role of lender of last resort. The importance of size in this sense cannot be overemphasized, since highly leveraged firms, exposed to the vagaries of the international market, live with the spectre of default. It was for this reason that the expression "octopus-like spread of the *chaebol*" came into wide circulation in South Korea. But the *chaebol* tentacles gripped not only the economy but eventually the state as well: big state and big business would have to sink or swim together. A credit-based financial system, mediated by an interventionist authoritarian state, became the basis of Korea, Inc.

The flip side of the state–big business symbiosis for many years was suppression of popular protests and the evisceration of labor as a political force. This pattern, common in East Asia, was in contrast to Western Europe where institutions of representative government were powerfully shaped by an effort to cope with such sectors. It also fundamentally differed from that of Latin America, where corporatist structures emerged from the demands of various landed, business and social groups, including labor, and where economic policies, such as ISI, obtained political legitimacy through (generally unsuccessful) populist attempts to redress great economic inequalities. True, oppressive political conditions for labor in Taiwan and South Korea were mitigated by firm-level paternalism; but labor remained weak and systematically excluded in both countries, shackled by considerations of national security and international economic competitiveness. This did not really change until the late 1980s, when martial law was lifted in Taiwan, and when mass protests drove Chun Doo Hwan from office. Thereafter labor organizing was rapid, particularly in Korea.

In short, the contours of state and society in South Korea and Taiwan were powerfully shaped by international conflicts, from the agonies caused by Japanese imperial ambition, civil wars, revolutions, and the Cold War. With the easing of Cold War tensions, combined with greater prosperity in Taiwan and South Korea, both political coercion and developmental frenzy have subsided – although economic growth proceeds apace. The greatest task for the 1990s is to redress the excesses of the past, in Korea to reassess the relationship between the state and business, and in both to find ways to institutionalize popular sectors which shouldered much of the burden of such rapid development.

CONCLUSION

This chapter started with the observation that social science theories often reveal more about the social scientists than the subjects of their inquiry (an argument that E. H. Carr once made about historians, as well). I have argued that the experience of late-developing Germany has much to inform us about the formation of the states in East Asia. This is a point sometimes made in parentheses but never fully elaborated on in the writings of Chalmers Johnson, for instance (Johnson, 1995).

If the biography of the author is as important as I have made it out, then perhaps I should explain the particular personal and historical grounds for insisting on the importance of the "political" (as Schmitt understood the term) as undergirding the economic mobilization of East Asian security states. The experience I draw on is the knowledge bred in the bones of anyone growing up in post-1949 Taiwan or postwar South Korea, namely the intense, emotional loathing of communism that was so successfully drilled into every school child, the constant drumbeat of admonition that national survival was contingent on economic development and military preparedness that demanded personal sacrifices. This is the kind of lived experience that is deeply internalized, even if it has long dwelt in the shadows of much Western imagination about the golden-era of the Pacific Rim and its supposed unfettered capitalism. It explains why the most ruthless societal mobilization for economic growth worked for so long.

Does this make these developmental experiences idiosyncratic, bereft of lessons for other developing countries? The answer, I think, is mixed. In a comparison of development in Northern Europe and East Asia, one scholar has argued that Austria, Finland, South Korea and Taiwan (the four countries he examines) shared four attributes of successful state intervention. First, old bureaucratic traditions were capable of providing competent administration; this is unquestionably true of all four. Second, again in all four, the wars they suffered shook up the prewar power blocs and rearranged the previous distribution of power among domestic elites, paving the way toward a less obstacle-strewn development strategy. In that sense, the history of South Korea and Taiwan might not be as unique as one might think. Third, each faced security threats of a kind possibly leading to their annihilation – which very nearly happened to South Korea and Taiwan in 1950. Last, in spite of their positions between two major international power blocs, all four were committed to the bourgeois legal order (if only in form sometimes) and respected private property. In the end, all four adopted policy tools that were remarkably similar: investment subsidies, price controls, credit rationing, and maintenance of interest rates at artificially low levels (Vartiainen, forthcoming).

What, then, are the lessons for development? The genius of the states in South Korea and Taiwan – and Finland and Austria as well – was in harnessing real fears of attack and instability toward a remarkable developmental energy. The pursuit of power and plenty, in the context either of the security state or of catching up with the rest of the world (more often both), has been vastly more effective in generating developmental energy than a general appeal to increased welfare, à la Latin American "populism."

REFERENCES

Amsden, Alice (1989) *Asia's Next Giant*, New York: Oxford University Press.
Clough, Ralph N. (1978) *Island China*, Cambridge, MA: Harvard University Press.
Cumings, Bruce (1981) *The Origins of the Korean War*, vol. 1, Princeton, NJ: Princeton University Press.
—— (1984) "The Origins and Development of the Northeast Asian Political Economy: Industrial Sectors, Product Cycles and Political Consequences," *International Organization*, 38 (1): 1–40.

Gerschenkron, Alexander (1965) *Economic Backwardness in Historical Perspective*, Cambridge, MA: Harvard University Press.

Haggard, Stephan (1990) *Pathways from the Periphery: The Newly-Industrializing Countries in the International System*, Ithaca, NY: Cornell University Press.

Hintze, Otto (1975), in Gilbert, Felix (ed.) *The Historical Essays of Otto Hintze*, New York: Oxford University Press.

Hirschman, Albert (1958) *The Strategy of Economic Development*, New Haven, CT: Yale University Press.

Jansen, Marius B. (1968) "Modernization and Foreign Policy in Meiji Japan," in Robert Ward (ed.) *Political Development in Modern Japan*, Princeton: Princeton University Press.

Johnson, Chalmers (1995) *Japan, Who Governs?* New York: W.W. Norton.

Kissinger, Henry (1979) *The White House Years*, New York: Little, Brown.

Krueger, Anne (1979) *The Developmental Role of the Foreign Sector and Aid*, Cambridge, MA: Harvard University Press.

Lewis, Reese Phillip (1993) "The Origins of Taiwan's Trade and Industrial Policies," unpublished Ph.D. dissertation, Columbia University.

Marz, Eduard (1991) *Joseph Schumpeter: Scholar, Teacher and Politician*, New Haven, CT: Yale University Press.

Park Chung Hee (1979) *Korea Reborn*, Englewood Cliffs, NJ: Prentice-Hall.

Schmitt, Carl (1976) *The Concept of the Political*, New Brunswick, NJ: Rutgers University Press.

Schumpeter, Joseph A. (1983) *The Theory of Economic Development*, New Brunswick, NJ: Transactions Books.

Vartiainen, Juhana (forthcoming) "The State and Structural Change: What Can Be Learned from the Successful Late Industrializers?", in Woo-Cumings, Meredith (ed.) *The Developmental States in Comparative Perspective*, Ithaca: Cornell University Press.

Wade, Robert (1990) *Governing the Market*, Princeton, NJ: Princeton University Press.

Woo, Jung-en (Meredith Woo-Cumings) (1991) *Race to the Swift: State and Finance in Korean Industrialization*, New York: Columbia University Press.

Woo-Cumings, Meredith (1995) "Developmental Bureaucracy in Comparative Perspective," in Kim, Hyung-Ki, Michio Muramatsu, T.J. Pempel, and Kozo Yamamura (eds) *The Japanese Civil Service and Economic Development*, New York: Oxford University Press.

Part V

15 What are the lessons from East Asia?

Henry S. Rowen

There are two extreme views on lessons from East Asia. One is that its experiences were so historically and culturally determined that little is relevant or transferable to peoples elsewhere. The other is that the East Asians succeeded largely because they adopted good economic policies and created good institutions and any country that emulates them will also do well.

The first position amounts to observing that those elsewhere are not "Confucians;" have not been occupied by or strongly influenced by Japan; are often not ethnically homogeneous; are less likely to have been exposed to wars and social upheavals; are less likely to have been motivated by serious threats to their survival; have not been occupied by, aided or protected by Americans; and do not have tens of millions of achievement-oriented, educationally-focused, entrepreneurial Chinese people. They might have a few of these attributes or their equivalent but nothing like the whole set.

The other view, that they need merely to follow the practices of the East Asians, raises two questions: one is which of the East Asians, because there are significant differences among their circumstances and policies. The other is that implementing good policies and creating functional institutions in very different political and social environments is no small task, one that many governments are now struggling with.

The question addressed here is what *specific* lessons might be gleaned from the East Asian experience? That is a subset of a larger question: what should the slow growth countries do to grow faster? Many experiences from around the world provide evidence on the broader question, including negative lessons from the socialist and other highly statist economies. The distillation of all these experiences has resulted in what, for short, is called the neoclassical economic policy package. The experience of the East Asians is a major source of that canon, indeed has contributed to it being expanded. For example, the recent emphasis on growth with equality through the wide distribution of opportunities, not redistribution, has been stimulated by evidence from that region. Another example is achieving universal secondary schooling rather than allocating a large part of the national budget to tertiary education, as often is done elsewhere.

The preceding chapters makes it clear that, despite some commonalties, there is no single East Asian "model." Even Japan, as Raphael and Rohlen put it, supplies several "models." Policies and institutions varied widely, although there are systematic differences between the Northeast and Southeast. Some governments severely limited foreign direct investment while others welcomed it; some channeled capital and imports to designated firms while others did not; some had state-owned banks while others did not; easier access to imports by firms based on their export performance in some countries but not in others. Hong Kong had as close to a laissez-faire economy as was to be found anywhere in the world. However, all had superior macroeconomic stability (based on relatively independent central banks and finance ministries staffed with trained people), engaged heavily in foreign trade, invested heavily in primary schooling (and most of them also in secondary schooling), had low levels of government consumption, encouraged private savings, invested in rural areas and infrastructure, did not penalize agriculture, had low ratios of income inequality and were above average in protecting economic liberties.

Some of what they did was heterodox. As Root points out, state-owned enterprises were prominent in Indonesia, Malaysia, the Republic of Korea, Singapore, Taiwan, Thailand – and, of course, China. Many, especially in early years, practiced import substitution. State-controlled banks were common as were restrictions on financial markets. And forms of rent-seeking prevalent in the developing world are present, notably in Southeast Asia.

These variations supply an incentive to go behind policies to more basic factors. This book provided a set of them under the headings of Effective Governance, Achieving and Learning Societies, Growth with Equality, and External Influences.

Effective governance

This is arguably the most important one for reasons related to those famously expressed by Thomas Hobbes. This observation might seem banal were it not for the fact most developing country governments have not possessed it. They have taken on far too much and done poorly in them.

Japan has long since not been a developing country but its influence has been so great that the character of its governance is most salient. Raphael and Rohlen describe a country that has long had competent rule: meritocratic, with well educated, honest bureaucrats, and stable politics. Woo-Cumings shows how that system was transferred to Korea and Taiwan and how it was seen as a model in post-colonial times.

Has there been a more effective government than that of Singapore? As described by Quah it included, above all, an intense focus on economic development while meeting basic needs, fostering education, creating a meritocracy, minimizing corruption, curbing crime, and more. Root asserts that it is wrong to attribute such effectiveness simply to authoritarian rule for many authoritarian regimes have been ineffective. The ingredients in Singapore's effectiveness include a legacy of British law and governance (arguably given too little recognition by Quah), the incentive of a precarious national situation, a population largely consisting of high-achieving ethnic Chinese, and, above all, exceptional leadership. Some of the aims and practices of that leadership are often criticized in the West, but its efficacy is indisputable.

Effective governance requires competent bureaucracies. These existed early in some countries, notably Japan, Hong Kong, Singapore and Malaysia and got better in others, notably in Korea and Taiwan. Some of this competency derived from tradition in the Sinic countries, some from Japanese and British legacies and some from later American training and influence. Root sees these bureaucracies as having become partners in growth. He gives weight to institutional innovations, especially business associations and government–business consultative bodies as information brokers between private and public sectors. These politically authoritarian regimes did not operate top-down in economic matters; there were two-way exchanges.

Corruption hurts growth, especially where payments are uncertain and through incentives to create (profitable) red tape. It often existed at the top, especially among politicians (although evidently not in Hong Kong and Singapore) but, with exceptions including Indonesia, Thailand, China and the Philippines, it did not penetrate deeply in most of these countries. Apparently this was because of established norms and the high importance attached to performing effectively.

In Indonesia, Wardhana describes a government that got macro-economic and international economic policies right, in contrast to the experience of most developing countries, while Dasgupta tells about remarkable reduction in poverty in that vast country. What accounts for such effectiveness? The definitive answer has yet to be supplied but evidently some combination of the destruction of the communists in the blood-letting of 1965, the continued fear of Chinese-supported insurgents, socially (and privately) beneficial arrangements between Chinese entrepreneurs and the military establishment, the good use of well-trained technocrats (the "Berkeley Mafia"), good examples in Northeast Asia, and having perhaps the "right" amount of oil are explanations. (This last point means having too little oil to make manufacturing unattractive or to permit enjoyment of an easy life but enough of it to generate resources for investment in rural infrastructure, education and health. Remarkably, this happened.)

Taiwan's is not the only East Asian government with an effective technology strategy but it has been extraordinarily successful. Lin describes a focused national effort that resembles a wartime mobilization one – an image that fits the situation of Taiwan.

Pei argues that early crises in almost all of these states so discredited old and failing policies that succeeding governments were able to introduce radically better ones. A similar process has been at work recently around the world. Improvements in policies in Latin America followed on the debt crisis of the 1980s. Even more striking was the crisis of the Soviet Union in the late 1980s that led to its disappearance and the discrediting of the socialist model. India's liberalizing policies beginning in 1991 were prompted not only by recognition of the general failures of socialism but also by a macroeconomic crisis.

According to Haggard, institutions are an inadequate explanation for governments' behavior, i.e. crucial areas of policy being largely left to technocrats because of pressures from abroad, from banks, and from security threats, as well as the need for foreign firms with crucial technology and access to markets. He also sees governments as having become dependent on business. Why didn't this induce the usual rent-seeking so widely prevalent? Although not absent, it was contained by the incentives to perform that are addressed here. Haggard also describes a growing demand by business for rational – as opposed to arbitrary – regulation with limits to crony capitalism and with a predictable legal framework.

Only touched on lightly in this book is a high negative factor for effective government: ethnic divisions. This is evident in much of sub-Saharan Africa, the Middle East, South Asia, the Balkans, the Caucasus and Central Asia. East Asia has either not had this problem in severe form or its governments have managed it better. Singapore's attentiveness to racial harmony has been described by Quah: the protection of minority rights, the universal availability of public housing and (from a liberal Western perspective less attractive) prohibitions on religious agitation and restrictions on the press. Malaysia's method, after the 1969 ethnic uprisings, has been preferential treatment of Malays, described in the educational sector by Snodgrass, while leaving enough scope for the Chinese and Indian segments of the population to keep them motivated and more or less satisfied. Indonesia's ethnic mix, often troubled, has been managed in large part by wide sharing of the benefits of growth.

Achieving and Learning Societies

Japan is the quintessential learning society. This was a striking aspect of the Meiji period when, as Raphael and Rohlen describe it, the elite decided that the country's survival required selecting from Europe and America, modern institutions and technology and adapting them to Japan's needs and culture. Its adaptations and innovations are at least as important to understand as its borrowings. They included means of sharing information widely, the *keiretsu* (main bank) system of industrial organization, company unions combined with lifetime employment (for larger firms) and having much of workers' pay in the form of bonuses that vary with the success of the firm.

The educational achievements of the East Asians can be fully understood only through international comparisons. Snodgrass points out that in 1960, East Asia lagged Latin America in educational attainment in the adult population but was ahead in primary and secondary enrollment ratios for their income levels; in short that it was building for the future. Elsewhere, there was widespread neglect of primary and secondary schooling education with government spending on higher education for children of the elite. Stevenson shows comparative achievement tests data and how the Northeast Asian educational systems work to produce these achievements including much training of teachers and their relatively high pay. Behind these school factors is also strong family support.

South Korea, as described by Snodgrass, is truly an educationally-committed country. By the early 1990s, Korea had the widest educational coverage of any developing country. Earlier, in the 1960s and 1970s when the country was much poorer than it is today, students' families paid two-thirds of educational expenditures; this high private spending has continued. At the tertiary level, enrollment reached 42 percent, higher than in most European countries, much of it supplied by private institutions and paid for privately. Moreover, educational costs per pupil were low and its quality high.

The story in Malaysia is different. There, educational opportunities were tipped in favor of ethnic Malays whose schooling had lagged that of the Chinese. Only since 1991 have ethnic quotas been weakened. Helping Malaysia, as in Korea, have been policies that generated a strong demand for skilled workers.

Education has played a crucial, but not a simple, role in the demographic transition along with family planning practices. Koo observes that it led to fewer but higher quality workers. The demographic transition was linked closely to the great expansion in secondary schooling. By the 1960s, primary schooling was universal and university education was beyond the resources of most families. But at the secondary school level, increasing enrollments not only contributed to fewer births but also to a more productive workforce. Koo and Snodgrass also give great weight to the demand for labor. Koo shows that education is not sufficient without market-oriented policies using the examples of the Philippines and Singapore: the former had a high level of education, bad policies and slow growth while the latter had not as high education, good policies and high growth.

With few exceptions, developing countries do not create technology, they acquire it from advanced ones. This form of learning requires certain government policies and the right kinds of institutions. A formula for failure, one all too widely apparent, is to trade little, block foreign direct investment, send few students to advanced countries, discourage licensing foreign technology, and spend much of the nation's science and technology budget on institutes isolated from businesses. Lin's description of Taiwan's technology strategy shows that these errors were avoided. Other East Asian countries pursued different strategies. South Korea, following the practice of Japan, discouraged foreign direct investment (a standard method for getting technology) but, again following Japan, licensed technology from abroad on a large scale. Singapore and Malaysia sought multinational firms that would bring technology to them. The government of Hong Kong adopted a hands-off position. All worked because all permitted or encouraged learning from the rest of the world while building domestic institutions.

Growth with equality

Japan, as in many other ways, was a model for rapid growth with relatively low income differences. Taiwan then became noted for growth with equality, South Korea's income differences were relatively small, and Indonesia made a successful effort to reduce poverty. Why did this happen? One reason is that these authoritarian regimes (not including Japan) lacked legitimacy. Spreading the benefits of growth helped supply it. As Dasgupta puts it, they did not have political democracy but they had a kind of economic democracy. And, again, the precarious national situation of many fostered an all-in-one-boat mentality.

Dasgupta describes how Indonesia achieved good growth with a large reduction in poverty. Stated baldly, the strategy seems unremarkable: support for agriculture, supplying basic services such as roads, rapid expansion of primary schools, and public health (family planning, maternal and child health, disease control). Such a strategy was not much adopted in other regions. And, as in Singapore, there was little income redistribution in Indonesia. Trade created a demand for low skilled labor that helped raise incomes of the poor.

External influences

Japan set the pattern in the nineteenth century in a novel way. Fearing takeover by the colonial powers, its elite decided to modernize by adopting their technology and some of their institutions but modified them to meet Japanese tastes.

Woo-Cuming's chapter centers on external influences, in the sense defined here. She deals with three that strongly affected South Korea: legacies from Japan, the threat from the North and the influence of the United States. The first left a meritocratic bureaucratic structure, a tradition of state-led development and a pattern of large conglomerates. The threat from the north produced social cohesion and national mobilization.

The United States furnished economic and military aid and protection – and, as a by-product, many Koreans were educated in the US.

Interactions

Another way to view these contributions is through the interaction of policies and institutions. History supplied institutional legacies in the form of British, Dutch, French, Japanese, and American colonialism. These were then modified through the influences of wars, trade, technology, and good policies. The growth of strong private firms, in part through foreign trade, vested interests in less regulation and objective rules. Government bureaucracies and firms came to specialize in the things that each did best. Over time, political institutions evolved with, as Pei observes, tactics in intra-elite conflicts and against oppositions becoming moderated. Ruling elites came to see useful roles in semi-open elections – eventually in quite open ones in some countries.

In short, many virtuous circles were at work.

Index